# Creating Successful Acquisition and Joint Venture Projects

# Creating Successful Acquisition and Joint Venture Projects

## A Process and Team Approach

JOHN E. TRIANTIS

**QUORUM BOOKS**
Westport, Connecticut • London

**Library of Congress Cataloging-in-Publication Data**

Triantis, John E., 1944–
    Creating successful acquisition and joint venture projects : a
process and team approach / John E. Triantis.
        p.  cm.
    Includes bibliographical references and index.
    ISBN 1–56720–252–7 (alk. paper)
    1. Consolidation and merger of corporations—Management.   2. Joint
ventures—Management.   I. Title.
HD58.8.T74   1999
658.1′6—dc21        98–41037

British Library Cataloguing in Publication Data is available.

First published in 1999

Quorum Books, 88 Post Road West, Westport, CT 06881
An imprint of Greenwood Publishing Group, Inc.

Printed in the United States of America

The paper used in this book complies with the
Permanent Paper Standard issued by the National
Information Standards Organization (Z39.48–1984).

10 9 8 7 6 5 4 3 2 1

To the memory of my mother

# CONTENTS

# ILLUSTRATIONS

# ACKNOWLEDGMENTS

Strategic business development has been an integral part of my life for a long time and it is difficult to be certain from which projects or from whom I have learned. However, I am grateful to my former supervisor at AT&T Laslo Gross for giving me the opportunity and guiding my involvement in the first acquisition and joint venture projects. I am also indebted to Bill Ohnsorg for the insights he provided on the business development process.

In preparing this book, I have received assistance from and I am thankful to John Hendricks and Hansen Long for offering many useful thoughts on an earlier draft of the manuscript. In addition, I would like to thank my former mentor Elizabeth C. Bogan for her instructions on how to write and Virginia McRae for her expert advice and assistance in structuring the book.

The support of my wife during the preparation of the manuscript has been invaluable and enabled me to focus on completing the task. Also, I wish to express my thanks and appreciation for the material support made available by Adrienne Scott and Fran Libasci in the preparation of the manuscript when I was a member of AT&T's Global Market Intelligence group. Finally, I wish to acknowledge the support of James Sotirhos without which none of this would have been possible.

# PROLEGOMENA

# 1

# INTRODUCTION

A great deal of management time and attention is dedicated to acquisition and joint ventures of medium to large companies with the expectation of immediate and large payoffs. Generally, the returns from these activities tend to be lower than expected, they take much longer to realize, and the majority of these projects fail. The main reasons for the failure of acquisitions and joint ventures to create value for shareholders of the acquiring company or the parents of the joint venture entity are, respectively:

1. There is little or no chance that one can find the appropriate company to acquire for sound reasons, at a reasonably good price, and be able to implement and manage it appropriately so as to obtain expected synergies.
2. It is extremely difficult to maintain the initial personal relationships, partner objectives, and joint venture clarity of purpose in the long run.

Acquisitions and joint venture projects belong in the domain of strategic business development. Strategic business development is the set of functions and activities oriented toward implementing the strategic vision of a company through acquiring or merging with other companies and forming joint ventures and strategic alliances. It is a very different function from market development, which focuses on managing existing markets through pricing, marketing, promotional approaches, and marketing and distribution agreements. Strategic business development is concerned with the long-term growth of a company, whereas market development deals with short-term financial improvement considerations.

Strategic business development encompasses all activities directed to planning, identifying, assessing, negotiating, financing, and implementing mergers, acquisitions, and joint ventures and strategic alliances. For the purpose of economy of words, strategic business development is referred to as simply business development in this book. Likewise, merger and acquisition projects are lumped together under the heading of acquisitions while strategic alliances and partnerships become synonymous with equity joint ventures. The differences between the various types of strategic business development initiatives are treated in the appropriate chapters.

## ACQUISITION AND JOINT VENTURE ACTIVITY RISES

Since the early 1980s, the global economic environment and financial markets have been marked by a departure from traditional business and financing strategies. The environment has been characterized by an increased level of acquisitions and joint ventures. Financing, especially for large international projects, has shifted from traditional balance sheet financing to the more creative approaches of structured project financing. Leveraged buyouts and third-party financing have contributed significantly to the increase in domestic and worldwide acquisitions and joint ventures, respectively.

A number of factors beyond financial engineering and the use of debt to finance acquisitions and joint ventures are responsible for the increased level of acquisitions and joint ventures. The most important reasons for this increase are: industry deregulation around the world, differences in market development and competition, and increased global capital mobility and entry of new players and investors. Also, consolidation of operations and strengthening of financial performance, companies positioning for growth in new markets, new technologies and commercial products, and globalization of business and trade are contributing factors.

The causes of this upward trend are expected to be present over the foreseeable future as well. However, financial considerations, new technologies, and applications of those technologies are expected to contribute to further increases in acquisition and join venture activities. As industry deregulation and planned privatizations around the world increase, opportunities to restructure old, poorly run government companies will present themselves to investors with cash and the stomach to invest in foreign countries.

## PURPOSE, IMPORTANCE, AND BENEFITS OF THE BOOK

### Purpose of the Book

Acquisitions and joint ventures are difficult, expensive, and risky projects regardless of the level of planning and talent invested in them. As is known to most participants in these projects, the majority of them fail with amazing regularity. Yet, paradoxically, companies and investors persist and continue to engage in acquisition and joint venture activities. It is this paradox, or more precisely, what underlying processes, structures, and systems are required to enhance the success rates for these projects, that motivated my writing this book.

The purpose of this book is to examine the reasons for their high failure rates and show how to create successful projects using the right teams and processes. It starts with the premise that the execution of long-term strategy of a fairly large company will most likely involve some acquisition and joint venture activities. Because of their significance in disciplined decision making in acquisition and joint venture projects, we discuss world-class business development groups, the project processes, and practices. We also examine the crucial issues in the creation of shareholder value in strategic business development projects. The basic concepts of organizational structures, processes, and practices discussed in this book are universal and they apply to domestic as well as international business development and to any industry.

### Importance of the Book and Benefits to the Reader

This book fills a void in the existing literature and supplements it with its description of the teams and subteams, the intricate processes, and world-class practices involved in the creation of successful acquisition and joint venture projects, as well as the major issues involved in moving projects through these processes. Therefore, its significance lies in sharing the broad, practical experience of many years in business development and project financing. Having seen what works and what does not, practitioners in this area will be able to increase the success rates of these types of projects.

The reader will benefit by the principles, practices, and guidelines the author has observed and actually practiced in both successful and unsuccessful business development projects and organizations. The uniqueness of this book is the extensive coverage of the preparation involved, the project team, the organizational issues, and the key processes in assessing, negotiating, financing, implementing, and extracting synergies in acquisitions and joint venture projects. The key feature of the book is the treatment of all strategic business development topics at the practitioner's level and dealing with mundane considerations such as creating a project workplan, a business plan, building a monitoring system, or securing corporate approvals. First, the reader develops a good appreciation of the reasons acquisition and joint venture projects fail regularly and why the project team must embrace world class practices. Then comes understanding of the success factors.

The discussion enables the reader to understand the structure of a world-class business development organization, its mission, and its character. The discussion of the teams involved, their specific responsibilities, and the resources, skills, and experiences required to evaluate, negotiate, and implement acquisitions or joint ventures helps in preparing for and executing these types of projects. Examination of the critical success factors in identifying and screening companies and the role of strategy and development of objectives enables a reader to follow the steps of the opportunity assessment, negotiation, and implementation process.

The book emphasizes the value of an orderly transition of responsibilities encapsulated in plans that enable the project team to develop a business case, provide a recommendation for approval, and go from deal closing to actual operations. It also stresses the development of the assumption set, picking the appropriate method of valuation, identifying and quantifying project risks, quantifying tradeoffs in negotiations, quantifying expected synergy costs and benefits, scenario and sensitivity analysis, and sanity checks to perform to ensure a sound financial analysis and project valuation. Knowing that one can manipulate financial models to swing positions and show different results, our intent is to direct focus on the factors that really make a difference and ensure quality analysis and evaluation.

The challenges in doing acquisition and joint venture projects in emerging countries give the reader a unique perspective on the likelihood of success and on the issue of project risks. Hence, the need for sound due diligence, good legal agreements, and effective financing to ensure project success. However, an even greater benefit for the reader is appreciation of the importance of the implementation subteam and the processes it goes through to translate paper agreements into actual operations. This helps in being effective in assessing and harnessing synergies.

Answering the question of how one judges project success and performance of the new entity enables the reader to argue that in order to judge performance, one needs to monitor elements beyond the usual financial variables and look at strategic returns on investment. To ensure success, one needs to set objectives, create operational targets, and link performance to management objectives. However, the reader would be given an incomplete picture of what is involved in doing projects without a mention of impediments, the influence of politics, and the conflicts that arise along with guidelines on how to manage impediments. Finally, he or she appreciates why a world-class acquisition or joint venture process ends with a review of the recently completed project from start to finish.

## THEMES, CLARIFICATIONS, AND CAVEATS

### Recurring Themes

A number of key success factors in acquisition and joint venture projects make up the themes in this book. The following are themes that surface repeatedly in every chapter and are crucial in ensuring project success:

1.   Strategic considerations drive all business development activities.

2.  Know what you are getting into and what you want to get out of a project.
3.  Establish appropriate processes and teams to manage these processes.
4.  Manage projects to established processes and not to externally imposed timelines.
5.  Transition subteam responsibilities appropriately and maintain continuity of purpose.
6.  Quality project assessment and discipline in decision making are a must.
7.  Undertake and structure only financeable projects with sound economics.
8.  Establish open, unimpeded, and constant communication, input, and feedback channels.
9.  Use experienced managers in project teams and develop expertise and skills.
10. Plan and prepare well for acquisition and joint venture projects.

### Project Process Issues

The complexity of acquisitions and joint ventures makes treatment of all areas and issues in one book physically impossible. Consequently, the book focuses on providing the basics of the process and team approach to creating successful projects. The acquisition process is examined only from the buying company's perspective and the reason for this is that the seller's interests are best described by investment bankers. The processes and team requirements discussed here need to be tailored to the particular needs of a company and professional advice should be sought to adopt the practices and guidelines offered.

Ignorance of how to do things has rarely stopped corporate managers from pursuing business development activities they believe are worth pursuing, including acquisition and joint venture projects. This is an expensive approach to experimenting with the company's long-term growth because of the high cost of acquiring or creating joint venture companies, the external advisor fees, and the human resources expanded on these projects.

A number of questions are raised frequently, such as: Why do you need processes for acquisition and joint venture projects? For a number of reasons, but also because of the egos of certain corporate managers sitting at the top who think they know how to do anything. Also, if there is no process in place, projects would simply be dictated because they fit those managers' personal plans and views of what is good for the company. The follow-up question is: Can you omit steps in the processes outlined and still have a successful project? This is possible, but not likely. By following all the steps outlined, you increase the chance of a project being successful. Are all steps important? Yes, some more than others, but importance varies according to context and the project's peculiarities.

In this book, we emphasize the need for strategy to drive projects. But, can you have financially successful projects not based on strategic considerations? Certainly. In the short run, the company gets the benefits of financial engineering. However, what does a company do with pieces that do not fit the long-run scenario? It divests because the core business is not attended to and the company realizes it has to focus in areas where it has a competitive advantage.

That is, it goes back to strategic considerations.

### Resource Requirement Issues

Acquisition and joint venture projects have extensive human resource requirements of teams, subteams, and management involvement. What if resources do not exist within a tightly run company? How does a company create a successful project if it does not have the complex business development organization structures described? Why is the engagement of expensive investment bankers necessary? These are questions raised for good reasons and following are our explanations.

In any well-run project, only a few senior managers are involved, but they are prepared and briefed by business development professionals. Organizational structures serve needs of different companies and should be adopted to the specific needs of the company. That is, one can scale up or down the structures and subteams described: Responsibilities can be compressed to fewer subteams using fewer managers as experience in doing acquisitions and joint ventures increases. Another approach is to scale down expectations and play only in your league. If a company does not have the resources and does not want to invest to build organizations and expertise, then perhaps it should not be contemplating acquisitions or joint ventures. Alternatively, it could engage external experts to do the project.

The number of project participants in the subteams described in this book appears to be a luxury and a frequently asked question is why are so many subteams necessary or how can a small company afford this luxury? First, no company large or small can afford luxury or waste. Second, the project team consists of a small core of three or four members who draw functional experts as needed, but who do not spend all their time on the project. Third, subteams are created to increase efficiency through division of labor and the core team members participate in more than one subteam.

Companies with limited resources usually rely on outside experts to do acquisition and joint venture projects. If a company needs to engage outsiders, then hire a trusted consultant to orchestrate the project and provide guidance; however, expect shortcuts in the process and less attention to details and the company's needs. If this is unacceptable, then the company needs to create internal capabilities, train a few people, and motivate them to stay on.

### World-Class Practices

We make frequent reference to world-class practices in doing acquisition and joint venture projects because they result in effective execution and successful projects. These are not our rules; they are experiences and practices of successful project teams that repeatedly have come up in our benchmarking studies of best practices in the strategic business development and financing areas. For example, the company strategy driving acquisition and joint venture projects is a principle practiced by successful project teams. Why? Because conceptually and practically it makes sense, it ties things together, it produces results, and it motivates behavior consistent with the project goals and objectives.

There is repetition of world-class practices by design to ensure that their significance is well understood. Our approach is to go from the broad concept, to a narrower principle, to specific practices. Why? Because the topics are too broad to cover only once. Also, world-class practices involve many complex functions, many stakeholders, numerous success factors, and few chances of coverage without duplication given that there are several dimensions to cover in each principle or practice. For instance, the acquisition and joint venture opportunity assessment process world-class practices require discussion from a number of dimensions: the key issues involved, the steps of the process, the subteams responsible, and guidelines on how to do the project successfully.

# 2

# WHY ACQUISITIONS AND JOINT VENTURES FAIL

## INTRODUCTION

Acquisition and joint venture projects are expensive, difficult to execute well, and risky, despite the large management and financial resources invested in them. More than 75 percent of them fail with amazing regularity, a fact known in advance to participants. Paradoxically, despite being aware of the danger of failure, companies persistently engage in acquisition and joint venture activities to achieve their long-term growth objectives. The present chapter examines this paradox and provides some insights as to why acquisition and joint venture projects fail.

Acquisition and joint venture project failures are costly, not only because of the huge loss of invested financial and human resources, but also because of the tremendously large opportunity costs involved. Ordinarily, such projects take many months to complete. Human resources dedicated to a project work exclusively on that project instead of an alternative, such as an internal expansion program or a new product initiative. Additionally, a large amount of senior management time is consumed in briefings and progress reviews of an ongoing project in order to pave the way for corporate approvals.

When one understands the real costs of an acquisition or joint venture project, develops an appreciation for the chances of creating success, and knows and internalizes the reasons for failures, then one appreciates what is required to create a successful project and whether it makes sense to undertake the project. The decision to undertake a project is based on three key considerations: (1) identifying and adding up all the project costs and benefits in order to create a true picture of what is at stake; (2) calculating the project success rate *a priori* so that the decision whether to proceed takes into account the many elements required to produce a successful project; and (3) knowing the company's capabilities to evaluate, negotiate, and implement a project successfully.

In the sections that follow, we look at how to assess the chances of producing a successful project by assigning probabilities to the various major steps involved. Then, the recent record of acquisition and joint venture successes is examined in order to determine to what extent it confirms expectations. After reviewing the usual explanations given for project failures, we discuss the root causes of failures in order to avoid them. The chapter concludes with a summary of the factors causing projects to fail and recommendations on how to avoid making a project part of the failure statistics.

## LIKELIHOOD OF SUCCESS AND THE RECORD

### Estimating Project Success Rates

For acquisition and joint venture projects to be successful, every aspect of a project needs to be executed flawlessly. Even if there is a 90 percent probability that the right target or joint venture has been selected, success is not guaranteed because a number of other considerations affect the success of the project. These include having a good project team, clearly articulating project objectives, conducting effective negotiations, paying the right price, implementing the project effectively, having compatible cultures, developing a sound business plan, harnessing all expected synergies, and operating with a superior management team.

If only the above ten considerations affect how successful a project will be and the probability of being successful in each of these areas is 90 percent, then the probability of doing everything right in the project is equal to the product of the probabilities of success in each area. That is:

Probability of successful project =
  0.9 x 0.9 x 0.9 x 0.9 x 0.9 x 0.9 x 0.9x 0.9 x 0.9 x 0.9 = 0.35.

Therefore, as the number of factors that affect a project's success increases, the probability of having a successful project is reduced. For example, if the determining factors are increased to twenty, which is closer to actual experience, the probability of a successful project becomes about 12 percent. If we reduce the probability of success of each of the twenty factors to 80 percent, then the probability of project success is reduced to about 1 percent.

Understanding all the elements involved in creating successful acquisition and joint venture projects and the likelihood of success in each helps ensure that a project will succeed. The historical evidence surrounding failure of acquisition and joint venture projects and the causes for the low probability of a successful project are discussed below. Pointing out what causes acquisitions and joint ventures to fail raises the question: If those causes are eliminated, can successful projects emerge? The answer is yes.

## The Recent Record of Acquisition and Joint Venture Success

In 1995 there were about 6,000 mergers and acquisitions (M&A) and another 10,000 to 12,000 strategic alliance or joint venture projects. Two-thirds to four-fifths of them are considered strategic failures. At the same time, because demand was greater than supply, prices rose, multiples and premiums increased, and project risks climbed. According to a Coopers and Lybrand study [M.S. Porter (1996b)] 89 percent of the companies surveyed indicated that quickly integrated target companies had less difficulty overcoming the differences in cultures, information systems, and administrative procedures than those that were merged more gradually.

The Mercer Management Consulting study [M.S. Porter (1996a)] has evaluated some 300 major acquisitions of publicly traded companies, each with price tags higher than $500 million. According to the study results, more than half the acquisitions are not successful. A large number of acquisition projects destroy shareholder value because of the way the merged entity is handled; it is managed by accident. The Mercer study also indicates that post acquisition management is more important than the price paid for the target and that companies effective in integrating the acquired companies are more successful in creating value.

The Warwick Business School study [V. Houlder (1997)] examined roughly 300 British acquisitions, each worth more than $12 million, that took place between 1991 and 1994. It found that a large proportion of the acquired companies were, for the most part, ignored by the buying company. This caused frustration among one-quarter of their managers and led to an inability to obtain cooperation to harness synergies. About 50 percent of the acquired companies were kept at arm's length, 15 percent were fully integrated, and only 9 percent were described as "symbiotic." The same study points out that companies successful in transferring knowledge and expertise were rare and that about half of all the transactions ended in failure. Why are so many companies slow to integrate, and why do the buying companies ignore the acquired firm? The study concludes that after all the effort spent on closing the deal, there is no energy left for the post agreement and implementation period.

When it comes to strategic alliances, it is a given that at least 50 percent will fail if judged on financial merits alone. The true range of joint venture project failure is closer to 75 to 85 percent if measures other than financial considerations are used. Booz-Allen & Hamilton's study [B.P. Sunoo (1995)] indicates that of the 20,000 new alliances created between 1987 and 1992, about 40 percent were considered failures in 1995, and this does not include the alliances terminated since the study was completed. Booz-Allen & Hamilton attributes strategic alliance failures to the following factors:

1. Failure to pick the right partner
2. Failure to obtain agreement up front on goals and objectives for the new entity
3. Lack of relationships and right chemistry
4. Inadequate and erratic communications
5. Interference by parent company with the joint venture's operations

According to an interesting Arthur Andersen survey [Arthur Andersen Consulting (1995)], 76 percent of telecommunications industry executives believe that most companies will engage in some form of acquisition or joint venture project. Ninety-three percent of the respondents state that their own companies are partnering aggressively, but the majority (54 percent) felt that the long-term prospects for joint ventures were fair, 9 percent thought they were poor, 34 percent thought the prospects were good, and 2 percent thought they were excellent.

Regardless of what the precise estimates of failure are for acquisition and joint venture projects, what is important to understand is that the majority of these projects fail mainly because of poor and slow project implementation and integration. In light of this fact, why isn't more emphasis placed on skillful implementation and integration and why isn't sufficient attention paid to creating value for shareholders? Is the record complete, or is there something missing? While the explanations given are correct, they do not fully explain the root causes and the mechanics that lead to failure. The next section looks at the usual explanations for project failures.

## POLITICALLY CORRECT EXPLANATIONS FOR FAILURES

Inherently, high-level management evaluations of acquisition and joint venture project failure do not perform detailed assessments and look into the details of root causes. On the whole, they offer politically correct explanations because it is deemed inappropriate to cite participant incompetence, management interference, and bad decisions. However, even these high-level explanations offer lessons to be learned by those engaged in acquisition and joint venture projects.

*1. Hostile takeovers.* One reason often cited for failure of a particular acquisition is that it was really a hostile takeover in which financial engineering was the only consideration. Such a motivation is not conducive to an environment of respect and cooperation. Because the project is poorly integrated, failure follows.

*2. Overpaying for the acquisition.* From time to time, acquiring companies maintain that overpaying for the acquisition caused it to fail. For this to be true, either the success of the project is judged on the basis of financial returns alone, or no strategic returns on the investment are expected or have materialized. In either case, the implication is that the acquisition was pursued for one reason: financial returns.

*3. Lack of strategy.* A third reason for failure is lack of strategic rationale in most acquisitions and joint ventures. In world-class companies business development professionals engage in strategic and operational gap analysis in order to identify the target or partner company that can fill those gaps. On the other hand, in most companies, short-term considerations and a desire to fix a market position problem quickly result in absurd decisions to pursue projects to rectify the situation.

*4. Implementation delays.* Failure to integrate quickly is another reason given for the failure of acquisitions. This implies that there is little consideration given to the integration versus autonomy issue. It shows a lack of understanding that autonomy and outright acquisition of a target company are inconsistent objectives in one project. In other words, going back and forth on this issue delays integration and creates a divergence of expectations between the acquiring and the acquired companies. This divergence then creates conflicts of objectives and poor execution of the implementation plans.

Two more reasons offered for the failure of joint venture projects are conflicts over joint venture partner objectives and an inability of the partners to work together. While these reasons are certainly sufficient to wreck a joint venture company's success, they also reflect root causes inherent in these projects. The politically correct explanations usually given for acquisition and joint venture failure are valid, but they do not tell the whole story. They account partially for the regularity and massiveness with which such projects fail. Although not ordinarily discussed, other reasons in addition to the ones already examined work together to cause projects to fail.

## ROOT CAUSES OF PROJECT FAILURES

Acquisition and joint venture projects are costly and difficult to execute successfully because there are a number of steps in a complex process, each of which has to be done correctly to result in success. The major reasons for project failure are lack of strategy and clear project objectives, wrong reasons for pursuing acquisition and joint venture projects, and inexperienced project teams. The second set of reasons for project failure includes unreasonable expectations, lack of understanding the project process, and incomplete project assessment.

The third-order factors causing project failures are biased estimations of revenues, costs, and investments; succumbing to external pressures; and failure to address project risks. Implementation problems due to a variety of underlying reasons, failure to transfer responsibility, and poor chemistry and relationships are the fourth set of project failure causes. If left unrecognized, each of these factors can by itself or in combination with others cause projects to fail.

### Lack of Strategy and Project Objectives

Lack of strategic rationale is characteristic of most acquisition and joint venture projects. Quite often, the long-term strategy is either nonexistent or poorly articulated, or the project team members do not fully understand the strategy because they are not immersed in it. As a result, projects are initiated for the wrong reasons, are driven by edict, and are selected to meet the immediate company or specific business unit needs.

The reason that lack of strategy results in project failure is very simple: If you don't know where you want to go, any road will take you there. Without a clear, well-communicated, and understood long-term strategy not even a strategic gap analysis that has meaning can be performed. Without a thorough strategic gap analysis, it is not possible to create a clear profile of a desired target or a partner company. Absent a clear profile of the company one should be looking for, any company will do. This is a serious omission in preparing for projects and drives down the probability of successful acquisitions and joint ventures. On the other hand, a clear long-term corporate strategy that is internalized by project team members enables them to perform a sound strategic gap analysis. After a sound strategic gap analysis, the project team proceeds to the operational gap analysis, creates a clear profile of the company it should be looking for, and develops appropriate screening criteria.

> *Strategic gap analysis refers to a comparison of today's business definition against the desired state of the company's long-term position, which is done for the purpose of identifying the company's strengths and weaknesses. On the other hand, operational gap analysis is the identification of the gaps between the desired characteristics in the company's operations and the actual state of affairs.*

In acquisition projects, conflicts in strategy develop because either a strategy was not in place or it was not well communicated and understood by all project participants. In joint venture projects, there is a third reason that conflicts in strategy develop: unstated expectations concerning partner and joint venture entity strategy are not met, and the interests of the joint venture projects diverge.

At times, even if there is a clearly articulated long-term corporate strategy, projects fail because of lack of clarity of project purpose and objectives. That lack indicates that an operational gap analysis was poorly conducted. That is, it was not apparent to the project team what specific terms and conditions should be negotiated with what trade-offs and at what price. Therefore, clarity and continuity of purpose and objectives in the project are essential ingredients for success. When clarity and continuity are missing, project team behavior is not channeled in the right direction, judgment of success is clouded, and often conflict results. If project objectives are not clearly stated up front, so that they can be negotiated and consensus obtained, there is a high probability that conflicts will follow.

Hostile takeovers are routinely given as a reason for failure of acquisitions, but that is not sufficient to cause a project to fail if it is based on strategic considerations, precise project objectives, and sound financial analysis. Hostile takeovers result in failure when the only motive for the acquisition is financial engineering. When strategic and operational fits have entered the acquirer's calculations, hostile takeovers can be successful.

*Example: Review of a large U.S. corporation's fifteen-year acquisition program determined that its poor record was due to lack of strategic rationale behind its acquisitions, despite a high level of technical expertise of project teams and attractive project financials. Acquisitions and strategic alliances were pursued on the basis of opportunistic considerations, but no effort was made to strengthen its core business or to develop a competitive advantage in the industry.*

## Wrong Motives for Pursuing Projects

*1. Financial engineering.* Quite often, financial engineering, i.e., the manipulation of a company's operations to improve short-term financial statistics, surfaces as the incentive to engage in an acquisition or joint venture project. Although financial considerations are important in all decisions, undertaking a project with the expectation that financial synergies alone will make the project a success and improve the company's financial picture usually dooms the project to failure. Hostile takeovers are especially likely to fail when they are motivated only by financial engineering because there is a lot more involved in creating a successful project than simply satisfying financial expectations.

*2. Individual business unit objectives.* From time to time, individual business unit objectives set in motion and drive forward an acquisition or a joint venture project simply because these objectives are deemed to be in the unit's best interest. Such an assessment should be made by the corporate business development organization after examining all alternatives and evaluating the proposal against a set of objective criteria. Otherwise, by pursuing a project that meets one business unit's objectives can result in misallocation of corporate resources.

*3. Market share.* Acquiring market share is another motive that does not by itself justify undertaking acquisition and joint venture projects. Acquiring market share does not necessarily enhance the company's profitability or create a sustainable competitive advantage. Also, a host of costs and risks are involved in acquiring market share that are not apparent at the outset. However, if the acquisition of market share is part of the corporate strategy because it results in creating a competitive advantage or produces some other significant strategic return on investment, then pursuit of market share through a project is entirely appropriate.

*4. Access to R&D and technology.* Desire to acquire a new technology or access to unique R&D capabilities is by itself not a sufficient reason to pursue an acquisition or a joint venture project. However, many projects are undertaken for this reason simply because alternatives have not been explored in adequate detail. On the other hand, to the extent that acquisition of new technology and access to unique R&D capabilities is part of the corporate strategy and leads to a sustainable competitive advantage in capturing and maintaining market share, then that motive is likely to contribute to a project's success. By itself, acquisition of new technology and R&D capabilities usually satisfies interests and objectives of individuals, not the collective corporate interest.

*5. Bargain deals.* Naïve expectations, such as purchasing a bargain target company or forming a joint venture at minimal costs because it may produce high returns on investment, should be warning signs that such projects are most likely headed for failure. The truth is that there are no bargains left for amateurs in the acquisition and joint venturing area. Besides, what may appear to be a bargain often has a lot of hidden problems that become apparent in the not-too-distant future. Resist the temptation to undertake a project only because it seems to be a bargain. Ask for more evidence that an opportunity exists and be alert to potential problems.

6. *Complementarity of operations.* The quest for complementarity in acquisitions and joint ventures is another motive of questionable value if it is not based on solid strategic and operational gap analysis. Looking for complementarity in such projects is often indicative of misguided company expansion plans and a quick and easy way out of the problem of stagnant growth. Equally dangerous is the view that complementarity necessarily results in synergies, because that view assumes ability to implement a project successfully and to harness synergies that result from doing the project. Untested assumptions about complementarity generally lead to project failure.

7. *Risk diversification.* Diversifying outside the company's core business becomes fashionable from time to time because it is viewed as a good way to reduce risk. If the acquisition or joint venture project is in the same business as the parent company, then there is a possibility that the project will be successful. On the other hand, almost all diversification acquisitions in which buyer and seller are in a different businesses —and almost all joint ventures in which the parents and the joint venture company are engaged in entirely different pursuits— are doomed to fail. This is because few synergies can be obtained from areas in which the acquiring or parent companies have little or no expertise.

8. *Internal politics.* Internal company politics create impediments to successful execution and cause failure. When the decision to undertake a project is an attempt to bring peace and neutralize various constituents who cannot reach a consensus, look for trouble. If there are problems in reaching a decision on how to execute the long-term corporate strategy and in creating alternatives, then there will be problems in the evaluation of a particular opportunity, in negotiating, in implementing a project, and in operating the new entity.

9. *Potential gains.* In some instances, acquisitions and joint ventures are pursued with a casual attitude that if the project does not work, the new entity can be sold at a profit. This gambling attitude should have shareholders concerned because it does not produce the right kind of behavior to create a successful project; the escape door is wide open, and the motive to succeed does not have the highest priority.

10. *External pressures.* One of the most frequent inappropriate motives for undertaking an acquisition or a joint venture project is external pressures and influences. Often, certain external advisors convince senior management that there are unique strategic advantages to pursuing a particular project, and that the benefits are so clear there is no need for costly project assessments. It is inappropriate to pursue a project simply due to external influences because external advisors do not have a complete picture of the strategic and operational gaps of the company. Therefore, while external advisor suggestions and recommendations are welcome, they should always be subject to thorough internal scrutiny and assessment.

*11. Buyer's obsession.* Finally, the acquirer's obsession with the deal itself is a wrong reason to pursue a project. Such an obsession develops while doing the project assessment and examining the potential synergies and possibilities to do many things. It is fueled by the tight time lines that project teams operate under and leads to a one-track mindset: Complete the transaction as soon as possible to obtain the benefits expected in the deal. Obsession with the deal itself is the wrong reason to continue involvement in a project or consummate a transaction because when present, voices of reason and factual evidence are ignored.

Why do so many companies engage in acquisition and joint venture projects for the wrong reasons? The root causes are traced to lack of knowledge on how to do these projects effectively, and this problem is not acknowledged. As a result, strategic considerations do not drive projects and individual interests dominate. In addition to wrong motives driving projects, inexperienced project participants cause project failures because they omit many steps of the process designed to ensure project success.

*Examples:*
- *A medium-size U.S. company would invest in high-return, quick-payback acquisition projects, with little regard to acquiring companies to fill its strategic gaps. In fact, it had no long-term strategy. Eventually, most quick-payback acquisitions turned sour and had to be sold to maintain a 12 percent return on investment.*
- *One division of a U.S. company acquired a company for about $98 million, while another division spent $23 million to create similar capabilities internally. This is a classic case where different business units pursue their own business development projects, but could easily have been prevented if a corporate business development group had been managing the company's acquisition program.*
- *A European company formed a joint venture with a small high-tech firm in Asia to get access to its R&D and product development capabilities. Due to cultural differences, synergies did not develop and the European company sold its interest in the joint venture to another Asian company. Probing into the causes of failure revealed that an inexperienced project team did the project evaluation and had not considered cultural compatibility and chemistry issues.*
- *A U.S. firm proceeded with the acquisition of a smaller U.S. firm even after it was shown to its management team that the negotiated terms and conditions were unfavorable. The acquisition proceeded because, in the minds of senior managers, success was associated with immediate project closure.*

## Inexperienced Project Teams

A major root cause of acquisition and joint venture failure that does not receive much attention is the widespread inexperience of project teams and other participants in these projects. The lack of experience is spread throughout the entire business development group. In other types of projects, one may learn on the job, but acquisition and joint venture projects demand expertise in doing every aspect of the project correctly and efficiently, because the opportunity to go back to alter some aspect is not an option.

In many instances, senior management has little appreciation of the processes involved, what it takes to do projects effectively, and the qualities of the company being acquired. Even in cases in which there is some experience in acquisition and joint venture projects, senior executives find it difficult not overseeing and influencing the management of projects. The problem of senior management over-involvement is really one of delegation: experienced business development managers rarely exist within a company.

Limited mastery of planning and preparing for negotiations, of distilling clear positions on issues, and of understanding the process and issues on the part of all subteams involved results in prolonged negotiations, poor agreements, overpayment, and eventual failure. Also, when negotiations are taken over by sponsors, business unit heads, or outside experts, failure results because these individuals do not have the intimate knowledge of every issue that the project team has.

Ignorance of subject matter and the process has not stopped people from undertaking acquisition and joint venture projects because the view is that they can learn from the investment bankers or the outside consultants engaged in the project. However, if there is ignorance of acquisitions and joint ventures and the processes involved, it is impossible to assess what should be done at every juncture. Besides, the first wrong move made when there is ignorance of subject matter and lack of experience is to pick inappropriate project advisors.

*Example: A U.S. corporation did its first acquisition ever outside the United States with a project team never involved in an acquisition before. There was no subteam working the implementation issues and the acquired firm was neither integrated nor left autonomous. The price for the target company included a substantial premium because of large expected synergies, but the project failed to produce any synergies and the acquired firm was sold at a loss.*

### Unreasonable Expectations

Unreasonable expectations start with a fictitious strategic fit and a nonexistent operational complementarity for a given project. Unreasonable expectations can often be traced back to ignorance of the subject matter and the processes involved, inappropriate individual motives, and some outside influences, but at the senior management level they are the most damaging because they are difficult to alter.

Just as damaging are unstated expectations on the part of project participants concerning a multitude of issues that differ from those of the project team. Such expectations are the by-product of hidden agendas, lack of experience, or implicit assumptions that go untested. For example, senior management may have synergy expectations that are inconsistent with the implementation plan. Also, expected target company or joint venture partner contributions are usually not stated up front in an effort to create good will among all involved. As expectations go unchecked, they build up, and when the other party makes its position known and presents its demands, frustration develops and the negotiations derail or fall apart.

Building up expectations concerning synergies is a grave error on the part of any project participant within a company. Eventually, the real picture emerges and then the damage cannot be contained. Also, competitive advantage expectations being sold by internal project stakeholders as part of the project rationale introduce inefficiencies in the decision-making process and create difficulties in the implementation phase of the project. There is no bigger disappointment than expected synergies and competitive advantage not materializing out of an expensive acquisition or joint venture project.

### Lack of Process Understanding

Lack of understanding of the acquisition and joint venture project process is a big part of an inexperienced project team's problem and another root cause of failure. Successful implementation requires a methodical and disciplined approach, and completion of each step in the appropriate fashion. Precise execution of the steps in the process cannot take place when there is uncertainty about the process, the approach, and the timing of execution.

The omission of steps in the process creates problems in the execution and implementation of projects, as do steps in the wrong direction, steps initiated out of sequence, and steps executed poorly. For example, conducting a due diligence when the decision to acquire a company has not been firmed up, or undertaking a project in an emerging country without first checking the local business laws and legal requirements, is entirely inappropriate and sends wrong signals. Sending wrong signals to the outside world repeatedly affects the way a company is viewed and valued by investors and should be avoided.

When there is little understanding of the process, the acquisition or joint venture project is usually taken over and driven by investment bankers or external consultants. While there are advantages to professionals taking over the process, they do not have an intimate knowledge of the company's strategy and needs and are motivated by a different set of objectives. The results are that artificial time lines are imposed on the project evaluation and negotiation phases and little attention is paid to implementation issues because such issues do not affect closing the deal. The external advisors are gone once the deal is signed and the company's transition managers are left with a monumental implementation task and the responsibility of extracting synergies from the project.

When there is little appreciation of the project process and the process is taken over by external advisors, shortcuts are often taken to meet the tight, externally imposed deadlines. The result is an incomplete project evaluation and the negotiation of less-than-desired terms and conditions. This is a prescription for failure because every step in the process is as important as every link in a chain. Each is significant enough to make a difference in the success of the project. Also, shortcuts are not something an inexperienced project team can afford to take because they make it more difficult to assess the impact of various actions being initiated.

Sometimes, the view of the acquisition and joint venture projects is so casual that it results in limited discipline in the decision-making process. Work that should be done is left out, steps of the process are omitted, shortcuts are taken, financial assessments are manipulated, emphasis shifts from issue to issue, and forward thinking is put aside. Such behavior should be of concern to shareholders because lack of discipline in the decision-making process results in project failures and wastes significant and valuable company resources.

Lack of understanding the process of a project occurs widely and affects a project's success in a major way. Knowledge of process resides mostly with business development groups or with investment bankers. The former are rare and the latter are not very likely to share that expertise. However, this problem can be addressed by engaging consultants who specialize in coaching project teams through the processes of assessment, negotiation, and implementation.

*Example: Lack of understanding of process and unreasonable expectations on the part of a foreign government agency caused a joint venture between a European electronics firm and a former Soviet Union Republic to be abandoned and the European company to go out of business. A root cause analysis revealed that the foreign government's project team had never done a joint venture previously with an outside partner and the European company's project team did not invest time to educate its counterparts and manage their expectations about costs, benefits, contributions, and partner responsibilities.*

### Incomplete Opportunity Assessments

The major by-products of the lack of knowledge of subject matter and processes are shortcuts in the acquisition and joint venture project process, agreeing to extremely tight time lines, inadequate acquisition target and joint venture partner screening, and partial opportunity evaluation. The areas that ordinarily get incomplete assessment are strategic fit evaluation, testing of assumptions underlying the financials, negotiation trade-offs, risk impact assessment, present and future cost and investment requirements, project valuation, cultural due diligence, and implementation requirements.

As a result of incomplete assessments, projects carry expectations that are never met because they are not based on all the evaluations and checks that projects should go through. For that reason, incomplete assessments cause projects to fail. While emphasis is often directed at developing the case for the project based on its financials, the integrity of the financial evaluation is often questionable when left in the hands of an inexperienced project team.

Incomplete strategic and cultural due diligence and failure to assess organizational compatibility are reason enough to lead to wrong decisions and eventually project failure. Omitting steps in project assessment and implementation requirements creates the same problems in decision making and so does a quick and dirty evaluation of the target or partner company's organizational structure, its processes, systems, and networks. Most of the time, one is better off not doing a project at all rather than doing the project with an incomplete assessment.

*Example:* The pension liabilities associated with the acquisition of a small telecom manufacturing firm were not figured into the total acquisition costs because the due diligence was performed by a subteam with no previous experience in this area. The liabilities became apparent during the integration phase of the project and when they were included in the financial analysis, the project's net present value turned negative. That is, the project was a failure from the start.

### Biased Estimates of Costs and Benefits

Untested explicit and implicit assumptions lead to a false set of pro forma financial statements and an evaluation based on them leads to decisions based on shaky grounds. In most cases, revenue projections are overstated, while investment requirements and expenses are understated. This is due to lack of experience, misunderstanding of hypothesized relationships and implications, and failure to challenge the assumption set. Biased estimates of costs and benefits are symptomatic of lack of discipline in following a pre-established process which leads to overpaying to close a transaction.

Underestimated project costs are the norm in most projects. Several costs associated with doing a project are either not included in the estimates or are severely understated. Again, this occurs because of ignorance of process and how to go about doing all the tasks involved in acquisition and joint venture projects. For instance, senior management's time and involvement are not included in figuring out the real costs (i.e., the opportunity cost of the project). The full costs of implementing a project to the stage of ongoing operations are not fully accounted for nor are the decisions made with a good appreciation of the true costs and benefits. When costs are summed after project completion, the project is judged less successful than previously thought.

Unreasonably high synergy expectations coupled with underestimation of human resources required to evaluate, negotiate, and implement the project lead to decisions that on an *ex-post* basis are judged to be inappropriate. Also, excessive reliance on financial measures without a solid foundation of tested assumptions gives project participants a false sense of security and motivates decisions that ultimately lead to concluding a poor transaction. For example, if one believes that the financial picture of a project is very positive, that individual can be persuaded to give away some of the value created by the project over to the other side. In reality, the exact opposite should happen.

*Example:* The financial analysis of a British company's acquisition in the Pacific region was completed in record time, but failed to include an estimate of project implementation costs. Inclusion of the $7.4 million implementation costs would have caused a lower price to be negotiated or the project to be rejected. Ultimately this acquisition failed because of poor handling of implementation issues and an inexperienced liaison subteam.

## Caving In to External Pressures

When there is ignorance of the subject matter and the project process, external forces take over and the project process is driven by outside advisors, the target firm, or the partner company. When this happens, undue external pressure is placed on project participants to work under arbitrarily imposed and unrealistically tight time lines. This produces behavior focused on closing the transaction as soon as possible and worrying about implementation issues later. When the project team surrenders its charter and caves in to external pressures, the project is likely to fail regardless of whatever else takes place around it.

When the project process is driven by the target firm, the partner company, or external advisors, the project team manages to time lines and not to pre-established, tested processes. Under such conditions, the project team is not effective in understanding risks and issues and in assessing, negotiating, and implementing a project successfully. This leads to poor performance of the new entity relative to the expectations that the external advisors or the other side helped create.

When negotiations are taken over by outsiders, the emphasis is on closure and nothing else. In those instances, behavior is not based on open and uninhibited communication, but on secrecy and motivation inconsistent with corporate value creation. For instance, when there is no time to evaluate a situation or an issue completely, one tends to be cornered into agreeing to terms and conditions that ordinarily one would not accept. It is interesting that there is a strong correlation between project success and Japanese businessmen's consistent refusal to have projects pushed against time lines that do not allow sufficient time to communicate the situation to the entire team and to discuss the issues until a consensus is reached. That approach avoids the problem of making hasty and wrong decisions that quite often lead to project failure.

*Example: The acquisition of a small French information technology company was completed because the acquiring company was pressured to submit an inflated bid under threats that a competitor was allegedly submitting a high bid that should be matched. The second bid was approximately 15 percent lower than the acquiring company paid, or about $4.5 million. The higher price paid for the target company extended the break-even period by about a year.*

## Failure to Address Project Risks

In every acquisition and joint venture project a number of risks are associated with the execution of the business plan. In most projects, risk assessment and management are deferred until the implementation phase of the project. Ignoring the need to deal with risks in the assessment and negotiation phases is another root cause of project failures. When project risks have not been correctly identified, their impact is not quantified, evaluated, and included in the financial analysis, and they are not managed appropriately. The result is that those project risks lead to an understatement of the true costs of a project and the potential impact on the business case financials. Risks almost always materialize and disrupt the financial well-being of the new entity and the parent company.

Inadequate environmental assessment, incomplete opportunity evaluation and analysis, and untested assumptions are the factors responsible for not being able to identify project risks, to quantify their impact, and to realize the need to develop risk management and contingency plans. Failure to deal with project risks results in the negotiation of less favorable terms and conditions, inappropriate risk allocation and sharing, risk management plans not being developed, implementation problems, and unfavorable impacts on the new entity's operations and financials. That is, it results in project failure.

Failure to identify risks, quantify effects, and create risk management and contingency plans is correlated with ignorance of subject matter and project process, and with tight project time lines imposed by external pressures. Therefore, senior management and the project sponsor must ensure that project participants have appropriate training and experience and the ability to resist external pressures and artificial time lines. This is important because unmanaged risks always materialize and their financial effects can wipe out any gains from the project.

*Example: A joint venture of a U.S. company in India was dissolved because three project risks materialized simultaneously: Inability to obtain the tax holiday status expected, reduction of the operating license period from fifteen to ten years, and the financing being arranged by a local agent which cost twice the financing cost included in the business case. The financial loss to the U.S. company was in the neighborhood of $3.5 to $4.0 million. Lower cost was chosen over certainty of financing and insurance to protect against revocation of the operating license was turned down because of its cost: Two major risks were not managed appropriately.*

### Implementation Problems

Implementation problems arise because of the tendency of project teams to go through the evaluation phase too fast and the integration and implementation phase too slowly. This is exactly the opposite of what should take place. This phenomenon is explained by ignorance of subject matter and project process and undue external influence on senior management concerning the time lines and execution of a project. When implementation problems become severe, expected synergies do not materialize as expected, costs increase beyond what was estimated, and projects fail.

Unclear corporate strategy and project objectives can cause implementation problems, as can conflicting strategy and goals between the new entity and the parent companies or between joint venture partner companies. However, more often than not, senior management and other internal project participants have little appreciation of implementation planning and management of change. Consequently, human resources and financial costs are both underestimated.

Speeding through project assessment and going slowly in the implementation and integration phase of a project are a prescription for failure.

The main reason for this is that organizational and cultural differences are not recognized and accounted for in the business plan. The significance of uninhibited communications is brushed aside and the wrong chemistry develops. Furthermore, failure to integrate quickly and effectively creates false expectations on the part of the new entity's management team. All these factors create an environment in which conflict develops and little progress is made in extracting synergies.

Unreasonable business plans also create implementation problems and indicate either inadequate participation by the project implementation team in their development or undue external influence. The "not invented here" syndrome concerning process, systems, and networks of the target company creates implementation problems and causes friction and unproductive competition for resources. Finally, inappropriate transition of responsibilities, lack of continuity of purpose, and lack of strong support by senior management cause implementation problems. These lead to the inability to get the new entity's management team to share responsibility in harnessing synergies, causing the project to be judged a failure.

*Example: A large U.S. company acquired a small company, planning to integrate it into its operations. A budget crisis hit the buyer company and in its attempt to cut costs, it cut the project implementation budget in half. Delays in integration ensued, seconded managers were disillusioned, morale in the acquired firm dropped, the integration of the target company never materialized, and the firm was sold two and a half years later at a loss.*

### Failures in Transfer of Responsibility

Inexperienced project teams, lack of subject matter understanding, and inadequate project process knowledge result in drastic discontinuities and abrupt transfer of responsibilities. A smooth transition of responsibilities to the new entity's management team ensures continuity of purpose. An abrupt transition causes difficulties among the new entity's management team in accepting business plans in whose creation they were not involved and whose requirements and benefits they do not understand.

Failures in the transfer of responsibilities inadvertently lead to inadequate support for the autonomous new entity. This means that the new entity is managed on a part-time basis by a management team with little or no experience, which indicates absence of a sound transition plan. Also, unkept promises by people no longer involved in the project cause failures in responsibility transfer. Thus, the need for continuity of purpose and appropriate transitioning is great because without them, the ensuing implementation problems cause projects to fail.

Finally, inexperienced liaison managers and the absence of a strong steering committee are part of the responsibility transfer problem. One of the responsibilities of the liaison team and the steering committee is to ensure that the business plan requirements and financial expectations do not fall through the cracks in the implementation or the transfer of responsibilities. Other responsibilities include creation of a sound governance structure, an effective organization, and a strategy consistent with that of the parent company. A third set is to ensure adequate financial and human resources support of the new entity by the acquiring or the parent company and to facilitate conflict resolution so that the business plan is fully realized.

*Example: A joint venture between two U.S. information technology firms failed because verbal agreements concerning partner responsibilities and contributions were not included in the joint venture agreement. The reason partner responsibilities were not included is that the information was not related to the negotiations subteam before the signing of the agreement. That is, there was a breakdown of communications.*

### Poor Relationships and Chemistry

In many acquisition and joint venture projects, the importance of relationships and chemistry is brushed aside as insignificant by participants not involved with implementation issues and who go away as soon as the deal is signed. This is especially true in the case of acquisitions where the negotiations are characterized by a competitive spirit and are viewed as a game where personal relationships do not belong. However, failure by the project team to create relationships at all functional levels with the seller, the target, or the joint venture partner results in a tremendously complicated and difficult job in negotiating and implementing a project successfully.

Poor relationships and chemistry are caused not only by external influences and interference, but also by emphasis on getting projects done as quickly as possible in the assessment and negotiation phases of the process. Cultural differences, poor all-around communications, lack of clarity of purpose and objectives, and lack of continuity of a common purpose and interest prevent relationships from forming and cause existing relationships to deteriorate. This leads to a lack of trust, which then makes implementation difficult, causing a project to fail.

In addition to too few relationships among management and functional experts in the entities involved, overemphasis on financial results and an undue reliance on legal agreements result in poor relationships and chemistry that is not conducive to cooperation. Concentration and undue emphasis on financial results indicates a lack of experience in doing acquisition and joint venture projects. Reliance on legal agreements may be beneficial for projects up to a certain point, but beyond that, it results in the projects being taken over by legal experts. Business issues are not being addressed, while relationships deteriorate and the wrong chemistry develops.

*Example: Because of cultural differences and organizational incompatibilities, a European company walked away from a joint venture company in Brazil that was expected to produce very large synergies for both parties. Financial losses* *to both parties were around $5.0 million. This was a small price to pay relative to the costs of forming the joint venture under the wrong chemistry and cultural incompatibilities.*

## SUMMARY

Acquisition and joint venture projects are costly and difficult to execute successfully because there are many factors involved in a complex process, each of which has to be done correctly in order to produce success. The major reasons for project failure are lack of strategy and clear project objectives, wrong reasons for pursuing acquisition and joint venture projects, and inexperienced project teams. The second set of reasons for project failure includes unreasonable expectations, lack of understanding the project process, and incomplete project assessment.

The third-order factors causing project failures are biased estimations of revenues, costs, and investments; succumbing to external pressures, and failure to address project risks. Implementation problems due to a variety of underlying reasons, failure to transfer responsibility, and poor chemistry and relationships are the fourth set of project failure causes. If left unattended, each one of these factors can, by itself or in combination with others, cause projects to fail. Once it is understood what causes projects to fail, what needs to be done to make them successful becomes apparent.

# PART I

# TEAMS AND PREPARATION

# 3

## STRUCTURE AND RESPONSIBILITIES OF THE BUSINESS DEVELOPMENT GROUP

### INTRODUCTION

Business development is the set of activities that create new markets and opportunities for a company and it is broken down into market and strategic business development. The former deals with developing short-term market opportunities and internal solutions, whereas the latter is concerned with long-term growth of the company through acquisitions or joint ventures. Business development groups are small groups formed for the purpose of identifying, screening, and working to conclusion acquisition and joint venture projects. They are usually part of the corporate strategy and development organization and are staffed by highly motivated managers with exceptional skills and backgrounds.

The scope of the business development group in world-class companies extends from assessing internal initiatives to mergers and acquisitions and strategic alliances. The business development group is the steward of the new business development function in the company, but the extent of involvement in these projects depends on its charter and the resulting organizational structure.

Acquisitions and joint ventures are interesting, high-exposure, and recognition activities in companies worldwide. Therefore, business development positions are desirable for highly motivated individuals or reserved for individuals intended to move rapidly up the management structure. At the same time, acquisitions and joint ventures are difficult, risky, and expensive propositions. Hence, the need to staff business development groups with skilled and experienced individuals who can work within established processes and are disciplined decision makers. These factors create some unique requirements for managers of business development groups to focus energy on creating win-win arrangements. It is from this area that most benefits can be derived in creating successful projects.

In this chapter we discuss key aspects of business development groups starting with the mission of a world-class business development group, its importance, its structure, and its character. We examine the characteristics of successful organizations, the capabilities, qualifications, and skill sets required along with the roles these organizations perform in the business development process. The responsibilities of the business development group from articulating the company strategy and developing project objectives down to the integration of lessons learned and the characteristics of world-class business development organizations and best practices are also discussed. Relationship management, constant vertical and horizontal communications, and adherence to established processes are the underlying themes of this chapter.

## ASPECTS OF THE BUSINESS DEVELOPMENT GROUP

### The Mission of Business Development

The mission of strategic business development is to implement the company's long-term strategy by acquiring or merging with other companies and forming joint ventures and strategic alliances. It encompasses planning, identifying, assessing, negotiating, financing, and implementing acquisitions and joint ventures.

Business development is different from market development, which focuses on managing existing markets through pricing, marketing, and promotions. Strategic business development is concerned with the long-term growth of a company, whereas market development deals with short-term financial considerations. There is, however, some overlap. In world-class companies, that overlap is where tremendous synergies are created through common understanding of the company's core business, its strategy, the market environment, customer needs, and the possibilities for growth.

A broader mission of the business development group includes the creation and implementation of vision and strategy through the development of new businesses, products, and services to attain growth objectives that result in increased shareholder value. Under this definition, creation of corporate strategy, business development, and project implementation reside in the same organization.

### Why Business Development Groups Are Important

An experienced business development group is crucial in creating a successful project by ensuring that strategic considerations drive all acquisition and joint venture projects, by defining the project and its scope, and by creating and assessing alternatives to the proposed project. It also brings into the project team individuals with the right skills and expertise and it ensures appropriate transitioning, continuity of purpose, and adherence to pre-established processes. In addition, an experienced business development group provides guidance and advice to the entire project team and senior management on every aspect of a project and manages the engagement of external advisors.

The absence of an experienced business development group from an acquisition or joint venture project is associated with confusion, lack of purpose, ignorance of process, poor negotiations, long delays in implementation, inability to extract synergies, and eventual failure. Thus, it is essential that the business development group has strong presence in the project from start to finish. Strong presence, in turn, necessitates an appropriately structured organization staffed by individuals with desired talents and motivated to create shareholder value.

The first requirement of a proficient business development group is knowledge of the company's business, products, and services and a clear understanding of its strategy. A thorough understanding of the processes, the risks and issues, and the multitude of interfaces involved is another important element in getting projects done. For project teams to be effective, they need to have clearly defined responsibilities. Here, the business development group assigns specific responsibilities because if the responsibilities of project subteams are not clearly defined, the result is confusion and conflict among project participants.

### Organizational Structures

A few organizational structures have been found to produce excellence in operationalizing strategy, identifying and assessing opportunities, implementing acquisitions and joint ventures, and integrating lessons learned. Two basic organizational structures are world-class in terms of executing projects in record time, and these projects have higher success rates than those of average organizations. The structures are flexible and adaptable to specific needs, overall company structures, and nature of business.

*1. The Central Business Development Group.* The simplest structure is one in which the corporate business development group reports to a corporate vice president of planning and business development, who, in turn, reports directly to either the company chief executive officer (CEO) or chief operating officer (COO), the president, or even the chairman. Under this structure, shown in Figure 3.1, each head of a business unit also has its own business development unit that deals with specific countries or regions of the world, but reports on a dotted-line basis to the corporate business development organization. The ultimate responsibility for acquisition and strategic alliance projects rests with the corporate business development organization. What makes this structure effective is the synergies created between the business unit and the corporate business development groups each operating with clear and common understanding of strategy and under established processes.

**Figure 3.1**
**The Central Business Development Organization**

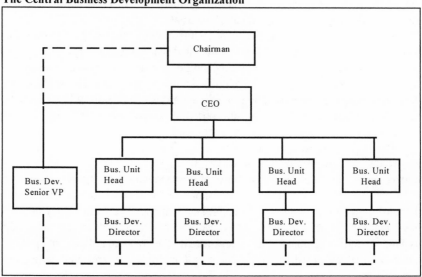

**Figure 3.2**
**The GE Model for Business Development Groups**

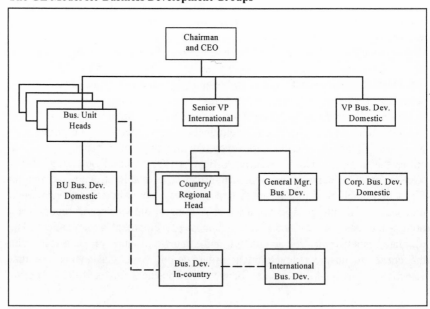

*2. The GE Model.* Another structure, highly effective and often imitated, is the GE business development organizational structure shown in Figure 3.2. Under this structure, each domestic business unit has its own business development group, the senior vice president of international operations has an in-country and a headquarters business development group, and the chairman or the CEO of the company has a corporate business development organization.

The GE model serves well its extensive acquisition program and appears to reflect a dichotomy between domestic and international business development. That is not really the case, because the in-country business development group reports on a dotted-line basis to the vice presidents of the domestic business units and works very closely with the international business development group. Also, the corporate domestic business development group has close working relationships with the other groups and provides assistance, advice, and guidance as needed. This organizational structure is more difficult to manage because of the several matrix management elements to it and is subject to being plagued with politics.

Starting with these basic structures, one can create a business development organization that meets a company's requirements. A thorough understanding of the business development process, simplicity of structure, and clearly defined areas of responsibility and accountability are the guiding principles in the design of business development organizations. However, the senior management's views define the scope of business development activities. For example, if senior management feels strongly about the linkage of strategy and business development, then strategy creation and business development reside in a single organization. If, on the other hand, more value is placed on the linkages between business development activities and implementation, then both functions come together under the business development group.

The central or corporate business development groups that operate successfully report to senior management, which enhances their credibility and authority. In every case, a flat business development organizational design is in place: The group is headed by a director-level manager and work is performed by a small group of associates who have extensive networks inside and outside the company and quick access to decision makers. This structure allows for speedy project assessments and approvals.

## Culture, Skills, and Backgrounds

A good business development group is a self-directed organization that knows its mission and its responsibilities and has the right mix of qualified people with appropriate skills and backgrounds. Teamwork on all levels and empowerment of business development associates form the basis on which these organizations build their strength and expertise. While project accountability resides with the project sponsor, there is active senior management support for business development associates leading projects, and recognition of successes and reward systems are in place to motivate appropriate behavior.

A broad spectrum of skills and backgrounds is required to create a world-class business development group, but emphasis is placed on diversity of backgrounds, well-rounded company experiences, and integrity. While technical competence is not a requirement, a good understanding of the company's business, its products, and services is necessary. This allows business development associates to be cognizant of issues that come up in acquisition and joint venture projects and become more comfortable with assuming risks.

Five to ten years' experience in acquisition and joint venture projects is often a business development group requirement and negotiation skills are a must not only for domestic projects, but international projects as well. Good analytical skills are essential along with skills in financial analysis and evaluation of projects in the presence of risk and uncertainty. Success in identifying, evaluating, negotiating, and seeing projects to completion requires perceptive and persistent individuals who can think clearly under stress.

Legal expertise resides outside business development groups; however, familiarity with basic legal issues is helpful as is some accounting and finance experience to oversee the due diligence work. Experience in large project management and consulting is of great value to guide clients through project assessments and to take projects from inception on through the approval processes. Finally, individuals with access to global information networks, contacts, and relationships are most valuable in world-class business development organizations.

Some business development groups grow talent internally and start with introducing new associates to the company's business, products, and services. Training in project valuations and financial analysis follows to ensure these areas are addressed adequately. Exposure to business development best practices is one of the most valuable investments that broadens their perspectives and introduces ideas for them to experiment with. Training in reviewing and analyzing right and wrong corporate decisions contributes toward developing the maturity level of business development associates and the art of negotiations is learned by doing it along with the negotiations subteam in a support function. Finally, training in project management is a basic requirement to enable associates to function effectively in this capacity and deal with the magnitude of issues that surface when doing acquisition or joint venture projects.

### Characteristics of World-Class Business Development Organizations

Some of the characteristics of world-class organizations are, to some extent, conditioned or influenced by the nature of the company's business and its strategic approach to growth. Characteristics common to every business development group that has earned the reputation of being a world-class organization are lack of internal politics, high level of teamwork, open communications and extensive cooperation, and flawless executions. Other characteristics common to all world-class business development groups are sound organizational structures, familiarity with strategy and screening, knowledge of established processes, and expertise in planning and execution.

Effective business development groups are characterized by flat organizational structures, the primary reason being to have quick and unimpeded access to senior management for timely decisions. We observe that business development groups reporting directly to senior management enjoy enhanced credibility and influence. This is particularly important in companies where intense competition prevails among business units.

In world-class companies, a clear corporate vision is translated into a clearly articulated strategy. The business development group has some role in the creation of strategy, but has full responsibility for operationalizing it. World-class business development groups demonstrate commitment to excellence, which results in sound project selection when pre-established processes are followed. Firstly, every acquisition and joint venture project has a champion or sponsor, a senior executive who is committed to providing support and is accountable for project success. This support translates to quicker assessments and corporate approvals. Commitment to excellence is evident in all work and output produced in intelligence gathered, analyses performed, support provided, and decisions made by experienced business development groups.

Talent, skills, experience, and established processes are one part of the equation in being a successful business development group. The other part is planning and execution. Excellence in planning and execution begins with scheduling the first contact with a potential acquisition target or the joint venture partner and ends with planning post-implementation audits for the project. Adherence to processes helps the project team to plan and execute flawlessly, but paying attention to detail is also required in order to produce quality outputs and decisions.

## BUSINESS DEVELOPMENT GROUP RESPONSIBILITIES

Acquisition and joint venture projects are complex projects to bring to fruition and, therefore, require the active participation and leadership of the business development group. This group is uniquely positioned to meet these responsibilities because of its role as the steward of the business development process.

### Pre-Evaluation Responsibilities

*1. Creation of corporate strategy.* This is an annual activity that begins with an assessment of company performance and industry trends, develops business unit objectives that become corporate objectives, and translates those objectives to financial and market targets. It results in articulation of the long-term vision of the company and how to get there. The business development group does not necessarily develop corporate strategy, but it does require clarity of purpose which enables it to operationalize the strategy. In the absence of clear strategy, even the best business development group fails to create successful projects.

The business development group helps senior management shape their vision, develop consistent long-term company objectives, and identify growth alternatives. Armed with understanding of the long-term strategy and the company's strengths and weaknesses, the business development group performs strategic and operational gap analyses to create a profile of desired targets or venture partners.

The business development group also identifies gaps in the corporate strategy articulated relative to implementation requirements. Because it is responsible for implementing strategy, the business development group forces discipline and clarity of purpose and cohesiveness in corporate strategy through dialog with the strategic planning group. Another area of responsibility is the development of alternatives to achieve strategic objectives. The creation of different options requires evaluation and ranking of options and eliminating marginal opportunities.

*2. Opportunity identification and screening.* Intelligence created by the business development group is unique information that enables trained professionals to develop scenarios on how to implement strategic objectives driven by the requirement to meet customer needs. It includes creating and updating data bases with target company data, competitive information, environmental assessments, industry statistics, analogs and comparables for purchase prices, analysis and interpretation of data base statistics, monitoring and identification of industry trends, and reports and recommendations.

Opportunity identification is an ongoing effort to select good projects where the corporate strategy and development group, individual business units, in-country business development groups, and individual unit business development groups participate. All these entities participate because they bring unique perspectives and have specialized contacts. More importantly, early participation in the selection process by all groups impacted results in developing project acceptance and support.

An effective business development group has continuous contact with business unit heads, outside consultants, investment bankers, and financing institutions, which enables it to conceptualize alternative opportunities and ways to meet customer needs. It establishes the qualitative and quantitative screening criteria of acquisition targets and strategic alliance partners with input from senior management. These criteria include measures such as revenue per employee, gross profit, and market share and are used to determine the value of alternatives and to identify associated synergies. It also evaluates the strengths of each alternative against the stated criteria, identifies resource requirements for each alternative, and assesses the feasibility and likelihood of success for alternatives. This helps the business development group to select and recommend projects for full-scale evaluation.

*3. Assessment of strategic fit.* Most of the value provided by the business development group in strategy implementation is the evaluation of the strategic fit of a project judged against the articulated strategy. In the hands of an effective business development organization, strategic and operational fit assessment is a powerful screening criterion and results in tremendous savings of time and effort throughout the assessment process. In addition to understanding corporate strategy, the company's products and services, its markets and customers, and the needs being served by the company's products and services, strategic fit assessments require an objective assessment of the company's strengths and weaknesses, the industry structure, and current and emerging trends.

*4. Formation of the Project Team.* Once a project is defined well enough and the preliminary screening is done, the business development group forms the project team to handle the project to completion. Because of the wide project experience and talents of the business development group, the appointed project team leader ordinarily comes from this group. The project leader, with help from the business development group, engages functional experts to create the core project team which, also includes a financial analyst, a lawyer, and an operational manager.

## Process and Project Management Responsibilities

*1. Stewardship of the business development process.* The stewardship responsibility belongs to the business development group. Stewardship ensures not only compliance with pre-established processes, procedures, and methodologies, but also effective management of projects and relationships throughout an extensive network of contacts internally and externally. Stewardship includes constant learning, monitoring and adopting best practices, and appropriate staffing, training, and exposure to diverse experiences, to ensure the continuity of the business development group as a world-class organization. The ability to use pre-established processes to navigate a project from identification to implementation expeditiously is found only in business development groups.

Successful execution of acquisition and joint venture projects requires exceptional project management capabilities and support from the business development group. Effective project management begins with clearly defined objectives and requires continuity of purpose and effective transitioning of responsibilities. It also includes well-defined deliverables and expectations of performance, a well-designed and reasonable project workplan, delivering the project within the budget prepared, and workplan flexibility and ability to adapt.

The business development group's project management responsibility involves a review of impacts across business units and coordination of efforts and deliverables into a cohesive approach in order to move projects forward. It ensures that efforts are not duplicated, that various projects are not in conflict with each other, and that synergies between various projects are maximized. When conflicts in strategy or project objectives arise, the business development group is responsible for resolving conflicts and ensuring that all participants have a common view and support the selected project. In addition, consulting senior management on the project process and guiding clients through the process is a necessary and high-return activity.

2. *Performance of sanity checks.* When corporate strategy is developed elsewhere, the business development group is responsible for performing sanity checks on the articulated strategy and developing other options. Individual business units create their own business strategies, which are then combined to form the corporate strategy in an additive manner. In reviewing the corporate strategy in order to implement it, the business development group identifies cross business unit strategy conflicts, assesses potential impacts of conflicts, and recommends reconciliation of individual strategies in the context of creating a consistent overall corporate strategy.

3. *Project communications.* Project communications involve intra-project team, inter-business unit, and external contacts and communications. The business development group manages communication channels and ensures the unimpeded flow of information vertically and horizontally, helps the project team develop documents used for internal reviews and progress reports, and often creates releases for external communications. Finally, it serves as a liaison to senior management and facilitates communications.

4. *Management of due diligence, consultants, and legal agreements.* The assessment of acquisition or joint venture opportunities is based on information provided either by the target firm, the potential partner, or by brokers and investment bankers. The business development group ensures the validity of the information provided and helps the project team in the early due diligence effort.

---

*Due diligence is an in-depth effort to examine, validate, or obtain information not shared in public documents related to financial, legal, human resources, and obligations. Its purpose is also to uncover misrepresentations concerning operations and claims of expected synergies.*

---

In the formal due diligence process, the acquiring company has a short time to review records and pick out inconsistencies and misrepresentations. The business development group assists the project team in this effort in overseeing the work of outside accountants, consultants, and investment bankers. It facilitates access to external resources, manages these resources, defines the responsibilities of external advisors and provides direction to accomplish the due diligence objectives.

The business development representative on the project team also helps to create and reviews legal documents and agreements drafted to affect the completion of the transaction and ensure that the project objectives are met and that legal documents reflect the desired terms. It creates the intent and business objectives, but the lawyers are responsible for drafting appropriate language that reflects those objectives.

5. *Consulting clients and managing approvals.* Consulting internal clients reduces reliance on and expense of external consultants, builds closer relationships between different groups, and produces better results. Consulting takes the form of walking clients through processes, sharing past experiences and discussing how they relate to the current project, demonstrating how impartial assessments are performed, sometimes doing the analysis or directing clients to appropriate experts, guiding the negotiations subteam through the process, and teaching clients how to perform certain analyses.

In most companies, there is a well-structured approval process in place to obtain approvals to proceed with a project and dedicate resources to perform the project evaluation. In effective business development groups, corporate approvals for recommended projects are a formality because there have been interim reviews, constant communication, and briefings along the way. In most instances this is not the case, approvals take as long to complete as project assessments, and this is a clear sign of a breakdown in communications and a poorly structured business development group.

Authorization to proceed with negotiations, acceptance of the negotiated terms and conditions, and making investment funds available also require corporate approval. Other decisions such as the degree of autonomy of the new entity, retention of senior target company executives, earn-out formulas, and new-entity strategy require senior management approvals as well. The business development group guides the project team in obtaining project approvals, it is responsible for obtaining independent internal and external assessments of the project valuation, it develops appropriate documentation and summaries for senior management and board of directors' review, and it prepares the project sponsor to present the business case to the CEO for approval. Because of past experience, it knows the key considerations and helps senior management come to a decision quickly.

6. *Transitioning of responsibilities.* Effective transition of responsibilities from one subteam to another and between the project subteams and the new-entity managers is an orderly transfer of responsibilities that moves projects from one stage of the process to the next smoothly and efficiently. Continuity of purpose in the project is an integral part of effective transitioning of responsibilities. The business development group ensures that effective transitioning is incorporated in the project workplan and monitors the transfer of responsibilities. This is accomplished through review of issues and progress to date at each step of the process, clear articulation of expectations for the deliverables of the next stage, and requiring the party handing off responsibilities to remain engaged until the next stage is completed in order to

provide assistance when required.

### Evaluation Phase Responsibilities

In the opportunity assessment phase, the business development group is responsible for several major elements and although it may not perform these functions, it ensures that they are well executed.

*1. Opportunity assessment.* In this stage, project participants understand the opportunity to create shareholder value, define the project scope, and structure workplans to evaluate it. It is a process that determines whether a project has what it takes to be successful. The process starts with examining how the proposed project satisfies customer needs currently not being met. It includes a strategic fit assessment and looks at alternative ways to achieve the same results. Human resource requirements are identified and financial assessment and business case development follow along with identification and quantification of risks and issues.

Opportunity assessments made by experienced business development groups avoid the commonly occurring symptom of inordinately high-cost acquisition and joint venture projects. That is, problems such as biased opportunity assessment in favor of sub-optimal alternatives, incomplete or wrong project assessments, drawn-out negotiations or incomplete negotiations, and poor agreements are avoided. Such opportunity assessments also prevent shifting of scarce corporate resources to projects that do not support the core business or new strategic directions.

*2. Risk identification.* A very important element in assessing value and managing projects effectively is to identify risks, quantify their impact, and develop plans to manage those risks or develop contingency plans. The business development group is uniquely positioned to add value in this area because it has a broad perspective of the opportunity, is involved in the early phase of assessment, understands the issues, monitors the negotiations, and is able to create alternatives on how to allocate project risks. Senior managers new to strategic business development look to legal agreements to mitigate risks or deal with uncertainty, but as their experience increases, they rely on risk management plans created by the business development group to mitigate project risks.

*3. Financial analysis, valuation, and evaluation of alternatives.* A key element of project success is sound financial assessment. The business development group plays a crucial role in managing the financial evaluation, ensuring that appropriate models and valuation methodologies are used, and challenging assumptions early in the process to ensure that objective business considerations drive the project financials. If assumptions reflect personal biases or political considerations, the business development group has an obligation to flush them out and eliminate them from the set of assumptions used. It also plays an important role in the determination of the methodology used in the development of financial valuations by questioning hypothesized relationships, models, and methodology used.

The business development group is responsible for the evaluation of alternatives to the proposed project. This entails evaluation of options along key dimensions of a project from strategic fit to cultural fit, which are key elements in determining the extent to which the two companies can work together, given the differences in management philosophy and business approach. However, no opportunity assessment is complete without understanding the impacts of errors in the assumptions used, possible divergence from the envisioned scenario, and risks materializing. The business development group outlines appropriate scenarios and is responsible for engaging the right project participants and overseeing the analysis and the evaluation of the range of impacts.

*4. Identification of synergies.* Identification of synergies is a major responsibility of the business development group. This takes place to eliminate proposed projects that do not close strategic and operational gaps identified or do not create sufficient synergies. Also, a comparison of the expected synergies from alternatives is made in order to rank those alternatives.

Synergy identification is followed by assessment of the likelihood of the synergies being realized given the project peculiarities, expertise, and talents of project participants. The business development group makes its expertise available and ensures that all costs and benefits are included in the calculation of net benefits when the project team quantifies the synergies. Additionally, it ensures that a balance between synergy costs and benefits is maintained throughout.

---

*Synergies are the extra benefits that accrue to the company because of an acquisition or a joint venture project. They are best exemplified by the expression that 1+1=3, 5, or more and usually refer to improvement in financial performance and market power directly attributable to the project and which the company could not achieve on its own.*

---

*5. Business case development.* Business cases are the means to formalize all that has been learned about the project and bring it together in one document. Traditionally, most of the emphasis in business cases is on the financials of the project and focus directed toward a single measure, the project's net present value (NPV).

---

*A business case is a document that brings together in a summary form the results of the various analyses and evaluations performed by the project team. It is an internal communication tool and it forms the basis that supports the decision-making and corporate approval process for a given project.*

---

A good business case brings together the elements of project assessment into a crisp summary and a set of recommendations to senior management, such as unmet customer needs satisfied by the project, strategic and operational fit, financial viability, alternatives considered, evaluation of risks and issues, sensitivity analysis, financing plans, and implementation and business plan requirements.

Acquisition and joint venture business cases are the responsibility of project teams. However, business development groups help to bring all the elements of project assessment together and develop a cohesive recommendation for a project. Besides obtaining or creating the business case information, the business development group helps create documents that record the negotiated terms and conditions and are used in communicating project status and progress. These documents include briefing packages for senior management and project status reports for external communications. The business development group also delivers a fair and reasonable representation of the facts of a project and provides its recommendation to senior management to pursue an opportunity.

### Negotiations Phase Responsibilities

*1. Negotiations support and guidance.* Negotiations begin the moment someone picks up the phone to call the person representing the other party. Most of the effort in negotiations, however, is concentrated toward the second half of the project time line. Here, the business development group makes a key contribution to projects through supporting the negotiations subteam. The support includes identification of the key issues in the project, development of the company negotiation positions on those issues, and guidance in developing and quantifying trade-offs and negotiating risk allocation and sharing with the other side. Having gone through other negotiations and seen how the process can be used to mitigate project risks, the business development group adds value and ensures that the understandings reached are included in legal agreements.

Negotiations are handled by a subteam which is usually headed by a senior manager, but is always supported by the core project team and advised by the business development organization. The reason for this is that the business development group knows how the process works, understands protocol, is familiar with issues likely to surface, has experience in preparing for negotiations, and knows what to look for. Consequently, it plays an important role in the negotiations from the start of the project and in some cases it assumes the responsibility of conducting the negotiations.

The business development group advises the negotiations subteam on all aspects, helps in the development of the negotiation strategy and plans, and ensures effective, all-around communications. Its responsibility is to ensure that the negotiations plan contains a thorough understanding of the other side's needs and positions on various issues, clearly stated project objectives and terms and conditions that must be obtained, and reasonable positions on all key issues impacting the project valuation. It also ensures a realistic timetable of negotiations with milestones and checkpoints, synergies accruing to both sides as a result of doing the project, and several quantified trade-offs of value to both sides.

2. *Governance structure of the new entity.* The definition of autonomy, the extent of integration of an acquired firm, and the governance structure of the joint venture company are responsibilities of the business development group. The reasons for the business development group's involvement in this area are its ability to translate strategic objectives into appropriate project structures, its knowledge of the issues and intricacies of the process and what is needed to produce success, its ability to provide guidance to joint venture steering committees and/or to lead its activities, and its ability to use its influence with senior management to gain support for the new entity.

Linkages with the parent companies must be established and maintained in order to provide effective management and issue resolution channels after deal closing and project implementation. That responsibility rests with the business development group, which appoints one of its managers to the steering committee, which, in turn, picks the joint venture's board of directors, creates the organizational structure of the new entity, and staffs key positions. It also assists the project team to select the liaison subteam to ensure continuous

> *The steering committee is a group of seasoned business development managers appointed to a team whose responsibility is to create the governance structure of a joint venture, develop the new entity's mission and strategy, and ensure consistency of goals and objectives with the parent companies. It also assists the joint venture board of directors and ensures effective transitioning of responsibilities to its management team and continuity of purpose and objectives.*

support from the parent companies and realization of the business plans of the new entity.

> *The liaison subteam is established in the post-implementation phase and is a group composed of managers from the parent company whose responsibilities include interfacing with the new entity, ensuring adequate support, and issue resolution.*

3. *Project structure and financing.* The business development group and the project team work closely with appropriate organizations to create efficient financing structure options for the project, to negotiate terms and conditions, and to develop the agreements that impact the terms of financing. Involvement

by the business development group in financing issues and in the financing subteam is advisable because financing requires a good understanding of how internal and external financing can be combined to arrive at optimal financing structures, what external financing options are possible, and what funding sources can be tapped for a given project.

### Implementation Phase Responsibilities

Project implementation determines the extent of an acquisition or a joint venture project success. Usually, project implementation is an afterthought, something that needs to be done after agreements are concluded. However, for successful business development groups, implementation planning is on equal footing with strategy and is part of the business development process. It anticipates human and capital requirements, plans integration into the company's structure, and plans how to extract expected synergies.

*1. Project implementation.* Appropriate project implementation is a key element of success for acquisition and joint venture projects, and the business development group is responsible for several areas: It oversees the formation of the implementation subteam, creates linkage to the core project team, advises on implementation planning, and establishes processes to resolve implementation issues. The business development group assesses the skills and human resources needed and helps the implementation subteam transfer responsibilities successfully. It also monitors implementation to ensure that the company's senior management team embraces the new entity management team, provides support for it, and dedicates resources to implement successfully.

*2. Extraction of synergies.* The business development group is responsible for the early identification of synergies in a project, is involved in the quantification of synergy costs and benefits, and assists in the negotiations of sharing the costs and benefits with the seller of a target company or with a joint venture partner. Knowing how to extract synergies, it assists the implementation subteam in planning synergy extraction, which is reflected in the business plan of the new entity. More importantly, the business development group adds value by helping the implementation subteam translate the findings and recommendations of the due diligence subteam into ways to create new synergies.

*3. Integration of lessons learned.* The business development group is viewed as the central keeper of knowledge and expertise in doing acquisitions and joint venture projects. At the conclusion of each project, the business development group representative on the project team performs an assessment of what took place in the evaluation, negotiation, and implementation phases of the project. This assessment is called postmortem analysis; it is done to extract valuable lessons learned and adds value by institutionalizing the lessons learned from every project undertaken. It is crucial to successful business development groups, which learn by reviewing how the process worked, the project team's successes and failures, unusual events that occurred, and project idiosyncrasies. Once the experiences and the lessons learned from a project are internalized by the entire business development team, they are made part of the process and become guidelines on how to handle a particular issue next time.

*4. Monitoring performance.* Monitoring performance of acquisitions or joint ventures is viewed as mundane and performed by first-level managers who track and report accounting information. Such a view of tracking does not allow for measuring the success of a project in terms of strategic return on investment being realized or to what extent management objectives are being met. Successful business development groups embrace a broader view of tracking and look at the new entity's performance in terms of traditional accounting information, strategic return on investment, and realization of management and entity objectives. This view results in much more effective measures of new-entity performance.

The business development group and the project team leader ensure that the implementation subteam develops operational performance targets and tracking systems to monitor and control the performance of the new entity. It also ensures that there is a linkage between the objectives of the implementation subteam and those of the new-entity managers with performance of the new entity in order to reward success in harnessing expected synergies and project implementation. When earn-out arrangements are warranted, the business development group advises the implementation and liaison subteams concerning the structuring of earn-out formulas and management of these arrangements.

---

*Earn-out arrangements are agreements in which payments made to recipients are determined by the extent to which stated objectives and business plans are realized. They are an effective way of negotiating a hedge against risks that impact the realization of business plan targets.*

---

## INTEGRATION OF LEARNING AND METRICS OF SUCCESS

### Transfer of Knowledge

After a project is completed, world-class business development groups engage in postmortem analysis, which examines how the project was handled from the day the idea was formed to implementation. The process is reviewed and evaluated, problem areas are identified, what was done well is highlighted, and the lessons learned in the project are recorded. Once the findings are fully understood and digested, recommendations are made on how knowledge obtained from participation in a project can be disseminated throughout the business development community of the company for incorporation in the process for future projects. It is important that the knowledge transfer take place because it builds the experience base, improves the organization's effectiveness and productivity, and results in much better handling of projects. The expectation is that mistakes made in a project are not likely to be repeated in the future, peculiarities of one project can shed light on future projects, and successes can be imitated.

A analysis by itself is of limited value if it does not include the views, input, and feedback of internal clients, peers, subordinates, and supervisors as well as the views of suppliers to the business development group and external participants. This 360-degree evaluation of the process and individual and team performance is the exclusive responsibility of the business development group, which includes the views of the acquired or the partner company because they provide a view from the outside. The views of internal client groups along with those of external parties provide the balance needed to ensure that appropriate learning is integrated into the business development process to enhance its effectiveness.

### Metrics of Business Development Group Performance

World-class business development groups are learning organizations. Because of that, they review all projects upon completion to assess what was done right, what went wrong, what were some major issues or problems and the causes of those problems, what solutions were developed, and major lessons learned. Experiences obtained in projects are recorded to ensure that effective knowledge transfer and use in future projects takes place. However, senior management also needs to assess the performance of the business development group and its contributions toward making a project successful.

A business development group is judged in terms of the results it produces in working opportunities through the established processes. Measuring results takes two forms: the quantitative measures approach versus the broader qualitative and holistic view. Both views of measuring success have merit, and use of both is encouraged when looking to assess business development organizational effectiveness and success. The quantitative metrics of business development group success include:

1.  The cycle time from identification of opportunity to completion of the project. This is a commonly used criterion, but needs to be tempered by the complexities of projects and unusual circumstances.
2.  Some measure of return on investment achieved. Project financial criteria such as NPV, net income, free cash flow, and return on assets are monitored on an ongoing basis and reported to senior management.
3.  The number of opportunities identified, assessed, and implemented in a year. Again, this is a measure that needs to be examined in the context of project team experiences and complexity of projects.
4.  The budget of the business development group relative to amount of revenue generated through new projects. This provides another incentive to institute an

effective screening process, to identify resource requirements early on, to be selective about expanding resources, and to eliminate projects of questionable value.

5. Realized synergies relative to identified synergies. This is a closely tracked measure because it shows how successful the business development group has been in evaluating synergies, negotiating synergy premiums, and implementing projects.

6. Number of deals consummated versus opportunities assessed. This measure tells two things about the business development group's activities: how good its screening and evaluation processes are and how focused it is on projects it engages in.

7. Number of successful projects over the company's strategic business development history. This is a broad measure of expertise residing in the business development group and experience accumulated through time.

The measures to evaluate and monitor the business development group's success in terms of less precise, qualitative criteria include:

1. Review of the project and evaluation of how well the process worked after the project is implemented. This includes assessment of implementation ease and to what extent project objectives were met.

2. Survey of project participants to obtain their views on how effective the business development group is. This is an effort to assess the internal client satisfaction and obtain input and feedback on the business development process. Survey participants should include functional experts, business unit heads, and senior managers.

3. Audits performed two to three years after a project has been implemented to determine success. The focus of these audits is to evaluate how the company's strategy has been helped by the project and how the actual costs compare with the expected costs and benefits of synergies.

4. The extent of internal politics present in projects and the extent to which the objectives of different business units are achieved. This determines the focus and effectiveness of the business development group in keeping impediments out of the project process.

5. Innovation in terms of methods, approaches, and techniques introduced in the business development process. This requires benchmarking with world-class practices to determine how close the business development group comes to following such practices.

6. The level of cooperation and communications within the team and with other corporate entities. This is reflected in the frequency of project team and senior management briefings, the consistency of status reports and messages delivered internally, and the speed of approvals.

7. Ability to learn from project experiences and transfer the knowledge gained. This requires a review of previous analyses to assess how successfully lessons learned in past projects were applied to current projects.

It is recommended that both approaches be used to develop metrics to judge business development group success on a project-by-project basis. In addition, one has to get beneath the surface to really understand success of acquisition and joint venture projects and institute measures to enhance it.

## SUMMARY

The most common and effective structure of the business development group is one where the group reports to a corporate vice president of planning and business development, who, in turn, reports directly to the company CEO. The business development group is involved in practically every aspect of a project and plays an important role in the validation of corporate vision and strategy, opportunity identification, project definition, and strategic and operational fit assessment. It participates in the negotiations phase, in the business case development, and in getting corporate project approvals. It also advises the project team on project implementation, monitoring and control issues, and extraction of expected synergies. Finally, it conducts the project postmortem and integrates lessons learned in the project process.

The contributions of the business development group are in every phase of the process and demonstrate the importance of this group in acquisition and joint venture projects. The culture of a successful business development group is examined along with the skills and backgrounds of the individuals making up this organization. The characteristics of world-class business development groups are reviewed and the metrics of success are outlined. In addition, transfer of knowledge and the value of organizational learning in improving processes and handling projects more effectively are discussed.

In world-class companies, the business development group is a key organization driving acquisition or joint venture projects with support from the project sponsor and the senior management team. Due to the central position it occupies and the linkages it provides for the entire project team throughout the project process, it is in a position to influence how projects are executed and ensure success. Therefore, senior managers should ensure that an experienced business development organization is established and maintained.

The roles and responsibilities of the business development group are broad and varied, but in each project they should be fairly well defined and understood by all project participants from the beginning of the project. Because of the big impact that the activities of the business development group can have on the success of the project, only experienced and seasoned associates are involved in acquisition and joint venture projects or assigned to the steering committee. Continuous learning, training, and accumulation of experience are essential in enhancing the effectiveness of the business development group.

# 4

---

# PROJECT TEAMS AND SUBTEAMS

## INTRODUCTION

Two major reasons for acquisition and joint venture failures are inexperience of project teams and confusion about roles and responsibilities, which result in conflict among project participants, work not getting done, issues not being addressed properly, and projects being led by external advisors. Negotiations take longer and desired terms and conditions are obtained at prohibitive costs to the company, implementations become difficult, synergies do not materialize, and the project fails to create shareholder value.

In acquisition and joint venture projects the time lines are tight, and there is no time for on-the-job training. Because of that, it is very important that the teams formed to handle projects are structured properly, the interfaces well defined, and the roles and responsibilities clearly understood. The right project team composition, understanding of project process, and effective execution are essential in creating conditions for success.

Senior management and sponsor involvement is required to ensure success and for that reason, the discussion in this chapter begins with the responsibilities of senior management and the project sponsor. The composition of the project team and the various subteams and responsibilities are examined along with those of external advisors. Recommendations on how to put together a strong project team are also presented.

## THE PROJECT TEAM

A narrow definition of an acquisition and joint venture project team is one that includes a business development representative, the team leader, the technical functional expert, the financial analyst, and the lawyer. This defines the core team, which is only a part of the entire project team. The extended team includes senior management, the project sponsor, the business development group's representative in the project, business unit heads impacted by the project, the negotiations subteam, the due diligence subteam, and the project financing subteam. In addition, it includes the human resources subteam, the public relations subteam, the implementation subteam, the liaison subteam, the steering committee, investment bankers and external advisors, and the new entity's management team. Figure 4.1 shows the various project subteams and their linkages.

The core project team consists of the project team leader, a business development expert, a technical functional expert, a strong financial analyst, and a lawyer, but from time to time, experts in various areas function as core team members. These experts get heavily involved in helping resolve issues and provide answers to important questions to move the project forward.

**Figure 4.1**
**The Structure of Acquisition and Joint Venture Project Teams**

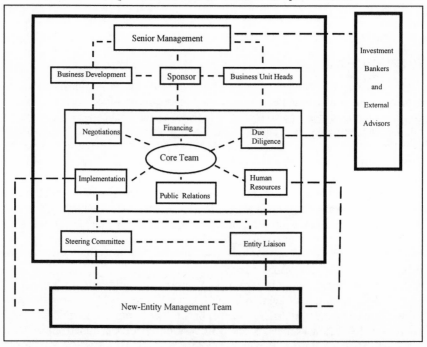

The business development group is always present in acquisitions and joint ventures —first, because it represents the corporate interests in the project, and second, because of the knowledge and expertise that resides in that group. A business development group representative is usually involved in a project from its inception, becomes the project leader, provides the linkage to corporate strategy and long-term goals, and advises the team on process and requirements.

It is a good idea to invite business unit heads to participate in the decision to undertake a project before it gets defined. Business unit heads may have alternative plans that are better than the proposed project or suggest a better project definition. Their buy-in and support of the project are essential in getting the project through the approval processes. If business unit heads are included in the project selection, they support the project through the entire process. Another reason for including them in the extended project team is that they can provide the functional experts for the project evaluation, negotiation, and implementation. Without this support, the project is likely to go nowhere and will be abandoned. Business unit heads also lend support and expedite project execution and approval. If they participate in the project selection, they use their influence to get the project through the approval process quickly and with minor modifications.

## DIVISION OF RESPONSIBILITIES

### Senior Management and Project Sponsor

Acquisition and joint venture projects go to senior management for approval of the project's merits and funding authorization. Projects involving substantial investment dollars require approval of the chairman and the board of directors. Since senior management must at some point be involved in reviewing a project, it is best that it be involved right from the beginning. There are several advantages to early senior management involvement:

1. Enhancing their understanding of the project rationale and merits. This reduces the briefings needed later in the process when status reports are necessary or when complications arise.
2. Getting commitment to support the project through the evaluation phase. This is an important consideration because it keeps the senior management team engaged in monitoring the status of the project.
3. Keeping communication channels open for periodic progress updates. Having committed their support for the project evaluation, senior managers require periodic updates and status reports, which produce further involvement and usually additional support to see the project to completion.

To be effective and contribute in the project process, senior managers involved in acquisition and joint venture projects must understand the business development needs of the company and the various alternatives that can meet those needs. They need to obtain the business unit heads' views on the proposed project and solicit reasonable alternatives. This is advisable in order to obtain their commitment and support for the selected project. Senior management reviews the project feasibility study, approves proceeding to the business development stage, and authorizes resources to complete the evaluation and negotiations phases.

Initiating contact with senior management on the other side, when required, is a role that no other group can carry out as effectively as the company's senior management team. It reviews progress of negotiations, authorizes major trade-offs, and approves key terms and conditions negotiated.

It also approves the business case for the project, including the implementation and the business plan for the new entity and all bids. This requires a final check concerning the value of the project and summaries of these documents are produced for senior management review. Furthermore, senior management briefs the chairman and, when necessary, the board of directors. When the project approaches completion of negotiations and closing, the project sponsor, the business development group representative, the project team leader, and the investment banker as a team prepare senior management to brief the chairman and the board of directors on the value of the project and obtain their approval.

Involvement of senior management through the project is important because that results in better appreciation of the project's strategic objectives and the extent to which they are met, and the need for support of the new entity's management team. That understanding helps senior management appreciate the project merits, approve the transaction, and provide the support needed for the new entity to be successful. Senior management's access to the project team and information comes from three channels: the project sponsor, the business development group, and business unit heads. The independent assessment required by senior management concerning the fairness of the transaction comes from internal experts not involved in the project and trusted external advisors.

The primary interface of senior management with the project team is through the project sponsor, although the business development group often briefs senior management on acquisition and joint venture projects and related issues. The project sponsor is basically the project champion. It is crucial that the sponsor is convinced of the value of the project in order to convince the senior management team of the project's merits, ensure availability of resources to execute the project properly, and obtain support for the project team's decisions.

---

*The project sponsor is a seasoned company executive with experience in strategic business development who is a member of the senior management team, or a well-respected business unit head designated to have oversight responsibility, obtain the required support, and bring the project to completion.*

---

In order for an executive to qualify as a sponsor of the acquisition or joint venture project, that individual must have an appreciation of the process, the skills required to manage a project successfully at a high level, and some previous experience with acquisition and joint venture projects. The sponsor must possess vision to see how the project can create shareholder value and provide guidelines and support to the project team, and since the sponsor oversees a team of highly skilled professionals, he or she must have the skills to communicate effectively. The sponsor is the main channel of communications between the project team and senior management and understands the issues involved and the needs of the two groups. In addition, this individual makes decisions when presented with factual evidence, but escalates a major issue to senior management and provides recommendations.

The formation of the project team is the responsibility of the business development organization, but the project sponsor influences the composition of the project team and stays close to the project until it is defined well enough to begin an in-depth evaluation. Once the project starts going through the assessment process, the project sponsor assumes a high supervisory role, but stays informed at all times about important issues and progress on the project. The sponsor's responsibility ends with the closing of the deal and the appointment of the liaison team and the steering committee.

## Project Team Roles and Responsibilities

The functions of the core project team start with developing the project workplan and ensuring that the project goes through each of the steps involved in the process. It works with the business development group to obtain the expertise and talent needed to execute a project successfully and performs some of the key functions in the evaluation, negotiations, and implementation phases if needed. The core team also provides support for the project subteams and assistance in resolving issues as they arise.

The core team interfaces with the project sponsor, senior management, the project team of the target or the joint venture partner, and investment bankers. It briefs senior management and manages the engagement of outside consultants and technical experts. Being a central interface for all internal groups and communicator of progress on the project, it ensures a smooth transfer of responsibilities and continuity of purpose and objectives at each stage of the project process. It serves as the central source of authoritative information and manages the project through the process to ensure efficient project approvals.

In addition to their assigned functions in a subteam, project team members have broader responsibilities. For example, team members are expected to ensure open and uninhibited communication between subteams since without this, subteams become dysfunctional and projects end up implemented unsuccessfully. Team members are also expected to cooperate and assist in their area of expertise and share experiences and expertise outside the narrow requirements of the job. Project team members must understand and deliver expected outputs in a timely fashion, which means they must support the project workplan requirements and voice objections when expectations are unreasonable or when better solutions are possible. Finally, they are expected to ensure effective transition of responsibilities and continuity of purpose. This requires supporting the receiving subteam with involvement until the project moves to the next phase so that there is continuity throughout the project.

The work of each subteam links with the work of the project team indirectly through the individuals on the subteam who are members of the core team and directly via the core team. Effective transition of responsibilities requires open communication channels and well-defined linkages with the rest of the larger team. This is important in bringing together the different inputs into a coherent evaluation and recommendation. Project team experience, open communications, well-defined linkages, and extensive cooperation characterize all world-class project teams.

### The Role of External Advisors

Besides internal professionals, the project team includes external advisors and consultants with expertise in different areas. It includes investment bankers, accounting and tax experts, legal advisors, independent technical consultants, market assessment professionals, and, in the case of large and complex projects, a chief negotiator and a financing advisor. There are two reasons for hiring external advisors: First, certain highly specialized expertise does not reside within the company. This expertise includes investment banking, due diligence, tax and valuation, and legal support. Second, the company has expectations that through external advisors, an independent assessment and objective view of the project value can be obtained which are not possible using internal teams.

The roles of external advisors are routinely defined by their specialty and the project requirements. In order to get maximum value from the engagement of external advisors, it is important that the business development group defines specific responsibilities for external advisors. In addition, the project team leader oversees the work of the external advisors because that work is linked with the project team's through the project team leader and the business development group.

Some acquisition and joint venture experts maintain that external advisors should not be involved in the early phases of the project assessment and negotiations. However, the project team must be eclectic and engage the right advisors from the moment the decision is made to pursue a project. The project team must assign responsibilities and manage the work of external advisors to maximize their contributions. Under such conditions, external advisors make a difference in creating successful projects.

## FUNCTIONS AND LINKAGES OF SUBTEAMS

### The Negotiations Subteam

For projects of average complexity, the negotiations subteam is made up of the chief negotiator, the financial analyst, and an experienced lawyer. The chief negotiator is usually a business unit head impacted most by a project, a business development manager, or an external professional negotiator in the case of complex projects. The negotiations subteam owns the responsibility of conducting the project negotiations. Contrary to the common belief that this subteam is the only group involved in negotiations, the core team and various experts provide the support needed in order for the negotiation subteam to function.

The negotiations subteam plays a key role in ensuring project success because its work impacts the structure of the deal, the terms and conditions of the purchase of the target company, or the creation of a joint venture entity. It also impacts the nature of legal agreements, the price to be paid to close the transaction, and how project risks are shared among project participants. The negotiations subteam links with the rest of the project team through the core team, the business development group, and the project sponsor, who gets involved when an important decision needs to be made and escalation is required. The functions of this subteam are described in greater depth in Chapter 12.

### The Implementation Subteam

The implementation subteam is a group of professionals charged with managing the transition from legal agreements to actual operating entities in accordance with company strategy and project objectives. The implementation subteam is staffed with experts in various key functional areas who also possess human element skills necessary to manage organizational change. The subteam is engaged as soon as it becomes apparent that the project is likely to close and stays involved until its responsibilities are transferred to the new entity, the liaison subteam, and the steering committee.

The implementation subteam manages change, disputes, and conflict in the critical transition moments of a project. How well it manages change determines to large degree how successful the project is and how much value gets created. That is why in world-class project teams there is heavy emphasis on the implementation subteam since its work lays the foundation for successful new-entity operations and harnessing expected synergies. Continuity in the work of the implementation subteam is so important, that members of this subteam are often seconded to the new entity.

The implementation subteam relies on the business development group for definition of strategic direction and the degree of autonomy of the new entity, on the core team and functional experts for support, and on the legal agreements negotiated to develop its plans. Its main contribution is in ensuring that the new entity's organization is appropriately structured, staffed, and supported to operate successfully. It also assesses the costs, requirements, and benefits of integration.

### The Due Diligence Subteam

Due diligence is a thorough examination and checking of every piece of information obtained from a potential target or joint venture partner. It includes investigation of all aspects of finances, marketing and distribution, human resources, organizational structure and company culture, technical capabilities, and customer and supplier relationships. The due diligence effort is important in ensuring project success because it verifies information presented to the project team, uncovers problem areas and hidden information, and forms the basis for sound recommendations and decision making.

The due diligence subteam consists of the financial analyst on the project team, accountants and tax experts, and experts in various functional areas in need of due diligence. The charge of this subteam is to help the project team in validating data and information used in the evaluation, to confirm expectations, ensure consistency of assumptions, look for opportunities for improvement, and provide recommendations to make decisions. It links to the work of the project team primarily through the financial analyst, but also through the functional experts involved in the due diligence work. The recommendations of this subteam are assessed by the project team and incorporated in the decision-making process.

### The Human Resources Subteam

The human resources subteam consists of experts from the personnel department, a business development representative, and a member of the implementation subteam. Senior management may get involved in the activities of this subteam when new-entity management contracts are required. The major function of this subteam is to define the skills inventory and requirements for the new entity's management team with focus on the technology and product development, marketing and sales, personnel, and financial management leadership teams. It also conducts the organizational and human resources due diligence, which requires assessment of existing skills and evaluation of salary and incentive plans, wages and benefits, and labor issues as well as assessment of personnel policies.

The human resources subteam negotiates termination of contracts of managers in the target company. Integration of a target company creates an opportunity to downsize the incoming organization, but often requires ending involuntarily the contracts of its senior managers. This needs experience in handling the emotional and financial aspects of contract termination. In addition, this subteam negotiates earn-out formulas and new contracts for the senior managers retained. New contracts for retained managers involve negotiation of a package that includes position and title, reporting structure, salary and benefits, incentive plans, performance requirements against stated objectives, and termination clauses. Finally, this subteam manages secondmends and transfers to and from the new entity. This cross-pollination is required to transfer knowledge and know-how between the new entity and the parent company and is best achieved by assigning key company managers to the new entity and promising new-entity managers to the parent company.

Participation of personnel experts in the project is important because of their ability to conduct an effective human resources due diligence. An appropriate organizational and human resources due diligence contributes a great deal to the success of a project in two ways: changing the governance and organizational structure of the new entity or, based on its findings, recommending complete disengagement from a project. The work of this subteam is linked with the project team's through business development and implementation subteam members assigned to the human resources subteam.

### The Financing Subteam

The project financing subteam is formed when it becomes evident that the deal is likely to be consummated and its role is to bring efficient financing to the project. It consists of the project team leader, the financial analyst, the business development representative, a corporate treasury manager, and external advisors. The functions of this subteam are to:

1. Review and assess the project from a risk evaluation perspective. In this step, it reviews the project business case with particular emphasis on the project economics and risks to determine whether financing enhancements will be required.
2. Evaluate several financing options and alternatives. In this step, the various schemes of bringing financing to the project are reviewed and screened, the costs and benefits of each evaluated, and the best two or three options evaluated for efficiency, certainty, and completeness.
3. Negotiate the financing aspect of the project deal structure. This involves negotiations of financing terms and conditions with the seller or the partner and funding institutions participating in the financing of the project.
4. Interface with financing advisors and the financing community. Financing advisors and participating institutions need help in understanding the project rationale and objectives, the relationships and assumptions behind the financials, and the risks involved in the project.
5. Negotiate terms and conditions and drafting of financing agreements. This is an iterative process in which proposals and counter-proposals are made, trade-offs are considered, and different risk allocation schemes are used to affect financing.
6. Implement the financing and monitor related activities. This involves managing the document creation supporting the requirements of institutions involved for timely disbursement of funds and resolving issues as they arise.

The contributions of the financing subteam impact project success because they impact the availability and speed of financing, the cost of funding a project, and the way project risks are allocated and managed. Its activities link with those of the rest of the project team through the business development representative and the financial analyst. It should be noted that in the case of off-balance sheet or limited recourse financing, the subteam includes technical and legal experts specializing in financing.

## The Public Relations Subteam

The public relations subteam consists of the project team leader and public relations experts who specialize in dealing with the press and external communications. Its linkages to the rest of the project team are through the project team leader. The reasons for the existence of this subteam and its significance are:

1. The formulation of consistent messages about progress on the project. Because of the significance of acquisitions and joint ventures in meeting the company's strategic objectives and seller or the partner company considerations, consistent, measured, and balanced messages need to be delivered externally.
2. The perception created by its announcements in the marketplace. The perception created by the undertaking of a project must be managed prudently by experts in shaping investor views that are consistent with company objectives and project costs and benefits.
3. The impact external announcements have on customers and suppliers alike. In addition to the investment community, customer and supplier fears and expectations need to be managed throughout the project to ensure continuity of the relationships in the post-implementation period.

The work of the public relations subteam contributes to project success by creating a set of expectations that are consistent with the project's objectives and its value to the company. Also, this subteam is the central point for all issues that have to do with external communications because it is important to deliver a consistent message throughout the life of the project. Investors, customers, and suppliers expect that, and this translates into three major roles for the public relations subteam: communicate progress on a project internally and externally as appropriate, work with and coach senior management for press interviews, and prepare and release deal announcements that deliver clearly and precisely the intended message.

Public announcements of a deal have market and competitive impacts because they shape the perception of a superior transaction that can benefit customers significantly. The intended audience of deal press releases is the investment community, the customers of the parent and the target companies (or the joint venture entity and the parent companies in the case of a partnership), and the suppliers of the new entity. As a by-product of this targeting for public announcements, customers of competitors are made aware of the benefits of the new entity to its customers and may be influenced to give their business to the new entity.

### The Tactical Support Subteam

As the name indicates, the work of the tactical support subteam is very different from that of the rest of the project team, but essential to ensure project success. Because of the tight project time lines and the highly pressurized environments, its activities help everyone on the project team and create lasting impressions on external participants in the project. The functions of this subteam cover a wide area; namely:

1. Preparing meeting rooms and materials for meetings. This involves detailed planning to ensure that all the physical arrangements and equipment requirements are taken care of and supplies are available.
2. Setting up meetings and publishing meeting minutes as needed. This requires extensive coordination and communications to ensure participation by all who need to attend meetings. Also, taking and publishing meeting notes requires understanding of issues and diligence in following discussions.
3. Providing phone coverage and secretarial support and making convenient and efficient travel arrangements. Effective secretarial support dedicated to the project facilitates the functioning of the project team and communications with senior management.
4. Maintaining the war room and the insider list. This is of tremendous help to the project team and senior management, who are continuously pulled in different directions dealing with the numerous issues that surface in the project.
5. Preparing presentations and distributing materials. This clerical support to the project team is of tremendous help because it frees up team members to perform knowledge-intensive functions.
6. Updating the project workplan on a continuous basis and tracking progress on various deliverables and budgets. The help of the tactical support subteam in this area enables the project team leader to manage the project effectively and communicate the status of the project to all team members simultaneously.

While mundane, these support functions are important to ensure timely execution of the project evaluation, negotiation, and implementation because they free up the project team professionals to focus on their areas of responsibility.

## POST-IMPLEMENTATION SUBTEAMS

### The Liaison Subteam

The implementation subteam ceases to exist as soon as the new entity is created and is fully operational. The responsibility of the interface between a new entity and parent companies is then handed over to the liaison subteam. This is a group of managers with experience in organizational issues who are basically the linkage that the new entity has into the parent companies' management. Sometimes, implementation managers become members of the liaison subteam to ensure continuity of purpose and maintenance of relationships. The linkages to the rest of the team are through the business development group, which monitors the activities of the new entity beyond the start of operations.

The work of the liaison team is important because it has a direct impact on the success of a project in several ways:

1. Ensuring adequate parent company funding for the new entity's business plan. This requires briefings of senior management on issues surrounding the business plan and the implications of financial and managerial support being withheld from the new entity.
2. Setting operational targets and objectives with the new entity's management team and obtaining parent approvals. This requires understanding the company's expectations and the new entity's capabilities as well as its management team's objectives and incentive plans.
3. Negotiating new entity reporting requirements to the parent company. Often, bureaucratic reporting requirements are placed on a new entity because of inadequate understanding of what is important to be tracked. Therefore, the liaison subteam needs to determine what is important to be monitored and negotiate reporting of appropriate variables and time schedules.
4. Managing secondmends and transfers in and out of the new entity in conjunction with the human resources organization. Working with the human resources subteam, the liaison subteam facilitates the rotation of managers in and out of the new entity and ensures continuity in transferring benefits in both directions.

### The Steering Committee

The steering committee consists of seasoned managers and professionals experienced in implementing acquisitions and joint venture projects. The functions of the steering committee are to:

1. Select the board of directors for the new entity. This is probably the most important contribution of the steering committee because in the process, the interests of the new entity and the parent company need to be accommodated. In the case of a joint venture, the selection of board members becomes more challenging because of different partner interests.

2.   Define the new entity's business area, its mission, and its strategy. This function requires understanding of company strategy, project objectives, and the strengths and weaknesses on both sides. It also requires vision in creating a mission that is consistent with that of the company.

3.   Interface with the new entity's board members and senior management on major issues. As the new entity becomes operational, a number of high-level issues develop that the steering committee needs to resolve with input from senior management.

4.   Review and re-define the degree of autonomy for the new entity. This requires an objective review of progress and a close working relationship with senior management and the new entity's board of directors to adjust the level of independence afforded the new entity. It usually occurs when there are major discrepancies in the new entity's performance versus senior management expectations which require reconciliation of the issues.

5.   Provide guidance on governance issues. Changes in the composition of the board of directors and major organizational changes in the new entity are reviewed by the steering committee and recommendations are presented to senior management. Sometimes, the steering committee is responsible for searching and screening new board members and key managers.

6.   Ensure consistency of strategies, goals, and objectives between the parent and the new entity as it is being implemented. On an ongoing basis, that responsibility is transferred to the liaison subteam and the business development group. Often, the business development group performs sanity checks on an annual basis to determine consistency of strategy, goals, and objectives of the parent and the new entity.

7.   Make sure the new entity is set up and managed properly to become a successful operation. The implementation subteam is responsible for making the project operational, but the steering committee uses its experience and influence to ensure that the new entity's operations are set on firm ground and have the support of the company's senior management team.

Ordinarily, the steering committee consists of a member from the business development group, a senior industry expert, and a member with organizational structure and human resources skills. The work of the steering committee is linked to the rest of the project team's work through the business development group and the implementation and liaison subteams. It takes place right along with and complements the work of the implementation and liaison subteams, while dealing with a different set of issues. The implementation subteam and the steering committee develop a common approach to the new entity and agree on a common set of operational performance targets. The liaison subteam and the steering committee are in constant communication to ensure that there is no conflict in their approaches and they coordinate parent company briefings and requests for support for the new entity.

## SUMMARY

The project team is composed of the core team and subteams that handle negotiations, due diligence, project financing, human resource issues, public relations, and implementation. The extended team includes the liaison subteam, the steering committee, investment bankers and external advisors, and the new entity's management team. It also includes senior management, the project sponsor, the business development group and its representative in the project, and business unit heads impacted by the project.

There is a vast area of expertise that should reside in a project team to produce success and the need for an experienced project team is apparent. The consequences of inexperienced project teams are also apparent. They include lack of subject matter knowledge, little appreciation for project process, incomplete project evaluation, ineffective negotiations, poor project implementation, discontinuities in the transitioning of responsibilities, poor support for the new entity, inability to harness synergies, and eventual project failure.

# 5

---

# PREPARING FOR ACQUISITION AND JOINT VENTURE PROJECTS

## INTRODUCTION

In world-class organizations where projects are always successful, equal emphasis is placed on the activities that take place before a project is evaluated, while it is being evaluated, and after the project is implemented. In this chapter, we concentrate on the activities prior to actually engaging in the project. These activities involve several important elements which, if not executed properly, can cause a project to fail. We discuss those elements and explain why they are important in ensuring project success.

Preparation for acquisition and joint venture projects involves organizational preparation and briefings, resource requirement assessment, and process-related work. Preparation is essential and contributes to project success in several ways. First, it helps the company clarify its strategic goals and objectives. The company's long term strategy needs are revisited in light of industry changes and it is always a good idea for goals and objectives to be reviewed and, if necessary, revised prior to engaging in acquisition or joint venture projects. Preparation leads to reevaluation of needs and definition of project objectives, which is done by identifying the gaps in strategy and operational capabilities. After strategic and operational gaps are identified, project objectives are developed and profiles of desired target or partner companies created.

Preparation involves examining different ways to accomplish objectives. After selection criteria have been established, the examination of alternatives results in selecting a balanced and objective solution. Using established processes the project team arrives at a project selection that represents a consensus decision and prepares senior management to receive the proposed project favorably. More important, however, is setting up the structure to handle the evaluation, negotiation, and implementation of a project. This structure includes the financial and human resources required as well as the analytical preparation and the development of approaches to dealing with different types of projects and engaging the right project advisors.

Preparation before the project goes through the assessment, negotiation, and implementation process helps make each process step successful and portrays a positive image to the selling and target companies, to potential joint venture partners, and to external advisors. A positive image from the start is essential in managing an acquisition or a joint venture project effectively. Otherwise, the project team is not effective and is seriously disadvantaged.

## THE STRATEGIC ASPECTS

### Strategic and Operational Gap Analysis

Preparing for acquisition or joint venture projects provides a good opportunity to revisit the corporate strategy and the underlying components. First, the core business definition, the company mission, and what the company aspires to be are reviewed. The core business definition evaluation entails an assessment of the company's main business, its product line and life cycles, and identification of its own strengths and weaknesses. The review of strengths and weaknesses applies to management skills, market position, technical competencies, cost structure, and financial performance. That is, it applies to all areas that determine a company's competitive advantage.

> *A company's business definition is the articulation of what constitutes its core business areas in the context of its mission statement. It is based on the company's deployment of assets and its competitive position in the industry and is a statement about the scope of the company, which then outlines the boundaries of the company's operations.*

Once the company's future business definition is acceptable to senior management, its strengths and weaknesses are evaluated and the mission of the company comes into focus. At this stage, it is critical for management to define what the company aspires to be in the long run, given the current state of technology evolution, market changes, and competition and industry structure changes. Once the mission of the company is understood and communicated throughout the management team, the review of the existing long-term strategy begins. That is, an examination of how the company plans to go from its current business definition to the one outlined by the mission statement is undertaken.

The review and development of the corporate long-term strategy entails identifying the key requirements to enhance the competitive position of the company and developing ways in which to deploy corporate resources so as to minimize the weaknesses and leverage and expand the strengths of the company resources. Once the corporate strategic objectives and requirements are defined, the strategic gap analysis begins by comparing the requirements of the strategy with the current state of affairs. At this stage it is determined whether the company's business units are able to meet those requirements internally or whether the company needs to engage in an acquisition or joint venture project in order to meet the strategic objectives. That is, the gap in strategic capabilities is identified and possible solutions are examined.

Using the findings of the strategic gap analysis as the starting point, the business development group goes on to the operational gap analysis where differences between actual and desired states are more measurable, such as market share, unit costs, technology, R&D, and product development. The purpose of the operational gap analysis is to measure the company's weaknesses through those differences and look for means to fill those gaps. This is a significant step because it defines the elements that a project should bring to the table and the desired profile of a potential acquisition target or a joint venture partner.

With strategic and operational gaps identified, the corporate business development group looks for internal solutions. It solicits alternatives from the business units and determines to what extent they meet the strategic and operational gaps of the company, and not only those of the individual business unit. When internal alternatives are exhausted and a greenfield approach to meeting the strategic objectives is ruled out, the focus turns to acquisition or joint venture projects.

---

*A greenfield approach is one in which a company starts from ground zero and builds with internal resources and talent the required capabilities under conditions it considers appropriate. Three key advantages of the greenfield approach are its cost-effectiveness, a stable growth, and the development of company resources.*

---

After the business development group and senior management have concluded that the best approach to meeting the company's long-term objectives is through acquisition or joint venture projects, there is one more step: the comparison between achieving the long-term goals through an acquisition or through a joint venture. This is a difficult decision for which senior management may wish to obtain additional advice from trusted external experts and consultants in order to develop consensus on the business development activity to pursue.

In world-class companies, the decision to acquire versus to form a joint venture is based on several key considerations:

1.   The extent of control over the new entity's operation. If a tight control is required, then the choice is tilted toward an acquisition because in joint ventures, control is shared and partner interests may, at some point, diverge.
2.   The cost of a merger or acquisition versus that of a joint venture. Here all direct and indirect costs must be considered: financial, management, technology contributions, access to markets, know-how, and the time involved in doing an acquisition versus creating a joint venture company.
3.   The human resources expanded in doing an acquisition versus a joint venture. This involves a comparison of the number of managers and the length of time required to work an acquisition with those required throughout the life of a joint venture project.
4.   The ability to prevent the technology, trade secrets, and processes that give the company an advantage from being leaked to competitors. This is a major consideration for technology companies, especially when R&D and product development are the sources of the company's competitive advantage.
5.   The availability of appropriate target companies to acquire. Often, the decision to form a joint venture company is dictated by the absence of companies to acquire that have the desired profiles.

### Defining the Project Scope and Developing Objectives

One of the first activities of the project team is to clarify and define the scope of the project so that it becomes workable. Then, the project goals and objectives are developed, discussed extensively, clearly articulated, and communicated throughout the project team. Unless the project team knows what it wants to get out of a project, the objectives shift and change to fit the circumstances and projects are likely to fail. Adequate time should be spent developing sound and realistic project objectives that are consistent with the company's strategic goals and communicating them to the entire project team.

Articulating what the project team wants to get out of the project is not sufficient; the team must also decide at the start how the company intends to use the new entity and the degree of autonomy it will be granted after deal closing. The project team conditions senior management expectations so that they can be managed accordingly and lists what it will settle for concerning major project risks. Having defined and articulated the project goals and objectives, the project team develops company profiles and screening criteria and in each subsequent step of the process it ensures continuity of purpose, goals, and objectives.

### Development of Alternatives

The creation of alternatives to the proposed project takes place both early in the process and after a project is defined. After an acquisition target or a joint venture partner company is selected and more information becomes available, other alternatives may be considered as the proposed project's position relative to other options changes. The creation of alternatives is an important part of the process because continuous comparison of the proposed project to other alternatives and finding that its ranking remains the same reinforces the value of the project. The affirmation that the proposed project is the most attractive alternative is important for independent project assessment experts looking for evidence to support the project selection.

Acting on the belief that internal growth is preferred to acquisitions and joint ventures, companies examine alternative business unit initiatives as viable alternatives. Then, the greenfield approach is investigated, whereby costs and benefits of creating a new entity and building the desired capabilities are compared with those of the proposed project. Then, the costs and benefits of acquiring versus venturing are examined so that it becomes clear which alternative dominates.

Often, external advisor alternatives come to the project team through senior management. In these cases, the issue of motives and confidentiality considerations should be considered. Only after all alternatives are considered and the proposed project remains the best option can the sponsor and the project team brief senior management about the project.

### Creation of Exit Strategy

Before contact is made with the seller, the target, or a potential partner, the project team should have an exit strategy in place, an escape valve that allows a graceful exit out of difficult situations. The exit strategy is important because it allows the project team to terminate discussions when the reality of the situation becomes evident and is drastically different from expectations or when the project goals and objectives cannot be met or if desired organizational and cultural compatibility is not present. It helps in protecting the company's image and reputation if there are serious issues with the background and reputation of a potential partner. It also protects the company's interest in the event the target or joint venture company pursues legal means to force the company into a transaction that is a poor alternative.

Depending on the stage of the project, the exit strategy formulation and communication takes different forms. Initially, it is made through verbal statements and in the memoranda of understanding or the letters of intent. Then, as the project firms up, it is included in the termination clauses of the agreements negotiated. As the project reaches the closure point, the exit strategy is redefined, updated, and included in legal documents with clear definition of the triggers for exiting an arrangement. The lawyer advises the team on the exit strategy options, on possible escape or termination clauses, and on the legal issues involved, and recommends effective ways to exit at different points in the process.

Exit from a project must protect the interests of all parties involved and preserve the confidentiality of information shared. Once the exit strategy is developed and contact with the target or the joint venture partner is made, the project team begins the process of gathering and assessing information from these companies. Also, the exit options of the other side must be identified and defined in legal documents.

## TACTICAL CONSIDERATIONS

### Senior Management Briefing

After it is determined that the best way to meet the company's strategic goals and objectives is through an acquisition or a joint venture project, the project sponsor is identified and the team formation sessions begin. In the session with the project sponsor, the business development group describes in detail how it arrived at the conclusion to pursue a given project. It presents the evidence in clear terms, discusses the risks involved in each approach, and the expected project costs and benefits, and solicits input and advice on how to brief senior executives.

Once the project sponsor is convinced of the value of a proposed project, the business unit heads are briefed again on the strategic needs of the company, the options available, and the rough estimates of costs and benefits of different options. The business units' alternatives are examined and compared to the greenfield and external options. When business unit heads are comfortable with the project, the sponsor and the business development group brief senior management and seek approval to initiate necessary contacts and develop the project feasibility study.

This is a time-consuming process, but it must take place right at the start because if it does not, serious problems and lack of project support may develop later. This lack of support derails many a project. Therefore, management briefings and approvals at the outset are most useful. The senior management briefings involve several key elements:

1. Review of corporate strategy and identification of the strategic and operational gaps. This is important to set the stage and enable senior management to assess the extent of the strategic fit of a proposed project.
2. Alternatives to fill the strategic and operational gaps and the costs and benefits of each alternative. Presenting alternatives to senior management is important to demonstrate that other options have been considered, but the proposed project is the best selection to fill strategic and operational gaps.
3. Recommendation of the business development group supported by preliminary evidence. Because of its charter and position in the organization, senior management looks to the business development group to provide its recommendation about a project based on good reasons and some evidence.
4. Expected resource requirements to execute the proposed project. This is necessary for senior management to develop an appreciation of the financial and human resources required to execute the project and determine whether these resources are available in the company.
5. Expected synergies and shareholder value to be created by the project. In addition to strategic and operational fit, an acquisition or a joint venture must produce

synergies and create sufficient shareholder value to make it attractive. Synergies and shareholder value are usually measured in terms of net present value.

6. Request to proceed to the feasibility study phase. This is the objective of the initial briefing and senior management must be convinced of the value of the project given the risks involved in doing these projects.

> *Net present value (NPV) of a project or synergies is the discounted sum of the net revenue stream minus the investments required over the life of a project. The rate used to discount in NPV calculations is usually the company's weighted cost of capital.*

### Identifying a Sponsor and the Project Team

After the business development group has performed the strategic and operational gap analysis and is close to making the decision to develop a feasibility study, but before the briefing of senior managers, the project sponsor is identified with input from senior management, briefed on the various aspects of the project, and given the assignment of overseeing the project. The project sponsor is ordinarily a member of the senior management team, experienced in acquisition and joint venture projects, and capable of getting consensus and support for the project.

The project team leader is identified right at the start and has the responsibility of assembling the rest of the project team consisting of the subteams discussed in Chapter 4. When the entire project team is assembled, a team-building initiative is undertaken by the project sponsor and the team leader that includes training on the key issues and the process involved in acquisition or joint venture projects. Team building also includes building personal relationships and enhancing communications among the extended project team members, and understanding the linkages and dependencies as well as the outputs expected from each subteam at various junctures in the process.

The escalation process is the way in which issues and recommendations are brought to senior management. It is defined when the project team is assembled and everyone understands how the process works and the extent of cooperation and teamwork expected to make the project team effective. The project sponsor assumes the function of managing the relationship with senior management and the seller, and the target or the potential partner company explains the project security considerations and spells out the responsibilities of the project team. After this, the project team as a group begins preparatory work in the respective areas of expertise.

### Insider List Preparation

The insider list is a roster of company employees who participate in an acquisition or a joint venture project. It is prepared as soon as the project team is formed and briefed about the project. The purpose of creating and maintaining the insider list is to control sensitive information and to make sure that in the event confidentiality breaks down and information is used to benefit a certain party, tracing leaks is easier and limited to the individuals on the insider list. The insider list also covers external advisors, consultants, technical experts engaged in the project, and secretarial and clerical support staff.

The creation of the insider list involves a briefing of the confidentiality responsibilities of participants in the project and the provisions of company rules and the law concerning breaches of confidentiality. This is an important element in ensuring confidentiality and is highly recommended for every acquisition and joint venture project undertaken. Confidentiality is important because if compromised, it disadvantages the company and gives competitors knowledge of the company's activities. The project team has many other issues to worry about, and confidentiality and trust of project team participants should not be among them.

### Securing a War Room

The war room is a fairly large conference room that is properly equipped and is available to the project team twenty-four hours a day throughout the life of the project. This room should be available once the decision to move forward with the project is made. The war room is located within the company's private facilities and the physical access should be secured with a combination lock with entry privileges only for those authorized to enter the room for business on the project. The equipment in the room includes personal computers, multiple telephone lines, a fax machine, voice mail capabilities, large black or white boards, several easels, reproduction equipment either inside the war room or nearby, shredders, and document assembling equipment.

The war room got its name from rooms used as military command and control posts where all information from the field came in and was communicated to officers in a consistent manner and where decisions were made and orders given out. In acquisitions and joint venture projects, the war room serves exactly the same purpose as it does in military operations: As information comes in, it is evaluated in a central location, information updates on the project are posted in the war room, progress is recorded on the project workplan, new issues in need of attention are posted and those resolved moved to a different category, outputs expected and delivered are recorded for all to review, and pending decisions are posted.

The most effective way to manage acquisition and joint venture projects and communicate to project participants the project status is through the use of the war room. However, the security of the war room must be ensured at all times because of the sensitive information posted there. It is a good idea to have company security experts check the facility from time to time for devices that do not belong in such an environment. Also, use of voice recording equipment should be made after consultation with the legal representative on the project team.

### Engagement of Investment Bankers

Investment bankers are professionals who specialize in acquisition (and joint venture) projects and play a significant role in their execution because of industry expertise and experience in dissecting transactions and developing and evaluating financial synergies. They make contributions in negotiations because of their understanding of the motivation of sellers and broad experience in creating ways to meet their needs. Investment bankers have project valuation and deal-structuring expertise and knowledge of valuation methodologies, comparable transactions, and the implications of different deal structures. Their knowledge of market conditions, industry averages, and comparable transactions is essential in determining the bargaining power and the types of concessions likely to be obtained.

In addition to their experience in financing acquisition and joint venture projects, investment bankers offer advice that is invaluable in securing a reasonable transaction which can be financed effectively and come to closure effectively. Ordinarily, the engagement of investment bankers decision is based on past relationships. A review of relationships should be conducted periodically to ensure that the right investment house is engaged that has appropriate expertise in the industry the project is in. That is, the business development group must ensure that significant industry expertise resides in the investment bankers under consideration in order to maximize their contribution in the project.

A review of credentials of two or three investment banks and interviews with the industry experts of each bank is recommended before making the decision to engage one. Prior to engaging the investment bank with the most qualifications and industry expertise, the project leader should state the expectations and the envisioned roles and responsibilities of the investment banker right at the start. This is important because it sets the tone of the relationship and helps in defining and negotiating the terms of the engagement. Also, it helps in getting an understanding up front of the way the investment bankers intend to work with the rest of the project team, not only with senior management, which is a common practice.

### Selecting Due Diligence Experts

As in the case of investment bankers, due diligence experts in accounting and tax issues are drawn from firms with which the company has had prior dealings; that is, accounting firms involved in the tax preparation and the auditing function of the company. This practice has merit because of the sensitive information disclosed, but industry expertise is also an important consideration. Performing a due diligence on companies in a different industry requires expertise in that industry and knowledge of what is significant and of its norms and practices.

Accounting and tax advisors with expertise in specific tax areas are engaged to dig through volumes of financial data to uncover information and verify the representations made to the company. External legal experts are engaged in acquisition and joint venture projects when difficult questions or issues surface, and from time to time, technical experts and consultants are engaged for their opinions on financing, identifying, and managing project risks, and satisfying requirements of the funding sources.

As in the case of investment bankers, the business development group along with the project leader defines expectations, roles, and responsibilities of these experts, as well as expected outputs. They also define the linkages to the work of the project team and the relationships with internal experts on the due diligence subteam before negotiating the terms of engagement of external due diligence experts. It is important to work closely with external advisors and learn from their experience and knowledge.

### Business Unit Briefings

Individual briefings of business unit heads take place when enough is known about the proposed project to make the case for it. These briefings are an important step in the preparatory stage of doing an acquisition or joint venture project because such courtesy calls demonstrate that input from business unit heads is valued and sought after by the business development group and the project team The briefings communicate the particulars of the proposed project effectively and the business unit head reactions to the proposed project are solicited and discussion of alternatives is invited. The expectation is that business unit head buy-in and support for the project and concurrence to move forward are obtained.

Briefings afford business unit heads the opportunity to present their own initiatives to fill the strategic and operational gaps and alternatives to the proposed project. This dialogue is essential for all to understand the merits of the alternatives and to arrive at the selection of the most attractive alternative for all stakeholders. In other words, these briefings lead to consensus on the project. In addition, they are forums for discussions on business unit synergies expected and how each business unit will contribute to their realization.

## PROCESS AND PREPARATION

### Preliminary Screening

Screening of acquisition targets and potential joint venture partners is a challenging task and begins with the strategic and operational gap analysis, which basically defines the attributes that the target or partner company should possess in order to fill the gaps identified. The desired attributes, in turn, define the profile of the target or joint venture partner company that should be considered for the project. The profile developed from the gap analysis is an ideal target or partner company profile, with adjustments made to fit reality.

The desired company profile defines the key screening criteria. That is, the creation of the desired target or partner company profile enables the project team to develop screening criteria against which different companies and alternatives are compared. The criteria contain financial measurements and broader considerations such as market position, R&D capabilities, technological leadership and product development, and competitive positioning measurements.

Screening criteria are derived directly from strategic gap considerations before the decision is made to pursue a given project. If a project is selected without screening, the selection criteria can be shaped to fit the positive elements of the project, and in that case, emphasis is given not to the profile, but to individual measurements to justify the decision. This approach is dangerous and leads to valuable resources being wasted in assessing sub-optimal opportunities.

### Mini Due Diligence

In order to decide if a company is the right target or joint venture partner, information is gathered from public sources before and during the screening stage. The mini due diligence is part of screening and refers to the effort of gathering financial, marketing, technical, product, and other publicly available information. The primary purpose of the mini due diligence is to help with the strategic fit assessment and verify the existence of operational complementarity. It entails a product line review to determine product life cycles and market positioning and assessment of technological capabilities to determine how the company would benefit by the transaction.

The mini due diligence reexamines industry trends in order to make judgments about future developments. It looks at the customer and supplier sets to find out if a single entity can impact the company disproportionately after the transaction closes and identifies potential risk scenarios that help quantify the likelihood and potential impacts of the risks. In addition, it estimates costs and benefits of the transaction, paints a realistic picture of what should be expected by the proposed project, and performs a rudimentary financial analysis and rough estimates of shareholder value created. The mini due diligence is the first sanity checkpoint at the beginning of the process and helps make the decision to pursue the project. Since external advisors have not yet been engaged, the mini due diligence is the responsibility of the business development group.

### Resource Requirements to Execute the Project

An important part of the preparatory work in acquisition and joint venture projects is to identify the management talent required to do the project and estimate the costs involved. The cost estimates include senior management and sponsor time and travel expenses along with the business unit heads' time and expenses to participate in developing alternatives and consensus. Then, the cost of project team members' time and travel expenses are included, which are fairly significant over the entire process.

The cost of internal experts drawn from the business units is another element that is added to the total project cost. Also, the costs of engaging external advisors, their expenses, and success fees are identified. Since difficult issues arise in the course of doing a project that cannot be resolved by the advisors engaged, the cost estimate of bringing in additional, highly specialized consultants needs to be included such as, for example, an environmental due diligence expert, a foreign tax specialist, or a chief negotiator. Finally, an estimated price required to close the transaction is added to the total project cost, along with the projected costs of implementation.

The identification of human resources needed to do the project and the estimated financial cost of closing the transaction should be available for senior management to review at the first briefing on the project. This allows senior management to understand the extent of resources to be dedicated to the project versus engaging in everyday activities and managing the company's operations. Precision is not required, but it is important to make an effort to present an all-inclusive cost estimate and show how the resources are spread over the project feasibility, the first business case analysis, the deal closing, and the project implementation and synergy extraction phases.

### Expected Business Unit Synergies

Often, project synergies are the reason given by business units for doing a project. If that is true, then those synergies belong to that business unit, which should have the opportunity to do its own assessment of costs and benefits of the synergies and demonstrate how it plans to harness them. When the business development group initiates a project, dialogue and communication with the business units is essential. Since a key concern is the expected synergies, the first order of business in the preparation stage is to identify potential synergies, find out how business units can help in their realization, and assess the likelihood of the synergies actually materializing.

Once business unit synergies are identified, they are communicated clearly to the project team, which quantifies the expected costs and benefits. The next step is to demonstrate the ability to harness the expected synergies. It is crucial that internal discussions about synergy costs and benefits be held confidential until there is a need for disclosure in the negotiations stage. If the business unit expected to benefit from the synergies is convinced of their value, it commits to harness those synergies in the post-implementation period.

### Project Workplan

The project workplan is the blueprint for the evaluation, negotiation, and implementation phases of the acquisition and joint venture project process. The project workplan lists activities to be undertaken and it includes the subteams responsible for the completion of specific activities and specific expected deliverables spelled out in detail. It also shows the time frames for the expected deliverables, the dependencies among the various activities in the process, and the budget estimates for completion of each phase.

The value of the workplan is that it defines the overall project process, identifies sub-processes, and defines the major activities, timelines, expected outputs, and individuals responsible, as well as the linkages between sub-processes and dependencies in one place. However, the workplan is valuable only if it is updated continuously, if it ensures effective transitioning of responsibilities and continuity of purpose, and if the project timelines are realistic. Realistic timelines are important because they impact work quality in

**Table 5.1**
**Sample of Project Workplan Form**

| Project Activity | Subteam Respons- ible | Deliver- able Expected | Quality of Deliver- able | Delivery Date | Receiv- ing Party | Depen- dencies | Budget Expense |
|---|---|---|---|---|---|---|---|
| Feasibility Study | | | | | | | |
| Strategic Fit Assess. | | | | | | | |
| Synergy Identif. | | | | | | | |
| Financial Analysis | | | | | | | |
| — | | | | | | | |
| — | | | | | | | |
| Implemen. Planning | | | | | | | |
| Bus. Plan Creation | | | | | | | |
| — | | | | | | | |
| — | | | | | | | |
| Post mortem | | | | | | | |

all aspects of the project. Workplans come in different forms. Table 5.1 shows a convenient way to present information that makes project monitoring manageable.

### Sanity Checks

When the workplan is created, the project team embarks on a full-blown assessment of the project, but this is where sanity checks can prevent a lot of problems later in the process and a sanity check is advisable at this point. Ordinarily, the core project team performs the sanity check and the elements involved include the following:

1.  Ensuring a common understanding of definitions among project participants. This is essential in preventing misunderstandings and differences of interpretation on different issues.
2.  Reviewing project objectives to ensure common understanding and determine if they can be realized. It is intended to ensure continuity of purpose and is a reality check on project team support.
3.  Revisiting, understanding, checking, and testing the assumption set. As events unfold and new information comes in, assumptions are scrutinized and changed to reflect new knowledge.
4.  Identifying implicit assumptions. This is important because under strong project leaders, teams tend to think in similar patterns and this creates implicit assumptions that go unchecked.
5.  Checking for common understanding of project risks. This requires identification of risks, assessment of the probability of their occurring, an estimated impact on the financials, and the likelihood of project success.
6.  Identifying dissenting voices and understanding the reasons for dissension. This issue requires attention because minority views tend to diverge from the team's due to the backgrounds and previous experiences of these individuals.
7.  Obtaining an independent assessment or external advice on issues that are not clear. It is impossible to have all the expertise required to do acquisitions and joint ventures reside within the company. Therefore, external advice should be sought on issues that cannot be covered by internal experts.

## HOW PREPARATION HELPS

The benefits from the project team's preparation start with the strategic and operational gap analysis, which identifies strengths and weaknesses and creates desired target or partner company profiles, and the definition of project goals and objectives, which provide a common view and direction for the project team. The formation of the project team brings together the best talent in the company and the preparation of the exit strategy enables gracious termination of discussions while protecting the interests of the company. The mini due diligence and the preliminary screening verify information to avoid embarrassments down the road and the creation of alternatives ensures that the selected project represents the best value for the company.

The assessment of resources required to do the project enables senior management to determine availability and whether expected benefits outweigh projected costs. The selection and engagement of external advisors ensure coverage of all major issues by experts and provide another perspective based on broad experience. Also, business unit briefings to solicit input to the proposed project and support on a going-forward basis and the identification of synergies and estimation of costs and benefits are important since a premium will be required to close the transaction. In addition, the development of the project workplan facilitates an orderly project execution and effective management of activities in the project process. Finally, sanity checks prior to engaging in a full-blown project assessment prevent engagement of valuable resources to projects that do not create shareholder value.

Adequate preparation is strongly recommended because of the beneficial impact it has on all subsequent steps of the process and in ensuring project success. If adequate preparation does not take place, this is what happens:

1. The project is not driven by strategic considerations, but by individual business units' objectives and personal agendas.
2. The project team does not include the right players and functional experts nor does it have a clear picture of goals and what it wants to get out of the project.
3. Confusion concerning roles and responsibilities is present, and effective transitioning of responsibilities and continuity of purpose are absent.
4. Complications that damage the company's reputation occur when a project is exited.
5. Screening is based on ad-hoc criteria and unverified information, or criteria shaped to fit the circumstances.
6. Alternatives are not fully considered as an option and value creation is not maximized.
7. Neither resource requirements nor project costs enter the decision to proceed until late in the process.
8. Business unit discussions are held only when conflicts arise, by which point it may be too late to obtain consensus.
9. External advisors with previous company ties are brought in based on past relationships without appropriate screening.
10. Expected synergies and ability to realize them are not discussed and commitments to extract them are not made.

## SUMMARY

In this chapter, the project team functions during the preparation phase for acquisition and joint venture projects are discussed. The key elements in the preparation are strategic and operational gap analysis, definition of project goals and objectives, and the formation of the project team. Other important elements of preparation include creation of the exit strategy, a preliminary due diligence and screening, the creation of alternatives, and assessment of resources required to do the project. In addition, engagement of external advisors, business unit briefings, identification of synergies, the creation of the project workplan, and sanity checks prior to engaging in a full-blown assessment of the project are essential in preparing for a successful project execution.

Adequate preparation is strongly recommended because of the beneficial impact it has in all subsequent steps of the process and in ensuring project success. The consequences of inadequate preparation on the project are manifested in the project not driven by strategic considerations, but by individual business units' objectives with personal agendas. The assembled project team includes the wrong players or functional experts who do not have a clear picture of goals, screening is based on ad-hoc criteria and unverified information or criteria are shaped to fit the circumstances, and complications occur when exiting a project.

On the other hand, with adequate preparation alternatives are fully considered, resource requirements are understood, and project costs enter the decision to proceed early in the process. Furthermore, business unit discussions are held before conflicts arise and external advisors with appropriate credentials and experiences are brought in with appropriate screening and not based on past relationships. Finally, expected synergies and ability to realize them are discussed and commitments to extract them are made when the project team is well prepared. Then, there is clarity of responsibilities, effective transitioning of responsibilities, and continuity of purpose.

# 6

# RESOURCE REQUIREMENTS FOR ACQUISITION AND JOINT VENTURE PROJECTS

## INTRODUCTION

Most acquisitions and joint ventures begin with the idea of meeting some major objectives and are pursued to the evaluation and negotiation stage before management even knows whether sufficient human resources with appropriate skills exist within the company or the costs and benefits of the project. The omission of a resource requirement assessment right at the start is a serious flaw in the project process. Not knowing the total project costs and benefits before a full-blown project evaluation distorts the basis of decision making because it results in resources being expended without justification.

Quite often, acquisition and joint venture projects are started with project teams lacking required skills and experience to execute them. This indicates ignorance of process and results in project failure because project teams attempt to do the work of professionals without having knowledge of the process and the necessary skills and experience. When the limitations of project teams are realized and external talent is hired to do all phases of the project, costs increase and the entire project is run by outsiders whose interests may not necessarily coincide with those of the company. Therefore, it is strongly recommended that prior to engaging in acquisition and joint venture projects, senior management, with help from the business development group and trusted consultants, identify internal human resource constraints and estimate total project costs.

Ignorance of the range of costs and benefits at the start is a problem because scarce resources are engaged in projects that do not merit much consideration and such resources could be used in other, more productive endeavors. Whether resources are engaged in marginal projects is usually not known until well into the project process because a fair assessment of costs and benefits takes time. Hence, the significance of estimating project costs and benefits before the project team gets too deep in the assessment and negotiation process. This chapter deals with the assessment of resource requirements and costs involved in doing a project.

The costs associated with doing a project range between 5 percent and 12 percent of total project costs, which include the price paid for the target or the value of the joint venture company created. This estimate is derived over a number of projects and includes all implementation costs (ranging from 3 percent to 7 percent) down to the establishment of monitoring and control mechanisms. Since project execution expenses are a big share of total project costs, it is helpful for senior management to know the range of the proposed project's costs in order to make the decision to proceed before a lot of resources are thrown into the project. Make no mistake, however: identify and ensure the engagement of appropriately skilled human resources within the company first, but if you must, then hire all the external talent required.

## INTERNAL RESOURCE REQUIREMENTS

A broad set of skills, knowledge, and experience is required to meet the challenges of project evaluation, negotiation, and implementation phases, as well as the ongoing operations of the new entity. Here, the focus is on availability and cost of engaging these resources.

### Senior Management Involvement

The first element in the estimated project costs is the senior management's time invested in the project. It includes their participation in project activities such as understanding the strategic and operational gaps of the company and how the proposed project fills these gaps. This requires participation in briefings by the sponsor and the project team on project objectives, costs and benefits, and alternatives. It also includes identification of skilled human resources to dedicate to the project and to be seconded to the new entity. It is important for senior management to be involved in this in order to understand the opportunity costs and the need to engage external resources.

Senior management reviews the feasibility study and business case and this requires familiarity with major issues, follow-up, and monitoring project progress. It spends time in meetings with the project sponsor and the team leader, the business development group, and investment bankers in preparation for corporate approvals, and chairman and board of directors briefing meetings. It also initiates contact and meets with seller or partner company senior management and is involved in new-entity management team briefings and strategy sessions.

Often, the argument is made that senior management involvement should not be considered project cost but, rather, part of overhead. This view distorts the true cost picture because it ignores the principle of the opportunity cost. In addition to the cost of time spent on acquisition and joint venture projects, travel and related expenses should be included in the estimated costs as well as the cost of hiring external consultants to help senior management understand how projects are done and the resources required to implement them. When all activities of senior management are considered, costs become significant because acquisition and joint venture projects consume a disproportionately large chunk of their time. Ignoring this cost element is inappropriate and it is a good idea to engage an expert from the business development group to estimate these and other project costs.

### Project Team and Subteams

Acquisition and joint venture project teams were discussed in Chapter 4 and consist of the core team, subteams of experts, and the steering committee. The core team includes the sponsor, the team leader, a business development group representative, a financial analyst, a lawyer, and an operational expert. The subteams require internal functional expertise and external advisor experience in negotiations, due diligence, organizational issues, public relations, financing, and implementation. The liaison subteam and the steering committee require seasoned managers who play key roles in the implementation and the post-deal-closing phases.

The core team must include members with extensive skills and experiences in order to be effective. This is why the expertise of the business development group is needed to ensure that the right individuals fill the positions in the core team and the subteams. In addition to senior management, estimated project costs include participation of the project sponsor, the business development group representative, business unit heads, internal functional experts, external advisors, seconded managers to the new entity, the liaison subteam, and the steering committee.

After the business development group verifies the availability of appropriate human resources to work the project, it estimates the project team and subteam costs beginning with a human resource count, that is, the number of people involved in supporting the project. Then, their estimated project involvement is measured in management or occupational-level person-weeks and their loaded salaries and wages. From this, the financial analyst calculates the personnel expense component and travel and incidental expenses of team members. Next are the costs associated with engaging external consultants, which includes engagement fees, success fees, and all expenses. Finally, the costs associated with the physical facilities and equipment used for the duration of the project are estimated and added to the total project cost.

### Liaison Subteam and Steering Committee

Identifying managers to serve on the liaison subteam and the steering committee is a challenge, because qualified individuals to serve on these subteams, who have broad experience in both business development and managing organizational change are rare. Hence, extensive screening is needed to identify talent and experience to fill liaison subteam and steering committee positions. The liaison subteam is formed before the work of the implementation team is completed to handle the interface between the new entity and the parent company. This subteam requires managers experienced in implementing projects and able to resolve conflicts and issues raised by the new entity. These resources and travel expenses are significant and should be included in the total project cost.

The steering committee requires seasoned managers experienced in acquisition and joint venture projects. These professionals spend significant time establishing the governance structure and ensuring the right organization is in place, that the management of the new entity is functioning properly, and the strategies of the new entity and the parent company are in harmony. The steering committee human resources cost and travel expenses are also included in the total project cost. An additional consideration is to use the opportunity cost of the liaison subteam and the steering committee as a measure of their true costs because seasoned managers may be used in other company activities.

## EXTERNAL RESOURCE REQUIREMENTS

### Investment Bankers

Engagement of investment bankers is an expensive proposition because of their unique expertise and the extensive contributions they can make in acquisition and joint venture projects. Hence, it is important that the right investment bankers are assigned to a project because the project team needs to learn the unique processes, obtain some of their extensive industry data and insights, develop close cooperation and teamwork, and affect some knowledge transfer.

Investment bankers ordinarily charge retainer fees, engagement fees, and success fees for services and these fees range considerably across industries and clients. Since the business development group knows what industries different investment bankers specialize in, the common practices, and the range of customary fees, it selects the investment bankers. In addition to investment banker fees and charges, estimated travel and related expenses are included in the project costs as well as outlays for consultants specializing in unique areas or to assess crucial impacts.

Even more important than negotiating transaction fees is defining and negotiating the investment bankers' roles and responsibilities in a project in order to manage charges and maximize their contribution. Also, it is important to negotiate the type of experts to be engaged and actually work the project. If the company negotiates for a director-level person, the project team had better make sure that a director-level investment banker, and not a junior member, works the project's key issues. It is not a good idea to keep investment banker involvement to an absolute minimum, but it makes sense to plan and manage their activities to get the most benefit from their engagement.

*Example: The business development group of a U.S. world-class company works with three investment banks and insists that the engaged bank assign to its acquisition projects the chief industry analyst, a specialist in due diligence and negotiation issues, and a deal structure and financing expert in addition to the cadre of financial analysts.*

### Accounting, Tax, and Legal Experts

The negotiations, due diligence, and deal structure of acquisitions and joint ventures require expertise in several disciplines that are much too specialized to exist within a company. For that reason, project teams find it necessary to engage external experts in accounting and tax issues, pension liability actuaries, computer systems consultants, other due diligence specialists, and legal experts. Ordinarily, accounting and tax support in the due diligence effort comes from an accounting firm that performs the accounting and auditing function for the company. The reasons for this practice are that there is a close working relationship and trust between the company and the accounting firm and the accounting firm understands the industry and the areas the company needs to pay close attention to. The project team ensures that the right mix of internal experts and external advisors is assigned to work the project, with senior advisors working the key high-level issues.

*Example: In an acquisition of an equipment manufacturer, the cost of assuming pension fund obligations was omitted, but it was so high that it made the project unprofitable. In another project, the cost of cleaning up a manufacturing site cost the acquiring company more than the purchase of the target and caused the acquiring company to declare bankruptcy. In neither case were outside experts engaged.*

As in the case of investment bankers, the cost of engaging external accounting, tax, and legal experts includes the fees charged for professional services, the travel expenses, and all other expenses incurred. Therefore, it is important to specify the functions expected to be performed by these experts so that costs can be controlled, while maximum services are obtained from them. This is strongly recommended because the experts are put to work and focus on appropriate issues immediately. Furthermore, some project team members participate in the same activities and are the recipient of knowledge transfer necessary to build organizational capabilities.

## PROJECT COSTS AND CAPITAL EXPENDITURES

### Cost of Deal Closing

Estimating total project costs requires extensive work to identify resources needed and develop a reasonable estimate of what it takes to close a transaction. In acquisition projects, this cost estimate starts with the stand-alone fair market value and the market premiums are added. Information on premiums comes from comparable industry transactions, the expertise of investment bankers, or the business development group. The project team estimates a range of net synergies and assigns a part to the cost of closing the deal. This is because while the seller requires payment for identified synergies, the buyer is not interested in sharing future wealth; hence, the negotiated synergy premium is somewhere in the middle.

In joint ventures, the cost of closing the deal includes all fees, expenses, and investments required to close the transaction. In the case of foreign ventures, it also includes fees and charges for permits and payments to local agents to facilitate negotiations with foreign governments and closing. For both acquisitions and joint ventures, it is wise to add a cushion to estimated costs, say 3 percent to 5 percent, for unforeseen investment requirements and expenses to avoid surprises when actual costs exceed expectations after closing.

When it is necessary to pay a closing price range higher than dictated by comparable transactions, market conditions surrounding the project, or the negotiating position of the two parties, then earn-out formulas are used. The costs of earn-out formulas can be a significant component of the expected total project costs and are included in the total project costs.

---

*Earn-out formulas are contractual arrangements in acquisitions and joint ventures whereby payments are made to the seller or to the management team of the new entity only when certain target levels of operational or financial performance by the new entity are met.*

---

### Implementation Expenses

Implementation managers manage change and the organizational conflicts that come with it. Knowing that such individuals are a rare breed, the business development group ensures that individuals with the right backgrounds, skills, and experiences are brought into the implementation subteam. Project implementation expenses are a significant part of total project costs and often are omitted from acquisition and joint venture cost estimates. A good estimate of implementation expenses is in the 3 percent to 7 percent range of the acquisition price or the value of the joint venture entity created, with most projects falling toward the upper limit. Because implementation expenses are a large portion of total project costs, they must be estimated carefully in terms of human resource requirements, expenses related with implementation, and investments necessary to affect the implementation.

Salaries and expenses of managers of change involved in the project for a few months to ensure a smooth transition are included here, if they have not been included in the project team costs. Also, travel expenses and costs of hiring additional management talent and external advisors to assist in the transition are added. The cost of inspecting the new entity's equipment, inventories, and systems and their integration or replacement costs should also be included. These are costs of equipment or systems that from the beginning of the project have been determined to need replacement or systems work to integrate the new entity with the parent company's systems.

Defining new-entity monitoring and control requirements and creating operational targets are part of implementation, as is the identification of new equipment or systems needed to implement monitoring and control mechanisms. The costs associated with operational and financial reviews, audits of the new entity, and the development of new initiatives are included in order to obtain a complete picture of implementation costs.

### Terminating Existing Contracts and Creating New Contracts

The creation and negotiation of contracts for retained target or parent managers is a first-order priority for the implementation subteam as the project approaches closure. This involves a review of management skills and talents required for the new entity, interviews and selection, drafting, negotiating, and signing contracts, and paying out bonuses. The associated expenses go into the cost of terminating existing management agreements and creating new contracts. In addition, the costs of secondments to and from the new entity are included.

A key activity of due diligence is a review of customer and supplier contracts to understand the key customers, terms and conditions included in these contracts, and whether current contracts need to be renegotiated. In the case of joint ventures, a review of potential customers takes place and customer contract terms and conditions are drafted. The costs of these activities are included in the cost of terminating or creating new contracts as is the cost of customer notification such as mailings, personal visits, and promotional materials. In some cases, terminating customer contracts requires compensating customers and this expense is added to the total project cost.

Supplier contracts are reviewed to ensure that the firm is getting the best possible terms from arrangements with suppliers. This involves contract reviews, supplier site visits and inspections, and comparisons of terms and conditions offered by the various suppliers in the industry. The project team needs to be mindful of costs and the impact of contract termination due to a change in ownership because some contracts contain clauses stating that they expire upon sale of the firm. This means that contracts have to be re-negotiated by the new owners and the costs of drafting and negotiating new supplier contracts are included in the cost of creating new contracts.

### Future Capital Requirements

A major responsibility of the project team is to review the technical, operational, and marketing plans of the new entity to ensure that planned or anticipated capital expenditures are consistent with those plans. While in most cases future capital requirements are included in the business plan of the new entity, it is a good idea to review those requirements closely to avoid surprises and large unforeseen capital expenditures.

Capital expenditures related to integration of the new entity or implementation of the project and investments in system interfaces are items usually omitted from capital budgets. These are investments needed to install, combine, or replace manual or computer systems and monitoring and control mechanisms for the new entity. Investments in integrating the technology platform, product development, market and distribution channels, and plant and equipment required to harness synergies must also be included.

In the case of joint venture projects, the project team assesses the partner company's ability to meet future capital calls and contribute its fair share. This is especially important in the case of foreign joint ventures with government entities in emerging countries because the company may have to come up with the foreign partner's contribution. If there is doubt about the partner's ability to contribute capital in the future in order to expand the joint venture company's activities, an estimate of that capital requirement should be included in the total project cost and then arrangements should be made for the company to be compensated.

### Unforeseen Requirements and Expenses

The last component of the total acquisition and joint venture project cost is unforeseen requirements and expenses. Here, allowance is made for some extra expenses that cannot be anticipated. For example, when management is trying to close a project quickly, additional personal visits may be required by senior managers, which involves unexpected travel and incidental expenses. Estimates of unanticipated travel to meetings, the time spent, and the opportunity cost of senior managers are included in this item. The unforeseen-cost category also includes items such as taxes due by the target company or the new entity, overdue pension contributions, and contributions to benefit plans that have not been made but now become the acquiring company's liability.

Unexpected contractual liabilities are not uncommon in acquisition projects and need to be accounted for in this category. Risk reserves and insurance coverage premiums to protect from occurrence of certain project risks and provisions for risk management are also included in these costs. Unexpected investment requirements, costs of hiring additional management talent to implement the project, and external resources engaged to ensure smooth operations of the new entity are included here. Finally, allowance is made for unexpected expenses such as incremental expenses for foreign agent costs to facilitate contacts and ensure project closure.

## SUMMARY

The estimation of all project costs prior to engaging in a full-blown project assessment is important to ensure that the decision to proceed with the project is based on a reasonable set of financials. However, just as important is the identification of human resource requirements to do the project and it is crucial to determine up front whether a project can be executed successfully. Not identifying required management talent and in the absence of reasonable total project cost estimates, valuable company resources are wasted in the assessment phase for no good reason.

Often, project teams undertake the evaluation of an opportunity without understanding the human resource requirements and the total project costs. To prevent valuable company resources from being wasted, the project team must identify human resources needed to do the project and project costs early in the process. This brings discipline to the decision-making process and contributes to value creation. Once human resource requirements are fully understood, the project costs are estimated fairly well, and the project team can engage in a full-blown assessment of the project.

# PART II

# PROCESSES THAT MAKE THE DIFFERENCE

# 7

## SCREENING ACQUISITION TARGETS AND JOINT VENTURE PARTNERS

### INTRODUCTION

One of the reasons acquisitions and joint ventures fail regularly is incomplete assessment of the opportunity presented. There is often incomplete screening of potential target or joint venture partner firms in the beginning and once a project passes from initial screening to the evaluation phase, the focus shifts from strategic fit to the project financials, negotiating advantageous terms and conditions, and implementation and synergy extraction. After the initial assessment, most projects go through evaluation, negotiation, and implementation without subsequent strategic and operational reviews.

With inadequate opportunity screening, it is unclear which alternative best meets the strategic and operational needs of the company. Thus, a number of important stakeholders do not lend support to the project because they are not convinced it is the best approach to meet company needs. On the other hand, when a proposed project goes through thorough screening, even those opposed to it initially are convinced of the value of the project and support it. Therefore, since incomplete assessment can occur in all phases of the project, continuous screening up to deal closing is recommended.

The responsibility of identifying and screening potential targets, or joint venture partners, rests with the business development group. In world-class organizations, it is a full-time job to uncover unique opportunities to implement the corporate strategy before they become apparent to the broader investment community. That is, identification and screening of companies to be acquired amounts to hunting for bargains to close gaps in the firm's strategic and operational capabilities well in advance of being identified by competitors. Likewise, selecting among potential joint venture partners entails picking a partner to create a competitive advantage in the marketplace before a competitor does.

The first part of this chapter deals with screening acquisition targets and the second part discusses joint venture partner screening. A distinction is made between initial screening and ongoing assessment, which continues until the deal closes. Initial screening refers to screening performed in the feasibility phase of the project, whereas ongoing assessment is the screening taking place in the business case phase of the project. In this chapter we focus mostly on the early screening effort while the ongoing evaluation of a project is covered extensively in Chapter 8.

The role of strategy and strategic fit in screening of acquisition targets is examined first. Then, the possible acquisition types are looked at to determine the extent of the strategic fit and assess the synergy possibilities followed by the operational fit evaluation, the company profiling effort, and the development of screening criteria. The importance of financial evaluation and early due diligence in project screening is examined and the critical success factors in identifying and screening acquisition targets are reviewed.

Screening joint venture partners requires assessment of the motives for partnering and emphasizes clarity of purpose, consistency of strategies, and management compatibility. Implementation and project risk assessment in joint ventures are part of screening, as are partner experience and partner expectations.

## SCREENING ACQUISITION TARGETS

### Pre-Evaluation Phase Screening

Target companies are identified for strategic, marketing, or financial reasons, although they may be motivated by regulatory/legal, human resource, or other factors, but in most cases screening is done on an ad hoc basis or to justify decisions already made. Usually, a list of criteria with threshold numbers and qualitative statements is created to indicate that the identified company meets corporate requirements better than other alternatives.

In most companies, identification and screening of target companies is pursued so that immediate needs are met or due to commitments by different business units or because certain senior executives wish to be associated with an acquisition. However, to ensure that appropriate motives characterize identification and screening of targets, the business development group must do the screening to ensure that corporate strategy and objectives are the driving forces.

Most companies use an ad hoc target selection process that exemplifies an inadequate approach to implementing the long-term corporate strategy. On the other hand, successful business development groups identify and screen potential acquisition targets based on a clear understanding of corporate objectives, strategy, and direction. Seasoned managers perform the strategic and operational gap analyses to identify needs and develop project objectives and requirements, which then define the characteristics of projects required to fill those needs. Profiles of several companies that fill identified gaps and a few quantitative screening criteria are created. However, this is not always possible and it is important that they are stated clearly so that there is no ambiguity concerning the comparison of a prospective target against the screening criteria.

World-class organizations use extensive market intelligence, early due diligence, and customer input to understand industry trends and market forces, to create firm-specific information, and to assess the health of the firm's operations and future prospects. This translates into clarity of purpose and project objectives. Objectives keep the focus on what is important, guide the behavior of the project team throughout the process, and enable it to select one from a list of potential target companies. This requires a comparison on the basis of several attributes and a ranking of alternatives so that in the event the most attractive project falls through, the next project is selected.

### Strategy and Strategic Gap Analysis

The long-term success of a company depends on its ability to create profitable growth and create or maintain competitive strength. The ability to develop competitive strength, in turn, depends on a corporation's ability to shift resources from mature business to new business, markets, or technologies with growth potential. Planning for and developing long-term competitive strength is a function of strategic business development planning and entails assessing internal capability development versus acquisitions as a strategy of sustaining long-term profitable growth.

Corporate strategy is the foundation and starting point for all business development activities. It provides a clear statement of the senior management's vision and corporate mission and objectives. Therefore, business development groups must have a thorough understanding of the corporate strategy and expertise in performing strategic fit assessments of all identified targets. Prior to the strategic fit assessment, the business development group performs an in-depth strategic gap analysis, which identifies the company needs to meet its strategic objectives. The use of a strategic gap analysis matrix, shown in Table 7.1, is recommended to display the gaps and the benefits to be obtained by an acquisition.

In the first column, the business definition, the important areas and key drivers of the company, the technologies, the markets and distribution channels, and other strategic elements that are important to the company are listed. The present state of affairs is described in the second column, and the desired capabilities and competitive advantage being sought are articulated in the third column. A comparison of columns two and three shows the gap in the company's strategy listed in column four. The fifth column of the strategic gap analysis matrix is an assessment of benefits derived from filling the strategic gaps through an acquisition.

**Table 7.1**
**Strategic Gap Analysis Matrix**

| Strategic Elements | Current State of Affairs | Desired State of Affairs | Strategic Gaps | Benefits of Closing Gaps |
|---|---|---|---|---|
| Organizational capabilities | | | | |
| Corporate culture | | | | |
| Business definition | | | | |
| Managerial talent | | | | |
| Competitive advantage | | | | |
| Customer satisfaction | | | | |
| Cost structure and profitability | | | | |
| Product differentiation | | | | |
| Technological capabilities | | | | |
| Products and Services | | | | |
| Markets and channels | | | | |
| — | | | | |
| — | | | | |

## Acquisition Types

Because there are different strategic reasons for engaging in acquisitions, different possibilities exist to create synergies, and for that reason, target screening criteria vary by type of acquisition. The three types of acquisitions are the following:

1. *Vertical acquisition.* In vertical acquisitions the acquiring and target companies are in different industries, but have strong buyer-supplier relationships. This type of acquisition takes place primarily to control a certain production input. Therefore, the main criteria should be ease of implementation or the ability to digest the target company without major difficulties, relationships with other buyers, and exclusivity of contracts, patents, rights, or other factors that would create barriers to entry or create a sustainable competitive advantage through the acquisition.

2. *Horizontal acquisition.* Under this type of acquisition, the acquiring and the target firm are in the same industry. Horizontal acquisitions are undertaken to increase market presence or to achieve economies of scale in production, distribution, marketing, etc. In this case, compatibility of management styles and strategy, ability to implement, and technological platforms used by the buying and the target firms are the essential criteria. Consolidation of operations, cost savings, and other screening criteria are significant, but of secondary importance.

3. *Concentric acquisitions.* These are acquisitions in which the acquiring and target companies are related via basic technologies, production processes, or markets. These acquisitions represent attempts by the acquiring firm to move from its current business definition to a closely related business activity and they take place for the benefit of expected synergies in sharing resources, entering a market with higher returns, and ability to diversify through employment of combined resources.

The concentric type of acquisition is the most difficult in which to ensure success. Consequently, the target company must pass a list of screening criteria, starting with compatibility of management styles, consistency of strategic directions, and ability to implement the acquisition quickly and successfully. Current and future market growth and market share, revenue composition and growth, operating margins, current and future investment requirements, customer relationships, and operational consolidation synergies are other important criteria.

### Strategic Fit Assessment

An effective way to determine strategic fit between the acquiring and the target company is the strategic returns on investment approach. A strategic gap analysis is a pre-requisite to performing a strategic return on investment analysis to evaluate how the target company will enhance: organizational capabilities, the company's market presence and growth, R&D and technological innovation, meeting customer needs and customer satisfaction, competitive advantage, and financial gains and shareholder value.

Identifying and measuring strategic returns on investment in a target entails several elements beginning with an analysis of market position and underlying strengths before and after the acquisition to assess the project's contributions. The assessment of organizational capabilities and skills acquired determines the degree of improvement in the competitive position of the company, and the evaluation of operational profitability and cost structure reduction quantifies the expected synergies in the financial area. In addition, possible technology enhancements and product innovation and know-how in various processes determine enhancements in the company's competitive position.

Strategic fit assessment requires an evaluation of major enhancements in the product line and the commercialization of new technology. This helps to evaluate changes in the speed to market and the company's position in the industry. Review of customer satisfaction data and evaluation of input and feedback identify changes in customer perception of the products and services offered by the combined entity. It is also important to determine expected shareholder value creation in the business case, which amounts to comparing current with expected net present value to judge financial success. Furthermore, identifying the sources of and measuring the creation of sustainable competitive advantage to nurture those sources helps determine how the company can maintain a unique position in the marketplace.

Assessment of strategic fit starts with a review of the buying firm's business definition, which constitutes the first step in screening a partner or a target. The business definition of a firm entails an analysis of physical and human asset deployment, the products and services it provides, and the markets it serves. It is a self-assessment of the firm's production process that starts with inputs and ends with how goods and services are being provided to customers and how well the customer needs are met.

There are a number of factors that the business development group considers in a strategic fit analysis, and emphasis is placed on different factors when screening an acquisition target as opposed to a joint venture partner. Even within acquisition options, strategic fit criteria vary because different types of acquisitions require emphasis on different factors. Usually, strategic fit is judged in terms of compatibility of corporate vision and principles, sources of competitive advantage, business definitions, deployment and utilization of assets, and organizational culture and chemistry. Use of the strategic gap analysis matrix in Table 7.1 helps identify gaps and determine the extent of strategic fit.

*Example: A medium-size, high-growth U.S. corporation produced exceptional shareholder value for a number of years. When growth flattened out, it pursued acquisitions of small companies outside the United States, expanded their production and export capacity, and increased profits. This growth strategy worked well for approximately three years, but then profits followed a downward trend. A root cause analysis revealed that the competitiveness of its U.S. operations had declined substantially as new products were introduced and nothing was done to strengthen its R&D and product development capabilities. In addition, the only criteria used to screen target companies were market and profit growth because they were considered indicators of fit with the company's growth strategy.*

To avoid misunderstandings about sources of competitive advantage, the entire production process of both firms needs to be evaluated in terms of technologies used, management skills available, and whether financial considerations alone can create a competitive advantage. This evaluation is performed in conjunction with an examination of the utilization of physical assets and human resources, but a strategic fit assessment is incomplete if the organizational cultures and the chemistry are not evaluated properly. Compatibility of organizational cultures is difficult to ascertain because participant expectations are not expressed openly in the evaluation and negotiations phase. Furthermore, organizational designs appropriate for individual firms prior to acquisitions or creation of joint ventures may no longer be appropriate, and the policies, procedures, and systems may be incompatible.

### Operational Fit Assessment

Strategic and operational gaps are needs in the company's long-term strategy and its everyday operational capabilities. Strategic and operational fit refer to the extent to which those needs are met. While strategic gap and strategic return on investment analyses help assess the strategic fit and define goals in a project, the operational gap analysis is crucial in assessing how the target firm's operations complement and strengthen the operations of the acquiring company. Operational gap analysis helps measure how different the two organizations are, assess the complementarity in key functional areas, and determine areas likely to require substantial management attention. Operational fit is important because it determines the degree to which successful integration is possible and the level of synergies one can expect to extract.

As in the case of the strategic gap analysis, operational gap analysis involves listing key functional areas of the buying firm, its production processes, systems, and procedures, and an honest assessment of its capabilities in each area. This analysis is depicted in Table 7.2, with the list of skills, capabilities, and key production elements in the first column. Next to the buying company's current capabilities column, the capabilities that would enable the company to achieve its operational objectives are identified. In the third and fourth columns, the target firm's current capabilities are compared with the capabilities desired and the gaps in operational capabilities stated explicitly. The fifth column lists the benefits to be obtained by an acquisition that would help bridge the gaps identified.

A key element in determining operational fit is an analysis of the management and reporting structures of the two companies, as well as of reporting mechanisms and information and communications flows. Assessment of control systems, problem-solving approaches, responsibility assignments, and allocation of human resources comprises the second element followed by an assessment of product line compatibility, customer and supplier interfaces, and supporting structures. Through the operational gap analysis, the company needs are identified and the operational objectives for an acquisition project defined.

### Development of Profiles and Screening Criteria

Companies with good track records in acquisitions engage in investigations of firms that could be potential targets well before they approach them. Potential targets are drawn from competitors, parallel producers, vertical integrators, technical developers, targeted customers, and firms with outstanding distribution

**Table 7.2**
**Operational Gap Analysis Matrix**

| Key Operational Elements | Current Capabilities | Desired Capabilities | Description of Operational Gaps | Benefits From Closing Gaps |
|---|---|---|---|---|
| I. Production | | | | |
| Facilities | | | | |
| Processes | | | | |
| — | | | | |
| II. Skills | | | | |
| Know-how | | | | |
| Capabilities | | | | |
| — | | | | |
| III. Product Line | | | | |
| New product | | | | |
| Speed to market | | | | |
| — | | | | |
| IV. Financial | | | | |
| Rev/employee | | | | |
| Unit costs | | | | |
| — | | | | |
| V. Operational control | | | | |
| Benchmarks | | | | |
| Targets | | | | |
| — | | | | |
| — | | | | |

channels. From time to time, acquisition targets with fairly good profiles brought to the company by investment bankers are considered but, as a general rule, they are not bargains. Bargains are rare and must be uncovered through intensive basic research.

The results of the strategic and operational gap analyses identify the factors needed to build the profile of an ideal target that meets the strategic needs of the company and complements its operational capabilities. That is, the gap analyses identify the business areas, the capabilities and characteristics, and the competitive advantages that ideal candidates should possess. Once this is done, it is fairly simple to sketch the profile for a target company that includes the desired characteristics.

To develop the screening criteria, the business development group identifies the drivers of the project value expressed in terms of key variables, such as market share levels and growth, or thresholds of those variables. The identification and screening investigation entails searching among possible targets and applying the pre-established criteria against the target's profile in the following key areas:

*1. Strategy.* The strategic vision and the extent the target can enhance the acquiring company's competitive position, its product line, the technological capabilities, and the risks of managing the new entity.

*2. Market position.* The size of the firm, access to market share and growth, sales records and customer concentration, established distribution channels, customer satisfaction and relationships, and reputation with competitors.

*3. R&D and technology.* The R&D staff and its capabilities, the technological innovation and leadership of the firm, its new product introduction processes, and the speed of product commercialization.

*4. Financial performance.* Operating performance, profitability, stability of cash flow, foreign exchange risks, transfer pricing, tax considerations, and investment requirements.

*5. Human resources.* Reporting structures, management talent, educational backgrounds, labor supply, wages and benefits, staffing levels, and skills profiles.

*6. Other considerations.* The company ownership structure and legal issues, the labor environment, labor contracts, environmental issues, and product and technology transfers.

The development of screening criteria is important, but how these criteria are applied is what makes the difference between a sound and an inadequate opportunity screening. This the reason for recommending using experienced project teams in doing acquisition and joint venture projects.

### Financial Assessment

The purpose of financial analysis and valuation of a target or a joint venture in the screening phase is to develop a baseline project NPV to estimate shareholder value created and compare it with that of alternatives. Figure 7.1 shows the main steps involved in this process whereby the early screening stage is primarily concerned with steps 1, 2, and 6, but screening does not end until closing.

**Figure 7.1**
**The Financial Assessment Process**

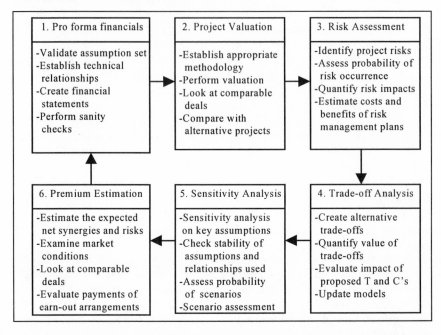

The screening of a target from a financial perspective entails an examination of past and future revenue trends, cash flows, and investment requirements. However, the most important element is understanding and validating the assumptions underlying the revenue, cost, and cash flow projections. The project team must not miss any indications that the books of a target company have been prepared in order to present the best possible picture to potential buyers.

Before moving to the business case phase, the project team identifies resource requirements, the management talent needed to execute the proposed project, the costs involved, and future investment requirements. Parallel to this, the revenue components and synergy costs and benefits are estimated so that new pro forma financial statements are created or existing ones validated.

> *Valuation of a company is the determination of its worth based on its economic value-generating capacity, deployment of assets, industry trends, and market conditions. Terminal value is the value of the company in discounted cash flow valuation methods beyond the forecast horizon, which is usually ten years.*

The early financial screening also includes a valuation of the premiums likely to be required to close the transaction. The important premiums to be valued are the market premium based on comparable transactions, the synergy premium determined by the net benefits to both parties of expected synergies due to the acquisition transaction, and the controlling-interest premium, which is based on the principle that there is one share price for partial acquisition of a firm, but a different share price if control of the target company is desired.

## Identification of Resource Requirements

It was explained earlier that identification and quantification of resource requirements is done to determine what resources are available to execute the project and ensure inclusion of all cost elements in the preliminary project financials. It also helps to assess the likelihood of successful project implementation. Internal resources are evaluated to decide the kind of external advisors to engage to complement the project team capabilities.

Identification of resource requirements has two parts: the identification of adequately trained and experienced human resources internally and the quantification of all costs of the resources to be expanded in the project. This is an activity that is recommended in the project feasibility study phase so that if project net benefits are low relative to project risks, the decision to withdraw from the project can be made early and save the company valuable resources.

Chapter 6 explained why it is important for the feasibility study recommendations to be based on reasonable preliminary estimates and include the following cost elements:

1. Senior management and project sponsor involvement to estimate the opportunity costs instead of treating their involvement as overhead.
2. The dedicated core project team and subteams, which include functional experts brought into the project when needed.
3. Engagement of investment bankers, accounting, tax, and legal experts, external advisors, and consultants.
4. Implementation-related expenses, including synergy extraction costs and the costs of the liaison subteam and the steering committee.
5. The total cost of closing the deal, including fees, customer and supplier contract termination, and premiums required.
6. Terminating and creating new senior management employment contracts, as well as incentive packages and earn-out arrangements.
7. Future capital requirements to cover capacity upgrades, geographic and market coverage expansions, and development of new technologies and product lines.
8. A fraction of total costs for unforeseen expenses and investment requirements in the neighborhood of 5 to 10 percent.

## Mini Due Diligence

Due diligence is the activity associated with uncovering and verifying information and data released by the seller or the potential partner firm and ensuring that there is no hidden information that may be damaging to the company. An important element in screening projects in the early (feasibility study) phase is a brief and reasonably broad due diligence right at the start of a project.

The first area covered in the mini due diligence before or during the feasibility study of a project is the investigation of financial statements and projections of the target or the potential partner and their cost structure and their profitability on each market followed by an assessment of human resources, the quality of the management team and labor force employed. Inspection of the physical plant and equipment, especially when a manufacturing facility is involved, is advisable as is a preliminary environmental due diligence to ensure no waste dumping and environmental contamination. The reputation of the R&D group and the technological capabilities of the firm are checked along with its product line, the product line life cycles, and the quality of the products and services offered. A review of market trends and assessment of the firm's market position and distribution channels are conducted in conjunction with an evaluation of industry structure trends and changes in the competitive environment.

The mini due diligence is handled by the business development group and internal experts. Again, it focuses on establishing the validity of information, confirming major issues and expectations, and checking the reasonableness of the assumptions used to develop project financials. The early due diligence effort is undertaken to increase management's confidence that the decision to proceed is based on reliable information and evidence. However, most of the due diligence effort occurs after the feasibility study.

### Critical Success Factors in Identifying Targets

To identify the right target, in addition to close strategic and operational fits, the business development group and the project team pay attention to some key factors:

1. *Early due diligence.* The due diligence step is normally undertaken when the decision is made to proceed with the acquisition. However, an early mini due diligence is recommended to find evidence of the target company's value and advantage; namely, to determine superior customer value, effective positioning, technological advantage, and unit cost superiority. An important element in this effort is to obtain direct customer input and determine the nature of relationships and customer satisfaction. Following this, the project team investigates all financial, legal, human resource, and environmental issues.

2. *Market, industry, country analysis and trends.* A thorough market share assessment by product and market segment and the growth patterns for the various product lines is a starting point and is followed by an industry structure analysis and evaluation of industry trends. The analysis also includes looking at the stage of the target firm's product life cycles and the power of customers and competitors. In the case of a foreign acquisition, an analysis of the country macro economic, political, and legal infrastructure conditions is a requirement.

3. *Revenue composition and market concentration.* The analysis of revenue by product line and market segment is a first step in the financial analysis. The makeup of revenues by different sets of customers gives an indication of

dependence on certain customers. The market size and growth, price information, and elasticity of demand are important elements in understanding how revenues are likely to evolve under price pressures and in assessing potential project risks.

*4. Organizational capabilities and compatibility.* Acquisitions fail mostly because of incompatibility of visions and values, strategic intent differences, and incongruent reporting relationships and control systems between acquiring and target firms. Therefore, organizational capability and management compatibility assessment are required to understand how to manage the implementation of an acquisition and how their capabilities can be brought together harmoniously. Early determination of capabilities complementarity and compatibility of management structures and cultures is essential because the sum of managerial talent and competence in the acquiring company plus that of the target is less than the demands placed on the combined entity. Autonomy and control expectations present in both firms need to be understood to determine compatibility of strategies and visions, and attitudes and cultures.

*5. Implementation and integration.* A critical factor for a successful acquisition is implementation of the acquisition and integration of the acquired company's operations with the buying company's operations. In this stage, the difficulty of implementing the acquisition and integrating the operations of the acquired into those of the acquiring company are evaluated. This assessment requires a team of managers who serve as catalysts in the implementation and know what strengths and weaknesses the company brings to the target.

*6. Test of synergy assumptions.* Often, an acquisition is pursued on the assumption that there are synergies to be obtained. This assumption is based on the impression that the implementation will be successful and that the new organizational structure will enable the acquiring company to harness the expected synergies. Many acquisitions fail because a number of such implicit assumptions are never articulated and the implications on the business plan are never examined. To avoid this problem, the project team should list and assess each assumption for validity and likelihood of occurring.

## SCREENING JOINT VENTURE PARTNERS

Joint ventures are cooperative business arrangements by two or more firms for strategic purposes. Usually, the arrangement takes the form of a new company that creates a new business entity and allocates ownership, operational responsibilities, and financial risks and rewards to each owner, while preserving a separate identity and autonomy. In other instances there is no equity involved, but merely a common effort undertaken by the partners to share risks in a project, such as the development of a new product. These arrangements are called strategic alliances, but our interest is in identifying and screening equity joint venture partners.

There are several motives behind equity joint ventures, such as market access, access to capital, access to resources or technology, risk reduction or sharing, regulatory requirements, production efficiency or cost savings, distribution channels, or market expertise. While the motives are numerous and varied, the intent is to enhance each partner's position and this is the focus of the pre-evaluation screening effort. Success in equity joint ventures is critically dependent on clarity of purpose, consistency of strategies and objectives, and partner experience in joint venturing. Hence, the early screening of potential joint venture partners focuses on these factors.

### Clarity of Purpose

Clarity of purpose means that the partners in a joint venture know exactly why they wish to engage in the joint venture, what they want to get out of the project, and, most importantly, what they are willing to give in return in terms of human and financial resources and other contributions to support the new entity. Developing clarity of purpose is the most important contribution the business development group makes in joint venture projects because it forces consensus and clear articulation of what the company wants to get out of the project.

Continuity of purpose in the feasibility study phase plays an important role in assessing the likelihood of the project goals and objectives being maintained as it moves through the evaluation process. It is also important that continuity of purpose is maintained when responsibilities are transferred from the negotiations subteam to the implementation subteam. Without effective transitioning of responsibilities that preserves continuity of purpose, the original project objectives are changed to fit the situation rather than meeting the strategic and operational needs of the company identified in the beginning. Clarity and continuity of purpose lead to effective screening because they enable the project team to determine to what extent the company needs are being met by the proposed project. Hence, the business development group and the project team leader ensure clarity of objectives and continuity of purpose throughout the project.

### Consistency of Strategies

The absence of consistency of strategies is probably the factor cited most frequently as the cause of joint ventures being terminated. A company may recover its financial investments in a joint venture, but the human resources expanded and the opportunities lost may be greater than the experience gained through the joint venture project. Therefore, a close scrutiny of the potential partner's strategy, goals, and objectives, stated or implied, is recommended.

When screening potential joint venture partners, the business development group and the project team ensure that both short- and long-term partner strategies, goals, and objectives are consistent across all partners. Conflicts of strategies are early warning signals that unless they are changed to be consistent with each other, the joint venture company is headed for failure. Identifying inconsistent partner strategies is another avenue through which the business development group brings discipline into the decision-making process.

Consistency of strategies goes beyond consistency of partner strategies. It includes consistency of the joint venture company's scope and business strategy with the business definitions and strategies of the parent companies. This is a crucial point because often, joint ventures created to enter a specific business or market change their business definition and enter one of the partner's markets. Such changes are created by significant strategy inconsistencies and conflict and result in joint venture dissolution or its sale to one of the partners.

### Partner Experience in Joint Ventures

How knowledgeable the partners are in joint venturing is a key determinant of venture success because having gone through joint venture company formations, the partners know the issues and what is needed to make the project a success. Therefore, when potential joint venture partners are being screened, the venture experience of the partners, the outcome of those ventures, how the joint ventures were dissolved, and how they view the venturing process are closely examined.

Partner experience influences ease of project implementation, success in the development of the joint venture strategy and business plans, efficient operation of the joint venture company, and free exchange of personnel between the parent companies and the joint venture company. However, partner experience in negotiating a joint venture arrangement based on the win-win principle is most helpful because it enables the partners to create an effective governance structure based on expected venture benefits rather than control considerations.

Partner experience helps tremendously in obtaining support for the joint venture company on an ongoing basis. This is important not only in the early stages when synergies are being extracted, but after that as well because with experience in joint venture formation come reasonable partner expectations. Therefore, the screening of potential partners should incorporate the element of partner experience in forming and operating joint venture companies. Experienced project teams do this as early in the process as possible to eliminate partners with little potential.

### Management Compatibility

Management compatibility assessment begins with an evaluation of similarities and differences of partner organizational and reporting structures. For example, if the organizational structure of one partner is a flat, thin layer of management while the other partner's is a pyramid with several management layers, decision making is quite different. The likelihood of being able to structure and maintain a successful joint venture under these conditions is small because different organizational structures reflect different management philosophies and styles.

The second step is the evaluation of the mindset of the key managers in the partner companies and a test for the existence of a win-win mentality. Understanding the motivation, the thinking patterns, and the approach to problem solving by the management team of a potential partner is important to determine whether a win-win arrangement can be negotiated and maintained. The presence of a win-win mentality is crucial in implementing and operating the joint venture company successfully and obtaining significant synergies. It is also important in determining how stable a joint venture arrangement can be and how synergy benefits will be shared among partners.

The third element in assessing management compatibility is the chemistry present in the interactions of the joint venture partners from the senior management teams down to functional experts. The right chemistry involves relationships at all management and functional levels, open communications, clarity and continuity of purpose, honesty in dealing with joint venture goals and objectives, willingness and ability to team and work together to resolve issues, and ability to disagree and yet be able to work together effectively. Differences in organizational and reporting structures usually result in poor joint ventures, but absence of a win-win mentality and the right chemistry are certain to result in failure after the joint venture is implemented.

### Implementation Assessment and Risks Involved

Screening also entails assessing how difficult it would be to implement the joint venture with a particular partner. The business development group and the project team need to provide answers to screening element questions. For example, what experiences and capabilities does the potential partner have in joint venturing and implementing such projects? Does the company and the potential partner have human resources to spare in the evaluation, negotiation, and running of the joint venture? Are financial resources available to meet current and future capital requirements of the joint venture?

These are basic questions followed by other questions such as: How large are the project risks and how can the risks be shared among the joint venture partners? Can the company afford to risk technology transfer and leaks of trade secrets to the joint venture entity, and ultimately to the partner? If a potential partner wishes to make in-kind contributions, how will they be valued? How likely is the company to extract synergies through the formation of the joint venture entity?

Another essential screening element is evaluation of the risks of partnering. The implementation risk factors are project risks which, if they materialize, would have severe, irreversible impacts, and terminate the joint venture viability. Reaction of the marketplace and competition to the joint venture is a risk, which requires delicate handling of announcements because when a successful joint venture is created, competitors follow.

The commercial business risks are risks associated with business revenues being below expectations and expenses above business plan predictions. Competitive developments can cause strategy conflicts to develop. This is a risk because industry changes induce changes in the joint venture strategy, which may be on a collision course with at least one parent company's strategy. Finally, there are exit risks from a particular joint venture. If joint venture termination and exit clauses are not adequate, there is a risk that one of the partners may not fully recover its investment and expenses in the project.

### Reasonable and Manageable Expectations

Joint ventures are normally formed with expectations in the minds of potential partners concerning gains and roles that are not articulated or are partially expressed. Part of the screening process, therefore, is to probe and understand the motives and expectations of the partners regarding the business definition and the strategy of the joint venture entity. Expectations about financial and human resource contributions to the joint venture need to be checked occasionally to ensure that when capital calls or requests for secondments are made, the partners will honor them. In addition, the partner views on how present and future costs and benefits are shared should be identified early in the process and plans instituted to condition these expectations.

Early recognition of partner expectations about managing the joint venture entity and the responsibilities of the partners is important because it is an indicator of the partner's expected role in the post-implementation phase. Finally, partner requirements and expectations related to the new entity's reporting and control mechanisms must be identified and differences reconciled before they become major issues.

After partner expectations have been identified and verified, the project team determines to what extent they can be managed in order to forge a reasonable win-win arrangement. If it is determined that a potential partner has unreasonable expectations and maintains rigid positions, the project team should rethink the choice of this partner. Unreasonable partner expectations in the assessment phase continue into the negotiations, implementation, and operations phases of the joint venture entity, and prevent it from achieving its original goals and objectives.


## SUMMARY

The early screening and the feasibility study screening are intended to eliminate marginal projects while the business case screening selects the best alternative and determines to what extent the proposed project meets the company's strategic criteria and its operational needs. Effective screening of acquisition and joint venture projects is important because it eliminates unnecessary involvement in projects with little promise for substantial value creation and because it conserves scarce and valuable company resources. Therefore, the identification and screening in the feasibility study should be done by team members experienced in such projects; preferably by the business development group. If the early project screening is done poorly, valuable company resources are wasted and projects take longer to complete or result in failure.

The key screening elements for acquisition targets include strategic and operational gap analyses, the establishment of desired company profiles, screening criteria, and the strategic fit assessment. They also include the operational fit and expected synergies assessment, financial assessment and project evaluation, identification of resource requirements, and early due diligence.

When screening potential joint venture partners, emphasis is placed on clarity and continuity of purpose, consistency of partner strategies and project goals and objectives, and determining the extent of organizational and management compatibility. Joint venture partner screening also entails implementation assessment and identification of risks involved, checking for partner experience in forming joint ventures, testing for reasonable and manageable expectations, and verifying a win-win mindset and sharing of costs and benefits.

# 8

# THE OPPORTUNITY ASSESSMENT PROCESS

## INTRODUCTION

The opportunity assessment or project evaluation process is a systematic way to evaluate a proposed acquisition or a joint venture project in the feasibility study and business case phases and forms the foundation for corporate decisions to proceed with a given project. Opportunity assessment follows the screening process and focuses primarily on the one target or joint venture company that was selected.

A complete opportunity assessment process involves several major stages or steps shown in Figure 8.1. In the hands of a competent project leader and an experienced project team, it is also an opportunity creation process because in this phase the project team understands the strengths and weaknesses of the company and the target or the partner company through the all-inclusive and thorough analyses it performs. It also identifies areas of possible improvements in revenue, expense, capital investment, and operational performance through evaluation of the target's operations and examination of its financial statements. The implementation plan assessment provides recommendations to create synergies beyond what was identified in the initial phase of the project.

The discussion of opportunity assessment in this chapter begins with the characteristics of sound assessments and proceeds to the internal analysis needed to make the right project selection. The strategic fit evaluation is a key step in the opportunity evaluation process and it is followed by the identification of resource requirements and the feasibility study. The feasibility study forms the basis for the decision to proceed to the next step, which is the business case phase. Sometimes, project risks and major issues are evaluated before the feasibility study is completed and sometimes in the business case phase, depending on how significant they are perceived to be at the beginning of the assessment process. The next step in the opportunity assessment is the financial analysis and project valuation and is followed by the evaluation of alternatives discussion, and the assessment of the negotiated terms and conditions. The major elements of the due diligence effort are reviewed along with the purpose and how to develop a business case and the chapter ends with a brief discussion of project financeability.

**Figure 8.1**
**The Opportunity Assessment Process**

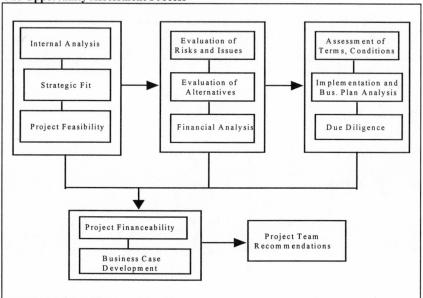

## GETTING TO PROJECT FEASIBILITY

### Characteristics of Sound Opportunity Assessments

Sound opportunity assessments are a prerequisite to successful acquisitions or joint ventures and are characterized by adherence to pre-established process and not to externally imposed requirements. Coverage of all significant concerns, continuity of purpose, validation and testing of assumptions, risk identification and quantification, and fact-based analysis are also key elements of sound opportunity assessments. Adherence to process ensures that a project moves through the assessment phases in the appropriate order and minimizes unnecessary external influences and delays. Thorough coverage ensures that all important issues are addressed adequately and that there are no surprises or embarrassments further down the project process.

Appropriate transitioning of responsibilities from subteam to subteam and continuity of purpose are key elements in project evaluations and required to create successful projects. When coupled with good coverage of the areas that need to be addressed, these two factors result in thorough assessments that preserve the original project goals and objectives. Additionally, they help decision makers get comfortable with the analysis and the project team recommendations. Articulation, validation, and testing of all assumptions result in sound and reasonable financials and analyses that can be traced back easily and allow for updates to be readily included in the financial models. This results in the assumption set being able to withstand scrutiny. Finally, fact-based analysis minimizes subjective input in the assessment and results in better decisions.

Well-defined roles and responsibilities of project participants, efficient coordination of inputs and deliverables, and a solid due diligence are other important elements of sound opportunity assessments. Well defined roles and responsibilities make effective transitioning of responsibilities and continuity of purpose possible. Efficient coordination of work produced and inputs into the next project phase requires extensive teamwork and communications, but it also creates strong linkages and speedy project evaluation. A sound due diligence ensures that the analyses and decisions are based on valid information and data so that there are no surprises after deal closing. Finally, clearly articulated findings and well-thought-out project team recommendations are a must in order to obtain corporate project approvals.

### Internal Analysis and Project Selection

Internal analysis is the assessment process phase initiated by the business development organization to understand the company's mission and long-term strategy, its markets and customers, and its own strengths and weaknesses. Armed with this, strategic and operational gap analyses are performed to reveal areas that the company needs to improve, that is, areas in which the target or the partner company is expected to make contributions and fill the long-term strategic needs and operational gaps of the company.

Three elements that come out of self-assessment are the project rationale and scope, a list of screening criteria to be applied in the selection process, and the project goals and objectives. Here, it should be noted that the screening criteria are not universal, but unique and tailored to the company's needs and objectives. A threefold approach that produces good results and is used to derive project screening criteria and objectives is the following:

1. Examining the market segments served to understand the customer base, distribution channels used, and how customer needs are currently being met.
2. Understanding the business definition of the company and the products and services it offers relative to its R&D and technical capabilities.
3. Evaluating how human and physical assets are deployed and determining the company's strengths and weaknesses in terms of costs and operating efficiency.

Part of internal analysis and self-evaluation is the determination of contributions the company is willing and able to make in order for the acquired company or the joint venture entity to become a successful operation. Other aspects of internal analysis are an evaluation of the company's ability to implement the project, the implementation costs, and whether the new entity should be integrated or granted autonomy. An integral part of project implementation evaluation is the ability to extract expected project synergies and their impact on the company's operations. The project selection among alternatives and the recommendation to move to the business case phase necessitate that a project pass all screening criteria and filters of the internal assessment process.

### Strategic Fit Assessment

The starting point in the strategic fit assessment is a complete understanding of the different business units' evolution and the strategy of the company as a whole, its products, strategies, and gaps that need to be filled by an acquisition or joint venture project. In this phase, strategic fit assessment addresses several key questions:

1.  How close the acquiring or parent company's business definition is with that of the new entity's charter. This is important because the project team needs to determine whether there is potential for conflict of the new entity's long term strategies with that of the parent company.
2.  How the proposed project can help the company reach its long-term objectives, that is, how the new entity can help the company circumvent the management talent, technical, and financial resource constraints it faces and how operating risk will be shared by the two companies.
3.  In what ways the new entity can help meet customer needs more effectively, help the company increase its market position and strength, and assist in developing or enhancing organizational capabilities and make the company more competitive.
4.  What contributions to the company's profitability the new entity can make and if it is the least costly and most effective solution.
5.  How the acquisition or joint venture project enhances the company's product line and its technological innovation and know-how.
6.  What significant synergies can be harnessed with reasonable effort and resources and how the new entity can help the company create a competitive advantage.
7.  Whether the risks are too high and offset project benefits. This is the essence of strategic fit analysis, which defines to a large degree the project team recommendation.

By addressing these questions, the project team can determine whether there is a close fit between the company and the target or the joint venture entity. The degree of strategic fit determines how well a project can be implemented and how successful it is likely to be.

### Resource Requirements

Identification of human resources required and the costs involved in executing a proposed project is a determining factor in the opportunity assessment effort. In the feasibility study phase, attention is directed toward skill set identification and verification and quantification of costs of resources to execute the project. In the business case phase, emphasis shifts to refining financial resource requirements to cover the identification of negotiation trade-offs, implementation requirements, and costs of risk management plans. Resource requirements evaluation goes beyond the closing date and calculates costs of resources to interface with the new entity, to retain management talent, costs of systems integration, costs of the new entity management team's learning the parent company business, and resources to be expended on synergy extraction.

The costs of resources needed to execute a project were discussed in Chapter 6. They include salaries and wages of project team members, travel expenses, overhead costs, fees of external advisors and consultants, the price to be paid to close the transaction, post-implementation costs, and some allowance for unforeseen expenses and future capital calls. In the business case development phase, the quantification of the costs of the resources to be expanded on the project is refined and a lot more detail added. This is important because resource requirements determine the ability of the company to execute the project successfully and the value created.

### Project Feasibility Study

The project feasibility study is a preliminary opportunity assessment that determines whether the project in question has the potential of being successful. It goes beyond the screening of a target or a joint venture partner and brings together several considerations essential in making the decision to proceed to the business case. The project team evaluates how customer needs will be met by the target or the joint venture entity, but this involves a clear project scope and articulation of objectives. For most projects, this constitutes an acid test because if the proposed project does not serve customer needs better, then the project rationale and objectives must be re-evaluated.

The strategic and operational fit of the proposed project formalizes the gap analysis and evaluates whether the benefits of filling strategic and operational gaps can be sustained over a long period and whether a competitive advantage can be developed and maintained. In the feasibility study phase, alternatives to the proposed project are evaluated and compared to the proposed project. Financial and risk considerations are important, but the focus is on how strategic objectives are met by each alternative. In this phase, risk identification and quantification is done at a more granular level than in the pre-screening phase. The project team seeks to understand the source and nature of risks, the probability of their occurrence, the financial impact, and a cost range for risk management. Skill and qualification screening and cost estimates are refined to determine whether company resources are available to dedicate to the project.

The economic viability of the project is determined by the first set of financials, which brings together in a systematic way all project elements, articulates assumptions and relationships, and determines shareholder value created. There would be no value to the feasibility study if there were no project team recommendations coming out of this phase. The recommendation is a synthesis of the analysis and evaluation performed to enable senior management to make the decision to take the project to the business case phase. Outlining the next steps in the execution of the project is needed for project participants to know what follows the decision to proceed and plan their activities. The steps outlined here form the basis of the project workplan.

With the completion of the feasibility study, the project team summarizes its findings in a brief document that communicates to management the results of the assessment and develops some assurance based on these findings. Providing a sound basis for decision making is necessary because at this juncture, management commits resources to develop a full-blown business case and pursue the acquisition or venture formation to closing.

## TOWARD MAKING THE DECISION

### Financial Analysis and Valuation

The two components of financial analysis of acquisitions or joint ventures are the stand-alone valuation of the target or the joint venture and the evaluation of the project impact on the company. Each component requires creating specific models to evaluate financial performance and determine stability of results. The financial analysis in the evaluation phase involves examining key areas of operations, such as engineering, product development, operations, sales and marketing, and accounting and finance. Consequently, it requires participation of experts from several functional areas who contribute to the development and validation of the assumption set. Once the project team is comfortable with the assumption set, it proceeds to develop project revenue projections. To do that, it performs a market and structural analysis, uses industry averages to compare its projections, and performs sanity checks.

Once revenue projections are made, costs are identified and calculated and the discount rate, tax rate, and depreciation rate for the project are determined along with an estimate of the project financing costs. Then, the current and future investment requirements are reviewed and estimated. These estimations are developed by project-specific models that capture key relationships in the new entity's and the company's operations. Using the financial models created, the financial analyst can quantify the value of trade-offs used in negotiations and evaluate terms and conditions coming out of negotiations.

The financial implications of the legal and tax structure of the transaction are included in the financial model and a project fair market value is then calculated. The next requirement in the financial analysis is quantification of expected synergies and identified risks and major issues. If premiums are expected to close the transaction, the project team estimates and includes them in the financial models. Also, a financial evaluation of alternatives is performed through the use of the resulting net present value (NPV).

Sensitivity analysis, scenario assessment, checking the stability of financial relationships, and sanity checks are an integral part of testing the project assumptions. These checks involve comparing the financial models' results with historical performance, industry averages, and past experiences. The valuation of the project includes the fair market valuation and calculation of premiums to close the transaction. Calculation of premiums benefits from investment banker and external expert input and advice on comparable transactions and common industry practices and averages. Once the project premiums are estimated, the project costs and benefits are included in the financial model, and the value created by the project is calculated and validated.

## Project Risks and Issues

Project risk refers to probable events whose occurrence impacts unfavorably the financial position of the company. There are risks associated with all strategic business development projects, but that by itself is not sufficient reason not to undertake such projects. Risks in acquisition and joint venture projects include implementation risks, commercial or business risks, and political risks in the case of international projects. On the other hand, project issues refer to substantial unresolved issues that impact the project adversely unless they are clarified, negotiated, or resolved to make the project successful.

Risk assessment involves identifying the sources, understanding their nature, and quantifying the major risks. Risk quantification amounts to evaluating the probability of the risks occurring, calculating the financial impacts, and assessing approaches to mitigate these risks. For risk assessment to be meaningful, the project team must concentrate on a few key risks. Then, it quantifies their impacts and calculates deviations from the project's baseline NPV. This is done by changing the assumption thought to involve a risk or be impacted by it, while all other assumptions are held constant and the project NPV is calculated. After risk impacts are calculated, the probability of each risk occurring is evaluated based on the collective project team assessment.

Risk assessment is important because it enhances understanding of potential deviations from the baseline NPV. It also determines the likelihood of the company achieving the project objectives and the impacts of key assumptions not materializing. This helps the project team select the best acquisition target or joint venture company and recommend to senior management the alternative most likely to result in the highest return.

Having obtained a good understanding of the sources and nature of the project risks, the project team searches for ways to minimize their impact through allocation, sharing, or outright elimination of risks. At that point, the project team estimates the cost of putting in place a risk management plan. The creation of a risk management plan involves negotiating risks away to third parties, and looking for ways to allocate risks among the parties involved. The former is a costly approach because it involves trade-offs that can reduce the project value drastically and the latter involves sharing risks based on ability to handle the risks, benefits received by the transaction, or the negotiating power of participants.

Obtaining commercial insurance when possible and available is a preferred solution, especially by the financing institutions involved in funding the project. Political insurance tends to be reasonably priced, but commercial insurance to cover business risks is expensive. Risk management plans also entail creating plans to alter the course of events and preclude unfavorable events from occurring or to minimize the impact of risks. This requires an evaluation of how a risk can be broken down into smaller components so that each risk component can be managed more effectively. It also involves creation of contingency plans to be activated when risks do materialize.

### Evaluation of Alternatives

Evaluation of alternatives to a proposed project entails examining all reasonable options available to the company in achieving its long-term strategic objectives. The assessment of alternatives involves examining each option in terms of several elements starting with the degree of strategic and operational fit and the reasonableness of assumptions underlying financial projections so that the NPV comparison is meaningful. The availability of human and financial resources required to implement the different options and the costs of these resources and the financial worth, expressed as NPV over the expected life of the alternatives, are compared.

Alternatives are compared in terms of certainty of realizing the expected project value and the risks associated with obtaining the expected business plans to get a sense of possible NPV variances for each alternative. The compatibility of long-term company objectives with those of the new entity is assessed to determine the likelihood of success in the post-closing period. Also, ease of implementation and integration is evaluated along with expected synergies, ease and costs of synergy extraction, and the likelihood of synergies being realized.

The evaluation of alternatives is a complex process that looks at these aspects and evaluates alternatives in their totality. One complicating factor in the evaluation of alternatives is the weight assigned to each of the components, and a useful tool that helps evaluate and rank alternatives is creating a matrix, such as the one shown in Table 8.1. The first column lists the major elements to be evaluated that are common to all alternatives, such as strategic fit, management talent, ease of implementation, and financial strength. Next show the importance of the particular element by assigning a weight to that element, with the sum of weights equaling 1. Then, assign a value from 1 to 10 to indicate the ranking of each element of an alternative. Finally, create a score for each element by multiplying the weight by the assigned value. Adding up the resulting scores of all the elements gives an overall index of how each alternative ranks. All alternatives are considered and their ranking shows how they compare to each other.

The evaluation of alternatives is a lengthy process that requires a skilled business development group and an experienced project team to assign weights and give the project elements appropriate values consistently across all alternatives. Also, objectivity in scoring each element is important for the evaluation process to be meaningful. Only then is senior management assured that the project selected represents the best possible alternative to meet the company's long term needs.

**Table 8.1**
**Evaluation of Project Alternatives Matrix**

| Elements to be Evaluated | Weight | Value Assigned | | | Ranking Score | | |
|---|---|---|---|---|---|---|---|
| | | Project A | Project B | Project C | Project A | Project B | Project C |
| Strategic fit | | | | | | | |
| Management talent | | | | | | | |
| Ease of implementation | | | | | | | |
| — | | | | | | | |
| — | | | | | | | |
| Net synergy benefits | | | | | | | |
| Financial strength | | | | | | | |
| — | | | | | | | |
| Shareholder value | | | | | | | |
| TOTAL | 1.00 | | | | | | |

## Assessment of Negotiated Terms

Assessment of negotiated terms is another important step in the opportunity assessment process because even though the decision to proceed with a project has been made, value creation is determined by the company's ability to negotiate expected terms and conditions. The strategic, operational, and financial assessment of terms and conditions negotiated validate the decision, and allow the project team to go back to the negotiating table with counter-proposals and tools to re-negotiate terms and conditions.

Effective assessment of negotiated terms entails quantification of the financial impact of various terms and conditions negotiated on the project NPV and it requires constant communication between the negotiations subteam and the project team. This is ordinarily done through the participation of a project team member in the negotiations subteam, usually the financial analyst, who conveys the results of negotiations to the project team. While the financial impact assessment is an important step, the project team assesses the strategic and operational impacts and the change in the project's overall attractiveness under the newly negotiated terms and conditions. The overall assessment is required because often changes in one condition impact other elements of the project which are not readily converted to dollars.

A skilled project team approaches the assessment of negotiated terms in a proactive manner by understanding the various types of trade-offs possible and quantifying each trade-off. The project team can quantify the impacts of proposed terms and provide efficient counter-proposals when input is provided from the negotiations subteam. An experienced project team constantly monitors negotiations and assesses negotiated terms to assist the negotiations subteam to move discussions in desired directions. In the event the terms and conditions insisted on by the seller result in the project NPV reaching the walk away threshold or if their strategic impact is unacceptable, the project team recommends that discussions be suspended or even terminated.

### Implementation Assessment

Project implementation and integration analysis take on increased importance once negotiations are under way and the project is likely to come to fruition. A key element involved in evaluating the implementation of the proposed project is the company's ability to implement the proposed project successfully. This involves an inventory of skills and assessment of management talent in the parent company and the new entity and an evaluation of human and financial resource requirements of the new entity. It also involves determining compatibility of organizational structures, processes and procedures, systems, and corporate cultures. This assessment basically determines whether a win-win arrangement is likely to be created by the project.

Assessment of the costs and benefits of business autonomy versus integration of operations is a key element that requires input from the new entity's management team to balance the interests of all parties. Implementation or integration costs include the compensation and incentives for the new entity's management team and are estimated in the business plan. In addition, expected synergies, likelihood of materializing, and ability to harness expected synergies are assessed.

Evaluation of human resources required by the new entity to operate according to the business plan is the first element in the process of staffing key management positions with the right people. This is followed by an inventory and assessment of management talent existing in the company and the target or the partner. Prior to filling positions, the implementation subteam determines the extent of compatibility between the company and the new entity's corporate cultures, systems, and organizations and institutes measures to adjust for these differences. For example, a talented employee of a large joint venture partner company assigned to a small new entity may be given training in how small companies operate and why they require different systems to operate efficiently. If cultural differences are too large to bridge immediately, external management talent may be hired to staff the new entity's organization.

Determining the degree of business autonomy versus integration is a difficult task and should not be decided a priori, but after careful examination of the costs and benefits associated with different options. In assessing autonomy options, the project team considers autonomy in terms of:

1.  Strategy, business definition, and operations. The key consideration here is the impact of each option vis-à-vis the company's mission and strategic and operational gaps.
2.  Investments and other financial decisions. Autonomy requires higher investments and it does not produce drastic cost reductions through consolidations. However, autonomy preserves the organizational structure that gave the target or the joint venture entity its attractiveness.
3.  Pursuit of new opportunities and business direction. This is another important consideration because in some instances, autonomy may be appropriate for investing in a new or risky business, but consistency of strategy with the parent company can be a sticky issue.
4.  Market segments served by the acquiring and the target companies. When the parent and the new entity are pursuing different geographic markets and consolidation of operations would not produce cost efficiencies, autonomy is preferred.

This approach to determining autonomy results in discussions among project participants and ultimately in a decision that is based on balancing of interests and control considerations. In acquisitions, a certain degree of integration materializes over time even if it was not part of the implementation plan, but successful acquisitions involve immediate integration of the target into the company's operations. On the other hand, successful joint ventures tend to retain a large degree of independence from the parent companies and operate autonomously as long as there is no conflict of strategies and objectives.


## DISCIPLINE IN THE DECISION-MAKING PROCESS

### Due Diligence

The due diligence effort is particularly important in acquisition projects because the buying company usually ends up assuming all responsibilities and financial obligations of the target. The first step is the legal due diligence where the lawyer on the team leads the investigation of legal issues and examines documents related to the legal status of the target, its contractual obligations with customers and suppliers, existing management contracts, and agreements with third parties. The intent is to uncover actual or potential problems related to legal obligations of the firm that can be passed on to the acquiring company and to make sure that adequate provisions are made so that the acquiring company remains unharmed after assuming the obligations of the target firm.

The second element of due diligence involves a thorough review of audited financial statements for the past three to five years and financial projections of the target or the joint venture company. Here, the due diligence subteam led by the financial analyst or an external accounting expert verifies all historical revenues, expenses, taxes, and investment data shown in the audited financial statements and pays particular attention to footnotes. Then, the financial projections and the underlying assumptions are scrutinized to ensure that there are good reasons for deviations of the projected from the historical data trends.

In the financial due diligence, all debt and equity agreements and tax records are examined to ensure no misrepresentations, hidden liabilities and obligations, or adverse impacts to the acquiring company in this area. If there are any, the target or the seller company is required to resolve all issues prior to proceeding with the acquisition or to make adequate provisions to eliminate any adverse impacts on the acquiring company.

Human resource due diligence is another key component that involves an assessment of management talent and the skills and quality of the labor pool. Items such as the average age and educational levels, wages and salaries, bonuses and incentives, training and skill upgrading, insurance and pension funding and liabilities, union activities, and labor unrest are scrutinized. This due diligence is crucial to the success of the new entity because if it reveals serious problems, the acquiring company has the option to acquire only the assets of the target firm. In this manner, it does not assume the problems or obligations of the target related to organized labor activities.

Environmental due diligence has taken on increased significance since the early eighties because of the enormous amounts of money involved in environmental cleaning liabilities. Environmental due diligence is a requirement in most acquisitions, not only in acquisitions of manufacturing facilities using hazardous materials. The environmental lawyer or engineer on the team traces the history of physical facilities and production processes and examines legal documents to ensure that no hazardous materials have been buried, dumped, or hidden in areas other than in reclamation centers.

Depending on the nature of the project, other forms of due diligence are required to ensure that all important areas are addressed, such as inspections of physical plant and equipment or valuation of inventories. While a due diligence usually starts after the decision to move forward has been made, an experienced project team engages in due diligence activities from the start of the project. The reason for this is to uncover misrepresentations or hidden information as soon as possible and either disengage from the project or require adequate provisions to compensate the company for adverse impacts.

### Business Case Development

The business case is an extension of the feasibility study and it is a living document in that it continuously updates project information, analysis, and data. It is a summary document of the project team's findings, it is used to communicate recommendations to the senior management team, and it forms the basis for making the decision to proceed to closing. Its importance is derived from rigor of analysis and discipline in portraying accurately all findings that go into developing this summary which is used to obtain corporate project approvals.

The development of the business case begins with a description of the background that led to the project and a definition of the scope of the project. After that, the project rationale and objectives are checked and articulated and the strategic fit of the project is re-evaluated. By this stage, alternatives have already been assessed and the business case demonstrates why the project represents the best option in meeting operational needs and achieving the company's strategic objectives.

Information and data obtained from the target or the seller company are assessed and key assumptions are evaluated by the project team to ensure reasonableness in the financial analysis that follows, which, ultimately, results in the valuation of the acquisition target or the joint venture company. Having done that, the project team re-examines the risks and issues associated with the execution of the project, quantifies the financial impact of potential risks, and develops ways to mitigate the risk impacts.

The project team monitors negotiations closely, incorporates the negotiated terms and conditions in the financial models, and assesses their impact on the project NPV. By this stage, the implementation subteam has developed the implementation plan fairly well and assessed the human resource and financial requirements reflected in the business case document. How the new entity is expected to operate in the post-acquisition environment is based on the business plan of the new entity, which is briefly described in the business case.

### Project Financeability

As negotiations are winding down and the preliminary business case is developed, the project team looks at the project financeability issue. The first elements to be evaluated in determining project financeability are the tax implications of the deal structure, the project economics, the operating environment risks, and the risk allocation approach. If the project is financeable, the financing subteam evaluates various financing options and alternatives. Often, financing is left to investment bankers who determine the option to fund the project. However, the financing subteam should share that responsibility and work with investment bankers or external financing advisors to select the best financing alternative for the project.

Once financeability is determined, costs and benefits of each type of financing are evaluated and the two or three most attractive ones are selected. The most efficient financing option is pursued, but in case that approach fails, the project team has other options to pursue immediately. Sources of financing are approached and the estimated costs and terms and conditions of the funding are incorporated in the financial model and reflected in the business case. Frequently, financing enhancements are required to support the financing of the project and the costs of enhancements are also included in the business case financials.

### Project Team Recommendation

Armed with the results and recommendations of the due diligence subteam and the business case analysis, the project team develops a unanimous recommendation for the project. The project team's recommendation summarizes the findings, is included in the business case, and influences the decision to pursue a project to completion because it is reviewed by senior management for corporate approvals. The recommendation contains a go/no-go proposal based on evaluation of the facts, includes a brief explanation of key supporting evidence, and outlines the next steps in completing the project.

The project team recommendation incorporated in the business case is structured in simple and clear language and becomes far more powerful when it contains a statement of potential adverse impacts of not following the project team recommendation. The project team recommendation is handed off to the project sponsor, who communicates and reviews the recommendation with senior management. If accepted as is, the project team recommendation then forms the basis for corporate approvals; otherwise, changes are made to satisfy senior management concerns.

## SUMMARY

In this chapter we discuss the key steps of the opportunity assessment process starting with the characteristics of a sound assessment process, which we stress because of their impact on the price paid to close the project, their influence on the decision-making process, and their impact on the ultimate success of the project. The first step of opportunity assessment is internal analysis and evaluation to determine the strengths and weaknesses of the company, identify gaps in long term strategy and operational capabilities, and create profiles of desired target or partner companies.

The project feasibility study determines whether an opportunity moves on to the full-blown assessment or the business case stage. If the project is judged to be the best alternative and to have sufficient value creation potential, risks are identified and quantified and the financial analysis begins. As negotiations proceed, the financial impacts of negotiated terms and conditions are assessed and different trade-offs are quantified and their impacts evaluated.

The due diligence effort validates the information used to build the case for the project and its recommendations are used in the project implementation and synergy extraction phases. By this time, the preliminary business case is developed, which includes the costs of the financing option selected. Having brought the key evidence together in the business case, the project team develops its recommendation, which weighs very heavily in the senior management's decision to approve investment requirements and expansion of human resources on the project. The emphasis in the opportunity assessment process is on adherence to pre-established processes, clarity and continuity of purpose, clear definition of roles and responsibilities of project team members, and effective transitioning of responsibilities. Teamwork, open communications, and efficient coordination of effort and inputs make a difference in the project evaluation phase.

# 9

## THE ACQUISITION PROCESS STEPS

### INTRODUCTION

The acquisition process is a series of steps and subprocesses that the project team follows to go from identifying a target to the postmortem analysis. The steps of the acquisition process serve some key functions in organizing the tasks involved into cohesive segments and dividing a large amount of work associated with doing acquisitions down to manageable segments that can be performed more easily. They also simplify the definition of roles and responsibilities among project subteams, define expected output and deliverables, and ensure effective transfer of responsibilities and continuity of purpose. In addition, they make up the plan of actions to be followed known as the project workplan, and create an audit trail to ensure that required functions are performed.

In this chapter, we discuss how a company goes from ground zero to implementing the acquisition and closing the project with a postmortem analysis. In addition to steps involved, roles and responsibilities of participants are discussed, as well as the interdependencies of functions performed. The steps and inter-relationships that make up a sound acquisition process help to explain how successful acquisitions are done and ensure shareholder value creation. When a step in the acquisition process applies equally well to the joint venture formation process, it is noted. Experience shows that unless an acquisition project team follows closely a set of pre-established and well-tested processes, the acquisition is certain to fail. On the other hand, even less than world-class project teams that follow a set of pre-determined criteria and sound project processes produce fairly good acquisition results on a consistent basis. While the acquisition steps are shown in a sequence, some of them can be performed in parallel.

## SETTING THE STAGE

The acquisition process involves several functions whose understanding by the team members is essential. Adherence to a sound acquisition process is a key factor that determines project success because by following a pre-established process, the project team capitalizes on past experience of success. How well each step is performed depends on the leadership of the project team, the skills and experiences of the project team members, and the extent of team building and communications. Also, help from the business development group, investment bankers, and external advisors in executing each step determines success. A schematic of the acquisition process is shown in Figure 9.1.

**Figure 9.1**
**The Acquisition Process**

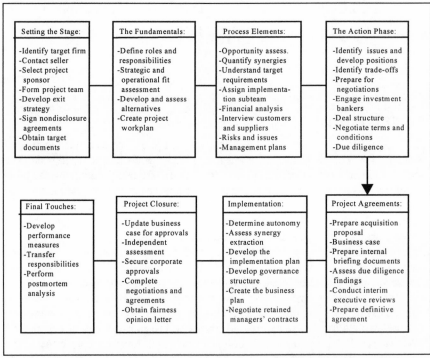

### Identifying a Target Company

The importance of strategic vision as the foundation of engaging in acquisitions or joint ventures is stressed a number of times and is repeated throughout the book because only through a well-developed strategy can sound screening criteria be developed. Once a strategic vision is developed, a gap analysis is performed, the project rationale follows from it, and the identification of the target company begins based on desired company profiles created.

Identification of a target is an activity performed by the business development group, but occasionally is done by upper management. Frequently, customers or suppliers of the acquiring company, investment bankers, financial advisors, brokers, the seller, or the target company itself present the opportunity to the company assuming that there are good reasons for the acquisition. However, only the strategic and operational gap analyses enable the project team to articulate the capabilities needed, develop the profile of an ideal company to acquire or partner with, and screen proposed alternatives.

When starting out to find a target company, the business development group has some key considerations in mind, which it uses to do the identification on a proactive basis. Operating and financial performance elements are easily understood criteria for judging value creation by an acquisition. However, knowing the company's strategic objectives, a world-class business development group performs strategic and operational gap analyses and a quick strategic return on investment assessment to identify potential acquisition targets. Armed with the desired company profiles it has created, it researches and screens firms in the same, related, or different industries, depending on the purpose of acquisition sought.

## Contacting the Seller

Initial contact with the seller is normally initiated by senior managers, but once interest on both sides is evident, contact at the working level is established. If the target is a subsidiary of a company, it is very important that contact and discussions are conducted with the parent. Senior management contact produces positive results in the case of joint venture projects because it creates substantial goodwill. In the case of acquisitions, senior management contact is used to demonstrate interest in the target. However, there are instances in which contact at working levels is preferable to determine the seller's interest in the transaction because potential problems in reaching agreement over basic issues may prevent the acquisition from materializing.

Initial meetings are used to sign nondisclosure agreements, develop a basic understanding of the other company's business, determine compatibility of cultures and management styles, and form impressions about commonality of strategic objectives. Release of confidential information or getting the other side to open up and share proprietary data should not be expected in early contacts. This comes with time, when the seller is convinced of the company's intent.

The team that participates in initial meetings must be able to articulate to the target or the seller the reasons they believe that make the project good for them and attractive for both sides. By the time a second meeting takes place, this team should have developed an exit strategy, in case deal breakers surface or simply because things may not work out as expected. Tact must characterize all discussions and one must always remember that the seller has just as many options available as the buyer.

### Identifying the Project Sponsor

A key requirement for a successful acquisition is the participation of a well-respected senior-level manager who serves as the project champion and supporter. Without a strong project champion, a project is characterized by delays, wavering back and forth, inability to complete the project, and eventual failure due to lack of senior management and business unit head support. The identification of a sponsor is the responsibility of the business development group initiating the project because it knows all senior managers, knows what it takes to do an acquisition, and can assess who would make a good champion.

Qualifications the business development group expects in the project sponsor are characteristics that make the sponsor a highly effective spokesperson and one who can move a project forward:

1. Senior management level or business unit head position. This is important in securing required resources to do the project.
2. Broad knowledge of the company's business. This helps understand how a target can be used to strengthen the company's core business and enhance its competitive position.
3. Thorough understanding of corporate strategy. This is necessary in visualizing the strategic and operational gaps and the benefits to be obtained from a project.
4. Highly seasoned and respected manager. This is a crucial element for this function in order to establish credibility and be able to obtain consensus and senior management support.
5. Interest and experience in external business development initiatives. This is a requirement for the sponsor to be effective in leading the project through the maze of the approval process.

### Forming the Project Team

The business development group usually appoints the project team leader, although the project sponsor provides input in that selection. The project team leader then assembles the team once the project is defined well enough to be workable. The project team consists of professionals who are experts in various functional areas and who rely on teamwork and collaboration to maximize contributions of all participants. However, it is essential that team members share common goals and objectives and maintain continuity of purpose throughout the project.

The project team is usually headed by a seasoned business development professional who obtains and maintains the commitment of team members and is responsible for the project workplan, the team's output, control of the process, providing guidance to team members, management of issues, and communication with external participants. Project team members are drawn from different functional areas including finance, operations, legal, technical support, marketing, corporate planning and strategy, human resources, and public relations. Senior managers are usually excluded from the acquisition project team because their presence does not allow for open team communication and interaction and their involvement results in decisions being made simply to satisfy senior manager wishes.

### Developing the Exit Strategy

One of the first activities the business development group and the project team undertake is to create the project exit strategy. Exit strategy refers to developing a reasonable, well-thought-out, and gracious approach to terminate discussions with the seller or the potential partner when it becomes apparent that project expectations are not met. This is important for a number of reasons, but also because the target or the seller may have extensive dealings with the acquiring company.

As important as the exit strategy is in preserving relations, it is even more important that a consistent message is developed concerning exiting discussions with the target because of investor considerations. That is, a consistent exit statement should be expressed in terms that are not specific, but are amiable, so that there is minimal impact on the stocks of both companies and if or when conditions change, discussions may start again with no hard feelings on either side. The exit statement is consistently communicated by the project sponsor internally and by senior management or preferably by a public relations expert externally so as to protect the interests of both sides and preserve the reputation of the company as a good party to conduct business with. A consistent exit statement is also important for managing the expectations of investors in both companies who like to be informed of progress on major activities.

### Signing Nondisclosure Agreements

At times, discussions about acquiring a target company are initiated on an informal basis and substantial information is shared. This exposes the company pursuing the project to potential legal problems if discussions take undesirable turns because claims may be made that the company benefited by proprietary information shared in the discussions. Therefore, it is recommended that the business development group have several variants of a confidentiality agreement available, prepare one for the company in question, and have it signed at the contact meeting or as soon as possible after that. No proprietary information or data from the seller or the target firm should be requested until the confidentiality agreement is signed and unless the acquiring company is willing to share similar information.

The confidentiality agreement covers nondisclosure of information shared, names of company representatives participating in discussions, the nature of the discussions and in some instances even that discussions are being held, and any terms, conditions, or tentative intentions and proposals. The confidentiality agreement should be signed by the manager representing the company and initiating the discussions and by a senior manager from the seller.

Outside the United States, requiring confidentiality agreements at the start of a project scares off people not used to a legalistic way of doing business. However, it should be explained that it is a routine company procedure intended to protect both sides. Foreign project participants find it far more acceptable to have nondisclosure clauses included in a memorandum of understanding (MOU) than to create a separate document dealing specifically with confidentiality. Therefore, we recommend using MOUs to record early understandings reached and include confidentiality and major exit clauses in them.

### Obtaining Proprietary Documents

After the initial contact meeting, the project team engages in follow-up discussions, documents are shared, and a fair amount of proprietary information is exchanged. Again, we stress that a confidentiality agreement should be signed before such documents are obtained from the target. This is because the company may be exposed to legal liabilities and because it is not a good business practice to get information without offering to honor the confidentiality of that information. One of the basic principles governing discussions and information exchange with the target firm which is worth repeating is the following: The rule of information exchange is reciprocity and the project team should not ask for information or data unless it is in a position to share with the seller similar company information.

Documents are obtained from the target throughout the course of discussions, but the most sensitive documents and financial information do not become available until the due diligence phase. Consequently, it is imperative that the project team know exactly what documents it needs to have access to at what point in the discussions, and negotiate for early release citing that timely assessment is beneficial to both sides. Documents obtained from the target or the seller are to be used in strict confidence by the project team and, in the event the acquisition does not materialize, returned with no copies made.

## THE FUNDAMENTALS

### Strategic and Operational Fit Assessment

Strategic and operational fit assessment of the target is an early analysis performed by the business development group and the project team in the feasibility phase. It determines the consistency of the target's long-term objectives with the company's strategy and how that strategy may be helped by the acquisition. A sound strategic fit assessment requires thorough understanding of the company's strategy, gaps in the strategy, and the target firm's long-term objectives. The operational fit assessment, on the other hand, involves an evaluation of complementarity of everyday operations.

Strategic and operational fit assessment also entails evaluation of the company's market position and strength before and after the acquisition, the impact of the acquisition on the company's organizational capabilities, and the expected impact on the company's cost structure and profitability potential. Also, enhancements in innovation and technology are assessed along with exceptional know-how the target brings to the company that will enable it to create a sustainable competitive advantage.

## Developing and Assessing Alternatives

Assessment of alternatives is essential to establish that the company's long-term objectives and operational needs are best met by the proposed project. The development and subsequent elimination of all but one alternative is also required to assure senior management that the proposed acquisition is the best course to execute the company's long-term growth strategy and value creation as opposed to:

1. Internal or business unit initiatives. This requires attention to ensure that parochial interests do not cloud perceptions of value created by alternatives.
2. Another external solution, such as a joint venture. Here, human resource requirements and costs and benefits of the two options must be examined closely to determine feasibility.
3. Acquisition of another target. It is a good idea to have screened more than one potential target in case the proposed acquisition does not materialize.
4. A greenfield approach. This option is often brushed aside because it does not produce immediate results, but a serious evaluation of this option as a long-term solution is recommended.

Assessment of alternatives involves evaluating which option fills what strategic and operational gaps and determining which alternative best meets the company's objectives and brings the capabilities it needs to become and remain competitive. This involves assessment of the financial value of each alternative, the degree of difficulty, human and financial resources required to implement the project, risks involved with each alternative, the extent of strategic advantage generated, and the likelihood of project success. Consequently, assessment of alternatives forms the foundation for the project selection and recommendation to proceed to the next phase.

## Creating the Project Workplan

The project workplan is developed by the project team leader with input from team members and it is the blueprint used by the team in getting the project through the process. The project workplan shows key activities involved in completing the project, the subteam owning each activity and individual members responsible, deliverables of each subteam, time lines associated with each activity, and estimated costs in performing each activity. Thus, the workplan enables the project team leader to monitor and control the process so that the project is completed by performing the activities outlined, in the time frames stated, and on budget.

In most cases, the project workplan mirrors the acquisition process outlined earlier. By spelling out the functions to be performed by each subteam, the project workplan facilitates effective transitioning of responsibilities and continuity of purpose from start to finish. Hence, since the workplan is intended to provide structure for the activities, it needs to be revised when major events occur to change the status of the project. Also, the project workplan is updated as activities are completed or new ones are added so that at any time it portrays the project status. Therefore, the project workplan is used as a tool to report progress to management and communicate future events and activities both internally and externally.

## KEY PROCESS ELEMENTS

### Performing the Opportunity Assessment

The opportunity assessment process was discussed in detail in Chapter 8. For most acquisition projects, it is preceded by internal company analysis before a target is identified and it begins after the project team is formed. Starting with the definition of scope and articulation of project goals and objectives, the team performs the strategic fit assessment and proceeds to develop the feasibility study. The feasibility study identifies the resource requirements and costs of doing the project and performs a preliminary financial assessment of the target, evaluation of project risks and issues, and evaluation of alternatives to the proposed acquisition.

As a project moves along the process, the project team analyzes the financial impact of negotiated terms and conditions, which are then incorporated in the business case. Parallel to that, the implementation subteam evaluates business autonomy issues, the implementation options, and potential costs and benefits of integration. While assessments take place, the information shared and claims made by the target are verified in the due diligence phase and the assumption set used is refined. Project evaluation is performed systematically in the business case phase and the findings of analyses and evaluations are summarized in the business case document, which includes a recommendation to senior management and an outline of the next steps to complete the acquisition.

### Quantifying Expected Synergies

For many acquisitions, the motivating factor is the potential synergies the buyer expects to obtain through acquisition of the target firm. Synergies mean different things to different project participants, but usually refer to enhanced financial and competitive performance, such as potential to shut down facilities, ability to consolidate operations and obtain cost reductions and efficiencies or access to new processes, R&D capabilities, technologies, product development, and actual products and services. Synergies also include access to new distribution channels and markets above and beyond what the acquiring company can achieve on its own and other factors that improve its industry standing and make the company more competitive.

A major responsibility of the project team is to identify and quantify expected synergies realistically and assess the costs and benefits of harnessing synergies. This is an important task because the seller and the target company have strong incentives to overstate synergies that may exist. Under no circumstances should the quantification of synergies be left to anyone other than the project team assisted by the business development group and the business units.

The project team reviews, scrutinizes, tests the implicit and explicit assumptions underlying these potential synergies, quantifies the costs and benefits of synergies, and assesses the likelihood of the synergies being realized as well as the risks associated with the synergies being realized. Quantification of synergies involves examining similar experiences and comparable acquisitions, realistic evaluations by functional experts, and discussions with the due diligence subteam to assign dollar values to statements of benefit.

### Understanding Target Requirements

The key driving factor for the seller is the price it can command in the marketplace and whether that price is tax-free. Therefore, behavior is geared toward maximizing the price it can get from the acquiring company. Occasionally, other factors that motivate the management of the target company to sell include access to the acquiring company's financial resources, technology, and R&D capabilities, branding of products and services, and assurances that the target's management will remain intact after the acquisition.

In order to value the target company properly and ensure successful implementation, the project team must understand the requirements the target or the seller company has stated or implied and the motives behind these requirements. Understanding the target's requirements is crucial in preparing the negotiation strategy and in actual negotiations because the project team can assess their impact and develop trade-offs or counter-proposals that meet requirements of both entities. It is also important in assessing the premiums that the seller may be asking and what constitutes equivalent trade-offs for those premiums.

### Assigning the Implementation Subteam

Success of an acquisition is primarily determined by two factors: the price paid and the ability to implement the acquisition effectively and obtain expected synergies. The price paid is determined by market conditions and the negotiating positions of the buyer and the seller. The ability to implement the acquisition and harness the expected synergies is determined by the qualifications of the implementation subteam, its expertise, and ability to execute the implementation and business plans effectively. As discussed in Chapter 4, this subteam is composed of experts in different functional areas who are responsible for transforming the target company after agreements are finalized and ownership is transferred to the acquiring company.

Implementation subteam members are identified by the project team leader early on and are involved in the assessment of the target, as core team members or functional experts. They are seasoned professionals in their areas of expertise, have experience in starting new companies and operations, and are able to manage organizational issues caused by drastic changes. They define the degree of autonomy the acquired company is to enjoy, or whether complete integration is the preferred option, and ensure that the implementation is executed effectively. Normally, some members are seconded to the new entity if it will operate autonomously and are responsible for the development of its business plan, which is evaluated and included in the business case.

### Performing the Financial Analysis

The purpose of financial analysis is to develop assumptions and quantify information and technical relations in order to create a reasonable set of financials and determine the value created by the proposed project. Financial analysis of an acquisition begins with an examination of the target's audited financial statements going back three to five years. Having been satisfied with their integrity, the project team proceeds to define the study horizon; review, challenge, and develop the assumption set; and determine the discount rate, the depreciation schedules appropriate for future investments, the tax rates to be applied in the analysis, and other model parameters such as dividend policy requirements, tax holidays, and import duties.

Future revenue streams are the most important element in financial analysis because they drive many other key variables and because a good part is determined by market conditions over which the target has little control. The target's future revenue is projected based on historical growth, information provided by the target, average industry growth expectations, pricing, marketing and promotions, and competitive considerations. Operating expenses are projected using historical relationships to revenues, other key variables, and by examining the post-acquisition requirements of the business plan. The third driving variable in financial analysis is capital investment requirements associated with implementing the acquisition and executing the business plan. Finally, quantification of implementation costs and expected synergies takes place and pro forma statements are created.

As discussions with the target firm progress, new information comes in and negotiations define the parameters for some variables. The updated information and negotiated terms and conditions are evaluated and reflected in the financial analysis, the purpose being to determine the price the company should pay for the acquisition and to estimate the project's worth to the company through its NPV. After financial statements for the target are created, the premiums likely to be required to close the transaction are estimated. After the price of the target and the value of the project to the acquiring company are determined, an analysis of issues follows and the risks to realizing the financial projections are identified, quantified, and reflected in the financial statements.

Project risk assessment gives the project team the information needed to create better baseline financial projections, define various risk scenarios, and create optimistic and pessimistic views around the baseline NPV projections. Having done the financial analysis, a seasoned financial analyst helps the negotiations subteam understand the key financial levers, create and quantify trade-offs, and guide the price negotiations toward the pessimistic view whereby a number of risks occur simultaneously. Financial analysis is required to help the project team determine the viability of the project and evaluate various financing options for the acquisition. External experts are invited to provide their assessment, but it is the project team's responsibility to ensure that the financing proposed meets the company needs.

### Interviewing Customers and Suppliers

The financial analysis incorporates a wealth of information through the development of financial statements, the price to be paid, and the estimated shareholder value. However, in order to determine how stable the financials are, the project team needs to obtain access to and examine the target's customer and supplier relationships. Visits with key customers are recommended to get a firsthand impression about their level of satisfaction with the target firm's products and services and determine whether large shares of sales are based on personal friendships that may disappear in the post-acquisition period.

Discussions with the target's suppliers is important to determine payment policies and practices, understand what competitors are doing, and obtain the suppliers' view of the industry's future and the target's expected demand for their products and services. Talking with the target's suppliers and customers takes place in the due diligence stage, but may be done earlier in the process by negotiating access to key suppliers and customers. This is important because it gives the project team another view of the target's operations, determines certainty of the revenue base, and strengthens the financial analysis.

### Identifying Project Risks and Issues

Issue analysis is an ongoing activity throughout the acquisition project. It brings to the forefront concerns expressed, it evaluates potential impacts of unresolved issues, and it seeks to develop solutions to the issues raised. On the other hand, systematic identification of project risks takes place once the assumption set underlying the financials is developed and the initial financial statements are created. At the same time, uncertainties related to realization of expectations are assessed so that risk management and contingency plans can be developed.

The essence of risk and issue assessment is a sound evaluation of assumptions underlying the financials and quantification of impacts on key financial drivers. The project team examines each key assumption, evaluates the likelihood of the assumption materializing, changes that assumption to fit a most likely scenario of events, and measures the impact on the project NPV through a financial model simulation. Thus, the impact of risks and issues associated with each key driver is the change in the project's baseline NPV. After key assumptions are changed to reflect risks materializing, the project's pessimistic NPV value is calculated. Risk management plans are created under this scenario with the cost of implementing these plans included in the overall project NPV.

### Developing Risk Management Plans

Risk management plans refer to plans intended to deal with unresolved issues and project risks, negotiate their allocation and sharing, and create ways to deal with them so as to mitigate the impact or eliminate the risks completely. Effective risk management requires each project risk identified to be broken down to smaller components, each component examined independently, finding ways and appropriate management talent to manage the smaller risk components, and coordinating the risk management plan efforts.

Risk management in acquisition projects takes several forms, the most common being pushing the risk back to the seller or the target through the use of agreements, negotiating the risk away to third parties, and allocating risks according to ability to handle. Other approaches to risk management include purchasing commercial insurance to cover certain risks and sharing the risk with the seller or other entities according to potential benefits received. Pushing risks to the seller is done in several ways, the most common being to lump all risks together and have the seller compensate the acquiring company for any portion of the new entity's business plan that is not realized.

Sharing risks with others is accomplished according to each party's interest in the project, expected benefits, and ability to handle risks. Two forms of risk sharing are use of earn-out formulas in which payments are made if certain thresholds are met and use of legal agreements to manage risk. These are effective approaches that minimize uncertainty when there are benefits to be obtained by the parties involved. Finally, commercial insurance may be a viable option to eliminate some types of risk; however, the project team needs to consider the costs of this option.


## THE NEGOTIATIONS PHASE

### Identifying Key Issues and Developing Positions

The first element the project team tackles in preparation for negotiations is to look at the major areas of concern, identify key issues for which the company wants certain outcomes to materialize, and develop the company's position on these issues. By company positions we mean the opening negotiation position, fallback positions, acceptable trade-offs, and walk away positions on issues identified as key financial drivers.

The key issues are identified and positions are developed in order to prepare the acquiring company's negotiations subteam to negotiate a better deal. This helps because key issues are areas of concern to both seller and buyer and are the focus of negotiations. Key issues are conditions to be attached such as, for example, a non-competing clause for a number of years in certain markets or geographical territories, or operating performance levels acceptable to the buyer, or a number of other levers the acquiring company wishes to control. The positions on the key issues reflect the entire spectrum from what the buyer ideally would like to get, to what it is willing to settle for, to what it will not accept and walk away from the deal.

Development of negotiating positions is of limited value unless several trade-offs are developed with roughly equal values to the other party. This enables the negotiations subteam to be flexible and innovative. If the acquiring company wishes to obtain a certain outcome in one particular area, although it should not offer, it needs to be prepared to give up something of similar value in another area so as to leave the seller as well off. Creation of equal-value trade-offs is a key element in moving negotiations forward quickly and bringing the deal to a close with both buyer and seller obtaining what is important to them.

### Identifying Acceptable Trade-Offs

Identification of trade-offs is probably one of the most difficult exercises for a project team because it requires good understanding of buyer and seller strategies and goals and objectives in the project. It also requires understanding the personalities of the target's project team and the representatives involved in negotiations and what they value. Hence, a fair amount of time should be spent in understanding what the seller wants and what key managers of the target think is important for them personally and for the target's future.

To identify acceptable trade-offs, the project team assigns value to each item being considered, but it is a complicated process to come up with dollar values for different items that have different risk profiles associated with them. Here, the experience of a seasoned project leader working closely with the financial analyst is invaluable in quantifying the value of the various trade-offs. Once reasonable trade-offs are developed, they are explained to the negotiations subteam members, who are then prepared to handle trading alternatives.

### Conducting the Due Diligence

The due diligence effort normally starts after the decision to acquire a target is made, but an experienced project team engages in a due diligence-like effort early in the process. While each project involves specific areas of detailed investigation, there are four primary areas of due diligence common to most projects: legal, financial, human resource, and environmental. Each area of due diligence attempts to verify all information released, uncover hidden liabilities or problems, and catch any misrepresentation before definitive agreements are signed. In certain types of acquisitions, the due diligence is complex and takes a long time to complete. This is due to a number of factors, such as multiple operations or foreign subsidiaries of the target with multiple cross-ownership, output purchasing, and transfer pricing arrangements with foreign subsidiaries. In those cases, the due diligence effort proceeds in parallel with the negotiations, and once the project team is satisfied with most of its assessment and findings, definitive agreements may be signed subject to no adverse due diligence findings being uncovered. Substantial negative findings in the due diligence process provide an easy exit for the company that would otherwise be buying the target firm and offer an opportunity to re-negotiate. However, such findings need to be handled with care when disclosed outside the project team and the target's representatives. The reason for this is that if the terms and conditions of the sale can be improved materially, the acquiring firm will be compensated for the negative findings of the due diligence.

### Preparing for Negotiations

The negotiations plan is developed by the core project team in conjunction with the negotiations subteam. The basis of the negotiation plan and the strategies of executing the plan is a sound understanding of the buyer's long term strategy and its goals and objectives in the project. The key elements of the negotiation plan are the key issues to be addressed in the negotiations, the buyer's positions on these issues, and the creation of trade-offs of equivalent value and concessions in order to obtain something of similar value.

Negotiations strategy refers to the approach used in conducting the negotiations and deals with styles to be used, trade-offs to be proposed, timing of certain events, and the "theatrics" in presentations and discussions. The negotiations strategy should fit the nature and personalities of the negotiations subteam comfortably, should be well understood, and should be memorized by team members like a play.

The advice often given the negotiations subteam is to push for the best deal on the acquisition price. While the price paid for the target is certainly important, the terms and conditions of the sale and the implementation of the acquisition are just as important in determining project success. Therefore, the acquiring company's negotiations subteam should under no circumstances force ridiculous terms and conditions or humiliate the representatives of the target or the seller. It should look for ways to give them a reason to claim that the terms and conditions obtained are fair so that project implementation can proceed smoothly.

### Engaging Investment Bankers

Investment bankers serve a number of valuable functions in acquisition projects. They advise on the valuation approach to be used, provide information on comparable transactions, participate in project negotiations, perform an independent assessment of the acquisition, communicate positions to the target's advisors, and prepare the fairness opinion letter.

> *A fairness opinion letter is a document produced by the investment banker engaged by the acquiring company. The letter states that they have reviewed the project economics, the financial analysis, and the methodologies used, and that in their professional opinion, the terms and conditions and the price to be paid to close the transaction are fair, in line with market conditions, and that the project creates reasonable shareholder value.*

Another area where investment bankers provide value is in financing the project. Their value is in providing ideas and advice, helping to create a financing strategy, and developing alternative funding structures. They also help negotiate financing agreements and underwrite part of the financing. Therefore, the project team needs to work closely with them to develop the right financing package for the project and learn from them.

Despite the investment bankers' potentially large contributions, the project team must evaluate their engagement. In addition to timing the engagement of the investment banker, the business development group must specify the areas of investment bankers' responsibility and obtain agreement on the terms of engagement. Most importantly, the project team must retain control of the project and not allow investment bankers to dictate time lines, company positions, and terms and conditions to be agreed to without consideration by the project team. The project team leader should, from time to time, remind investment bankers of the purpose of their engagement.

### Developing the Deal Structure

Project structure refers to how an acquisition or joint venture project is defined, what is encompassed in its scope, and how such a project is to be executed. On the other hand, a deal structure of an acquisition or a joint venture is a different concept and normally encompasses:

1.  The legal type of acquisition, that is, purchase of stock versus assets.
2.  The tax treatment of the transaction; that is, taxable versus tax free.
3.  The specific financing structure used to fund the project.
4.  The governance structure of the new entity.

In the first part of the deal structure the project team determines the company's views on the risks of assuming the target's liabilities. In the second component it determines the tax treatment of participants, while in the third element it shows how the acquiring company pays for the purchase of the target. In the last part of a deal structure, the project team outlines how the new entity is to be organized and managed in the post-acquisition period.

The type of structure to be pursued is determined by the assessment of risks involved in assuming the liabilities and obligations of the target firm when purchasing its stock. Otherwise, a stock acquisition is pursued because the value of the target is derived from the assets as well as from the contributions of its labor force. The financing aspect of a deal structure is the funding mechanism, which is determined by tax considerations, the company's ability to raise the capital needed, financing costs involved, risks assumed by the buyer, the terms and conditions of the transaction, and the governance structure of the new entity.

### Negotiating Acquisition Terms and Conditions

Actual negotiations of the terms and conditions of the acquisition are done by the negotiations subteam, with input and guidance from the business development group and investment bankers, and support from the entire project team. The negotiations subteam is made up of a senior manager (usually the project sponsor), a seasoned financial analyst, a lawyer, a business development manager, and a key technical person. The charge of the negotiations subteam is to bring negotiations to completion and obtain as many concessions on key issues outlined in the negotiations plan as possible.

Effective negotiations in acquisition projects entail few key considerations on the part of the negotiations subteam, the first being understanding the strategy and objectives in the acquisition of the target, the seller, and the acquiring company. Knowing what trade-offs are possible and their value to the seller and being empowered to propose, evaluate, and agree to different trade-offs is important; that is, having the ability to introduce new terms and conditions and be flexible on proposals. Also, developing a sound negotiations strategy with a number of fallback positions and contingencies and being well prepared with facts and figures to support its positions and proposals is essential. However, in some cases even when all these requirements are satisfied, negotiations stall. To get negotiations going again, new proposals are presented, but if this approach fails repeatedly and no progress is made, the negotiations subteam needs to review the situation, understand the causes of failure, and, if appropriate, activate the exit plan and disengage from discussions.

## GETTING TO PROJECT AGREEMENTS

### Preparing the Acquisition Proposal

After major negotiation issues are settled and the business case is updated, the project team submits a proposal to the seller. The acquisition proposal is a document indicating interest from the acquiring company to submit a tentative bid for the target, subject to due diligence findings and other key conditions. It is a brief document spelling out the intent of the acquiring company, the price range to be paid, and key conditions that must be met for the acquisition to materialize. At the same time, it allows exit from the arrangement if the required conditions are not fully met to its satisfaction.

The acquisition proposal is a carefully drafted document, by the lawyer on the team, with input from the team and investment bankers after approval of the interim business case. It is reviewed by the project team, the investment bankers, and senior management and is delivered to the seller through the investment bankers. Because the acquisition proposal is a document that obligates the buyer to go through the acquisition once the conditions laid out are satisfied, it is important that conditions included adequately protect its interests and create value.

The different types of legal agreements involved in acquisitions and joint venture projects are examined in Chapter 20. The project team needs to review carefully the typical conditions attached to the acquisition proposal, which include factors such as the following:

1. The representations and warranties of the companies are true and correct.
2. The companies have performed and met, in all material aspects, their obligations.
3. The acquisition proposal can be voided by mutual consent of the companies.
4. The buyer can withdraw the proposal if the seller modifies its recommendation in a manner adverse to the buyer or accepts a third-party bid.

### Developing the Business Case

The business case for acquisitions or joint ventures is a summary of the analysis, assessments, findings, and recommendations of the project team. It forms the basis for the decision to proceed with the proposed acquisition and obtain corporate approvals. It is updated continuously to reflect new information and its value is derived from two attributes: the rigor of analysis and the discipline in portraying accurately the evaluation of the proposed acquisition target and reporting all the findings, and its use as a means to communicate the project status, make recommendations to senior management, and in some cases to the outside world such as financing institutions and external investors.

The business case is an extension of the feasibility study and it is a living document that seeks to continuously update, verify, assess, and reflect the most recent information received and analyses performed. Most people view the business case as a document dealing only with financials; however, that impression is incorrect. The truth is that the business case brings together in a summary form the key assumptions made, the findings of the strategic fit assessment, the results of analyses done, and the assessment of alternatives. It also includes the project valuation and its impact on the acquiring company, the evaluation of risks and issues, the negotiated terms and conditions, the sensitivity analyses, the implementation plan for the acquisition, and a summary of the business plan.

### Preparing Internal Briefing Documents

One of the responsibilities of the project team is to communicate internally on an on-going basis the status of the project and progress made, report issues raised or resolved, report important findings, solicit help from senior management when necessary, provide recommendations, and handle communication problems. The first internal briefing document is the feasibility study, which introduces the project and gives the project team's assessment of the opportunity up to that point along with a recommendation to proceed to the next phase.

Prior to negotiations, the project team prepares a list of key issues to be negotiated and shares the negotiations plan and strategy with senior management to obtain their support. The acquisition proposal document is developed and shared with senior management to inform them of what is being proposed and obtain concurrence. When negotiations are finished, the final business case is prepared and shared with senior management to obtain corporate approval for the funds to invest in the acquisition.

After major agreements are concluded, the project team obtains an independent assessment of the project, usually from a centralized corporate staff, and a fairness opinion from investment bankers engaged to ensure that the price paid for the acquisition target is in line with market condi' 'ons. The independent assessment report and the fairness opinion letter are part of the package used to brief senior management. They verify and support the project team's assessment and that the price paid is fair for the shareholder value expected to be created.

### Assessing Due Diligence Findings

The due diligence effort entails reviewing a lot of documents, creates new knowledge, and verifies the information disclosed by the target. Often, no significant new findings are brought to light, but from time to time new information surfaces, misrepresentations are exposed, and hidden facts and obligations are revealed. When that happens, the project team examines the new evidence closely, assesses the implications to the acquiring company, and decides whether to proceed with the acquisition, subject to corrective action being taken to address the problems, or to terminate discussions.

Occasionally, even when faced with negative due diligence findings, companies proceed with acquisitions because of the view that after deal closing, they will have full control of the new entity and at that point can address all problems. However, it is advisable to terminate discussions when significant negative findings are exposed rather than proceed with the acquisition. The reason for this is that unless drastic changes occur, such as most of the target's management being fired, past problems are likely to persist and new ones develop and compound existing problems. Since this creates an environment of mistrust, emphasis should be attached to the assessment of the due diligence findings and the recommendation of the due diligence subteam.

### Conducting Interim Executive Reviews

Senior management has a strong interest about what happens with an acquisition project because it is impacted by the outcome of the project in several ways. Therefore, the project team has the responsibility to keep company executives informed on a regular basis or as the situation warrants. This is an opportunity to communicate the status of a project, report on progress made, bring to the fore concerns, risks, and other issues, and request the support of senior management. Another good reason for conducting interim executive reviews is to obtain direction and guidance from senior executives on how to deal with broad impact issues, get a unique perspective on the strategic issues involved, and feel their positions on the project.

Periodic project reviews and briefings are conducted by the project sponsor with help from the project team leader. While these reviews are information sharing in nature, the real benefit is that with each review the project sponsor obtains the tacit approval of senior executives to proceed to the next step in the acquisition process. Experienced project sponsors and team leaders use interim reviews to keep senior executives involved in the acquisition project and obtain unofficial interim approvals and continued support for the project. By the time the final business case is developed, senior executive approvals are only a formality.

### Preparing the Definitive Agreement

Definitive agreements are the final acquisition proposal and final agreement that governs the sale of the target. Most project teams look to the legal staff to produce these agreements, close the deal, and wrap up the project. However, definitive agreements are a responsibility shared by the project team and the legal staff because a number of business issues are involved that need to be addressed first and then put into legal language.

The nature of the final proposal is dictated by the reaction of the seller to the initial proposal, the course of negotiations, and terms and conditions the parties are willing to accept. The final agreement governing the purchase of the target reflects the negotiated terms and conditions and includes clauses that protect the acquiring company in case the claims made by the target do not materialize. Protection against risks is sought through earn-out formulas included in the agreement, whereby the price paid for the target is determined by the extent to which the agreed-upon business plan materializes and expected synergies are extracted.

While the project team is responsible for business issues in the final acquisition proposal and the purchase agreement, the legal group's contributions go beyond the drafting of the agreements. Regardless of experience in this area, it is recommended that the project team seek the advice and counsel from seasoned M&A lawyers because their expertise in developing deal structures, including governance and financing structures, is invaluable in ensuring coverage of all issues. Their understanding of terms and conditions to be obtained with various deal structures, especially concerning governance and financing, helps tremendously in funding the project. In addition, their skills are helpful in assessing integration potential, earn-out formulas, and clauses in the final agreement likely to prevent the deal from closing quickly or cause implementation problems.

## PREPARING FOR THE IMPLEMENTATION

### Developing the Implementation Plan

Success of an acquisition is mostly determined by the extent of strategic fit, the price paid for the acquisition, the way implementation is executed, and synergies actually extracted. Strategic fit assessment is done early in the process and the price paid is determined by the financial analysis, the terms and conditions negotiated, and market conditions. How the acquisition is implemented is driven by the project's implementation plan. The implementation plan is a guide that shows how the acquiring company wishes to manage the transition in ownership, the associated management changes, and its intent to run operations of the new entity in the post-acquisition period.

The implementation plan is developed by a team of managers who are responsible for making the transition work and are likely to be seconded to the new entity to make things happen. The project team is involved in this activity to ensure consistency of objectives across the process, to reflect implementation plan information in the business case, and to provide support for the implementation subteam. The key concerns of the implementation plan are defining the degree of operational autonomy or integration of the new entity with the acquiring company and identifying and selecting the management talent to run the new entity and develop appropriate compensation plans. Another key consideration is assessing implementation costs and creating a realistic business plan with sufficient future investment funding included to ensure that no constraints to realization of financial projections are imposed. Also, creating a reasonable implementation plan and time line likely to materialize and harness the expected synergies is important. However, dealing with organizational change dynamics, personnel issues, and politics of positioning for power, both in the acquiring and in the new entity, are the determining success factors.

### Creating the Business Plan

The business plan is a subset of the implementation plan, which shows how each of the financial statement line items will be managed to ensure that financial projections materialize. Thus, it deals with financial data and assigns responsibilities to implementation managers. The business plan is the implementation subteam's responsibility, but the project team participates in its development to assess reasonableness and summarize it in the business case. It is based on the new entity's business definition, scope of operations, and mission statement and is typically made up of subplans related to the major functional areas:

1. The human resources plan. This includes the organizational structure envisioned for the new entity, staffing policies, skill development and training, compensation, and other personnel issues.
2. The operational plan. This plan includes production schedules, consolidation of facilities, changes in processes, and describes how to achieve performance targets.
3. The technical plan. It is mostly concerned with R&D activities, development of new technologies, and product introduction and commercialization for the company to remain competitive.
4. The marketing plan. This plan includes marketing, sales, promotions, advertising, pricing, and product line management.
5. The financial plan. It includes detailed financial projections and a wide spectrum of measurements along with financial reporting requirements.
6. The synergy extraction plan. This is where the specifics of how synergies are to be created are outlined and the costs and benefits involved are shown along with the responsibilities of project participants.

A good business plan is characterized by completeness of coverage of business operations, contingency and backup plans, and assignment of responsibilities to capable functional experts along with consistent objectives, reporting structures, and control mechanisms. The business plan is the heart of the implementation plan, and for that reason, a lot of attention is given to its development. Senior management should review the new entity's business plan to determine likelihood of realization. A sound implementation plan enables the project team to fine-tune its execution and obtain desired results.

### Negotiating Retained Managers' Contracts

Success of an acquired company's operations can be traced to organizational structure, human resources policies, and superior management talent, which is expected to create value under a new ownership structure. When these elements are present, the acquiring company should keep all key managers to ensure that there is continuity in its successful operations. It is important that mechanisms are established to have retained managers work with the implementation subteam to transfer knowledge to the acquiring company, regardless of the degree of autonomy contemplated. When managers of the target are willing to join the new management team and are retained with new employment contracts, implementation proceeds smoothly and quickly.

Whether the acquiring company can retain exceptional managers from the target depends entirely on negotiated contracts. The key elements for retained manager contracts are:

1.  Positions in the new entity and corresponding titles. These are the most important considerations along with the reporting structure to the acquiring company's management team.
2.  Authority to make significant investment or new-entity strategic direction decisions because acquired company senior managers want to maintain their ability to impact strategic direction, which, often, is in conflict with the buyer's plans.
3.  Monetary remuneration, including bonuses and incentives. Remuneration is commensurate with authority and responsibility, which in integration cases declines considerably, but to retain management talent in the transition period, target company managers are compensated at higher levels. The retained managers' compensation contains clauses that tie remuneration to the new entity's performance in terms of meeting business plan financials and harnessing expected synergies.

## GETTING TO PROJECT CLOSURE

### Updating the Business Case

Once acquisition terms and conditions are negotiated, their impact on financials is updated and they are recorded in a summary form in the business case. When the implementation plan is developed and assessed, its financial impacts are captured and reflected in the business case. Likewise, when the risk analysis and plans are completed, the financial models are updated to incorporate all relevant information. As new data and information arrives, its validity is assessed and becomes part of the business case evidence. Assumption sets are tested, unreasonable or erroneous assumptions are rejected, and new ones are developed, reflected in financial models, and included in the business case.

When project information is updated in the business case, the project team portrays a complete picture and develops a recommendation for senior management to make the decision. The updates are summarized in the final business case for the purpose of using it to communicate the value created by the acquisition and obtain corporate approval to proceed to closing. Consequently, updates must reflect facts, clearly-spelled-out assumptions, and appropriate caveats to strengthen the business case foundations. Only then can the project team expect senior management to be convinced of the quality of analysis and the recommendation before them.

### Obtaining Independent Assessments

The project team assesses acquisition projects and is deeply involved with every issue in the project. Hence, obtaining an independent assessment and evaluation from another internal organization is highly recommended for all acquisition projects. If that experience does not reside internally, external experts should be engaged to ensure that the evaluation performed is indeed reasonable and accurate because:

1.  It is possible that the project team information, assessment, and analysis are erroneous or incomplete. Issues can go unchecked and basic elements escape the project team's attention because of tight schedules and operating under pressure.
2.  Interpretation of facts may not be entirely consistent or correct. This occurs because project team members often take definitions for granted and these definitions are not the same across all participants.
3.  Recommended processes may not have been followed. This can happen for a number of reasons, but is mostly traced to shortcuts and pressure to meet deadlines.
4.  Information and facts may have been omitted from the analysis. This occurs either because of ignorance on the part of the project team or because they were not considered important in the broader scheme of things.
5.  Personal biases and subjective judgments. They are occasionally introduced in the assessment process, but an independent assessment identifies such biases and requires explanations that satisfy impartial observers.

Independent assessments can be performed by a corporate business development group not involved in the project as well as by investment bankers engaged in the project. However, for this independent assessment to be of value, the party performing the assessment should not have a motive to produce a project recommendation one way or another. Therefore, while it saves time, it is not a good idea to have the independent assessment team do it in conjunction with the project team or while it is doing the project. Instead, it should be done separately from the project team's effort, probe the assumption set used, and test the accuracy of available information. It should confirm the reasonableness of analysis and methodology used in the valuation, and verify that the project team's recommendation is based on factual evidence.

### Securing Corporate Approvals

Acquisitions involve large sums of money to purchase the target. Because of the amounts involved, there need to be corporate approvals in public companies to authorize the acquisition and the investment funds required. Corporate approvals are obtained by following established processes and procedures, company authorization schedules and guidelines, and meeting corporate requirements. The project team is responsible for obtaining corporate approvals, with guidance and direction from the project sponsor and the business development group.

The corporate approval process begins with the project team and the business development group recommendation to the project sponsor who concurs with the recommendation. Then, it goes to business unit heads impacted by and likely to fund the acquisition for their concurrence. The chief financial officer of the business unit funding the acquisition and the corporate chief financial officer must concur and forward the business case to the corporate strategy and business development group for their concurrence. When that concurrence is obtained, the business case goes to the CEO, who, depending on the amount of the investment, may forward it to the board of directors for approval.

Throughout the approval process, briefings of senior managers involved in the decision take place to ensure a good understanding of the project, negotiated terms and conditions, shareholder value being created, and risks associated with the project. Once independent assessments are obtained, an executive summary of the business case is attached to the package submitted to senior executives for approval and goes to the CEO and the chairman of the company for their authorization. Finally, depending on the size of the acquisition, the board of directors must be briefed on the value of the project, approve the acquisition, and authorize investment funds.

### Completing Negotiations and Agreements

Simultaneously to corporate approvals, the project team concludes the due diligence effort. The negotiations subteam completes unresolved issues, and the implementation subteam begins to execute the integration and the new entity's operational plans. To prepare for closing, the legal team works closely with the project team and investment bankers to update the acquisition agreements and review contracts to ensure that the acquiring company's interests are protected.

In this phase of the acquisition process, things tend to move very quickly and it is recommended that the project team and the business development group remain engaged and monitor all aspects of the project to ensure progress is made toward closing. As negotiations wind down, definitive agreements are signed and closing takes place. With closing, the project team updates for the last time the business case document to reflect last-minute changes in the terms and conditions of the acquisition. Also, the project team briefs the project sponsor, who, in turn, communicates the status of the acquisition to senior management.

## THE FINAL TOUCHES

### Developing Measures of Performance

The core project team and the implementation subteam work closely to develop the governance and reporting structures, control systems, and operational performance measures for the new entity. The creation of effective reporting structures is important in the transition period to ensure that integration takes place rapidly and that there is transfer of know-how to the acquiring company's management team, especially in the case of autonomous new entity operations. Control mechanisms and systems are needed to ensure:

1. Congruence of mission statements, supporting business definitions, and consistency of acquiring and acquired company strategies.
2. Integrity of new-entity financial reporting systems to meet informational needs of the acquiring company.
3. Proper execution of the business plan by the acquired company to prevent abuses by disgruntled employees, which are common in consolidations and work force reductions.
4. Management of financial resources in accordance with the acquiring company's long-term strategy.

Development of performance measures must include input from the acquired company because it is a sensitive issue and needs to be handled carefully. Ordinarily, it entails creating financial ratios to determine how well the new entity is doing. We recommend that the new entity's objectives be established first, then management objectives be developed based on those objectives, and then operational performance measures be created that relate to those management objectives. In doing this, a complete management performance system is created that has a number of measurements tied to it beyond typical financial ratios and measurements.

### Transferring Responsibilities

Once closing occurs and project implementation begins, operational performance measures are developed, and the process of transferring responsibility from the project team to the implementation subteam takes place. The transfer of responsibilities involves creation of the new entity's mission statement, goals, and objectives; ensuring a smooth transition to managing to the new entity's business plan; and implementing organizational and reporting structures, control mechanisms, and performance measures. Most importantly, however, transition of responsibilities involves maintaining continuity of purpose and preservation of the initial goals and objectives.

Once implementation is well underway, the implementation subteam gradually disengages from the project and the liaison subteam assumes responsibility for managing the interface between the acquiring company and the new entity and between the new entity and the outside world. Since a number of managers on the implementation and the liaison subteams are also members of the project team, a complicated process becomes manageable because of the teamwork established.

As the project team and the implementation subteam phase out of the process, the liaison subteam ensures continuity of purpose in the project because it is responsible for realizing expected synergies. In essence, the implementation subteam manages the transition to the new entity and the integration of the entity or establishment of autonomous operations. To that extent, the implementation subteam develops plans to bring required resources to realize the business plan projections and harness the expected synergies. However, the liaison subteam actually ensures senior management support for the new entity and availability of human and financial resources to implement the project successfully.

### Performing the Postmortem Analysis

After the acquisition is completed, the implementation has taken place, and the new entity's operations have begun, the business development group monitors the acquired company, if allowed to run autonomously, or the integrated operations with the acquiring company. It also performs the project postmortem analysis to identify what was done well in the execution of the project, what was done poorly, what went wrong, and lessons learned in the process. The main benefit of a postmortem analysis is that experiences are shared within the company, expertise is developed, and the organization learns and becomes more effective in future acquisition projects.

Postmortem analysis is done by a seasoned business development group associate who can penetrate through organizational politics, facades, and barriers to get to the facts and root causes and obtain open and unbiased input and feedback on the project team's performance and the value of external advisors to the project. This associate identifies what needs to be recorded not for the purpose of assigning blame or punishing anyone, but for the benefit of learning from the acquisition, synthesizing the significance of findings into concrete recommendations, and communicating them to senior management and the rest of the project team.

Once performed, the postmortem findings are reported to the project sponsor and the project team in a meeting where the findings are discussed along with lessons learned. Finally, the postmortem analysis findings are written up along with recommendations about future projects and become part of the acquisition documents library.

## SUMMARY

The elements of doing an acquisition project are important links in the chain of events that take the company from the long-term growth strategy to buying a firm that helps achieve that strategy. In this chapter, the process steps, the responsibilities of project participants, and the significance of the process are examined.

The key groupings of steps in the acquisition process follow the major project phases: namely, screening, evaluation, negotiation, financing, implementation, and synergy creation. Emphasis is placed on the process elements that result in developing the acquisition proposal, negotiating win-win arrangements, assessing project risks, and extracting expected synergies.

A sound acquisition process is made up of clearly defined functions and steps that must take place in the right sequence and where effective transition and continuity of purpose is preserved to execute an acquisition successfully. A sound acquisition process enhances the definition of responsibilities and accountability of project participants, provides a checklist of functions that must be performed, and ensures effective transitioning of responsibilities and continuity of purpose, in addition to forming the basis for a good workplan.

# 10

# STEPS OF THE JOINT VENTURE FORMATION PROCESS

## INTRODUCTION

Strategic alliances are agreements between companies to work jointly and cooperate in formal arrangements for mutual benefit. Like any other business arrangement, they have costs and benefits associated with them, but the biggest cost is the requirement to share knowledge, experience, technology, and know-how with a partner who may be a partner for only a short time. Managing and balancing costs and benefits in any strategic alliance is the single most difficult challenge in these arrangements.

Joint venture projects take longer to complete than acquisitions. However, the joint venture formation process has many parallels and common elements with the acquisition process. When doing joint ventures, project teams follow most acquisition steps with minor adjustments and some joint venturing unique steps. Therefore, our attention now focuses on those steps of joint venture formation that are unique to it or different in emphasis or approach.

In this chapter, the discussion of joint venture formation focuses on partnership arrangements, which are the result of two or more companies contributing equity to form a new entity. We begin with the types and purposes of alliances and the importance of following pre-established processes. After that, we examine the identification and cultivation of the project sponsor issue and revisit the development of project objectives before contacting potential partners. Next, we cover the importance of the initial contact and the confidentiality agreements required to protect the interests of the parties involved. Then, we discuss screening of potential joint venture partners and the need to understand partner motives, needs, and requirements. The steps of the joint venture formation process emphasized are assessment of cultural and organizational compatibility and relationship building, establishing the right chemistry, and creation of effective communications.

Because partners have common interests, the joint project workplan they create is discussed along with the role of MOUs and managing senior management and partner expectations. The basics of negotiating a deal to create a win-win arrangement and the development of the governance structure are briefly discussed before we focus on the development of the joint operational plan. Financial analysis, the identification of risks and issues, and the development of the project business case are examined along with the assessment of the joint venture project financeability. Since win-win arrangements are crucial to ensure that the joint venture survives, we discuss the need to verify their existence and the due diligence effort throughout the project process. The chapter ends with a discussion of the venture steering committee, the liaison subteam and interfaces, the joint venture agreements, and monitoring and controlling the new entity.

## BACKGROUND AND PREPARATION

### Types and Purpose of Alliances

It is useful to review the different types of strategic alliances in order to understand the sources of problems in executing joint venture projects. Strategic alliances are business arrangements driven by senior managers, they are characterized by close operational linkages, and the partners have vested interests in the other's future success. They have cooperative management styles, they are not based on control but on sharing power, and they tend to be reciprocal relationships sharing strengths and advantages. Strategic alliances do not usually involve equity participation and investment. Consequently, they do not have the same level of commitment as arrangements that involve investment.

Strategic partnerships usually involve minority equity stakes and licenses, purchaser-supplier agreements, and long-term support arrangements such as franchises. Even if they involve minority stakes, these partnerships do not operate autonomously, but are managed by both companies. Joint ventures, on the other hand are formal alliances that involve equity and the formation of a new entity managed by a separate management team.

Generally speaking, the purpose of strategic alliances is related to one of the following considerations:

1. Leveraging strengths that the partner brings to the joint venture for mutual benefits.
2. Maximizing the impact of combining resources with those of another company and bypassing the constraints on the company's ability to execute its long-term strategy.
3. Sharing the costs, benefits, and risks of engaging in new business areas or new markets.

Occasionally, strategic alliances are formed to obtain access to cheaper sources of capital and local foreign markets and to influence the industry structure. Yet, another reason is to obtain access to R&D, technology, processes, and trade secrets, and this should be a constant reminder to project team members.

## Importance of Process in Forming Joint Ventures

The formation and assessment of joint ventures is a long and complex process that requires a skillful project team following established guidelines in order for a project to be successful. As in acquisitions, the venture formation process begins with the definition of the company's long-term strategy, followed by a gap analysis to determine areas of strength and weakness. This results in the creation of desired partner company profiles and appropriate screening criteria according to the purpose of the joint venture entity to be created.

The first element of a joint venture evaluation is the strategic fit assessment of the joint venture with the company's long-term strategy. A preliminary project financial analysis and its impact on the company is performed, and risks and issues are identified along with alternatives, which are compared with the proposed venture. At this point, the project team prepares a feasibility study summarizing preliminary findings, communicating progress, and obtaining approval to proceed to the next stages of the project, which is development of the business case and formation of the joint venture.

There are three important reasons for following pre-established joint venture formation processes. First, these are complex projects involving many areas of competence to understand and assess properly. When a pre-established process is followed, personal agendas and subjective judgments tend to get eliminated. Second, most partners do not know what is involved in forming a joint venture and how to go about doing it; the pre-established processes serve as guiding maps to teams. Finally, following established process takes away pressures to conform to unreasonable external requirements and time lines. This is important because long time requirements are accepted more easily if they are part of a process.

## The Joint Venture Project Team

The project team is assembled by the business development group as soon as the opportunity is identified and, as in acquisitions, it is made up of professionals and managers considered experts in their particular functions. Almost invariably, the joint venture project team is headed by a seasoned business development professional. To qualify for participation in the project team, individuals should be experts in their functions and sensitive to joint venture issues, experienced in assessing business development opportunities, good negotiators, and outstanding team players. In the case of foreign joint venture projects, understanding of foreign cultures and ability to deal with differences in doing business are essential. Unlike acquisitions where senior management participation is discouraged, joint venture project teams benefit by senior executive participation especially when they are experienced in joint venture formation. Foreign joint ventures require this type of participation to demonstrate importance of the project and commitment of the company to the joint venture.

For foreign joint ventures, the project team should have members experienced in doing business abroad who know what to do when there are no business laws governing business transactions or when there is no understanding of basic financial concepts. In the case of joint venture companies in developing countries, the project team needs to display sensitivity to local issues and needs while, at the same time, striving to create a win-win arrangement. In addition, it needs to deal with common local partner fears concerning the distribution of costs and benefits of the joint venture. Finally, all project team participants should understand what constitutes acknowledgment, agreement, and commitment in the local culture.

### Identifying and Cultivating a Project Champion

Joint venture projects are long and complex propositions with a lot of ups and downs in the process. Often, the project team and senior management are discouraged by the difficulties of forming joint ventures, withdraw support, and even pull out of a project prematurely. This is especially true in foreign ventures where differences in cultures and negotiating styles result in long delays and frustrate headquarters management. For these reasons, having a strong project champion is essential to promote the project to senior management and help them understand the peculiarities of joint venture formation. Otherwise, a joint venture project has little chance of surviving internal criticism, especially if other alternatives are available and the joint venture is viewed as difficult to manage.

In identifying a joint venture project sponsor, the business development group looks for similar qualities in this individual as the ones required of the acquisition project sponsor. However, all these qualities must be present to a high degree in order for the sponsor to be effective. This is particularly true when striving to create win-win arrangements: The project champion must believe in the principle and value of win-win arrangements and be committed to this type of negotiations. Because of the long time involved in negotiating joint venture formations, the project team must be in constant communication with the sponsor, reporting status, progress, issues, and outlook. Therefore, in order for the project sponsor to be informed, involved in the project, and committed to see the project to completion, the sponsor must be engaged on a full-time basis and must invest a lot of time in the project.

### Developing Project Objectives

Strategic and operational gap analysis and development of project goals and objectives are the foundation for sound opportunity evaluations and successful joint ventures. As in acquisitions, thorough understanding of the company's corporate strategy and operations is essential in producing a sound strategic and operational gap analysis, producing potential joint venture partner profiles, creating appropriate screening criteria, and developing company objectives in the joint venture project.

Teams with sound project goals and objectives tend to form successful joint ventures because project objectives are guiding principles that constantly remind project participants of the reasons for involvement in the project. Sound objectives are consistent, founded on reasonable partner expectations, clearly articulated and well understood by all participants, and frequently communicated to the project team. The development of clear company objectives for joint venture projects is important for assessing:

1. Compatibility with the potential partner's objectives. This is important because consistency of objectives usually translates to ability to work together to achieve common goals.
2. The influence of objectives on expectations about roles and responsibilities and partner contributions. The better defined the objectives, the easier to manage expectations.
3. Ability to maintain continuity of purpose and justify the joint venture alternative when the project appears to be going nowhere.

### Initial Contact and Confidentiality Agreement

Negotiations in joint venture projects begin when the first contact is established with a potential joint venture partner. Consequently, the first step should be taken seriously and executed by well-briefed and seasoned senior executives in order to demonstrate the partnership's importance to the company. Another reason for senior executives initiating contact is to share with the potential partner the company's goals in the project and outline expected benefits to both parties. This is essential in order to establish an environment for the right chemistry to develop from the beginning.

In acquisition projects, signing of confidentiality agreements at the start of substantive discussions is a must in order to protect both firms. For joint venture projects, confidentiality agreements need to be signed, but usually not before the parties feel comfortable with each other and when truly confidential information is released. Although joint ventures involving competitors are not very common, they occur from time to time. In those cases, confidentiality agreements are signed up front and extreme care is exercised in sharing only required information.

## KEY STEPS IN JOINT VENTURE FORMATION

### Screening Potential Partners

Screening potential joint venture partners is a long process because it requires probing into highly confidential information, which is a high-risk area for potential partners. Also, information sharing requires a certain level of trust, which in some cultures does not occur quickly or freely. Therefore, while proactive joint venture partner profiling provides direction, actual partner screening does not take place until serious discussions are underway. The first step in partner screening basically defines four elements of joint venturing:

1. Partner roles and responsibilities. Identifying strategic and operational gaps helps define partner contributions, roles, and responsibilities.
2. Desired partner company profile. This includes financial characteristics, organizational structures, management compatibility, and partner expectations.
3. Resulting screening criteria. These are requirements, thresholds, and yardsticks against which potential partners are compared or measured.
4. Assumptions to be verified. These are areas to be checked because they define what needs to be done to create a successful partnership.

Consistency of project objectives for both entities is important regardless of whether the companies are competitors, in different industries, in related industries, in supplier-customer relationships, in different markets, or have other relationships. As discussions begin, project teams assess partner experience in joint venture formation because it guides them in determining how to help the potential partner view the situation from the company's perspective. Also, joint venturing experience determines the reasonableness of partner expectations. This should not be taken for granted and should be checked at each step of the joint venture process even when dealing with companies that have done joint venture projects previously.

Organizational and cultural compatibility and the right chemistry are particularly important to the success of a joint venture project. Therefore, project teams assess how differences in reporting structures and control mechanisms in the partners may present problems in dealing with issues raised by the joint venture entity. For example, having a highly structured, hierarchical reporting structure and rigid management control mechanisms on the one side and a fairly flat and fluid reporting structure on the other frequently results in problems in dealing with joint venture issues because of different approaches used in resolving issues.

Ability to meet current human resource and financial obligations to form the joint venture and future capital requirements needs to be verified to establish that a potential partner is in position to deliver. Partner obligations extend beyond financial obligations and include:

1. Management talent contributions to be made through secondmends to the joint venture company and liaison subteam assignments.
2. Markets, technology, and processes to be brought to the joint venture to make it competitive in the marketplace.
3. Contributions of physical assets, human resources, and access to contacts, connections, and influence to handle local joint venture issues. Both ability and degree of willingness to contribute by the potential partner are verified in the screening phase.

Technology transfer to the joint venture entity invariably translates to technology transfer to the partner. Because of this, the implications of technology transfer must be assessed in projects where technology, unique processes, and trade secrets are the source of competitive advantage. The project team should evaluate whether appropriate safeguards and securities should be put in place to provide adequate protection or whether joint venturing is appropriate at all.

### Understanding Partner Requirements

A key element of partner screening and assessment is understanding the company and the partner needs in the joint venture and the first issue examined is technology or knowledge transfer to the joint venture and ultimately to the partner. Technology or knowledge transfer is often the reason and a requirement for partners to engage in joint venture activities. Thus, it is important that project teams understand which partner benefits by technology or knowledge transfer, what the partner wants to get in this area, and how much it is willing to forgo or contribute to the joint venture in order to get it. That is, they need to understand the terms and conditions to be negotiated for both parties to get what they want and the price to be paid in terms of trade-offs.

Market coverage, channel distributions, and market share objectives are other partner requirements to be assessed to determine whether a partner can deliver on expectations in this area. Project teams also assess partner abilities and help potential partners see the company's contributions and requirements. They evaluate potential partners' revenue, expense, profit, and investment requirements to determine ability to deliver on financial requirements.

The company and potential partner's willingness to contribute and the nature of the contributions are assessed early in the project. This is important because partners think they only have to contribute financial capital and some technology or know-how. However, partners are often required to contribute physical assets at market values below their own valuation. Likewise, potential partners may have contribution requirements and expectations of the company based on different valuations far above those of the company.

Sharing technology and know-how in the joint venture entity and contributing production processes and trade secrets are often required to place the joint venture company in a competitive position. However, project teams need to identify how receptive potential partners are to seconding experienced managers and technical experts to the joint venture. Partner company expectations and requirements play a crucial role in balancing costs and benefits associated with the joint venture entity. For that reason, project teams include in their assessment differences in organizational and cultural approaches and try to determine whether the partner will take the lead on certain issues.

### Determining Cultural Compatibility

The right chemistry is a key ingredient of success in forming and operating joint ventures. The right chemistry is created when good relationships are formed, the partner strategies and objectives in the venture are not in conflict, and there is a fair amount of trust and support of the partner's and the joint venture company's management team. Additional elements that project teams examine to determine cultural compatibility between the partners involve compatibility in the following areas:

1.  Partner mission statements. They are statements about what the company wishes to become in the long run, they reflect senior management's vision of the future, and they form the basis of the company's strategy.
2.  Organizational and reporting structures. They are important because they determine how decisions are made and what supporting and reporting structures are required for the company to function according to its business philosophy.
3.  Philosophy of business and problem-solving approach. In this area, project teams needs to understand the policies of the company concerning employees, shareholders, customers, and suppliers. They need to review how major decisions have been made, the participants, and how decisions were modified when required.
4.  Management talent contributions. The type of managers seconded to the joint venture reflects the depth of the management team and the importance a partner ascribes to the joint venture. This is significant because it determines the ability of the new entity's management team to function effectively.
5.  National cultural differences. This is a sensitive area in the case of foreign ventures and requires understanding the foundations of behavior and thinking patterns that determine the outlook of the partner and its expectations in the joint venture.

The majority of joint venture companies formed around the world fail on a consistent basis and the successful ones only last an average of three years. Therefore, it is important to determine cultural compatibility in the early stages of the assessment phase and at that point decide to exit if the project team believes cultural incompatibility may cause the joint venture to fail. A good approach to determine cultural compatibility is to score a potential partner on each of the factors discussed so far and decide what is the cut-off point of compatibility. A cutoff point in the 75 percent to 80 percent range of the perfect total score is recommended. Below that, continuing discussions with a potential partner is of questionable value.

### Communications and Relationship Building

Unimpeded horizontal and vertical communications are crucial in joint venture projects among the project team, the sponsor, senior management, and the potential partner's project team. In joint venture formations, project teams are in constant communication exchanging information, obtaining clarification on issues, and moving the project through internal processes in the respective companies. In this process the project teams are doing most of the negotiation in an informal way and resolve many issues before the negotiation subteams address remaining issues in formal negotiations.

In joint venture formations, project teams seek understanding and clarification to appreciate where a potential partner is coming from and eliminate common misunderstandings. They seek understanding of partner strategy; project goals and objectives; implicit and explicit assumptions made; requirements, expectations, and sensitivities; and organizational and cultural differences. They seek clarification of information exchanged, positions stated, and questions posed by the potential partner. To be successful in obtaining understanding and clarification, communications between the two project teams must be uninhibited and based on open and honest discussions.

Communication between project teams in joint venture projects is facilitated a great deal when there are personal relationships, not only between project sponsors and high-level managers, but also between project team members. In fact, when relationships develop at every functional level, information flows freely and things move forward quickly. These relationships, however, take time to develop and senior management on both sides must understand that relationship building is a key element in joint venture formation that pays more dividends than hard and quick negotiations.

### Developing the Joint Project Workplan

When the feasibility study analysis is completed and it is decided to form a joint venture company, project teams create their own workplan for internal processes, but coordinate their completion. This is not sufficient and the project teams come together to create a joint work plan for activities they perform jointly. The joint workplan begins with the development of a joint business definition and assessment for the joint venture company. Then, the joint venture financial analysis and valuation are performed given the different views of the partners, and setting up the governance structure and creating the management organization of the joint venture follow.

The agenda and negotiations timetable as well as a list of key issues to be negotiated are included in the workplan along with the implementation plan, which includes partner contributions acceptable to both sides. Putting together the joint venture business plan and developing a common business case for corporate approval are significant components. The workplan elements include the joint venture agreements and legal contracts that give partners legal rights and outline major responsibilities, developing the financing of the project required for all phases, and establishing operational performance targets and incentive plans to motivate appropriate behavior. Finally, obtaining corporate approvals from both companies, or from appropriate agencies if the joint venture partner is an arm of a foreign government, and developing reporting requirements and control mechanisms are joint workplan components.

The development of the joint workplan opens the formal negotiations phase because the project teams begin with different reference points and are not likely to have identical ideas and positions on many of the issues examined jointly. Therefore, relationships and effective communications must be given a high priority in order to produce win-win arrangements. Through the joint workplan, experienced joint venture project teams agree to perform a number of functions together after they have done their own analysis and proceed quickly to obtain closure on outstanding issues.

## FORMING THE JOINT VENTURE ENTITY

### The Role of the MOU

Early discussions with potential foreign partners in emerging countries are difficult for companies from developed countries to conduct. Often, people push to have documents signed to demonstrate progress to the home office. Usually, potential foreign partners are not willing to sign legal documents because they consider them unnecessary that early in the process and inappropriate. However, they may be willing to sign a memorandum of understanding (MOU) that states that the partners intend to work together to form a joint venture company to achieve a common objective. For experienced foreign partners, MOUs are documents stating the two companies intend to work together and nothing beyond that. In those instances, the value of signed MOUs is questionable.

When dealing with experienced joint venture partners, MOUs play a different role. They summarize the results of early discussions and indicate the commitment of the partners to work jointly to form a joint venture company. In addition, they may contain confidentiality-of-information clauses as well as termination-and-exit clauses from discussions and may be used to communicate the project status. The MOU is usually signed by high-level managers from both partners and is witnessed by project team members after having resolved difficult issues and reached agreement on basic issues.

Sometimes, MOUs are signed as the first step in the process toward development of a joint venture company. These are instances where at least one of the partners is not experienced in joint venture formation and needs to be coached along. In such situations, MOUs contain confidentiality and exit clauses, outline several next steps of the process, and assign specific responsibilities to the partners. Such MOUs are often used to condition partner expectations and point out expected contributions.

### Managing Partner Expectations

A difficult challenge in joint ventures is balancing partner costs and benefits, and the key to managing effectively the cost-benefit balance is to manage effectively the partner's expectations of the joint venture company. Therefore, project teams should understand the goals and objectives and the areas in which the partner has vital interests, concerns, and fears. Management of expectations is a full-time job throughout the life of joint ventures and covers the following key areas: goals and objectives concerning technology and know-how; sharing of marketing and trade secrets; operating profits; financial and human resource contributions and in-kind contributions; and management and control of the joint venture.

The project team is responsible for identifying the partner's expectations concerning these key areas, managing these expectations, and monitoring the evolution of the partner's strategy and goals and objectives because they influence the formation of expectations. As project teams begin to communicate openly the position of their company on key issues early in the process, the partner's expectations are beginning to get influenced and shaped by the input provided by the other. This process has two by-products: a number of items are resolved before they become issues, and by managing expectations continuously, few major issues are left for formal negotiations since managing expectations is another form of shaping partner positions.

### Creating Win-Win Arrangements

Negotiations in the venture formation phase are of a cooperative nature where the parties seek a common ground to accommodate each other's needs. Joint venture negotiations characterized by hard bargaining are candidates for failure because the purpose of a joint venture is to benefit both parties and not to obtain maximum concessions from the potential partner. On the other hand, negotiations where expectations are set and managed appropriately tend to be cordial and, more often than not, result in successful venture formations and operations thereafter.

A joint venture deal is negotiated with the view in mind that it is not a zero-sum game where what one partner gains the other loses, but rather one in which there are solutions benefiting both partners. This means that while the project team develops positions on key issues, the negotiations strategy is not to maximize partner concessions but to move both parties to positions where benefits to both are enhanced. Also, the essence of win-win arrangements is to strike a balance between costs and benefits for all partners. This type of negotiation requires a seasoned negotiations subteam with ability to see things from the partner's perspective and a clear understanding of project goals and objectives of the partners.

If the purpose of establishing a joint venture is to push the risk of a new undertaking outside the company's current operations, test its viability, and then acquire the partner's interest, win-win arrangements are impossible to achieve. In these cases, negotiations are conducted in the same manner as acquisition negotiations and the project team is advised to be cautious and examine partner motives closely.

### Creating the Governance Structure

How a joint venture company is organized is important because it reflects the strategic and operational fit of the partners through the selection of the legal and governance structures implemented. The governance structure of the joint venture company consists of the board of directors and the organizational structure is created to run the affairs of the new entity. The governance structure is intended to provide appropriate leadership, continuity of purpose, and management of the negotiated win-win arrangement. That is, it provides the forum to define how project risks and rewards are shared on an ongoing basis and how the joint venture evolves to meet market challenges and parent company expectations.

The governance structure consists of three bodies, each assigned a different set of responsibilities: The board of directors, the management team, and the steering committee. The board of directors is made up of seasoned senior executives from the partner companies and occasionally one or two outsiders recognized for their contributions in bringing the firms together. The main responsibilities of the joint venture's board of directors are to provide the joint venture company linkage to the owners and at the same time create the mission, vision, and strategy of the new entity. The board of directors must be given authority to define the scope of the joint venture's operations consistent with the strategies and business definitions of the parent companies, develop governing policies, and establish fundamental organizational values.

The management team of the joint venture includes talented individuals from the parent companies and employees seconded to it because of their unique management, technical, and operational skills, experiences, and qualifications. The management team is responsible for overseeing the joint venture's day-to-day operations, achieving its business plan, and harnessing the expected synergies. In addition, it executes the strategy adopted by the board of directors, provides focus, and motivates the work force to produce the results expected by the parent companies.

The steering committee is made up of key project team members and its main functions are to facilitate vertical communications in the joint venture company, as well as between it and the parent companies, and to manage high-level partnership issues. It provides advice to the board of directors and guidance to the management team concerning joint venture company policy in operational areas. In the implementation and early operations phases, it monitors performance at a high level and conducts reviews to ensure that goals and objectives are met. It also uses its influence to resolve issues before they become problems.

## JOINT ANALYSIS AND PLANNING

### The Joint Implementation Plan

The joint implementation plan refers to the plan the partners develop together to establish the joint venture's operation. It is developed by the implementation subteams and transforms the joint venture from a paper construct and legal agreements to a real company. The joint implementation plan covers a wide spectrum of organizational dynamics and political considerations and it is an important responsibility because it reflects partner agreements and sets the course for the new entity.

The joint implementation plan affirms the definition and scope of the joint venture and is another place where partner understandings are checked. It shows how the execution of the joint venture formation will take place and outlines the steps of the process along with key milestones and issues to be addressed. The joint implementation plan includes human resources, financial, and in-kind contributions to be made by the partners. Contributions to the joint venture cover current investments and expenses as well as future capital requirements. The plan also outlines reporting structures and control mechanisms instituted. This is significant in ensuring operational success because it shows how joint venture decisions are made and approvals from the parent companies are obtained.

The joint implementation plan outlines each partner's responsibilities, defines their leading and supporting roles and expected deliverables, and suggests how project risks will be managed. The implementation subteams examine the benefits, costs, resource requirements, and the likelihood of the expected synergies being realized and recommend how expected synergies will be extracted. The plan also outlines the process of issue resolution because conflicts arise for many reasons, especially in the start-up phases of a joint venture, and it is a good idea to create a process to resolve issues.

The joint implementation plan becomes part of the business case, and because of its importance, it should be reviewed by an independent organization to ensure that it is a reasonable and feasible plan. It also forms the basis of the new entity's business plan and the two together form the blueprint of how the joint venture is to be created and how it will operate to achieve intended objectives. To ensure that the operational and business plans are realized, implementation subteam members from partner companies are seconded to the joint venture company. Secondments produce positive results because people who created the joint plans now assume responsibility for executing them, realizing the synergies, and delivering what the parent companies expect from the joint venture.

### Joint Venture Risks and Issues

It is important for each partner company to identify the risks and issues it faces in the project, quantify those risks, and communicate them to the partner for consideration in the risk allocation and risk management plans. Exchange of information must be selective and sensitive to the potential partner's feelings so that it does not give the impression that it is viewed as a cause of risks and issues present in the project.

Joint venture partners face a different set of risks and issues going into a joint venture project because each partner has a different set of goals and objectives in the project as well as different management talent and expertise available to be dedicated to the joint venture. In addition, partners make different contributions, have different responsibilities in the new entity's operations, and have different expectations about the other partner's contributions and commitment.

The exchange of risk assessment information helps partners understand how the other side views the project and the other party's tolerance for and ability to manage risk. It is another forum for project teams to manage partner expectations by sharing with them their views of the venture. At the same time, it enables project teams to assess the risks and issues faced by the joint venture and develop risk management plans. However, each partner still needs to assess and manage its own risks and issues separate and apart form the assessment and management of the joint venture's risk and issues. Then, the joint venture has a higher probability of being successful because each party has risk management plans consistent with those of the joint venture.

## GETTING TO THE DECISION

### The Project Business Case

In the joint venture formation process, the project team prepares its company's business case and, in conjunction with the partner's project team, develops the joint venture company's business case. The company's business case is done in an iterative fashion, but uses the same approach and examines the same factors as business cases of acquisition projects. The joint venture's business case is based on the analysis done for each of the partner companies as well as on the business plan of the joint venture.

The emphasis in joint venture business cases is on using appropriate measures to characterize the value of the new entity on a stand-alone basis as if it was a company with long-standing operations. In fact, the valuation of the joint venture company is done as if it was a firm with operating history and expected to continue to exist into the future. The discount rate used in the financial analysis and valuation of the venture should reflect an implied cost of capital for the joint venture entity and gives partners a fair indication of value created by their investment in the joint venture. This is important because it gives project participants a good idea of the new entity's value in the event termination of the joint venture becomes necessary.

The business case development sequence recommended is to first complete most of the company's own business case analysis using assumptions the project team considers appropriate, including its own cost of capital. Then, the project teams get together, review and revise assumptions used, and perform the business case analysis from a joint venture company perspective. After the joint venture business case analysis is completed, each partner's business case is finalized and internal approvals obtained. This iterative approach allows for project evaluation from each company's perspective separate and apart from how the other partner views the project, but then allows for reconciliation of different views into a common evaluation for the joint venture.

### Venture Financeability and Options

Most joint ventures are financed through equity investments funded by internal company funds. Joint ventures with foreign partners in developing countries usually involve a hard-currency purchase of equity by the company from the developed country and either local currency purchase of equity or in-kind contributions to the joint venture by the foreign partner. A few joint ventures are financed through external debt and equity funds or on the strength of their cash flows with limited recourse to the parent companies. This approach is becoming increasingly popular in financing joint ventures with limited impact on the balance sheet of companies involved.

Financeability of a joint venture on a limited recourse basis is determined by the business plan, the project economics and financials, and the supporting business case analysis. Business case assessments particularly valuable in developing financing solutions and used by financing institutions begin with thorough analysis of the joint venture's revenue component. Here, attention is paid to demand and pricing elements, growth, and stability of demand along with competitive trends in the industry. Then, project risk analysis and plans to allocate risks or mitigate their impact are considered and parental involvement and guarantees in risk management are given substantial weight. Finally, current and future investment expectations and cash flow projections of the joint venture are evaluated. This is a significant requirement because financing institutions do not like surprises or additional funding requests. Credit enhancements from the parent companies may be required if the strength of the joint venture cash flows is judged insufficient to cover the venture's obligations.

### Verifying the Win-Win

Project teams must keep in mind that win-win arrangements are the foundation of successful joint ventures. Hence, they strive to create and verify the win-win nature of all understandings, agreements, and negotiated terms and conditions continuously. The verification of win-win arrangements entails several considerations, starting with consistency of partner objectives in the project. This involves checking consistency of partner missions and strategy and consistency of project objectives with that strategy. Then, understanding the partner's strategic return on investment follows. In addition to return on some financial measure, strategic return includes market positioning, access to new distribution channels, access to R&D capabilities, and other considerations that impact its competitive standing in the industry.

Checking chemistry and communications continuously is essential in verifying win-wins. It involves evaluation of personal relationships and formal and informal communications channels between project teams and partner management teams. Managing partner expectations and reflecting their views in the joint venture is just as important. This step requires assessing how partner perceptions are managed relative to the company's views concerning sharing costs and benefits. Clarifying partner roles and responsibilities is also important to ensure that they understand expected deliverables and that continuity in the joint venture is sustained.

Considering partner needs and balancing costs and benefits is a crucial win-win element. This requires understanding partner motives, needs, and expectations in order to judge whether there is balance of costs and benefits for each partner and between partners. Maintaining continuity of purpose throughout the joint venture's life is another step in verifying win-win arrangements. It involves checking for support structures, such as experienced steering committees and professional liaison subteams, that can sustain win-win arrangements negotiated when the joint venture was created.

### Joint Venture Due Diligence

In joint venture projects, there is no due diligence phase per se; it is an ongoing effort from day one until signing of legal agreements. The main project team responsibility in these projects is to ensure open and unimpeded communications and flow of information by establishing relationships at all functional levels. Having done this and created the right chemistry, the project team can obtain and verify information shared in the course of discussions with the potential partner.

A key question that the project team needs to answer in moving forward with the partnership is whether the partner has appropriate motives, can maintain willingness to contribute to the new entity, and possesses the required financial and human resources. Following that, it ensures that the goals and objectives of the parent companies are consistent currently and beyond commencement of operations. Interfaces and control mechanisms needed to provide financial and management support in operating the joint venture effectively are evaluated. In addition, the question of how to maintain balance of costs and benefit for both partners in light of changing operating conditions and partner goals and objectives in the post-venture formation period should be addressed.

A form of due diligence takes place when the project teams jointly develop the new entity's financial view, the joint implementation plan, and the common business case. During this effort, assumptions the partners are using to assess the value of the joint venture are examined and revised accordingly. Expectations are also revised and reflected in operational and financial positions of the partners. Partners come to discussions and the joint effort with their own impressions and wishes that need to converge to a common ground. As more information becomes available and is verified, initial positions are revised as partner and joint venture requirements unfold, and agreements are reached concerning project valuation, its implementation, and the new entity's business plans.

Aspects of what a potential partner brings to the joint venture are revealed in the course of discussions, and as the creation of the common joint venture view takes place, the project team re-verifies the important items. First on this list is the existence of assets, patents, and licenses to be contributed to the joint venture, followed by legal claims and court filings. Financial strength and availability of human resources to be contributed to the new entity are ascertained as is the potential impact on current customer and supplier relationships. Finally, the value of partner technology and processes to be contributed to the joint venture needs to be verified. Under any conditions, legal and regulatory due diligence takes place regardless of the partner's background and financial strength. This is particularly important when the partner is a foreign company or a developing country's government entity.

When the joint venture partner is a foreign country's government entity, the due diligence effort takes on increased importance and clarifies the impacts of that government's actions on a host of issues such as:

1. The legal and tax status of the joint venture company, the laws governing its operations, authority of an agency to enter into and ability to execute joint venture agreements, and authority and ability to contribute to the joint venture company financial, human, and in-kind resources.

2. Ownership rights of assets and revenue streams and obligations of the foreign partner, currently and in the future, as well as ability to convert local currency profits to hard currency, availability of hard currency, ability to repatriate profits and permits, and documentation required and ability to distribute profits outside the host country once the joint venture company obligations are met.

3. License and permit requirements to conduct business in the host country, duration of licenses, the nature of the exclusivity of operating licenses and the envisioned time span, and expiration terms, as well as technology, management, and know-how transfer and local production requirements, and export quota obligations to be fulfilled.

4. Requirements of various central government ministries, agencies, and departments and compliance with local government rules, performance requirements of the joint venture entity, and investments and expenses required to achieve those performance targets, as well as social obligations, support for development programs, and expected contributions to pension funds.

5. Political and commercial project risks, enforcement of contracts and business agreements, as well as existence of privatization plans and whether the foreign partner would have the ability to transfer the ownership interest to a third party, termination and exit clauses, exit obligations, terms and conditions, and how the joint venture entity will be valued.

## ENSURING JOINT VENTURE SUCCESS

### Establishing the Steering Committee

The steering committee is created by the project sponsor and consists of seasoned managers and professionals experienced in implementing acquisitions and joint ventures. The main function of the steering committee is to establish the new entity's first board of directors and select and nominate individuals with strong interest to ensure joint venture success. It interfaces with the board of directors and senior management to resolve major issues, in the start-up phase of the venture's operations, and reviews or redefines the new entity's degree of autonomy to ensure the interests of all parties are adequately addressed.

Ordinarily, the steering committee has a member from the business development group and one with organizational and human resources skills. The work of the steering committee is linked to the implementation and liaison subteams' work through the business development group. It takes place along with and complements the work of the implementation and liaison subteams, but deals with different issues. The implementation subteam and the steering committee develop a common approach to the new entity and agree on a common business definition and strategic objectives. Also, the liaison subteam and the steering committee are in constant communication to ensure that there is no conflict of approaches and to coordinate parent company briefings and new-entity requests for support.

The creation of the steering committee contributes to the success of a joint venture significantly. In fact, absence of an experienced steering committee results in long implementation delays and unresolved partner conflicts, which eventually result in project failures. The reason for this is that the steering committee sees that issues are addressed and the essential ingredients of success are included in the project implementation and the transition phase. Most importantly, however, the steering committee initiates discussions, seeks to enhance relationships, and obtains senior management support for the new entity's management team.

### Forming the Venture Interfaces

The appointment of an experienced liaison subteam member from each parent company is crucial to the success of the joint venture. This is important because when the work of the steering committee is completed, the liaison subteam becomes the interface channel. It is preferable that liaison managers have experience in joint ventures prior to this assignment and understand that the interests of the joint venture and the parent companies may from time to time be on a conflicting path. The main function this subteam performs is being the linkage and communications channel between the parent companies and the joint venture in the operational phase. In that capacity, liaison managers monitor the joint venture operational performance, communicate developments, identify issues to be addressed by the parent companies or the joint venture itself, ensure resources are dedicated, escalate issues, and obtain satisfactory resolution.

The creation of interfaces and relationships between the project sponsors, senior executives, and members of the project teams at every functional level in the parent companies is important to establish early in the process. Interfaces and relationships between the parent companies and the joint venture are just as important. Development of relationships and interfaces is an expensive but high-yield investment because it establishes communications and creates a structure through which issues are worked out effectively. Interfaces at every level are required to assess the joint venture project appropriately and to ensure on-going communications, enable the creation of effective control mechanisms through these interfaces, and ensure successful joint venture operations.

### Concluding Joint Venture Agreements

In this step of the process, the project team is responsible for structuring sound joint venture agreements. The agreements should reflect the tone of negotiations between the partners and summarize verbal agreements reached by the project teams. In most cases, the importance and strength of joint venture agreements lie with the outline of partner obligations to the joint venture and the explicit definition of each party's roles and responsibilities. This is so because while partner obligations remain, the project team members who reached agreements with handshakes have often gone on to other projects. That is, the continuity of relationships fades with time and so do initial intentions, especially when the joint venture is under competitive pressure and is not meeting parent financial expectations.

The challenges in joint venture projects are balancing costs and benefits of the parties involved in a flexible manner and ensuring continuity of purpose throughout the life of the project. Therefore, joint venture agreements need to reflect that need for balance as well as the win-win spirit of the joint venture formation. And, because conditions that brought the partners together change over time, the joint venture agreements must contain clear and effective exit clauses for both parties.

It is advisable to include clauses in the joint venture agreement concerning valuation of future in-kind contributions, the valuation methodology to be used if termination becomes necessary, and the rights and obligations of the partners at the exit point. Also, in the case of a foreign government agency partner, legal agreements need to be tight enough to protect the investment, the rights, and the interests of the foreign partner on a going-forward basis in the event of government changes, changes in business laws, planned privatizations, and other eventualities.

### Operational Targets and Performance Monitoring

By their nature, joint ventures are autonomous operations from the two parent companies with a management team that reports to the joint venture board of directors and is responsible for meeting the business plan. As such, they have a fair amount of discretion on how they choose to organize to meet competitive challenges and conduct business operations after the start-up phase. Control of joint venture operations is exercised by the partners and the joint venture's management team through systems and reports created by the implementation subteam with continuous monitoring by the liaison subteam and periodic reviews of control systems by the steering committee.

Operational performance targets are first created in the business plan of the joint venture, are reviewed on a regular basis by the liaison subteam, and revised as market and business conditions change. Operational performance of the joint venture is measured by financial targets, but also in terms of strategic return on investment and several other areas, such as development of entity management talent able to perpetuate the win-win situation created and competitive positioning of the joint venture. As in the case of an acquired company, performance measures developed for the joint venture should be closely tied to the joint venture management team's objectives. This produces clarity of objectives and focus on important elements.

## SUMMARY

In this chapter, we discuss the elements of the joint venture formation process that are unique in clarifying participant responsibilities and those that are different than the corresponding steps in the acquisition process. The emphasis in the joint venture formation process is on creation of relationships at all levels and effective communications, management of partner expectations, creation and verification of win-win arrangements, partner experience in joint venturing, effective transitioning and continuity of purpose, and maintaining the right chemistry.

Identifying and managing partner expectations is a key element in the process as is the creation of a win-win arrangement through the project negotiations and their subsequent verification. The governance structure of the joint venture entity, which establishes the board of directors, defines the high-level organization, and sets in motion the formation of the entire joint venture organization, is reviewed. In addition, identifying risks and issues and developing risk management plans in joint venture projects are a major effort because they call for enforcing the terms and conditions of agreements. This also helps in preparing for possible joint venture termination, buying out the partner, or walking away from it with financial losses, but valuable experience gained. Finally, verifying and maintaining the win-win on a continuous basis is important in joint venturing as are effective linkages into the parent companies and strong interfaces to ensure ongoing parent support.

# 11

---

# PROJECT WORKFLOWS AND TRANSFER OF RESPONSIBILITIES

## INTRODUCTION

Transitioning of responsibilities in acquisition and joint venture projects refers to the orderly transfer of responsibilities from one subteam to the next; that is, going from one phase of a project to the next in the most efficient manner. The most important element in effective transitioning is preservation of continuity of purpose in the project and the benefits resulting from that continuity. Continuity in acquisition and joint venture projects includes continuity of purpose and direction in the project, of project goals and objectives, of effort, and of functional and personal relationships.

Transitioning of responsibilities in acquisitions and joint ventures is needed to bridge gaps in understanding broader issues due to the division of labor required between subteams. While specialization enables the project team to handle a wide range of issues efficiently, integration of outputs is challenging because of differences in team member backgrounds and skills. It also makes the process work smoothly and effectively by providing a structured approach to passing on responsibilities. Transition of responsibilities prevents discontinuities in the project process. The way to preclude discontinuities in the process is to communicate the workplan requirements and the project status to the entire team frequently.

Transition of responsibilities focuses the project team on the workplan requirements and the underlying intent and purpose because project team members understand that a good part of project success is directly related to their effort; therefore, executing on the workplan effectively is a must. It also enhances communications and relationships among project participants, and forces clarity of definitions and interpretations. Open and continuous dialog and good working relationships are the foundations of effective transitioning. By definition, appropriate transfer of responsibilities cannot be effected unless there is uninhibited communication among team members and cooperation marks all interactions. Finally, effective transitioning compensates for the emphasis commonly placed on closing by focusing on post-closure activities. That is, it offsets the negative impacts of closure orientation by shifting the focus onto project goals and objectives that must be met in the post-closure phase.

In many projects, after the deal is closed momentum and effort dissipate and there is little continuity and attention to the transfer of responsibilities, which makes it difficult to ensure successful project implementation and new-entity operations. Because of that, newly acquired companies or joint venture entities are often managed on a part-time basis and are unable to harness or create expected synergies. The reason for such failures is that continuity of purpose and project goals are lacking and as a result, projects perform poorly relative to potential.

The purpose of transitioning is to hand down activities and responsibilities in an orderly and effective manner, enhance project team communications and relationships, and ensure continuity of purpose, project goals, and objectives. Consequently, transitioning responsibilities contribute a great deal to success of acquisitions and joint ventures. In this chapter, we discuss the elements of effective transitioning, the contributions of each subteam, the benefits of planned and effective transitioning, and what happens when there is ineffective transfer of responsibilities.

## ELEMENTS OF CONTINUITY

### Continuity of Purpose

Continuity of purpose is the preservation of the original spirit and intent of pursuing a project and a key requirement for well-planned and well-executed transfer of responsibilities in the project. Continuity of purpose extends from conception of the idea to do a project that fills the company's strategic needs down to measuring the performance of the new entity's operations. Continuity of purpose translates the corporate strategy, goals, and objectives into reality by clarifying their significance and making their achievement part of the process. That continuity of purpose turns verbal and paper agreements into actual operations and creates a mission to achieve the goals and objectives set out at the beginning of the project.

Responsibility for ensuring continuity of purpose extends from senior management down to all the project team members. Senior management expectations are set at the first project briefing and cultivated throughout the process to ensure engagement in the project. One element required to ensure that the project mission is accomplished is maintaining continuity in senior management expectations and involvement past the closing date, past project implementation, and into ongoing operations of the new entity. Focusing on continuity of management expectations keeps the organizational memory active and senior managers involved and working toward accomplishing the project objectives.

Continuity of purpose within project subteams is crucial to enhance and broaden personal and functional relationships that are important in making the process work smoothly and effectively. When the entire project team works with continuity of purpose in mind, it is oriented toward open and uninhibited 360-degree communications, it plans and transitions responsibilities effectively, and ensures that activities that must be addressed are attended to.

Besides continuity of purpose in personal and functional relationships, continuity of purpose is required in the project screening, evaluation, negotiation, and interpretation of verbal and written legal agreements. Without that continuity, transitioning of responsibilities becomes difficult and implementation takes longer to achieve because when an issue comes up, individuals involved in earlier stages need to be brought in again to resolve it. This wastes valuable resources because it is a backward-oriented process as opposed to a forward-looking process based on effective transitioning of responsibilities.

Finally, continuity of purpose is essential in clarifying project risks and requirements to make the project successful. When a discontinuity of purpose develops in the transfer of responsibilities, the likelihood of a successful project is small. If there is no continuity of purpose when allocating and sharing the project risks, the position of the company is on shifting ground and risk management becomes difficult. Without continuity of purpose in defining and understanding what is needed to have success in each step of the process, the project team faces conflicting views and confusion. Hence, continuity of purpose in the project should be given the attention that project goals and objectives are given. The project leader should enlist the help of the business development group in ensuring continuity of purpose and make this a top priority because with continuity of purpose, transitioning becomes more effective and produces results.

### Continuity in Functional Areas

Focus on key elements, continuity of purpose, and excellent communications are essential in order for functional responsibilities to be performed well in the evaluation, negotiation, and implementation of an acquisition or a joint venture project. In the case of implementing legal agreements, continuity of purpose is required for understanding verbal agreements and their role in shaping the definitive agreements. This is particularly important in the case of joint venture projects where continuity in the rationale and appreciation for the impact of terms and conditions are reflected in the agreements. That is, understanding the motives behind the agreed-to conditions makes their implementations easier. Continuity of purpose is also important in the interpretation of clauses of agreements consistent with project objectives because the implementation subteam cannot determine whether certain clauses in agreements are consistent with the project's original intent if there is no continuity of purpose throughout the project process. Continuity of purpose keeps the organizational memory refreshed, which overcomes impediments to meeting project goals and objectives.

In the risk management area, continuity of purpose is important in guiding the development of risk-sharing and risk allocation arrangements and the creation of risk management and contingency plans. These plans are created with one thing in mind: to achieve project objectives and realize the expected shareholder value. Continuity of purpose ensures that balance is achieved at all risk management levels because no activity is undertaken unless it directly supports the project objectives. Commonality of understanding of project risks and of the risk impacts, along with continuity of purpose in risk management and contingency planning, is required to enable the project team to complete these functions successfully.

Continuity of purpose in harnessing synergies is what makes the difference between ability to realize synergies and project failure. Continuity of purpose here includes continuity of project goals and objectives and of synergy expectations, as well as continuity in the understanding of needs, strengths, and weaknesses of the parent company and new entity. It also includes preservation of consensus, of approach, and support for the project to get or develop synergies and continuity of personal and functional relationships at all levels.

Continuity of personal and functional relationships is required at all levels for the project team to be successful in setting the agenda and conducting negotiations, in conflict resolution, and in elimination of impediments during the entire project process. Continuity of purpose, continuity of organizational memory, continuity of project leadership, continuity of personal and functional relationships are all essential in being able to implement a project successfully and create a viable new entity. These are differentiators that world-class business development groups leverage to the maximum.

## TRANSITION OF RESPONSIBILITIES

The common practice in most acquisition and joint venture projects is for subteams to hand off responsibilities to someone else and then phase out of the project as quickly as possible. The right practice is to have workflows proceed along pre-established processes and effective transition of responsibilities where continuity of purpose is the guiding principle. The common practice results in confusion, long delays in implementation, and eventual project failure. The right practice creates the conditions for focus, efficient project evaluation, negotiation, and implementation, and, eventually, project success.

### Transition Plans

Continuity of purpose results in an effective transfer of responsibilities between subteams and effective transitioning reinforces continuity of purpose. However, effective transitioning requires planning and understanding workflows and the rules of handing off responsibilities to another subteam. Transition planning begins with a clear outline of process, workflows, and handoffs of responsibilities, which ordinarily is part of the project workplan. It also defines in clear terms what is handed by one subteam to another and includes deliverables, quality characteristics, time frames, and how deliverables are handed off. Additionally, it reviews the project objectives at each junction and the status of major issues. This is a key element in ensuring continuity and should not be omitted under any circumstances.

Transition plans reflect agreement about what needs to be monitored into the next step of the process by the team handing down responsibilities. They also reflect how involved the handing-down subteam should be in the transition. Articulating the project team's expectations of the subteam assuming responsibilities in its area of expertise is another element of transition plans; in this step, the obligations of the receiving subteam to understand the inputs received and voice its assessment of the inputs are made clear. Figure 11.1 is a helpful tool to understand project workflows, responsibility transfers that must take place, and the types of key issues involved in each transition.

**Figure 11.1**
**Project Workflows and Transfer of Responsibilities**

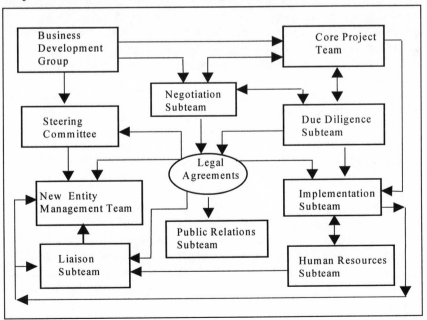

Review of the recent record of acquisition and joint venture success indicates that unclear objectives, lack of systems and cultural due diligence, project team inexperience in project implementation, and slow implementation and integration are the main reasons for project failure. These problems are related to lack of continuity of purpose in the project and lack of effective transition of responsibilities. Therefore, it is recommended that the project team leader assign top priority to ensuring continuity of purpose and planning the transition of responsibilities.

## The Transition Process

The main theme and benefit of transitioning is continuity of purpose and the result of continuity of purpose is effective transfer of responsibilities. Transitioning of responsibilities starts from the originator of an idea to undertake an acquisition or a joint venture project as a solution to the company's long term strategic objectives to the business development group. The originator of the idea may be senior management, external advisors, business unit heads, or a business development professional.

Regardless of who develops the idea for a project, there needs to be a transition to the business development group to review the concept because that is where the responsibility for initial project assessment resides. In order for the business development group to perform the initial screening and assessment of the proposed project and available alternatives, it must understand the motives and expectations of the senior management team. The idea of pursuing a project and the rationale behind it are passed down so that appropriate goals and objectives can be developed. Since the business development group is the central driver of the process, it helps the project team leader to ensure continuity of purpose and effective transitioning of responsibilities.

*1. Transition from the business development group to the core team.* Once the project and its scope are sufficiently defined, consistency with corporate strategy and strategic fit are ensured, and preliminary goals and objectives are created, the project responsibility is transitioned to the core project team. Because continuity of purpose is important, a business development manager usually becomes the project team leader. The core project team refines the project goals and objectives and assigns responsibilities to the subteams. Also, throughout the process, the core team ensures appropriate transfer of responsibilities and continuity of purpose.

*2. Transition from the core team to the negotiations subteam.* The core project team hands off to the negotiations subteam the responsibility of conducting the negotiations while the core team retains the responsibility of providing support and guidance to the negotiations subteam. It should be stressed again that handing off responsibilities does not mean dumping the responsibilities on another subteam. Instead, it means an orderly transitioning of responsibilities where the handing-off subteam remains engaged until it becomes apparent that its presence is no longer required.

*3. Transition from the negotiations subteam to other subteams.* The negotiations subteam hands off some responsibilities to individuals involved in drafting legal agreements, some back to the core team, and some to the human resources subteam. That is, once it negotiates the project terms and conditions, the negotiations subteam moves to the background and other subteams take over the responsibilities to implement the negotiated terms and conditions. Specific responsibilities are also handed off to the due diligence subteam to begin its work and develop project recommendations. In cases where there are two-way responsibility hand-offs, both subteams need to remain engaged until their work is completed and responsibilities are transitioned to a third party.

*4. Transition from the legal subteam to other subteams.* Legal agreements are the key outputs in acquisition and joint venture projects, another being project valuation. Transitioning takes place from the legal subteam and the agreements concluded to the various subteams:

- The implementation subteam responsible for turning agreements into real organizations and operations. Attention is paid to satisfy the terms and conditions of the agreements and ensure that the company's interests are fully met.
- The human resources subteam to begin its investigations, new-entity-management contract negotiations, and design the new entity's organization. The focus here is on senior management contracts and earn-out formulas as well as creating a management structure compatible with that of the company.
- The steering committee to ensure compliance with the key clauses in the definitive agreements. This is important in creating the new entity's governance structure and ensuring consistency of business definitions and strategies.
- The public relations subteam to commence its work to share the negotiated transaction internally and communicate externally to achieve the desired impact.
- The liaison subteam to ensure compliance of the parties with the terms of the agreements on an ongoing basis until their termination.
- The new entity's management team to be aware of its responsibilities under the terms and conditions of the agreements. Especially important are its obligations in fulfilling the performance targets and meeting the business plan requirements.

*5. Transition from the implementation subteam to the new entity's management.* The hand-off from the implementation subteam to new entity's management team is a crucial linkage in the process and requires a lot of attention, sensitivity, and care. While many responsibilities are transitioned directly to the new entity's management team, the interface responsibility is handed off to the liaison subteam, which functions as an ombudsman with referee roles assigned to it. By this point, responsibility for oversight of the new entity's governance structure and its management team have been transitioned from the business development group and the implementation subteam to the steering committee, which eventually is phased out.

Thus far, we have described a time sequence of workflows and responsibility transfers in the project process. Depending on the nature of the project, some transitioning may take place earlier or later in the process, but the importance of orderly transition of responsibilities throughout the project process needs to be emphasized.

### Going from Agreements to Operations

The purpose of acquisition and joint venture projects is to create new entities to meet the company's strategic needs. However, getting from entities created by legal and verbal agreements to actual operations involves responsibilities being transitioned and passed on before the new entity comes into being and operations commence. The step of implementing agreements is transitioned to the implementation subteam, to the human resources subteam, to the liaison subteam, the new entity's management team, and the steering committee. It is a difficult task because of political considerations, organizational sensitivities and dynamics, and potentially adverse impacts on individuals. Hence, the project team needs to pay attention to major links in project implementations.

*1. The financing subteam and human resources subteam links.* The responsibility of developing financing to fund the project is transitioned by the core team to the financing subteam and the corporate treasury group. Corporate treasury ordinarily assumes a leadership role in developing financing options and implementing the alternative selected. Once that step is completed, the responsibility of implementing the governance structure of the new entity — outlined by the core team— is now transitioned to the steering committee and the human resources subteam. Also, the task of staffing the new entity's management organization is transitioned from the implementation to the human resources subteam with continuity of purpose ensured in each step. The human resources subteam is responsible for negotiating retained management contracts and secondments, but once the operations of the new entity begin, responsibility for movements in and out of the new entity are transferred to the liaison subteam.

The human resources and the implementation subteams are handed off the responsibility of identifying and staffing the new entity as required by the core project team and the steering committee. Having put the board of directors in place, the steering committee looks to the human resources subteam to develop the management structure and staff the skeleton organization of the new entity it created. The responsibility of staffing mid- and lower-management positions and occupational teams is then transitioned to the management team of the new entity. In this manner, continuity of purpose is preserved and ensured at each stage.

*2. The implementation subteam link.* Setting new-entity objectives is mostly done by the steering committee and the implementation subteam. However, as that responsibility is transitioned to the liaison subteam and the management team of the new entity, objectives are further refined but continuity of purpose permeates all activities. Resetting the new company's objectives is a responsibility residing with the management team of the new entity as internal planning begins.

The implementation subteam develops the business plan for the new entity and begins putting it into action along with developing operational targets and creating operational performance criteria. Likewise, the plans to harness synergies originate with the implementation subteam. These responsibilities are then transferred to the liaison subteam and the new entity's management team according to the transition plan, which requires review of status and continuity of purpose at each transfer point.

*3. The liaison subteam link.* The management of interfaces and relationships with the acquiring or the parent companies is the responsibility of the liaison subteam, which stays with it until all implementation issues are resolved, synergies are harnessed, and the new entity is successfully operating on its own. At that point, the interface function ends and the relationship management responsibility is transitioned to the entity's management team. Integrated monitoring and feedback and control mechanisms are designed and started by the implementation subteam, but the responsibility of seeing these systems completed and working as expected is transitioned to the liaison subteam and the management team of the new entity.

### Contributions of Effective Transitioning to Project Success

Effective transitioning is a challenging coordination, motivation, and communication effort even under an experienced project team leader and the best of circumstances. For that reason, all participants in world-class project teams play an important role in the transitioning process to ensure continuity of purpose. This, in turn, ensures project success if everything else is handled appropriately. Every time there is transitioning of responsibilities, the receiving subteam benefits by the review of progress, explanations of status of various issues, and continuity of purpose being preserved.

*1. From the business development group to receiving subteams.* The benefits to the core project team, the negotiations subteam, and the steering committee from an effective transitioning of responsibilities from the business development group are a good understanding of corporate strategy, goals, and objectives; a clear definition of the project along with project goals and objectives; and continuity of purpose. These benefits are affected by the business development group's unique position because it oversees adherence to process and guidelines, works with the subteams and the steering committee, monitors and ensures that transitioning is executed appropriately, and advises subteams and the new entity's management team.

*2. From the core project team to receiving subteams.* The main contributions of the core project team in transitioning responsibilities effectively to the negotiations, due diligence, and implementation subteams are in-depth understanding of issues and analyses performed in assessing the project and expertise and advice in evaluation and project process. Also, providing access to internal and external experts and advisors and ensuring that the right resources are brought into the project are of tremendous help.

Since the core team is a central point of contact that coordinates subteam outputs, forms a linkage in the work and outputs produced, and is a communication channel reaching the entire project team, it provides focus on adherence to pre-established process and continuity of purpose and goals and objectives in the project. Finally, its engagement until the end of the project and ability to assist in resolving issues is a major benefit to the project subteams.

   *3. From the negotiations subteam to receiving subteams.* In the case of the negotiations subteam transferring responsibilities to the core team and the due diligence subteam, transitioning is a two-way arrangement. The core project team hands off the negotiations responsibility to the negotiations subteam which, in turn, hands off to the core team the responsibility of resolving issues as they come out of the negotiations process. Similarly, transitioning to the due diligence subteam flows in both directions: The due diligence subteam hands off to the negotiations subteam responsibilities related to its findings and the negotiations subteam creates and hands off new assignments to the due diligence subteam. In this instance, the transitioning process is more complex, it requires unimpeded communications to achieve desired results, and the subteams' engagement is longer. Lastly, the transition from the negotiations subteam to the implementation subteam is mostly via the legal subteam and the negotiated agreements.

   The benefits flowing from transitioning of responsibilities from the negotiations subteam are a reasonable assessment of negotiations, support requirements from the entire project team in order for negotiations to be successful, an orderly approach to two-way interactions, and continuity of purpose throughout the negotiations process. The complexity of two-way transitioning requires that the project team leader must be able to manage organizational issues, complex relationships and processes, and corporate politics.

   *4. From the due diligence subteam to receiving subteams.* The transitioning process from due diligence subteam to the core team is two-directional whereby responsibilities are handed back and forth as they arise and then transitioned to other appropriate stakeholders. The findings of the due diligence subteam and its recommendations are key benefits of transitioning to the core team and the implementation subteam. Reinforcement of key issues to be attended to and continuity of purpose also flow out of effective transitioning from the due diligence subteam.

   *5. From the implementation subteam to receiving subteams.* The implementation subteam plays a key role in the transitioning process and is a crucial linkage between deal closure and successful operations. Its transitioning to the human resources subteam, the liaison subteam, and the steering committee covers a number of key areas beginning with the business plan and the status of progress on the business plan execution, the monitoring of legal agreement execution, and human resources requirements and staffing of the new entity. The benefits obtained include operational targets and performance criteria, plans to harness synergies and progress in that area, and operational monitoring and control and feedback systems. However, the most important contribution the implementation subteam makes is ensuring continuity of purpose, which is absolutely crucial in creating the conditions for the new entity's sound management and the project success.

*6. From the liaison subteam and steering committee to the new entity's management team.* The liaison subteam and the steering committee also transition responsibilities to the new entity's management team and continuity of purpose is the most important element in these transitions. Here, consistency of strategy, project goals and objectives, benefits of harmonious relationships, and commonality of interests are repeated and emphasized. Then, and only then, the direct interface with the parent companies, the support for obtaining resources from the parent company, or exchanging managers, oversight of the entity's operations, management of human resources and issues, and the synergy extraction are transitioned to the new entity's management team.

When an effective transfer of responsibilities takes place, the new entity's management team benefits by preserved continuity of purpose, which enables it to pursue and achieve project goals and objectives. Effective transitioning also contributes a great deal toward the development of management objectives consistent with the parent company's strategy and the project objectives. In addition, continuity of purpose and effective transitioning are important in the implementation of agreements, risk management, harnessing synergies, and resolving conflicts and issues.

## SUMMARY

The themes of this chapter are project workflows, effective transfer of responsibilities, continuity of purpose, and their inter-relationship. Continuity of purpose and its significance in successful project execution is discussed first. Then, the nature of transition plans and use of project workplans in creating transition plans are discussed. The advantages of continuity of purpose and transition planning are a clear direction for project participants, understanding of responsibilities by all involved, and a clear picture of each subteam's deliverables.

The benefits of effective transitioning and continuity of purpose are reviewed and why continuity of purpose is so important in successfully completing the key functional areas. Continuity of personal and functional relationships at all levels is emphasized because it facilitates project team success and helps in conflict resolution and elimination of impediments in the project execution. Continuity of organizational memory and continuity of project leadership are essential in creating and implementing successfully a viable new entity and are characteristic differentiators of world-class project teams.

# PART III

## PROCESS GUIDELINES AND AREAS OF FOCUS

# 12

## ACQUISITION AND JOINT VENTURE NEGOTIATIONS

### INTRODUCTION

Most people believe that acquisition or joint venture negotiations constitute a well-defined phase after the decision to proceed with the project has been made. In reality, however, negotiations start from the moment contact is made with the target or the potential partner and the tone of discussions is set during the first one or two meetings. Negotiations continue until the last minute before the final draft of agreements is signed and details of implementing the agreement are sometimes negotiated after signing. Owing to the importance of negotiations, care is exercised to ensure that professionals make up the subteam responsible for the project negotiation process.

Negotiation is a process in which the parties involved make preferences known, articulate needs and wants, present and assess trade-offs, exchange views, and agree on issues to bring a project to closing. Most acquisition negotiations efforts center around developing a preliminary offer, presenting that offer, holding back-and-forth discussions on the validity of the offer, and creating a final offer. Successful negotiation teams, however, invest large amounts of time developing key negotiation points; developing initial, fallback, and walk-away positions; formulating trade-offs and contingencies; and developing the negotiation strategy.

The negotiation approach depends on the nature of the project. Most acquisitions require rigid, price-focused, and technically oriented negotiations, while joint ventures require a cooperative, win-win negotiation approach. However, all effective negotiations require two sets of important elements: first, a thorough understanding of the company's strategy, a clear articulation of project goals and objectives, what the company is willing to contribute to the project's success, and continuity of purpose throughout the project; and second, good communications between seller and buyer project teams and relationships at all functional levels. Simply put, negotiation subteams can only be effective if they have clear negotiation objectives, that is, know exactly what they want to get out of a project. They should understand what can be traded, remember the objectives throughout the negotiations, communicate effectively, and establish relationships with the seller's project team.

In this chapter, we open the discussion of acquisition and joint venture negotiations with some important guiding principles. Then we explain the importance of having an exit strategy from the start of the project and move on to discussing the negotiations plan. The composition of the negotiation subteam is discussed and the importance of preparation is emphasized repeatedly. The development of positions in the negotiation plan and the creation and quantification of trade-offs are discussed next because they are essential in guiding negotiations to successful completion.

The characteristics of good negotiation plans are listed and negotiation of risk sharing is treated here. The importance of feeling the other side's position and setting and managing project expectations are given attention before we describe how other cultures negotiate. The need to link negotiated terms and conditions with financials is discussed briefly and the focus shifts to project agreements and the role of outside advisors in negotiations. Creating a win-win is a main theme, the importance of communications and relationship development between negotiation subteams is emphasized, and the need for postmortem analysis of project negotiations is raised.

## ENSURING SUCCESS IN NEGOTIATIONS

### Characteristics of Good Plans

Good negotiations plans are rare among project teams that are not experienced in acquisition and joint venture projects primarily because the focus is on getting the project done within externally imposed time lines. On the other hand, world-class project teams create on paper and use detailed negotiations plans characterized by thorough understanding of the company long-term strategy and project objectives and reasonable understanding of the seller's or the joint venture's partner positions on key issues. They identify significant issues and the company positions on them reflect project team consensus and focus on a few, major-impact issues.

Good negotiation plans include other properties such as identification and quantification of several trade-offs valued by the other side, recognition of issues likely to surface, and development of alternative solutions. In addition to identification of project risks and creation of contingency plans, they focus on win-win arrangements at all times, balance costs and benefits to the parties involved, and have sanity checks to ensure that negotiations are moving in the right direction.

There is continuous communication and approval of negotiated terms by senior management and the assessment of financial impact of negotiated terms and conditions is done on a real time basis. Two other key ingredients of successful negotiations are effective transfer of responsibilities to the negotiation subteam and continuity of purpose in the negotiations. Without them, it becomes difficult to focus on key issues and negotiate advantageous terms and conditions for the company.

### Guiding Principles for Negotiations

Following are some guiding principles found to help in conducting acquisition and joint venture project negotiations effectively. While these principles and guidelines are universal, project teams need to adjust them to fit the particulars of the situation and place more emphasis on some and less on others.

1.  Know yourself first and know exactly what you want to get out of the project.
2.  Know what you are willing to give up in exchange for things you really value.
3.  Prepare extensively and understand the needs and positions of the other side.
4.  Establish criteria that define success and what constitutes agreement.
5.  Perform sanity checks throughout the entire negotiations process.
6.  Have an exit strategy with appropriate clauses ready for each stage of the project.
7.  Pick a team of professionals to develop a sound negotiation plan and do the negotiations.
8.  Relationships are very important. Respect individuals on the other side and their positions and accept differences in negotiation styles.
9.  Style is not as important as substance. Keep your eyes on substance.
10. Focus on a few important issues; do not let your energy get diffused in many directions.
11. Understand definitions, assumptions, the particular business jargon, and basic financial mechanics.
12. Develop and quantify several trade-offs, remain flexible, and introduce them as needed.
13. Follow closely the findings of the due diligence subteam and its recommendations.
14. Stay connected to the project financials and the assessment of the project team.
15. Understand the project risks and insist on risk sharing with the seller or the joint venture partner.
16. Manage project participant expectations early on.
17. Limit the role of external advisors in the negotiations to pre-determined activities.
18. Do not let external time lines dictate the course of negotiations. Instead, follow established and approved processes.
19. Do not let others do the agreements for you, only the phrasing language and the legal documents.
20. Always strive to create win-win arrangements.
21. Communicate, communicate, communicate.
22. Establish a quick decision-making and escalation process and ensure that senior management is available during negotiations.
23. When it is time to walk away, exit negotiations gracefully.

### Creating a Win-Win

Whether a win-win arrangement is needed comes up in every acquisition project because the key point in getting a good deal is the price paid for the target. The less the price, the better the deal. This is a myopic view of success because successful acquisitions entail several components beyond price paid.

They include key elements such as deal structure, payment terms and conditions, risk sharing, retaining key target managers, appropriate project implementation and integration, achieving objectives through the business plan, synergy extraction, and control of the new entity. These are areas the seller can help with.

The negotiation subteam must have a broad view of what constitutes success and strive to create win-win agreements at all times because they are the only stable and beneficial arrangements for all involved. Acquisitions fail even when the lowest possible price is paid because the management teams of acquired companies were unhappy with the terms of the deal and quit soon after the acquisition. In one case, the seller refused to supply components to the acquiring company after closing under the terms enjoyed by the target. Why? Because the acquiring company used arm twisting in negotiations to extract concessions and the lowest price.

In the case of joint ventures, win-win arrangements are a must for the joint venture to succeed. Here, balance of costs and benefits to all participants is the guiding principle and expecting project teams to seek only win-win arrangements is essential. In both acquisitions and joint ventures it is a good idea for the entire project team to always ask whether a win-win arrangement is being pursued and achieved. This does not mean leaving value that rightfully belongs to the company on the negotiation table. It does mean though, that the negotiation subteam takes a broad view of success to maximize project value by adding value to the other party in the process.

## PLANNING FOR NEGOTIATIONS

### Exit Strategy

An exit strategy is a consistent and plausible set of reasons for wishing to terminate discussions. The need to exit midstream in negotiations arises often because of the nature of acquisition and joint venture projects. Hence, the need to have an exit strategy from the beginning to be able to terminate discussions when necessary. It is important to have an exit strategy from day one because the expectations of the project team on key issues may not be met from day one. That is, initial contact is made under the assumption that there is room for both sides to benefit from doing the acquisition or the joint venture, but often, this premise is not consistent with reality and the other side's views.

Development of an exit strategy is recommended because it prepares senior management for that eventuality when conditions are appropriate and enables the project team to cease discussions under civil terms. In addition, it allows continuation of pre-existing relationships without being affected adversely by acquisition or joint venture discussions. However, there must be clearly articulated criteria up front and triggers for exiting that the project sponsor agrees to. While the need for having an exit strategy is stressed, the project team must think twice before exercising this option and assess the costs of exiting a project. Also, the negotiation subteam needs to understand that the style of exiting is just as important as the reasons for exiting.

## The Negotiations Plan

The negotiations plan is an element of acquisition and joint venture projects that people talk about, but rarely put down on paper. This is a major shortcoming because if it is not written, a complex plan cannot be checked for consistency nor can it be effectively communicated and accepted by the project team. That is, it cannot be executed nor does it allow for close coordination and monitoring of negotiations progress until too late in the process. Therefore, the negotiations plan must be a written document with enough flexibility to facilitate an effective negotiations process.

Effective negotiations plans are based on identification of key terms, conditions, or issues and succinctly spelled out desired outcomes as well as development of company positions on the issues identified. Effective negotiations plans reflect an understanding of the other side's needs and key issues and positions on those issues and identification and quantification of risks and how risks are to be shared or allocated. They also include creation and quantification of trade-offs acceptable to both parties and development of a quick decision-making and escalation process. Furthermore, they incorporate identification of alternatives on major issues and formulation of contingency plans and of sanity checks, walk-away positions, and triggers to exit.

The project team identifies key issues that cover a wide spectrum of areas in which the company wants certain outcomes. Key issues include the business definition, project terms and conditions, performance thresholds of financial variables, retaining target company management talent, and joint venture board of directors composition. Negotiation plans address joint venture partner contributions, specific implementation types for acquisitions, execution of joint venture business plans, earn-out formulas, and risk sharing. It is equally important to spell out clearly the ideal or opening position on identified issues, positions considered second-best or fallback positions, and positions that if demanded by the other side would cause the negotiations team to exit, that is, the walk-away positions.

Organizing the issues, positions, and common understanding by negotiation participants is important in determining how to maneuver and be effective in negotiations. To that extent, the approach to organizing relevant information summarized in Table 12.1 is highly recommended. The tabular approach is helpful in organizing compactly a lot of information and helps focus the negotiation subteam on the issues. This matrix is also used as a communication tool by the negotiation subteam, by the public relations subteam, and for discussions.

The need for creating a quick decision-making and escalation process is apparent and cannot be over-emphasized even for negotiation subteams with extensive experience and a good measure of authority to make decisions. The reason for this is that under the pressure of negotiations, the negotiation subteam may not be in the best position to make major decisions on its own. Also, to be certain that desired outcomes materialize, sanity checks are performed not by the negotiation subteam, but by the project team collectively.

**Table 12.1**
**Company Positions Matrix and Negotiations Plan**

| Key Issues, Outcomes, Desired Terms and Conditions | Opening Position | Fallback Position(s) | Walk-away Position | Other Side's Position | Possible Trade-offs |
|---|---|---|---|---|---|
| Issue #1 | | | | | |
| Issue #2 | | | | | |
| — | | | | | |
| — | | | | | |
| — | | | | | |
| Issue #n | | | | | |

People not familiar with acquisition and joint venture projects view walk-away or exiting negotiations as a negative outcome, which should not occur. This view is often shared by senior management once a project is well into the assessment and negotiations process. The reason for this view is that closing an acquisition project or completing a joint venture represents success, whereas not doing the acquisition or the joint venture project represents failure. Therefore, it is important that walk-away positions and an exit strategy are developed in sufficient detail for senior management to review and approve prior to negotiations taking place. Here, the project sponsor can facilitate things a great deal.

### Negotiation Subteam Composition and Responsibilities

The negotiation subteam in acquisition or joint venture projects usually consists of a senior-level manager (usually the project sponsor), a seasoned financial analyst, a lawyer, an operational manager, and an experienced business development manager. However, in joint venture projects where negotiations are an ongoing event, the negotiation subteam composition is less well structured. For example, technical and operational issues and requirements may be discussed among functional experts and agreements reached with little or no input from other project team members.

In acquisition negotiations, the negotiation subteam handles all substantive issues; however, there is continuous interaction and communication with the rest of the project team. In fact, input and advice from the project team is sought on key issues to ensure that all aspects are covered and the assessment of experts removed from the emotions of negotiations is shared with the negotiation subteam. A major requirement for a successful acquisition negotiation subteam is close linkage to and continuous open communications with the rest of the project team.

Owing to the nature of joint venture projects, the entire project team is engaged in some form of negotiation. However, when complex issues that involve exercising authority are brought to the negotiation subteam, they solicit input and advice from the sponsor and other senior managers. In any case, the responsibility for what arrangements are agreed to between the joint venture partners rests entirely with the project team leader and the project sponsor. For that reason, continuous communication and seeking of input and advice from the project sponsor are required for successful resolution or negotiation of difficult issues in joint venture projects.

### Importance of Preparation

Effective negotiations are possible only when there is adequate negotiation subteam preparation for this phase and preparation starts with understanding oneself first. In acquisition and joint venture negotiations, preparation starts with the project team acquiring a thorough understanding of its own company, its mission, the long-term strategy and goals, its strengths and weaknesses, what it expects to get out of the project, and what it is willing to give up. Having done this, the project team moves on to understand the other side's needs.

An understanding of the other company is developed along the lines of the target's or the partner's mission, strategic goals, needs to be met by the project, and assessment of expectations in the project. Once the understanding of the other side has evolved to the point where the project team knows the other side well enough to make reasonable judgments and predict behavior, consistency checks are performed to identify areas of negotiation or potential conflict. At that point, the effort turns to the identification of key issues, the development of positions on these issues, and the creation and quantification of trade-offs that would be of value to the other side.

Alertness and openness to potentially attractive proposals and flexibility in developing counter-proposals are two major benefits of preparing for negotiations and both are increased by rehearsing negotiations and considering what-if scenarios prior to actual negotiations. Development of contingency plans is essential in ensuring that negotiations move forward under desired conditions and planning for the unexpected enhances the negotiation subteam's flexibility. Also, time spent considering risk allocation and risk-sharing alternatives enables the negotiation subteam to bring proposals to the negotiation table as needed. Finally, developing a profile of the other negotiation subteam is helpful in developing relationships and understanding motives and negotiation styles.

### Development of Positions

The identification of key issues is followed by the development of positions to be negotiated to achieve project success. The project team identifies key issues for negotiation and which cover a wide spectrum of concerns and impact project financials substantially. The key project drivers on which to develop positions are issues or terms and conditions related to company strategic strength before and after the project, human resources issues, items of major impact on project financials, and implementation and operational concerns.

The development of positions on key issues begins with identifying a desired, preferred, ideal, or optimum outcome for each issue. This is called the initial or opening position. Understanding that opening positions are only ideals, negotiation subteams do not view the opening positions as threatening or unreasonable. Instead, opening positions are viewed as defining the area where eventual solutions lie.

Having developed opening positions, the project team then considers changes and quantifies the impact of those changes to the initial positions. This creates a set of second-best positions that would be acceptable to the company. These positions are called fallback positions, and although individually acceptable, they might not be considered acceptable collectively. That is, while settling for a second-best position is fine on one issue, if second-best positions are accepted on all issues, the project is usually considered a failure and reflects badly on the negotiation subteam.

The next step is the creation of walk-away positions, which, if insisted upon by the other side, would cause the negotiation subteam to walk away from discussions. However, walk-away positions should serve as triggers to propose trade-offs that were developed earlier. If trade-offs intended to jump-start negotiations are rejected repeatedly, walk-away positions serve as guides for the negotiation subteam to rethink its approach or even cease discussions. Because termination of discussions is generally viewed as a negative outcome, project teams remain flexible to help negotiation subteams avoid exiting discussions. On the other hand, pyrhic victories in negotiations do not make sense in the business world. Therefore, balance is needed in this area and the business development group should be consulted for advice in this matter.

### Development and Quantification of Trade-Offs

In the context of acquisition and joint venture project negotiations, trade-offs are packages of concessions and moves to new positions that enable the negotiation subteam to give something to get something of equivalent value from the other side. Trade-offs are difficult to develop because they require knowledge of what is valued by the other side and how much value is assigned to it. However, this is the essence of negotiations, that is, the art of being able to identify what the negotiation subteam wants to trade in exchange for something else and estimate its value to the other side.

Trade-offs should be developed for each key issue and important area for the company and the target or the partner company. The development of trade-offs is important because it gives the negotiation subteam some control over the course of negotiations, it enables it to make moves to brake stalemates, and it allows both sides to get what they want. When trade-off impacts are quantified, they become powerful tools to lead the negotiations.

Trade-offs are ordinarily quantified by changing the financial model assumptions and inputs to incorporate alternative positions or reflect contemplated concessions and calculate the impact to the bottom line of the company. However, this type of quantification may not be possible for each issue. In those instances, the negotiation subteam uses subjective valuations, which become subject to discussions at the negotiating table. For this reason, it is important to create a number of trade-off combinations and be ready to use them as needed.

## ESSENTIAL ELEMENTS OF NEGOTIATIONS

### Feeling the Positions of the Other Side

The best advice to help a negotiation subteam prepare for negotiations is to ask members to put themselves in the shoes of individuals on the other negotiation subteam. This helps a great deal in obtaining a better understanding of their goals and objectives and how they feel about certain issues. World-class negotiation subteams operate effectively by constantly asking the questions: "How would we feel if we were in their position?" and "what would it take for us to agree to the specific proposals from the other side?"

The exercise of putting the negotiation subteam in the position of people sitting across the table helps in several ways by:

1.  Enabling the negotiation subteam to see things from their perspective. This allows subteam members to see alternatives and trade-offs of value to them more objectively.
2.  Conditioning the negotiation subteam's expectations closer to the other side's. This lessens the strength of feelings toward certain positions and narrows the gap on issues to be negotiated.
3.  Making the entire project team behave more reasonably. The result of a more balanced behavior is that it makes the achievement of win-win arrangements possible.

It is recommended that the entire project team and not only the negotiation subteam engage in understanding the needs and feeling the position of the other side. In addition, development of relationships, liberal use of goodwill, and avoiding taking things personally are recommended. Taking things personally results in confrontations that have no place in professional negotiations.

### Negotiating Risk Allocation and Sharing

Project risk is the threat that the occurrence of an event or action will impact adversely project financials and the ability of the company to achieve its objectives in the project. If the threat becomes reality, the company engaged in an acquisition or joint venture project will suffer a substantial loss. The more severe the potential for loss and the more likely it is to occur, the greater the project risk. In acquisition and joint venture projects, risks are shared among participants. However, how those risks are shared is the most complex areas of negotiations, because of differences in views about which party owns what project risks.

In acquisitions, the seller expects to get paid a substantial premium above and beyond the fair market value of the target for synergies expected to be created with the buyer. Most frequently, synergies are not realized, but if they are, they are smaller than expected and cost a lot more to extract than originally envisioned. Therefore, the project team should negotiate an agreement with the seller whereby the seller shares in synergy extraction risk, has an interest in, and supports, the actualization of the acquired firm's business plan.

Once risks are identified, their impact is quantified and negotiations focus on either avoiding, passing to the other project participants, or sharing risks. However, existence of risks, probability of occurrence, and potential impacts are viewed from different perspectives and become the subject of extensive discussions. An efficient approach to handle project risks is to allocate them on the principle that the party most able to handle the risk owns it. Otherwise, both parties share the risk on an equal or equivalent basis when risks materialize.

The common approach to handle project risks is the creation of risk management plans in which parties that have an interest in the project share risks and create conditions to ensure that they do not materialize. However, if and when risks do materialize, both sides assume the impact on an agreed-to formula. On other occasions, it makes sense to share the cost of insurance to cover both parties when risks materialize. In any case, risk sharing is negotiated effectively when risk allocation is considered along with trade-offs and risk management plans.

### Dealing with Outside Forces

Negotiations in acquisitions take place secretly and only those close to the negotiation subteam are informed about the nature of the discussions, agreements reached, and outstanding issues. However, negotiations do not take place in a vacuum, which means that external influences and forces are acting upon the negotiation subteam and the course of negotiations. External forces considered influences on the negotiation subteam are the influence exerted by senior management positions and egos, positions of investment bankers engaged in the project, assessments of external advisors and lawyers, and externally imposed time lines and other demands by the seller.

The views and feelings of key project stakeholders are important and should be reflected in positions developed, but must not be allowed to interfere with negotiations while they are going on. For that reason, externally imposed time lines and wishes not part of the approved negotiations plan should be rejected outright. Also, adherence to pre-established process should guide the project team during negotiations, balanced with advice and input from experts and interested stakeholders. However, since the negotiation subteam is responsible for the outcome of negotiations, it screens input from project participants.

A sound recommendation on dealing with external influences is a four-step approach:

1.  During the development of positions on major issues, seek input from key internal stakeholders, and once consensus is obtained, announce it as the company position, which is now fixed.

2.  Have the project sponsor share with senior management the company position on major issues and obtain approval for the negotiations plan and the time line the project team views appropriate.
3.  Obtain input and advice from investment bankers continuously, but ensure that the negotiation subteam is responsible for the outcome of the negotiations.
4.  Negotiate the agenda, establish a reasonable schedule, and check off items as agreement is reached to prevent revising negotiated issues.

## Setting and Managing Expectations

Expectations in acquisition and joint venture projects are formed as soon as two entities establish contact, but are better defined as the project proceeds and formal negotiations begin. Hence, it is crucial that identification, conditioning, and management of expectations begin from day one. Identification of expectations amounts to understanding the other party's wishes, needs, and objectives in the project. Conditioning of expectations occurs when negotiation subteams put themselves in the other side's shoes. Management of expectations takes place when expectations are shared openly and the other party's view is shared in the same manner.

Unreasonable expectations can be traced to a number of factors, such as no previous experience with acquisitions and joint ventures and little or no appreciation of the other party's position on key issues. They are also due to different negotiation styles, whereby unreasonable positions are used as opening positions from which to retreat, and to disparity of negotiating strength. The negotiation subteam is advised to understand the source of unreasonable expectations and manage them by educating the other side and informing them of options open to the company.

Occasionally, when negotiations get stalled for a long time, both sides realize that it is due to differences in definitions. Therefore, the first thing negotiations subteam should do in discussing an issue is to seek clarification and definition of that issue so that both sides have common understanding; otherwise, confusion and disagreement result. Once common understanding of a point is achieved, definition of expectations becomes easier and their revision becomes possible through trade-offs and alternative positions. Another suggestion for negotiation subteams is to be prepared to revise expectations on every issue at each stage of negotiations and remain flexible to adopt a new position that may contain higher value than previously held positions.

## Linkage of Negotiations to Financials

The quantitative assessment of acquisition or joint venture projects is performed through a financial model, which is a set of actual or postulated relationships that express how different technical and operational components interact to produce revenue, expenses, investment requirements, and a summary measure such as net present value (NPV) of the project. The project team should understand well the key drivers, issues, and assumptions behind project financials, translate positions on different issues into appropriate assumptions and inputs to models, and simulate their impact on the project NPV.

As negotiations progress, inputs to the model get modified and initial assumptions change. These changes are incorporated in the financial model and the impact of negotiated trade-offs is monitored as events unfold so that at any point, the negotiation subteam knows how the project value changes by the negotiations. Financial model runs are performed throughout the negotiations in a continuous process of creating model updates, input revisions, assessment, and feedback in order to evaluate the impact of negotiated terms and conditions on the project NPV.

In parallel to continuous monitoring of inputs, assumptions, trade-offs, and updates of the financial model, communication of these changes to the rest of the project team and senior management takes place and assessment and feedback is provided to the negotiation subteam. This loop is essential to keep project stakeholders informed about progress made, perform sanity checks, and evaluate whether there is a need for intervention or corrective action and, if necessary, focus negotiations in different directions.

### Project Agreements

The purpose of acquisition and joint venture legal documents is to formalize various agreements reached during the course of project development and negotiations. The essence of legal documents is to capture agreed-to terms and conditions in a manner that adds value to the implementation process. Therefore, the business issues, commercial factors, and understandings drive the development of legal documents. World-class project teams have a lawyer in the core team and work closely with external legal counsel to draft acquisition and joint venture agreements because good legal agreements are the foundation of good relations after agreements are signed and projects are implemented.

Successful negotiation subteams are advised by lawyers in negotiating project terms and conditions and the lawyers on both teams draft the language and create documents formalizing the negotiated terms and conditions. It is better for the project team to work with the lawyer to draft a proposed document, rather than for the lawyer to draft the agreement and then seek input from the project team. The reason for this is that for the most part, business considerations, not legal considerations should drive agreements. However, legal considerations must be given equal attention because of potential adverse impacts if not handled appropriately.

Closing of an acquisition or a joint venture project refers to the signing of the definitive or purchase agreement and the joint venture company formation agreement. In order to arrive at this point, the due diligence effort must be complete and affirmative, and a number of legal documents and agreements must be created, negotiated, reviewed, and approved by the project team. Often, one of the parties uses closing as a means to extract concessions from the other side and usually this results in schedule slippages and last-minute changes in the legal documents. When closing is used as an excuse to obtain concessions, the negotiation subteam is advised to ensure that attention is not taken away from key issues, the findings of due diligence, and project fundamentals. In addition, attention to agreement details must be maintained to ensure inclusion in the final draft of the legal documents.

## FACTORS THAT ADD VALUE

### The Role of Outside Advisors

Outside advisors in acquisitions and joint ventures are usually financial and tax experts, legal counsel, investment bankers, and industry experts or consultants. The reason for engaging outside advisors is to provide expertise not residing in the company and an independent project assessment. In the area of negotiations, outside advisors should remain outside the negotiation subteam although they are involved in monitoring and assessing negotiations and providing valuable input and guidance to the negotiation subteam.

Outside advisors create more value by helping negotiation subteams prepare for the negotiations, assessing proposals of both sides, and advising on technicalities, rather than actually participating in the negotiations. This applies to all projects except those for which professionals are brought into negotiations to squeeze the best possible deal from the other side. Otherwise, the role of external advisors is to provide unbiased evaluation and assessment of negotiated terms and conditions, perform sanity checks, and provide advice and guidance.

When the negotiation subteam lacks expertise in negotiating successful deals, outside advisors play an important role in negotiating the transaction. Outside advisors also participate in negotiations to bring balance in negotiations dynamics when the other side brings in experts in certain areas to influence the direction of discussions. The third case for using outside advisors is in negotiations stalemates to get the negotiations moving. In every case, the role of external advisors must be well defined and their activities and involvement controlled. Otherwise, resulting agreements may not contain the elements considered important by the project team.

### How Other Cultures Negotiate

When negotiating with representatives from other cultures, language barriers and cultural differences often stand in the way to negotiating effectively because the focus is on style and not the substance of discussions. When the negotiation subteam is engaged in negotiations with people from foreign cultures, it is a good idea to receive cultural training before negotiations begin, become aware of differences in negotiating approaches and styles, and learn to respect those differences. When the negotiation subteam realizes that not everyone views the world from the same perspective and that it is not necessary for everyone to behave and react in the same manner in order to negotiate effectively, the focus shifts to addressing issues.

Respect for individuals from foreign cultures and sensitivity to their views of the world go a long way toward creating goodwill. Thus, the negotiation subteam needs to take time to get to know the team from the foreign entity and develop personal relationships. World-class negotiation subteams understand the motives for certain actions and reactions of people from foreign cultures and then proceed with negotiations by focusing on obtaining agreement on issues, checking their understanding of agreements, and verifying those agreements. It is important for the negotiation subteam not to insult a foreign team by opening negotiations with unreasonable initial positions because it may be perceived as a signal of not being seriously interested in getting to an agreement.

In our culture, agreement ordinarily means that both sides intend to fulfill their obligations under that agreement and if they fail to do so, the agreement can be enforced and provide restitution to the party harmed by the party not meeting its obligations. In other cultures, agreements take a lot longer to conclude and do not necessarily have the same implications as signed agreements in North America and Western Europe. Acquisitions of foreign entities become definite with the closing when title of ownership passes hands; prior to that, agreements are only checkpoints along the road to the closing.

When negotiating foreign joint venture agreements, the negotiation subteam must ensure that a win-win is created and should not conclude that a signed joint venture agreement implies that a win-win situation has been achieved. The significance of this is that the foreign partner may not follow through on conditions of the joint venture agreement if it is not viewed as a fair and equitable transaction.

### Outstanding Issues and Conditional Agreements

Occasionally, definitive acquisition and joint venture agreements are signed and closings concluded with some issues unresolved. Usually, these are difficult issues to negotiate within the time lines of the project workplan and agreements are signed subject to outstanding issues being resolved to both parties' satisfaction. These are called conditional agreements and are often used to close a transaction when both parties believe they have an understanding and can resolve issues to their satisfaction past the closing date. At times, circumstances dictate that since negotiations have produced agreement on most issues and a few outstanding issues remain, definitive agreements are signed in view of no-deal threats due to factors such as expiration of offers, licenses, and permits, and introduction of new offers.

Outstanding issues in acquisition projects are handled through conditional agreements on the basis that both parties share in the final resolution of an issue in acceptable ways. For example, if agreement on retained executive compensation is not achieved by closing time, an interim earn-out compensation formula can be used until it is finalized to both parties' satisfaction. In joint venture projects, more issues are left outstanding at the time of closing than in acquisitions and most of them have to do with managing the operations of the joint venture company. However, in these cases, the steering committee and the liaison subteam end up resolving the outstanding issues to the parent companies' satisfaction.

Conditional agreements should be used only when necessary, the reason being that with conditional agreements, the negotiation of issues is pushed out in time. Postponing negotiation of issues is to the seller's or one partner's advantage, especially when they are in a better negotiating position to begin with. Another reason for this is that if issues are left for the steering committee to negotiate post-closing, it is at a disadvantage because it does not have the support of the entire project team the way the negotiation subteam does.

## Communications and Relationships

Successful acquisitions and joint ventures are characterized by constant and open communications and good relationships at all functional levels with all entities participating in the project. This extends to successful negotiations as well where open horizontal and vertical communications enhance the negotiation subteam's effectiveness through constant input and feedback from the rest of the project team, senior management, and outside advisors. Also, the negotiation subteam establishes the right chemistry and good relationships through effective communications, which help in negotiating win-win arrangements. Finally, open communications are needed to affect continuity of purpose and effective transitioning of responsibilities.

The importance of good communications and relationships extends beyond negotiating terms and conditions and project agreements to project implementation and the new entity's operational phase. Unless good channels are established and open communications take place at all times, the negotiation subteam cannot be effective. Just as importantly, if bad chemistry and lack of personal relationships characterize interactions of the negotiation subteams, negotiations drag out and are not likely to produce successful agreements. Therefore, development of personal relationships at all functional levels and open communications in all phases of acquisition and joint venture projects are recommended.

## Negotiations Review

Acquisition and joint venture negotiations are excellent learning experiences for negotiation subteams because of required understanding concerning the company's strategy, business scope, and strengths and weaknesses. Understanding the industry, business definition, and personal needs and objectives of the other side developed during negotiations is valuable experience. A great deal is learned about the acquisition target or the partner, the management teams involved, and strengths and weaknesses of the companies and their negotiation subteams.

Since world-class companies and business development groups are learning entities, they want the learning and experience gained in negotiations institutionalized and the way they do that is through a negotiations review and analysis. The analysis is performed by the project team and led by a seasoned business development manager to ensure learning is passed to following projects. The negotiations analysis includes evaluation of the course of negotiations, the lessons learned, what was done well, what was done poorly, which processes were effective and which were not, and what contributed or distracted from success.

The postmortem analysis for the entire project is performed at the end of the project when the new entity is operational. However, it is recommended that the negotiations analysis be performed soon after this phase is concluded when events that took place are fresh in the minds of participants. Also, a written report should be prepared that includes recommendations on how to use lessons learned to improve effectiveness of negotiation subteams in future projects. Additionally, project teams should share findings of the negotiations analysis with other project participants and senior management.

## SUMMARY

The purpose of this chapter is to enhance understanding of the process and provide recommendations on how to conduct negotiations effectively. The discussion begins with creation of the exit strategy, the negotiation plan, and the negotiation subteam composition. The importance of preparations by the project team is emphasized and development of positions and trade-offs is given broad treatment. Also, characteristics of effective negotiation plans are discussed as is the need to negotiate risk-sharing arrangements.

A helpful practice in conducting effective negotiations is feeling the position of the other side on key issues and identifying and managing expectations of the parties involved. Other cultures tend to negotiate differently and we bring up that issue, but the need to link negotiated terms and conditions with project financials is more important than the form of negotiations. The role of outside advisors is discussed and the importance of communications and relationships development in the negotiations phase is emphasized again. Finally, assessment of what took place during negotiations after the project is completed helps the entire project team become more effective in negotiations of the next project.

# 13

# DEVELOPMENT OF THE BUSINESS CASE

## INTRODUCTION

The business case process of a project is a systematic approach to evaluate acquisition or joint venture opportunities. It culminates in the creation of a document that summarizes work done in assessing the project, presents key findings, and contains the project team's recommendations. It is an expanded version of the feasibility study, but it goes deeper into the analysis and brings discipline to the decision-making process. In all world-class companies, the business case forms the basis of the decision to invest in a project and produces the analysis needed to communicate the necessary information internally and externally.

The development of a solid business case is important for a number of reasons. First, it checks the project rationale and objectives against alternatives, and second it ensures review, evaluation, and summarization of all elements of a thorough assessment. It also raises questions and forces the project team to answer them in a satisfactory manner. A good business case is a communications tool that preserves continuity of purpose and forces discipline in decision making, thereby resulting in decisions made for the right reasons and supported by facts and analysis. Finally, it increases the likelihood of successful projects being executed and shareholder value being created.

In this chapter, we discuss business case development and review the process and key components. Because assumptions underlying the analysis are important in determining project value, we discuss the development, validation, and testing of the assumption set. Project resource requirements are examined next and the issue of alternatives to the proposed project is considered. Risks and issues are a central element in the business case financial evaluation and are treated accordingly. Then, the deal structure of a project is discussed along with impacts of negotiated terms and conditions on financials and project value.

The business case financial analysis components are briefly considered along with valuation requirements. Financing, implementation, business plans, and business case recommendations are discussed. Next, we focus on the characteristics of quality business cases and the discipline required to produce them. To ensure that objective evaluations are performed, we consider independent business case assessments and the chapter closes with a treatment of the uses of the business cases internally and externally.


## THE BUSINESS CASE DEVELOPMENT PROCESS

The business case process varies from project to project, but in all cases it entails development of information to aid in assessment, evaluation of data and evidence, and examination of key risks and issues. The steps of the business case development process shown in Figure 13.1 lead to convergence to the project team's recommendations and the next steps. The key processes involved mirror the discussion of the business case document sections.

The first element of the business case is a thorough explanation of factors leading to the decision to undertake an acquisition or a joint venture. The reason for this is to provide background information for participants absent in the early project stages. The decision to pursue a project is based on the results of gap analysis where mission and strategy are articulated and the company's strengths and weaknesses are identified and evaluated. Here, the project scope is defined by specifying the new entity's business and the markets, elements of the production process, or distribution channels it will own.

The background leading to the proposed project and the definition of its scope form the basis for developing the rationale for an external business development project versus internal growth. Then, the project team examines alternative solutions and selects one approach to filling the company strategic needs. Also, based on the findings of the internal analysis phase, key project objectives are developed that are intended to achieve the strategic objectives of the company. The development of project objectives enables the project team to articulate succinctly what the company wants to get out of the project, but objectives must be realistic, non-conflicting, and directed toward realizing expected synergies.

The strategic fit assessment of an acquisition or a joint venture takes place in the feasibility study phase, but it is reviewed again in light of new information produced since then. It evaluates how the implementation of the project would fill strategic gaps and meet the company's long-term objectives. That is, it examines the fit in terms of markets served, product or service offering, and human and physical assets employed. It does this through a strategic return on investment (SRI) analysis and provides answers to the questions of how the project helps the company circumvent management, technical, and financial resource constraints and in what ways the new entity shares in the operating risk going forward.

**Figure 13.1**
**The Business Case Development Process**

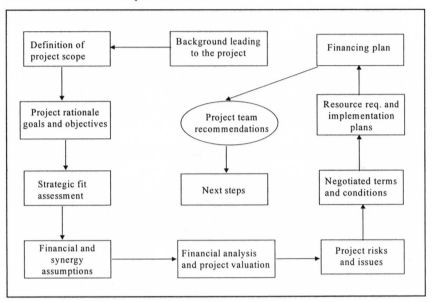

Strategic fit assessment evaluates how the new entity meets customer needs better and helps the company increase its market strength and what organizational capabilities are strengthened or developed with the implementation of the project. The SRI analysis determines whether the target or the joint venture brings low-cost solutions or enhances the profitability of the company and whether there are technical, operational, and financial synergies that are profitably obtainable. Furthermore, it shows in what ways innovation and company know-how will be affected by the project and whether the project results in some form of sustainable competitive advantage for the company.

## COMPONENTS OF THE BUSINESS CASE

### Development and Validation of Assumptions

It is important to articulate the base case assumptions made as the project moves through the assessment process before undertaking the financial analysis and to question data obtained, information sources, and postulated relationships. Often, implicit assumptions are made without the project team being aware because certain things are taken as being true or given by experts or upper management. Every time statements are made with potentially significant impacts on the assessment, the team needs to question the premises and classify them as facts or assumptions. This helps to determine the strength of the basis of financial results and allows the project team to revise assumptions when more information becomes available.

> *Base case or baseline scenario refers to what the project team views as the most likely scenario to materialize. It defines the project scope, assumptions, and relationships reflected in the financial model and estimates the value most likely to be created. The base case or baseline scenario forms the benchmark against which other scenarios are compared.*

During the evaluation phase, and especially the due diligence process, questions are raised concerning the assumptions behind the financials or the assessment of an issue. Questions are answered after careful examination, and in that manner, the assumptions are validated, changed, or rejected. The results of the due diligence, therefore, are an important aspect of assumption development and validation. The other aspect of assumption validation is the sensitivity analysis and the what-if scenario analysis performed in the financial evaluation stage whereby the impact of changes in the assumption set on the financials is assessed.

Because assumptions determine the project value and its assessment, we recommend a methodical approach in validating assumptions starting with considering the purpose and use of each assumption. The project team then identifies the origin and examines the nature of each assumption and possible motives behind assumptions developed by affected parties. In the third step, it compares key assumptions made with experiences and situations encountered previously and looks for facts to support major assumptions. Also, the project team obtains external assessment of the assumption set and concurrence on the major assumptions. To determine how the project value is impacted by variations in key assumptions, it uses sensitivity analysis, and to ensure consistency of assumptions, this approach requires the project team to conduct sanity checks throughout the evaluation process.

### Resource Requirements

A key element in determining project success is the assessment of financial and human resources needed to evaluate and implement the project. Financial resources include assessment and implementation expenses; external advisor, consulting, and investment banker fees; current and future investment requirements; and future expenses associated with monitoring and controlling the operations of the new entity.

Assessment of human resource requirements begins with determination of resources needed to close the deal, implement the project, and operate the new entity. It also involves evaluation of the pool of management talent in the acquiring or parent firms and the new entity and external management talent required to operate, monitor, and ensure success of the entity. Human resource requirements include quantity and quality dimensions of management and skilled labor. Another consideration of resources allocated to an acquisition or joint venture is the balance of management talent drain versus enhanced management skills and experiences obtained by participating in the operation of the new entity.

In addition to human resource requirements of an acquisition or a joint venture, financial resources required to close a project are considered in depth in the business case. Here, costs and expenses are identified and calculated and current and future investment requirements are estimated to arrive at a reasonable estimate of what it takes to complete the project. One important cost element that ordinarily escapes the attention of project teams is project implementation costs and investments and expenses related to synergy extraction. These costs are significant and can change the financial picture of the project. Hence, the project team needs to include them in the business case financial analysis.

## Consideration of Alternatives

Identifying and assessing alternatives is an ongoing business development group effort, which involves continuous review of the company's strategy, strengths and weaknesses, profiling of target and partner companies, and developing screening criteria. Strategy-driven objectives determine alternatives considered which are discussed in the business case and are used to support corporate approvals. The first alternative considered to a given project is an internal option that achieves the same strategic goals. The internal option assessment is then followed by the assessment of the joint venture and acquisition alternatives.

In most cases, the internal option to achieving the company's long-term strategic objectives is not considered because of the long time required to develop the necessary competencies to close the strategic and operational gaps. Instead, quicker solutions are sought through acquisitions or joint ventures, which basically buy growth for the company. While this approach may produce desired results in terms of financial growth, it usually does not capitalize on the company's strengths and competitive advantage.

Comparison of alternatives is first made in terms of the degree of strategic fit, followed by the financial value of each alternative. Since acquisitions are considered the quickest way to achieve the company's strategic objectives, one or two target companies are evaluated and the one best suited to fill the strategic and operational gaps is picked. Occasionally, joint ventures are considered as alternatives to acquisitions and are ordinarily rejected despite lower up-front investments because of the long time required to consummate a joint venture deal. When the venturing approach is selected, different joint venture arrangements are considered. The alternatives are ranked according to strategic fit, project NPV, risks involved, and ease of implementation. The alternative that has the closest strategic fit, creates most value, and is least risky is picked.

### Project Risks and Issues

In acquisitions and joint ventures, risks are events that, if they occur, impact significantly the financial projections of the new entity and the acquiring or parent companies. Project risks are variances from the base case NPV with specific probabilities associated with their occurrence. Issues are major areas of concern that suitable solutions must be created or appropriate terms negotiated to make a project financially viable. The difference between risks and issues is that it is much easier to control the latter than to control the former. Stated differently, project risks can be mitigated or even eliminated through management plans, but project issues require negotiation or development of contingency plans.

To assess project risks and issues, the project business case analysis focuses on areas common to all acquisitions and joint ventures, starting with product demand growth projections and price stability in the forecast period and technological innovation and market changes that may occur. The industry structure, trends, future evolution and developments, entry of new competitors, and the power of customers and suppliers are considered. Also, the ability to execute and implement a project according to plans and availability of financial and human resources to execute the project successfully are examined along with future capital requirements. Furthermore, ability to identify and harness expected synergies with reasonable expenditures; organizational and cultural compatibility, policies, and decision making; and ability and costs of retaining managerial talent in the new entity are evaluated.

Issues addressed in acquisitions and joint ventures are usually project-specific and their resolution becomes an objective of negotiations. If issues are not successfully negotiated, they either impact project financials adversely or become project risks and uncertainties. For example, if a given license to a joint venture is expected to give it access to a geographic area or market, but the market is to be defined by a foreign government body, this is an issue to be resolved by or negotiated with that government entity. If the market access of the license can not be negotiated and viewed with certainty, its outcome becomes a business risk handled through a risk management plan.

Risk management and issue resolution require thorough understanding of all project aspects. The project team performs this function with input from external advisors specializing in these areas. Identification and quantification of project risks and issues is a difficult and expensive task, but it reveals potential impacts on the project financials and defines the areas to negotiate certain conditions or outcomes. In addition, it brings out factors that must be evaluated carefully in judging value creation by a project; that is, it forces discipline on the decision-making process. Once impacts of risks and issues are fully appreciated, risk management and contingency plans are developed and their costs are estimated and included in the business case analysis.

### The Deal Structure

The project deal structure is reflected in the business case to provide required information for corporate approvals about an important element in project assessment. For most purposes, a deal structure is how payment is structured for an acquisition or a joint venture. A more accurate definition of a deal structure includes key negotiated terms and conditions, the legal classification, and the tax implications on both buyer and seller companies. It also includes the way the project is financed, the governance structure, and the manner in which the new entity is organized.

It makes a substantial difference what type of acquisition method is selected to effect the transaction because it impacts the tax basis of the target company's assets; for this reason, deal structuring is synonymous with picking the legal and tax framework for an acquisition. Legal and tax status considerations in a transaction determine whether a project involves acquisition of stock or acquisition of target company assets. The sale of a company is effected in two ways: sale of its stock to the acquiring company or sale of its assets. The sale of stock approach can also be a statutory merger, which occurs when two corporations combine so that one disappears and one remains in existence or a consolidation, which is effected when two corporations combine into a third entity.

The acquisition method defines the tax basis of the target and is a key factor in determining the acquisition economics. Acquisition methods fall either under those that result in a new cost basis for the target company assets or under those that leave the tax basis of the target company assets unchanged. The legal and tax considerations of acquisition methods are summarized in Table 13.1.

**Table 13.1**
**Legal and Tax Considerations of Acquisitions**

| Legal Considerations | Tax Considerations | |
|---|---|---|
| | *Taxable Acquisitions* | *Non-taxable Acquisitions* |
| Acquisition of stock | 338 transactions | Type A reorganizations |
| | Stock acquisitions | Type B reorganizations |
| Acquisition of assets | Asset acquisitions | Type C reorganizations |

*Source:* J.H. Marren (1985), p. 17.

### Negotiated Terms and Conditions

In order for a project to receive a fair independent assessment and corporate approvals, the business case must contain the negotiated key terms and conditions. In the case of acquisitions, key negotiated terms and conditions include the price paid for the acquisition and earn-out formulas, premiums included in transaction costs, payment terms and means of payment, and target company management contracts and incentive programs. For joint ventures, key terms and conditions included in the business case are partner roles and responsibilities; financial investment and in-kind contributions; sharing arrangements for revenues, expenses, and profits; capital requirements and expected capital calls; future support required from the parent companies; and exit clauses.

Inclusion of negotiated terms and conditions in the business case is motivated by the need to ensure inclusion in the financial analysis and impact assessment and present a convenient summary of the deal highlights for management review and approval. It also helps explain impacts on the strategic positioning of the new entity, determine how project risks are shared, and assess the likelihood of new entity success. Hence, negotiated key terms and conditions must be articulated briefly, clearly, and precisely in order for senior management responsible for approving the project to understand the deal negotiated and pass judgment on it.

### Financial Analysis and Project Valuation

The financial analysis forms the basis of project assessment because it summarizes nicely the interaction of various factors into the widely understood concept of net present value, which allows one to assess the impact of input changes and compare different alternatives. The financial analysis of acquisition and joint venture projects includes several elements that must be well understood and evaluated, starting with a market and industry structure analysis to assess the evolution of the industry.

Evaluation of economic and operating environments to determine market and financial projections stability follows with assessment, verification, development, and validation of assumptions to ensure consistency of projections. The cost of capital and discount rates are determined because of their central role in project valuation, and identification of tax and depreciation rates are considered, given the state of competition in the industry.

Pro forma financial statements are developed that form the basis of project evaluation followed by identification of key financial drivers to focus the project team effort and assessment of negotiation trade-off impacts to prepare the negotiation subteam. In addition, negotiated terms and conditions are evaluated to assess changes in the project value and costs of risk management plans are quantified to assess certainty of value creation. Finally, scenario and what-if analyses are performed to assess the likely range of project NPV outcomes.

The other side of the business case financial analysis is concerned with project valuation and is essentially the same for both acquisitions and joint ventures. Project valuation involves calculation of the project net present value based on the projected cash flows of the project and estimation of residual project value using an appropriate methodology. It also involves review of comparable transactions in the industry, quantification of the value and impact of market premiums, and determination of overall project valuation.

### The Financing Plan

Most business cases deal with project assessment and do not include a financing plan primarily because financing projects is viewed as a treasury function and treasury organizations are not usually involved until the need for financing arises. This is a serious omission because financing costs are not included in the business case valuation and financeability issues are not handled appropriately in this phase. On the other hand, world-class project teams are mindful of financing requirements and include a financing plan in business cases. This enhances project valuation accuracy because it includes financing costs and makes the project easier to finance.

For the purposes of the business case, a financing plan outlines how the project in question is going to be funded, the sources of funding, the allocation of project risks, and the cost of financing. Key determinants of financing options for acquisitions and joint ventures discussed in the business case include project economics, cash flows, profitability, and tax considerations for target shareholders and tax considerations of the acquiring or partner companies. Other determinants of financing options are the current debt/equity structure of the acquiring or partner companies, ability to use their balance sheets, project risks, risk-sharing arrangements and parental guarantees, accessibility to funding sources, and ease and cost of financing.

### The Implementation Plan

Project implementation is probably the most important and least appreciated aspect of acquisitions and joint ventures. Project implementation refers to the process of transforming a signed acquisition or joint venture agreement into actual new entities and it encompasses all activities and resources needed to make the transformation. Implementation plans are developed because of the multitude and complexity of activities to be performed, issues to be resolved, and objectives to be accomplished.

The importance of the implementation plan lies with several of its properties. To begin with, it enables the implementation subteam to transform agreements into entities efficiently and helps to organize the new entity so as to preserve the linkage to the company's strategy. Also, it captures expected synergies, identifies new possibilities for synergies, and develops a realistic business plan for the new entity. Finally, it develops control mechanisms to ensure that business plans are routinely realized. Because there is change associated with implementing acquisitions or joint ventures, the implementation subteam and plan are viewed as agents of change. Therefore, both must be flexible and able to deal with organizational and human issues associated with change.

The implementation plan is basically a workplan whose key elements are contained in the business case including the degree of autonomy versus new-entity integration into the company's operations and a description of the transformation process, the timing involved, and participant roles and responsibilities. The new-entity organizational structure is included in the implementation plan as is the identification and procurement of financial and human resources to implement the project.

New-entity high-level reporting structures and control mechanisms are created along with management secondments and development of incentive plans and earn-out formulas. A realistic business plan for the new entity is developed, key operational performance objectives, criteria, and measurements are defined, and criteria to measure project success are established.

### The Business Plan

The implementation subteam develops the new entity's business plan, which is a significant part of the implementation plan. Key considerations in developing a business plan are ensuring that linkage to the company's strategy is preserved and realism of expectations and objectives throughout the plan. The common business plan elements are the new entity's mission, goals, and objectives, the operational plan, the human resources plan, the marketing plan, the financial plan, and the monitoring and performance reporting plan. The project team reviews the business plan and key features are included in the business case.

The development of the new-entity mission and goals and objectives is the area in which consistency with the company strategy is preserved. Input is obtained from the steering committee and the new entity's board of directors to balance the company's mission statement, goals, and objectives against the interests of the new entity or the partner. The human resources plan identifies the new entity's requirements for management and skilled labor talent, describes how key positions are to be staffed, provides management incentive plans, contains earn-out formulas, and deals with transfers in and out of the new entity. The operational plan describes how the new entity will operate on a day-to-day basis to achieve its objectives and outlines responsibilities of different groups in the new entity.

The marketing plan describes the competitive landscape, market opportunities and challenges, and how the new entity's products and services are developed, priced, marketed, and promoted. When these elements come together, investment requirements are calculated, revenues and costs are estimated, and a fairly detailed pro-forma financial plan is developed, which the new entity is expected to meet. Additionally, the business plan describes the reporting requirements of the new entity and the monitoring and control mechanisms instituted to ensure that the business plan objectives are met and reported to the parent companies.

### Business Case Recommendations

The primary function of the project business case is to provide a convenient summary to communicate findings and assessment internally and externally and obtain corporate approvals. Hence, it is important that the business case provides brief, but clearly and accurately stated and well-supported recommendations for the project. For senior management to grant project approvals, the business case recommendations must be specific and the reasons for the recommendations convincing and supported by adequate evidence. Also, business case recommendations must have the benefit of review and comment by the legal organization and the concurrence of independent reviewers.

The business case recommendations include statements on the substantive issues of the project: namely, whether to proceed with the project or not, that the negotiated price and the total cost of the transaction compared to shareholder value created is fair, and that project risks are adequately covered through the risk management plan. They also affirm the type and certainty of financing to fund the project as the most appropriate. However, business case recommendations would be incomplete if they did not include the project team's assessment of the implications if the project is not approved and implemented and what happens next.

Often, when corporate approvals are required to proceed along the project process, negotiations may still be going on and issues may still be outstanding. In that case, recommendations are made based on the terms and conditions already negotiated and conditional approval is sought to proceed with the project, subject to certain outcomes materializing and desired terms and conditions obtained. When conditional approvals are sought, the recommendations of the business case are also conditional. However, under no circumstances should business case recommendations be made unless they reflect project team consensus and agreement on major issues.

## ENSURING BUSINESS CASE QUALITY

### Characteristics of Quality Business Cases

Most acquisition and joint venture project business cases tend to be voluminous and are developed to support the project team recommendations. When the purpose of the business case is to ensure disciplined decision making, the focus shifts from volume of paper and lots of evidence to providing a sound rationale for the recommendations. Therefore, the first characteristic of quality business cases is orientation toward creating strong arguments for recommendations and forming a sound basis for senior management decisions.

Quality business cases developed by experienced project teams are complete in the sense that all important aspects of project assessment, negotiations, structuring, financing, implementation, and synergy extraction are adequately addressed. It is important that only key elements of a project receive attention in the business case; otherwise, too many distractions are introduced. While completeness is a characteristic of a sound business case, it does not mean that the business case document should be voluminous. On the contrary, business cases must be brief and to the point or else they do not get read. Furthermore, accuracy of assessment and clarity of description are necessary for a business case to be effective. Finally, brief but fully supported recommendations are the most important elements of quality business cases.

Other important elements of the business case for acquisitions or joint ventures are validity of the assumption set and quality of the evidence and analyses performed. The assumption set drives project financials and the decisions based on these financials. The quality of data and evidence used and the analyses performed must be reliable, factual, validated, and well considered. However, if strategic project rationale is absent from the business case analysis and continuity of purpose is missing from it, the quality of the business case is dubious. Hence, the need to ensure their presence through the business case development process.

### Discipline in Business Cases

Variation in discipline employed in business case development results in various degrees of discipline in decision making. Consequently, the business case process requires the project team to practice and ensure discipline in business case development. The first factor in business case discipline is a common understanding of major definitions and nomenclature in the project, followed by an understanding of assumptions involved in the financial analysis and other aspects of project assessment. The third element of discipline is factual and reliable evidence, which is validated and cross-checked, and the fourth is appropriate methodology used and objective analyses performed.

Once financial models are developed that capture key relationships in the project, risks and issues are identified by experts in functional areas, and potential impacts on project financials are quantified, given a consensus probability of occurrence. The reason for this is that when the project team looks at project value, risks and issues related to achieving that project value must be considered simultaneously. To demonstrate that risks and issues identified are not going to impact its value significantly, risk management and contingency plans are developed and the costs of those plans estimated and included in the business case financials.

Unless alternatives to the proposed project are considered in sufficient detail, the project business case does not stand on firm ground. For example, for a business case to recommend approval for an acquisition or a joint venture without having examined other alternatives is inappropriate because other alternatives may yield higher shareholder value than the proposed project. Therefore, the project team needs to have benchmarks against which to compare the results of the business case.

Having arrived at a project valuation, the project team has one or more independent entities pass judgment on the project valuation and the business case. The reasons for independent assessment are to ensure that relevant information is considered and reflected in the project evaluation and increase the level of senior management comfort about the business case. Also, to protect senior management and the board of directors approving a project from exposure to litigation, a fairness opinion letter based on the independent assessment from qualified agents, such as investment bankers and outside experts, should accompany the business case document.

### Independent Assessment

Independent assessment of acquisition or joint venture business cases involves thorough review of data and information available, findings of due diligence, appropriateness of methodology used, stability of financial models, and objectivity of analyses performed during project assessment. This definition of independent assessment includes the due diligence effort and review of the business case assumptions and analysis. It also includes an examination of negotiated terms and conditions, the implementation plan, the terms of financing, the new entity business plan, and the synergy extraction plan.

The purpose of the independent project assessment is to ensure that business case recommendations are sound and that senior management decisions are based on factual information, stable financial models, projections using reasonable approaches, and complete and unbiased analysis. By ensuring that analysis is unbiased and the project valuation is reasonable, independent assessment ensures that there is a high probability that value is created by the project. As a result, it protects senior management and board members involved in approving acquisitions and joint ventures against future litigation.

Independent project assessments are performed first by corporate business development groups not involved in the project and then by investment bankers, whereas the due diligence effort is ordinarily undertaken by accounting firms. Since project assessment objectivity is the driving motive for independent assessments, the first order of business is ensuring reasonableness of assumptions, including revenue and expense assumptions, discount and depreciation rates, tax considerations, and valuation methodology and ensuring completeness of analysis and recommendations based on information and evidence.

While independent assessment is performed by individuals other than the project team, members of the team participate in this effort by sharing and reviewing jointly assumptions, data and information, financial models and model outputs, and methodology and project valuations. Sharing includes negotiated terms and conditions, risks and issues and risk management plans, implementation and business plans, and financing plans. When project assessment components are viewed jointly, omitted items are identified and interpretations of data and information other than the project team's are considered. At the end of this process, the recommendations of the project team should be fully supported by the independent assessment team.

Independent assessment of the project business case document is important because it is the final and authoritative check in the process and senior management relies on it. The independent assessment findings should concur with the business case findings and recommendations. Otherwise, the project evaluation is questionable, and if this happens, the project team either goes back and addresses issues raised by the independent assessment team or decides the project is not worth pursuing, which is a rare event.

## USES OF BUSINESS CASES

The business case and its predecessor the feasibility study are summaries of analysis performed, data and information used, and findings up to that point for the purpose of sound decision making. However, the feasibility study and the business case serve a number of other important functions. Namely, they are tools to bring discipline in the decision-making process, communicate project findings and progress internally and externally, obtain corporate project approvals, and help the participating financing institutions in evaluating the project.

The business case is used as the official project team assessment in internal communications to deliver a consistent message and obtain stakeholder buy-in. Consistency of messages communicated internally is essential to ensure project team credibility and availability of resources to support project execution. Externally, the business case findings and recommendations serve as a communications tool that describes the project and its value on a consistent basis and in terms that the business community understands.

When limited recourse financing is pursued, the business case analysis and documentation are reviewed and scrutinized by financing institutions involved, since the business case analysis forms the foundation on which this type of financing is based. By communicating the nature of the project, the opportunity assessment, findings and recommendations on a consistent basis up the management structure, the business case serves as the means that facilitates management discussion and approvals.

## SUMMARY

The business case development is a central element of the opportunity assessment process and forms the foundation of decisions and corporate approvals for investments to close the deal. The discussion of this chapter centers around the development of the business case and its components and treats the main issues of this effort. The business case process is described first, followed by the development of the project assumptions. Identification of project requirements is emphasized along with the need to evaluate alternatives on a fair and impartial basis.

Because of the significance of project risks and their ability to swing project value and impact the attractiveness of the proposed project, risks and issues are discussed in some depth along with project deal structure. The significance of assessing negotiated terms and conditions and the project financial analysis are given appropriate attention. Then, the financing plan, the implementation plan, and the new entity business plan are discussed and the nature of effective project recommendations is considered. Issues such as the characteristics of quality business cases, discipline in doing business cases, and resulting decisions are reviewed and the chapter ends with a discussion of independent business case assessment and uses of business cases.

The emphasis in developing sound business cases is on adherence to pre-established process and project workplan, validation and testing of underlying assumptions, and thorough and quality financial analysis and evaluation. Also, continuity of purpose through the project, independent assessment by impartial parties, discipline in development of the evidence and data for the business case, and concrete and implementable recommendations expressed in clear language and with no uncertain terms are essential elements of sound business cases.

# 14

## PROJECT FINANCIAL ANALYSIS

### INTRODUCTION

Acquisitions and joint ventures are undertaken to create shareholder value and growth. It is crucial that decisions are made based on informed judgments concerning total project cost, return on investment expected, and risk involved in achieving the expected return. Therefore, extensive market, pricing, capital investment, and other financial data gathering and information is undertaken and analysis performed to effect a sound project assessment. Financial analysis begins with development and validation of assumptions; it is performed to explain the interaction of various inputs and relationships, and summarizes findings in pro forma financial statements. Financial statements are then used as the basis to develop project valuations by taking into account other market elements.

Ordinarily, the financial analyst on the project team is responsible for the financial analysis and project valuation. When only the financial analyst is involved in the financial analysis, it results in limited understanding of project dynamics and inadequate assessment. Effective financial analysis is performed by an experienced financial analyst working closely and communicating continuously with technical experts and external advisors. This is because it needs the benefit of different perspectives to account for various influences on the project financials.

A sound financial analysis in acquisitions and joint ventures has a broad scope, which opens the discussion in this chapter. The chapter proceeds to development and validation of the assumption set that underlies and determines project financials. A discussion of market and structural analysis that determines demand growth and price level sustainability follows. The issues of discount, depreciation, and tax rates used in the financial analysis and the financing costs of the project are examined and the total project costs and capital requirements are discussed.

The main ideas in financial modeling, the quantification of trade-offs, and the evaluation of financial impacts of negotiated terms and conditions are reviewed. The iterative nature of the deal structure financial assessment is discussed next followed by quantification of identified project synergies. Project risk assessment and the evaluation of the impact on project financials is reviewed and the quantification of project resource requirements is revisited. After that, the focus turns to evaluation of the business case and the new entity's business plan.

The discussion of financial analysis continues with the evaluation of alternatives to the proposed project and the sensitivity and scenario analysis required to understand key financial drivers and the impacts of changes in the assumption set. Validating financial projections through sanity checks is discussed and the chapter ends with the elements that characterize a world-class financial analysis of acquisitions and joint ventures.


## ENSURING ADEQUATE FINANCIAL EVALUATION

### Scope of Financial Analysis

The main responsibilities of the financial analyst are the development, validation, and monitoring of assumptions underlying the creation of the pro forma financial statements, the development of models, and the financial analysis and valuation of acquisition or joint venture projects. We have stressed repeatedly that assumption set creation is the most important area of financial analysis because the assumptions behind driving variables dictate the results. Also, by understanding the assumptions the financial analyst and the project team know if there is sound rationale and judgment behind financial projections and the reliability of these projections.

Selecting the methodology to follow in developing inputs and the governing relationships in the financial model are other areas of concern to the financial analyst. For example, product demand and revenue projections must be based on a reasonable, generally accepted, and sound approach. In addition, how relationships are specified in the financial model requires understanding of the company's own business and the industry, and the views of experts are solicited to specify appropriate relationships. For instance, what kinds and amounts of capital equipment are required to produce certain levels of output is an engineers' area of expertise that is brought into the financial model to enhance its predictive capability and the project NPV results.

Market and structural analysis are areas that require input from marketing and competitive analysis experts upon which the financial analyst builds financial projections. It is a team effort involving all project participants and experts from other parts of the organization. The creation of pro forma financial statements is a routine activity once the assumptions and relationships are well understood, the market and structural analysis performed, and both are incorporated in the financial model. However, it is important to ensure that the output obtained from financial models is reasonable and consistent with operating principles.

Review of comparable transactions and calculation of project value are also financial analysis responsibilities. However, input and guidance from investment bankers and other experts is required to ensure that relevant information is incorporated in the development of the acquisition price or the valuation of the joint venture. Because different industries have different ways of valuing a concern and because many market forces interact to determine the acquisition price, the input and judgment of outside experts is essential to understand current market forces in order to produce stand-alone fair market valuations.

In addition to comparable transactions and project value, financial analysis encompasses quantification of project risks, quantification of trade-offs and negotiated terms and conditions, sensitivity analysis, and scenario and "what if" types of analyses. Quantification of expected synergies and sanity checks are other major areas under the scope of project financial analysis.

### Characteristics of Sound Financial Analysis

Sound financial analyses are characterized by clarity of purpose. The financial analyst understands the objectives of the analysis and knows precisely what needs to be done to achieve them. That is, the financial analyst is guided by a pre-established process and proceeds methodically through the steps of the process. Understanding the industry and the business of the acquiring, the target, and the parent company is important, but understanding of relationships specified in the financial model is even more important.

Project team consensus on assumptions is an indication that there has been interaction with and input from functional experts. This results in clearly articulated assumptions that are tested for reasonableness. If assumptions are not clearly articulated, the project team cannot test their validity. Armed with good assumptions, a seasoned financial analyst develops concise, yet flexible, models with adequate explanations throughout the model worksheets.

Completeness is another key element of sound financial analysis and is the result of constant communication with the project team and functional experts throughout the assessment process. In this area, the project team ensures that all factors that influence project financials are incorporated in the financial models. It also ensures that there is an integrated approach to financial modeling and analysis, which means that project participants are well informed about everyone's work. In addition, the stand-alone analysis is performed first and is followed by analysis of impacts on the acquiring or the parent company.

Validation of information, data, and financial projections obtained takes place throughout the course of project evaluation and sanity checks are performed prior to sharing the financial analysis results outside the project team. Finally, the stability of hypothesized relationships and reasonableness of results are tested by the project team and independent assessment experts.

## FINANCIAL ANALYSIS BUILDING BLOCKS

### Development and Validation of Assumptions

Before an experienced financial analyst solicits, develops, and validates assumptions, effort is devoted to understanding the definitions of different terms and obtaining agreement by the project team, business unit heads, and other key participants. This is crucial in ensuring that project participants on both sides understand the same thing when discussing a particular concept or issue. For international projects, agreement on definitions and terms is as important as development of assumptions included in the financial model, especially marketing and financial terms used in business issues discussions.

Since the financial analyst and the project team are not expected to know all aspects of engineering, product development, operations, marketing, accounting, and other functions, they rely heavily on the expertise of functional experts on the team, in the greater organization, and outside the company. However, expert input should be reviewed and assessed by the project team and validated against benchmarks to ensure reasonableness of inputs. Since model inputs and assumptions determine financial results and subsequent decisions, heavy emphasis is placed on the validation of assumptions.

The market and structural analysis used as input to financial models is a key element and the foundation of financial analysis. The reason for this is that product demand, pricing, marketing, product life cycle management, competitive impacts, and industry assessment come together in the structural and market analysis performed by seasoned analysts who understand the industry well. However, because of the myriad of factors interacting to determine the existing market structure, the financial analyst focuses on major impact assumptions and concentrates on understanding the significant relationships in the company's business and the industry as a whole.

The key areas which the project team develops assumptions are product demand growth and product pricing over time, development of new markets and distribution channels, and management of product life cycles. On the other side, assumptions concerning technology evolution, entry of new market players and competitive impacts, and new product introductions need to be developed. The major relationships that require attention are the expense to revenue, pricing to demand, product output to capital requirements, and competitor entry to the company's market penetration.

A recommended approach in developing and validating assumptions starts with a thorough traditional industry analysis to get a good view of trends and the evolution of competition. Then, input and assessment by internal experts on key market, engineering, and operating areas are obtained along with industry association actual demand data and projections of prices and demand growth rates. Transactions involving comparable companies over the past two to three years are examined and the key levers of the financial model to focus on are identified, that is, variables with the greatest impact on the project NPV.

The project team creates assumptions for basic technical and financial relationships and then expands on them, but validates the assumption set with internal and external experts twice. Also, the stability of assumed relationships and sensitivity of the financial models with model simulations are tested. Furthermore, each assumption is tested separately and the entire assumption set is tested versus a different assumption set to determine reasonableness and stability of the assumption set and, consequently, the financial model.

## Market and Industry Analysis

Market and industry analysis in acquisition and joint venture projects is an essential element in understanding factors that determine the demand and revenue side of financial models. In these projects, one has only three to five years of revenue data from audited financial statements and no history at all in joint venture projects. This does not allow the project team to use statistical models in identifying factors underlying demand, measuring the strength of relationships, and developing financial projections. In view of this, the project team searches for alternative ways to perform the market and industry analysis.

Market and structural analysis for acquisition and joint venture projects examines the demand, price, and competitive elements of the revenue stream and its growth. On the demand side, it examines the history of the acquiring or parent company, the target's demand growth, and the life cycle position of its products or services. When this is not possible, it is useful to look at demand or revenue growth of companies similar to the target or the joint venture. A comparison of target or joint venture growth with industry growth reveals to what extent they are consistent, and the project team needs to identify what factors account for differences in growth.

Having performed this kind of analysis, the project team looks at potential changes in demand composition over the projection horizon, which is usually five to seven years. Here, factors such as new competitor entry, technological advances, and new competing products are considered, and the assessment of independent advisor or industry experts is obtained. To get a first-hand impression of demand growth sustainability, it is a good idea to talk with major customers of the target concerning its reputation, their satisfaction with the products or the customer care service provided, as well as their purchasing plans over the next few years. It is equally important to talk to the target's key suppliers to understand its expected input growth, payment practices, and its reputation.

On the price side of the revenue equation, the major underlying factors the project team needs to consider are industry restructure, consolidations, and mega-trends. Also, the level of expected synergies and complementarity of operations need to be investigated to understand profit margins and how competitively the new entity can price when faced with increased competition. The impact of technology and competing products, the threat of new entrants, and the impact on price levels are incorporated in the assessment of price developments. In addition, how the customer set composition and tastes are expected to change is included in the price analysis as well as the evolution of the products and services under study. With this analysis the project team assesses the sustainability of demand growth and price levels. Based on those determinations, reasonable revenue projections are made that reflect key factors that influence its components. Cost projections are easily obtained through past cost-to-revenue relationships and pro forma financial statements are developed.

### Discount Rate, Taxes, and Financing Costs

The discount rate used in financial analysis usually reflects the weighted cost of capital of the acquiring or the parent firm and the assessment of project risk. In some cases, the discount rate used reflects only the cost of capital of the acquiring or the parent firm, but not project risk. We recommend against the former approach because it is difficult to assign a certain percentage to the project risk prior to having performed a risk analysis. Even then, it is conceptually difficult to discount a cash flow by fixed additional percentage points when the probabilities related to various risks change over time and cannot be determined with any degree of accuracy.

Accounting for acquisition and joint venture project risks through discount rate adjustments should be avoided. Instead, a weighted average cost of capital should be used as the discount rate in the financial model and account for project risks separately through developing probabilistic NPVs for the project. The reason for this is that cost of capital impacts should not be mixed with the impacts of project risks because the resulting valuation is viewed as a risk-free NPV. That is not true and is another reason that risk-adjusted discount rates should not be used because project investment return measures are not clear.

Tax considerations and legal issues determine the type of acquisition effected and the costs to the acquiring and the seller or the target company. Also, tax incentives and tax holidays of joint ventures are important elements in financial analysis and valuation, especially in foreign joint ventures that are given incentives to delay repatriation of dividends. These elements have significant impacts on the effective tax rate that is used in financial analysis.

Depreciation policies and practices in the industry of the target or the joint venture are reviewed and the impacts on the parent company evaluated.

Different depreciation schedules are assessed and the one best describing the new entity's needs in light of its competitive position is selected. A key consideration in the selection of depreciation rates is the need of the new entity to remain competitive. Furthermore, benefits from different depreciation schedules should be balanced against the need to keep new-entity investment at levels that make it competitive.

The project deal structure impacts the type and costs of financing, which are incorporated in the financial analysis. The financing costs of a project include several elements, the most important being the project advisor retainer and success fees, returns required by debt participants' and equity investors, and debt- or equity-related fees and charges. Other financing costs include external consultant fees and charges, costs of developing legal documents and setting up procedures for disbursements, and insurance premiums to enhance the credit worthiness of the entity raising the funding. In addition, costs of providing parental guarantees or other forms of credit enhancements, and implementation costs involved in administering loan repayments and dividend disbursements are included in the financial analysis.

## THE CORE FINANCIAL ANALYSIS

### Costs and Capital Requirements

For ongoing concerns, there is a fairly stable relationship between revenues and expenses. As the demand for the products and services increase, production or output increases follow and the increase in production invariably causes a proportional increase in production costs. The stable relationship between the two holds true over a certain production range, which does not require additional capital, but beyond that range the output-cost and output-capital relationships change. Also, one must account for additional expenses for new product development as current offerings age and for price reductions and marketing and promotional programs to counter the impact of increased competition. Additionally, expected synergy revenues, costs, and investments in the acquisition or the joint venture should be reflected in the financial analysis once the project team is convinced of their existence.

The development of reliable new-entity expense projections is normally done in the business plan after the decision is made to proceed with the project. However, cost and expense projections are needed earlier as inputs to the financial model to arrive at the decision to proceed. As a practical compromise, operations managers help develop interim cost and expense projections because of their understanding of the company's operations and cost structure and their ability to extrapolate that experience to the new entity's operations. As the business case development progresses, cost data firm up and by the time work begins on the business plan, cost and expense projections become reliable estimates.

While the revenue-to-cost relationship is fairly stable, capital requirements do not enjoy the same relationship. When output increases beyond certain levels, capacity constraints are encountered that require significant capital outlays for new plant and equipment. Because of that, the project team needs to consider future capital requirements through planning of new-entity future activities. As in the case of cost development, preliminary capital requirements are used initially to assess project viability, but these estimates are eventually concurred to by operations managers. By the time the new-entity business plan is created, future capital requirements driven by changes in demand are well understood and fixed.

This is an iterative approach to develop financial data and analyze information. The project team begins the project assessment with little information and preliminary financial projections to develop the feasibility study and determine the project's economic viability. As the acquisition or joint venture proceeds along the assessment process and negotiations define cost and expense parameters, financial projections improve and are finalized by the time the business case is completed. However, the project team remains flexible to revise cost and investment projections even after corporate approvals have been obtained. With reliable cost and capital estimates incorporated in the final project valuation, the value of an acquisition or joint venture is known with some confidence.

### Financial Modeling

Financial modeling is the art of capturing important operational and financial relationships and creating models that are linked together to produce pro forma financial statements for the acquiring or the parent company and the new entity. Capturing operational relationships requires a good understanding of the acquiring and the target's business and how they operate versus how they will operate, in order to describe what happens to the financial side when changes in operations are introduced. Hence, a lot of input into the financial models concerning production, cost, and investment relationships comes directly from operational experts.

Assumptions underlying financial models are verified by the due diligence subteam and the entire project team and constitute a key input into the financial models. Depreciation schedules, tax rates, capital requirements, financing cost elements, and discount rates are additional major financial model inputs besides revenue and expense projections. Using the latest actual financial data and other key inputs, financial models are simulated to produce pro forma financial statements and the project valuation.

The role of financial modeling does not stop here. It goes on to testing various inputs and assumptions, quantifying the impact of risks, and assessing the value of trade-offs. It also incorporates newly negotiated terms and conditions and quantifies expected synergies. These extensions of financial modeling enable the financial analyst to create other scenarios, perform sensitivity analysis, and what-if analysis. Because these analytical capabilities are build into financial models, project teams and management rely on them to evaluate the impact of changes in inputs and summarize information in widely understood financial measures.

### Quantification of Trade-Offs

Trade-offs are packages of equal value that leave the company as well off as prior to trade-offs being effected. They are identified by the project team, quantified through simulations of project financial models, and are levers used to move forward acquisition and joint venture negotiations. Effective development and quantification of trade-offs requires thorough understanding of the key issues and the company's positions on these issues in order to alter the financial model input in such a way that the right trade-offs are created and their impacts appropriately simulated through financial models. It also requires understanding the other side's interest and how much value it assigns different trade-offs and concessions. Because of these considerations, the need to ensure appropriate changes in financial model inputs, and conduct the right model simulations, the financial analyst is part of the negotiations subteam. The financial analyst communicates continuously with the project team to validate trade-offs being proposed and assess the impact of changes to other proposals.

Once financial model inputs are revised and impacts quantified, the project's NPV is calculated and compared to the baseline NPV and the difference is the cost of trade-offs. The value of trade-off to the other side is then validated and communicated to the entire project team and the negotiations subteam, which proceeds with making the trade-off offer at the appropriate time. Most of the quantification of trade-offs takes place prior to the opening of negotiations, but offers and counter-offers made during negotiations are assessed through financial models in real time. Early trade-off quantification produces superior results and expedites negotiations tremendously when the project team, and the negotiations subteam in particular, are well informed concerning the value of trade-offs.

### Evaluation of Negotiated Terms

Acquisition and joint venture financial models start simply, and with sketchy information and data they simulate various financial relationships and calculate the project's NPV. As more information becomes available and the target or the joint venture operations are better understood, the complexity of financial models increases and the financial analyst needs to have a systematic way to assess changes in postulated relationships and terms and conditions surrounding the project.

Being a member of the negotiations subteam, the financial analyst participates in and monitors negotiations closely, and as a particular term is discussed, its impact is evaluated. Also, as terms of the deal are negotiated or project conditions are agreed to by the parties, the financial analyst evaluates their impact on the project's NPV and communicates the results and findings to the negotiations subteam and the entire project team. The financial evaluation of project terms and conditions is validated by the project team from different perspectives and the reporting of impacts is done through constant and open communications.

To ensure that the impacts of negotiated terms and conditions are appropriately quantified, the project team performs sanity checks and solicits input from external advisors —preferably investment bankers engaged in the project. The evaluation of negotiated terms and conditions examines the impacts on the project NPV and on how changes in the terms and conditions impact the strategic fit and the overall project rationale and objectives.

### Assessment of the Deal Structure

Financial modeling and analysis in acquisition and joint venture projects is done through an iterative approach. That is, inputs are linked to outputs through actual or hypothesized relationships, and as the project goes through the assessment process, new information is developed and the model inputs and relationships are revised. To initialize the financial model and analysis, a possible deal structure of interest to the acquiring or parent company is assumed. As project assessment goes on and terms and conditions are negotiated, legal considerations and the tax impacts of various structures are better understood and incorporated in the financial model.

Alternative tax treatments have a significant impact on the cash flows of an acquisition transaction, and in some instances, they determine the feasibility of the acquisition. The structuring considerations include the tax impacts and the cost allocation considerations of the transaction on shareholder value of the acquiring or the parent company. In parallel, the tax impacts on shareholders of the target are examined to establish benchmarks to be used to develop the company position and negotiation strategy.

Alternative payment methods for the acquisition are evaluated for their cost and tax implications on the project's NPV. Furthermore, various costs associated with financing the transaction and their impact on the tax bill are assessed. Finally, a balance in the cost/benefit relationship between the form of payment (cash versus stock, versus bonds) and structuring the payment form (conditions, timing, ties to performance, etc.) must be achieved to make the deal structure acceptable to all parties.

## ADDITIONAL ELEMENTS OF FINANCIAL ANALYSIS

### Identifying and Quantifying Synergies

Synergies in acquisition and joint venture projects are important because usually they are the main motive for many projects and because they have a significant impact on the valuation of these projects. The identification of project synergies occurs when screening of alternatives takes place. The synergy quantification effort starts when the implementation subteam is in position to make reasonable judgments about the existence of synergies, the probability of their realization, and the magnitude of the costs and benefits involved. In addition to financial costs, quantification entails estimation of human resources required to harness expected synergies.

Synergies may exist in a number of functional areas. Here, the implementation subteam examines closely all possibilities related to synergies in the area of R&D, new product development, product branding, new markets and distribution channels, production and cost savings, revenue synergies, and other synergies. If the acquisition or joint venture project is strategy driven, there are synergies to be harnessed in the area of efficiencies in realizing the company's strategic goals and objectives and in enhancing the company's competitive position in the industry. While identification of synergies is easy to do, quantification requires development of reasonable assumptions, clear processes to obtain them, and project team consensus.

Synergies are also identified and quantified or validated in the due diligence phase, but the degree to which synergies are harnessed depends to a large extent on planning and the implementation subteam experience needed to attain them. It also has to do with the skills of implementation and new-entity managers and their potential upward financial gain. However, most of synergy realization depends on how effectively the target is integrated or how quickly a joint venture begins to achieve goals it was intended to achieve. Therefore, the financial analysis must capture synergy realization considerations and use them as inputs to the financial model. It should be noted that adjustments need to be made to scale these considerations to levels that make sense for each project.

### Risk Assessment and Impact on Financials

The two key elements in quantifying project risks in acquisitions and joint ventures are identifying the objective function or measure of performance to be impacted and then measuring the risk exposure. The objective function commonly used is the project's NPV and a measurement of risk exposure is the deviation from the estimated base case NPV. The NPV deviation is calculated through sensitivity analysis of key drivers of the base case NPV or through scenario analysis of risk events that impact the NPV.

The major elements involved in risk assessment and management in acquisition and joint venture projects are identifying the source of risk, assessing the probability of risk occurrence, estimating the impact of the risk on the project NPV, and calculating the cost of developing risk management plans. The most significant types of project risks are deal structure risks, commercial or business risks, financing risks, implementation risks, ownership risks, political and regulatory risks, synergy realization risks, foreign exchange risks, and business plan realization risks.

Starting from a reasonable baseline scenario or the base case NPV, each risk is quantified by appropriately changing the input assumptions to the financial model and simulating the impact on the project NPV. The difference between the project NPVs is the impact of the risk. After all individual risks are quantified, the impact of all risks together is simulated to develop the worst-case scenario. The risk impacts are plotted in descending order according to their impact, the probabilities of occurrence are evaluated, and risks management plans are developed for the most likely risks with significant impacts. The costs of risk management plans are included in the financial model and the decision is made whether to proceed with the project.

### Quantifying Resource Requirements

The translation of human resource requirements into costs, the projected production output into capital investments, and the estimation of implementation costs are key elements of financial analysis needed to produce reasonable project valuations. Acquisition and joint venture human resource requirements include management and labor needed to operate the new entity as well as implementation managers, the steering committee, the liaison subteam, and on-going management support and control of the new entity.

To quantify these requirements, the project team obtains extensive input from the implementation subteam, operations managers, and human resources experts. Under human resource requirements, the financial analyst estimates costs of retaining target company management talent and incentive programs. In addition to loaded wages and salaries, travel and other related expenses are included.

Investment requirements are ordinarily tied to the level of output produced by the new entity not in a linear fashion, but in a stepwise relationship. Also, presence of economies or diseconomies of scale makes estimation of capital requirements to meet future output levels difficult to assess. Therefore, the advice of technical experts should be sought. Finally, capital upgrades and introduction of new technology complicate the estimation of capital investments required by the new entity in the study period. Hence, it is important that questions concerning these issues are raised, addressed by experts and the project team, consensus is reached, and adequate provisions are made for capital requirements in the financial analysis.

### Evaluation of Business Case and Business Plan

The business case involves a comprehensive project assessment to determine its viability as a stand-alone proposition. The business plan is the blueprint for the proposed new-entity operation. The former is much broader, encompasses elements of the latter, and examines all key elements needed to make the project successful. The latter is narrower in scope and deals with the details of how the new entity will achieve its business objectives and financial goals. However, ensuring consistency of the business plan with the business case analysis and results is an important element of financial analysis.

Evaluation of the business case requires understanding of the acquiring or parent company's strategic goals and objectives, validation of the assumptions and relationships underlying financial projections, assessment of valuation methodology, and analysis of results. On the other hand, business plan assessment requires familiarity with tactics to translate strategic objectives of the acquiring or parent company into new-entity financial results. The former requires knowing how to assess value, the later requires know-how to achieve expected value and harness expected synergies. The business case analysis has as its end goal estimation of a fair value for the project, while the end goal of the business plan analysis is to determine how likely is the estimated fair project value.

Before evaluating the financial aspects of a business plan, the project team reviews and assesses the other business plan components. Namely, it reviews the operations and human resources plans supporting it, the marketing plan, and the technical upgrades and product introduction plan. The purpose of this review and assessment is to ensure internal consistency within each plan, that no conflicts or inconsistencies exist between requirements of plans, and that requirements of supporting plans are reflected in the financial plan.

## COMPLETING THE FINANCIAL ANALYSIS

### Evaluation of Alternatives

Evaluation of alternatives is the part of financial analysis that creates benchmarks needed to compare the value of the project against alternatives that could accomplish the same long-term goals. Experienced project teams have several choices here, but use of the base case as the benchmark is recommended because it incorporates historical evidence, industry experience, extensive analysis, and assessment of outside experts. The primary reasons for comparing alternatives to the proposed project benchmarks are to identify other approaches and their resource requirements to achieve the company's long-term strategic goals and establish the means to compare the project's value to that of alternatives. This permits ranking of alternatives according to strategic fit, NPV, or other criteria.

Comparison of alternatives identifies risks involved in alternatives, compares potential impacts, and ensures that the selected project creates the most value for the acquiring or parent company's shareholders, given its risk profile. It enables the project team to develop a well-supported recommendation for project approval and creates a reasonable comfort level for senior management to approve the proposed project as the most advantageous in accomplishing the company's strategic objectives. It also meets the independent assessment requirement needed for senior management approvals. In the absence of alternatives evaluated, the business case is not likely to pass that requirement. Additionally, it ensures that senior management decisions are not exposed to legal challenges from shareholders questioning the value of a particular project.

Analysis of alternatives first involves looking at the option of achieving the company's long-term strategic objectives through internal initiatives. This defines the initial hurdle and first criterion that other approaches must surpass in terms of strategic positioning and creating higher shareholder value. The reason for this being an interim benchmark is that internal growth can support the core business better than other approaches, is associated with learning organizations, enjoys higher level of support internally, and is less costly.

The internal initiative approach is often ignored because it takes much longer to accomplish company objectives under that approach versus external options be they acquisitions or joint ventures. In most cases, because evaluation of alternatives is a time-consuming and complex activity viewed as producing limited benefits, it is performed at high levels and evaluates few key financial drivers and risks associated with each alternative.

World-class project teams take time to identify internal initiatives and assess internal options to achieve the company's long-term objectives in order to establish interim benchmarks against which alternatives are to be judged. The analysis required to perform a sound comparison of alternatives entails the following elements:

1. Strategic fit evaluation and determination of how the project helps the company meet its long-term objectives.
2. Expected financial results, stability of financial performance, and value creation analysis.
3. Evaluation of project risks and unresolved issues and how they impact expected value.
4. Ease and cost of implementation and capturing identified synergies.
5. Financeability, cost, and certainty, given the risk profile of each option.
6. Assessment of likelihood of achieving the shareholder value expected to be created by the project.

Because all these considerations are involved in assessing alternatives, each alternative is rated for each element. This requires a seasoned project team to select one alternative versus another by using the expressed views of senior management to assign weights to the ranking of each element. The following example demonstrates the complexity of assessing alternatives and selecting the optimum alternative for the company to meet its long-term objectives: Alternative $X$ has a closer strategic fit than $Y$, it has a lower shareholder value but is less risky than $Y$, it has a higher probability of being implemented successfully, it is more difficult to create or harness synergies, and it is just as difficult to finance than $Y$. Under that scenario, which project is more attractive?

To answer that question, we have developed a method to resolve inconsistent rankings of alternative projects and enable project teams to compare different alternatives. This method is shown in Table 14.1 where for each alternative, the project team provides its assessment of the value for each element or criterion of evaluation expressed as a number from 1 to 10. The importance or weight of that criterion in comparing alternatives is expressed as a number from 0 to 1 and the sum of weights over all elements equals 1. The

**Table 14.1**
**Evaluation of Alternatives Matrix**

| Elements of Evaluation | Alternative Projects | | | | |
|---|---|---|---|---|---|
|  | $A$ | $B$ | $C$ | — | $N$ |
| 1. Strategic fit: <br> Assessed value <br> Weight assigned <br> Score of alternative | | | | | |
| 2. Project NPV: <br> Assessed value <br> Weight assigned <br> Score of alternative | | | | | |
| 3. Risk impacts: <br> Assessed value <br> Weight assigned <br> Score of alternative | | | | | |
| 4. Financeability: <br> Assessed value <br> Weight assigned <br> Score of alternative | | | | | |
| 5. Implementation: <br> Assessed value <br> Weight assigned <br> Score of alternative | | | | | |
| 6. Synergies: <br> Assessed value <br> Weight assigned <br> Score of alternative | | | | | |
| **Total score** | | | | | |

scores for each of the criteria are the product of the value and the weight, which are then summed up to derive the overall project score. The alternative with the highest overall score is one that meets the company's objectives in the most effective manner.

### Sensitivity and Scenario Analysis

Sensitivity analysis is the assessment of impacts of changes in individual financial model inputs or assumptions on the model's outputs, the output usually being the project's NPV. Sensitivity analysis is done by varying one input at a time and simulating its impact. Scenario analysis, on the other hand, is hypothesizing certain conditions or events affecting the project inputs and assessing the combined impact on the output of the financial model. In scenario analysis, more than one model input is affected by the hypothesized occurrence of events and the impact on the project value is simulated. The what-if type of analysis is more often than not a hybrid of sensitivity and scenario analysis whereby impacts of several factors are simulated in isolation or simultaneously.

Sensitivity analysis is a useful tool in assessing how important each assumption, relationship specified in the financial model, or input variable is in determining the project's NPV. By simulating the impacts of changes in the various assumptions and model inputs, the project team obtains a corresponding set of NPVs that allows ranking of the importance of each input changed. Scenario analysis, on the other hand, enables one to determine what happens to the project NPV when hypothesized changes in the operating environment occur.

When probabilities are assigned to each scenario's occurrence, the resulting expected NPV is called a probabilistic NPV. This is useful in determining the most likely NPV of a joint venture, but is of limited use in determining the value of an acquisition because value is determined to a large degree by price paid to close the transaction. Nonetheless, scenario analysis can shed light on the likelihood of the new entity meeting its business plan.

Sensitivity and scenario analyses are used to identify the key drivers of project financials, simulate impacts of different project risks, and assess the magnitude of expected project synergies. They are tools in evaluating impacts, identifying what is important to focus on, checking the rationale behind assumptions and relationships, and testing the stability and reasonableness of financial results. Sensitivity and scenario analyses are often used to develop an NPV range within which the actual fair market value of a project is likely to be in the presence of uncertainty. Optimistic and pessimistic views and upper and lower boundaries of a project NPV are created by sensitivity and scenario analysis by simulating the impacts of an optimistic and a pessimistic set of assumptions.

### Validation of Financial Projections

A crucial element of acquisition and joint venture financial analysis is validation of key components of financial statements created for the project. Validation of financial projections means performing sanity checks on outputs of the financial model and the results obtained. This is done through simulations of financial models and review of resulting financial variables for the purpose of ensuring:

1. Consistency of findings of the market and structural analysis performed.
2. Consistency of financial results with expectations formed prior to model simulations.
3. Stability of financial results when various changes are introduced in the model inputs.
4. Reasonableness of magnitude and pattern of key financial variables.
5. Consistency with results of similar projects and comparable transactions.

In most projects, validation of financial projections is performed in the independent assessment stage and is usually done by an outside expert. However, world-class project teams do their own validation of financial projections to ensure consistency and produce a solid basis for senior management decisions. What-if kinds of analysis are also useful in determining the consistency of financial projections. Performing sanity checks prior to sharing the results of financial analysis outside the project team pays dividends by avoiding embarrassments when financial analysis results are released. Hence, it is important to have ongoing discussions and a project team review of the financial analysis and results obtained every time there is a significant change in model inputs or model parameters. This is especially important when evaluating impacts of negotiated terms and conditions, proposed trade-offs, and changes in implementation conditions. It is also valuable in the assessment of synergies at the operational level and changes in the project risk profile.

## SUMMARY

The financial analysis of acquisition and joint venture projects is a key element of project evaluation because it validates the assumptions driving the project financials, creates linkages between different elements in the new-entity operations and the parent company, and provides an acceptable framework for assessment. Objective financial analysis forces discipline in the project evaluation process and quantifies the value of trade-offs, risk impacts, and negotiated terms and conditions. It brings together and summarizes the project financial aspects and forms the basis for project valuation and the decision to proceed with corporate approvals.

The emphasis in this chapter is on practices that make for a sound financial analysis. Namely, we focus on completeness of analysis, which is essentially determined by the degree of adherence to the pre-established process, validation of assumptions and hypothesized linkages based on factual information, and an objective market and industry assessment. Best practices in financial analysis include a series of sanity checks with other benchmarks and industry averages, extensive sensitivity analysis to confirm stability of model linkages, and independent assessment of the model and the assumption set by internal and external experts.

# 15

# ACQUISITION AND JOINT VENTURE VALUATION

## INTRODUCTION

In acquisitions, the purchase price is a key factor in closing the transaction and project valuations are used to develop the target's fair market value underlying the price paid. Some fair market valuation techniques are based on past target company performance while others look at future or expected financial performance. However, the price to close a transaction and the fair market value estimated by various techniques can be substantially different. Target company valuation is a complex undertaking because of different approaches in the treatment of inventories, valuation of intangibles, and tax considerations involved as well as differences in valuation across different industries. In addition, prices paid for acquiring businesses vary widely with no evident reasons. For example, *Inc. Magazine* reported in its June 1996 issue that the asking price for a family-owned country store in New Hampshire was 6.5 times earnings while the asking price for a Florida travel agency was 1.2 and for an Oklahoma fitness center 127.7 times earnings.

The acquisition price paid for ongoing businesses is composed of the following five elements: the stand-alone fair market value of the target, the level of synergies expected in the transaction, the market premium to be paid, the tax liabilities or benefits accruing to the buyer and seller, and the negotiating position of the parties. The main focus of the chapter is on the first four valuation components.

The first part of the chapter reviews the stand-alone fair market valuation process, the steps involved, and commonly used valuation methods. Different approaches used to calculate terminal or residual value are reviewed along with the nature and the reasons for market premiums in acquisition projects.

Inclusion of synergies in acquisition or joint venture valuations is determined by negotiations and how badly a company wants to close the transaction and is discussed after market premiums.

The valuation of the net tax benefits to the acquiring company is another component of the price paid to close a transaction and follows the synergy valuation discussion. A brief account of project risks in the valuation process is presented to show how to balance the interests of the parties involved. Even after calculation of these price components, determination of the acquisition price is not complete because other factors enter the equation, such as the bidding situation and the negotiating power of the buyer and the seller. Negotiation power is discussed next with a review of the roles of project participants in the valuation process.

This chapter concentrates on considerations such as the joint venture valuation process, which is the same as in acquisition projects. While project valuations are complex undertakings and an art that takes years of experience to develop, following a pre-established process helps significantly. Also, good project valuations are characterized by completeness of analysis and consideration of key factors impacting value, and the final price is determined by project economics, interaction of market forces, and the negotiation process where balance of interests of project participants is essential.

## PROJECT VALUATION BASICS

### The Fair Market Valuation Process

In order for the estimated fair market value to be a good starting point in price negotiations, it must be based on a process that takes into account all relevant information and involves a sequence of the following steps:

*1. Identify and define what is valued.* It makes a difference whether a target company's stock is to be valued in whole or in part versus valuing those assets in whole or in part. Stock valuation, for instance, entails consideration of assets, liabilities, past and future financial performance, market and competitive positioning, introduction of technology, and change in customer set composition.

*2. Perform market and industry analysis.* In this step, the project team examines key factors that determine future market demand and pricing for the products of the target. It includes understanding of competitive threats, product and market positioning, and how technology is likely to influence and define products and services to be introduced.

*3. Obtain financial information and data.* At this stage, the project team develops intelligence about the target's financial performance and obtains audited financial statements for the past five years and information not publicly available. This is the first step toward developing an understanding of past performance and reasons for deviations from trends.

*4. Ensure consistency of data and information.* Once the data are obtained, the project team ensures their accuracy and that accounting definitions are consistent through time. Also, the due diligence subteam cross-checks information and validates its definition and accuracy.

*5. Develop the assumption set.* The assumptions and the rationale for assumptions and postulated relationships underlying the creation of financial projections and the interactions among financial variables are developed, checked, tested, validated with external experts, and made explicit.

*6. Perform financial analysis.* The inputs are prepared, checked one more time, and models are simulated in this phase. The financial analyst looks at several ratios produced by the financial model to determine performance of the target company and ensure consistency of financial model outputs with expectations.

*7. Interview key managers, customers, and suppliers.* These interviews are mostly conducted in the due diligence phase. They are intended to obtain closely held information and confidential data, determine customer and supplier relationships, understand company policies and practices toward customers and suppliers, and review major contracts. Interviews with the target firm's customers and suppliers, trade association executives, and the firm's bankers reveal information relative to its past performance, payment practices, future plans, and industry evolution.

*8. Revise financial statements and create projections.* Having completed all these steps, the financial analyst either revises the financial projections obtained from the target company or creates new financial statements that reflect the data and intelligence obtained. The projected financial statements then form the starting point for the fair market valuation of the target.

*9. Value the projected operations.* Using pro forma financial statements, the financial analyst calculates the economic value of the target firm's operations over the forecast period, which is usually five to seven years. This is done under more than one method of valuation to get a sense of the range of possible values.

*10. Value the residual.* A number of techniques can be used to estimate a company's terminal value, the most common being: book value, liquidation value, market multiples value, and income capitalization value. The book value and liquidation value methods are not really forward-looking valuation approaches and are less preferred than the other two methods. The market multiples method applies multiples of comparable companies in the industry to either earnings or cash flow while the income capitalization method discounts net income or cash flow of some forecast period by the discount rate and allows for a number of growth assumptions to be introduced in valuing the residual.

*11. Prepare the project valuation.* In this step, the project team adds the valuation of projected operations and the firm's value in perpetuity, reviews the results of various techniques, and prepares a valuation range to negotiate in. How the ultimate negotiating range is established is a complex process, but a useful starting benchmark is the fair market valuation of the target. It consists of the NPV of the cash flow projections and the residual value of the target, which is the stand-alone shareholder value created by the project.

In addition to developing the stand-alone fair market valuation, the project team prepares for negotiations and determines the price to be paid to close the transaction. The project team is assisted by investment bankers to determine the negotiation price range and goes through the following steps:

1.  Collect data on comparable transactions prices and market premiums and value any intangibles involved.
2.  Develop reasonable cost and benefit projections of expected synergies for the buyer and assess the value of benefits accruing to the seller due to the transaction.
3.  Assess the impact of project risks, evaluate different approaches to allocating and sharing risks, and assess the tax implications of the structured transaction on the seller and the buyer
4.  Add these components to the stand-alone fair market valuation range to obtain the range for price negotiations.

The valuation methodology used for acquisitions is applicable to joint venture valuations as well, the difference being that in joint ventures the market premiums are added only to determine the market value of required partner contributions. Otherwise, the project team follows the same process to assess the value of the joint venture company. This is an important element because the project team calculates the base price at which the company would be willing to sell its interest in the joint venture in the event of venture termination. Also, it needs to understand the price range the partner would expect for the sale of its shares in the joint venture.

### Methods of Fair Market Valuation

Negotiators stick to valuation methods that generate favorable results from their perspective, although several stand-alone fair market valuations are obtained from different methods. Hence, the need to create a range of fair market valuation. Balance sheet-based approaches are passive and do not reflect earning dynamics and economic potential of a target, which determine how much it can earn or return on the investment the buyer can realize from it. Therefore, the project team needs to be prepared with valuations obtained from a number of methods and develops a position in the range of value that defines negotiations.

Some commonly used approaches in the fair market valuation of acquisition and joint venture companies are the following:

*1. Book net worth.* This is a method that does not represent market value, but it is simply the difference between the assets and the liabilities of the firm as shown on its balance sheet. For a newly established firm, the book net worth may be close to the economic value of that firm, but is always used in conjunction with other valuation methods.

*2. Net worth of tangibles.* Under this method, only tangible assets are included in calculations of net worth. Intangibles such as new product development and goodwill are excluded in the initial calculations, but are added in later to bring this valuation result in line with valuations from other methods. This type of valuation is appropriate for projects where the business is related to fixed assets such as, for example, the value of holding company assets or real estate-related operations.

*3. Capitalization of net profit.* Known as the multiplier approach, this method compares the income flows of the firm with other investment opportunities with similar risk profiles. The net profit before taxes is capitalized at a risk-free rate such as the 90-day Treasury Bill rate to adjust for specific risks and other relevant factors.

*4. Discounted cash flow or net income.* Since the late 1980s this is the most commonly used method of valuation. It requires cash flow projections for a number of years in order to calculate the NPV of the cash flows. The value of the firm being appraised is then the sum of the NPV of the projected cash flows and the NPV of the residual.

*5. Price earnings ratio.* This method of valuation begins with the after-tax earnings of the company and applies the price earnings ratio multiplier to calculate the value of the firm. The price earnings ratio used is derived for companies comparable to the one being assessed by first dividing the after-tax earnings by the number of shares to get earnings per share and then dividing the selling share price by this amount. This is a widely accepted valuation method, but it is limited by the project team's ability to find really comparable transactions and does not include market premiums.

*6. Market price to book entry.* The development of an average ratio of market price to book equity of companies in the same industry is the first step in this method. Then, this ratio is applied to the book value of the company being assessed to develop the market value of the firm. This approach is of limited value unless an appropriately selected set of companies is sampled to include in the average market price to book equity ratio.

It is apparent that each method produces a unique valuation for the target or the joint venture company being appraised and these values can be substantially different. Therefore, the project team needs to understand the different values, what is included in each method, and decide which method is most appropriate to determine the target's fair market value. Nonetheless, the entire range of values needs to be considered in preparing for negotiations.

## Terminal Value Calculations

For an ongoing concern, the stand-alone fair market valuation consists of the value of its business plan and the terminal value of the firm. The terminal value determination requires a good understanding of methodology and models involved, the market dynamics, and industry economics and evolution.

For most acquisitions, the liquidation value and the book value approaches are not used because due to their nature, they are static measures that do not incorporate market dynamics. They are also not considered because their validity is limited since the life of the firm assessed is in question beyond the present. Instead, market multiple techniques and income capitalization or discounted cash flow techniques are used to establish the residual value of a firm expected to operate beyond the study horizon. The market multiple techniques are appropriate to use in the case of publicly traded companies; otherwise, the financial analyst must exercise caution when using them. Market multiple techniques commonly used to derive a terminal value are the price to revenue, price to cash flow, and price to earning ratios.

Which market multiple technique is appropriate to use in the residual valuation depends on the nature of the target's operations, comparable firms, and the industry. Factors such as current and expected profitability, future capital requirements, and growth differentials from industry averages are considered to determine which ratio to use. Most industries use market multiples specific to them. For instance, in the oil industry the market equity to the number of barrels of oil reserves ratio is used, while the valuation of a cellular telephone company uses the market capital to some area's population.

Income or discounted cash flow capitalization methods of estimating residual value look at net income or cash flow of the target firm either in the last forecast period or the average of the last three to five forecast periods and discount them by the appropriate discount rate. Ordinarily, no growth is assigned to the residual value because it is generally accepted that in the long run, a company tends to achieve a steady-state growth where competition forces revenue and expense growth to levels that maintain a steady level of profitability. On some occasions, growth is included in the residual value when the industry is expected to experience tremendous growth after the forecast period or when inordinate productivity gains are expected due to new technologies being introduced.

The residual valuation can have an inordinate amount of influence on the determination of the stand-alone fair market valuation and it is an area of concern to the project team and the negotiators. In most cases, professional advice and assistance in valuations is recommended in bringing in that expertise. However, the project team must be aware of the limitations of each technique and use all information available to make adjustments to calculated values. Also, in the case of cash flow capitalizations, the project team examines carefully the proportion of the value due to forecasted operations versus residual value. In all cases, however, the project team needs to use common sense, outside expert advice, and independent review of the fair market valuation range prepared for negotiations.

### Roles of Project Participants

Owning to the complexity of project valuations there is a need for assistance from outside advisors regardless of the expertise that resides within the project team and the business development group of the company. The project team performs the analysis and project assessments required. However, help and advice of investment bankers and outside experts is needed in acquisition price negotiations because of their familiarity with comparable transactions, access to market data and financial ratios of companies in the industry, and their judgment on the validity of reasons to pay market premiums or obtain discounts. The market intelligence that investment bankers bring on the competitive nature of bidding for the target is unique and their ability to determine where the other side stands on the stand-alone fair market valuation, market premiums and discounts, and tax implications makes them indispensable.

The project team is assisted by external advisors in gathering intelligence concerning all aspects of project valuation, assessing the project valuation, passing judgment on it, and using it appropriately. Likewise, the internal independent assessor for the project ensures that the price paid for an acquisition is in line with comparable transactions. This is done by obtaining information from external advisors and help in interpreting market data and financial ratios. Also, the internal independent assessor ensures that the terms and conditions of the purchase agreement are consistent with the tax impacts of the transaction.

The role of the external advisors in an acquisition project is established in clearly articulated terms in the engagement letter. Of course, a number of factors determine the functions that external advisors perform depending on the complexity of the project, the level of expertise residing within the project team, and the experience of senior management with acquisitions. However, a number of standard functions are expected to be performed by investment bankers and external advisors, such as advice on stand-alone fair market valuation methods to be used and analysis of the range of resulting values. Other functions include research on market data, ratios, and market premiums or discounts for comparable industry transactions and assistance in verifying tax impacts of the deal structure and assessing influence on the price to be paid. Other investment banker contributions include intelligence on the process and competitive nature of the bid for the target and preparation of the fairness opinion letter that establishes reasonableness of the transaction and fair value creation.

The role the acquiring company's senior management plays in determining the price to be paid for an acquisition varies a great deal based on personalities involved and level of interest in a given transaction. However, the senior management functions in this area are to:

1.  Develop comfort with the determinants of price and understand the key elements of the bid price to be submitted.
2.  Ensure that the market premiums required to close the transaction are consistent with the company's long-term financial goals.
3.  Determine how expected synergies are shared with the seller and how the seller shares in the risks.
4.  Approve the established range of the bidding price based on the recommendations of the project team, the independent assessor's report, and the investment banker's fairness opinion letter.

While participants in acquisition projects perform specific functions, determining a fair bid price involves a lot of teamwork and it is an integrated approach to decision making. It is only through integration of work performed by the project team, the evaluation of the internal independent assessor, and the expertise of outside advisors and the intelligence they bring that senior management can make informed decisions. The integration responsibility is shared equally by the business development group, the project sponsor, and the project team leader.

## KEY VALUATION CONSIDERATIONS

### Market Premiums

The mechanics used to arrive at the acquisition price involve a complex process requiring specialized knowledge and expertise in negotiating the price for a target company since the fair market valuation only establishes a range of value. Hence, other market influences need to be accounted for because in addition to the fair market valuation, the price paid is determined by expected synergies, market premiums or discounts, tax impacts on the buyer and seller, and the negotiating power of the parties.

There are several reasons for adding premiums to the fair market valuation, which are related to the interests of buyers and sellers of a company. On the other hand, opposite motivation results in discounts over some fair market valuation range and experienced negotiators are acutely aware of these motives. The reasons for adding premiums to the fair market valuation are the following:

*1. Controlling ownership.* This type of premium is due to the buyer's wish to acquire a sufficiently large interest in the target company in order to control all aspects of the company's strategic direction and operations.

*2. Privately held firms.* This premium is paid for closely held companies with no market for their shares and it has to do with the view that the market value of those shares is higher than the book value of the firm's equity. In reality, this may not be true because investments in closely held businesses are virtually locked in.

*3. Sale of target components.* Often, buyers are interested in only part of a company, whereas the seller wants to sell the entire firm. In such cases, premiums are paid over the fair market valuation because sale of a component reduces the price the remainder of the target company can command.

*4. Valuation of intangibles.* When the fair market valuation method excludes the value of the target's intangibles from financial calculations, premiums are paid to account for the value of assets such as trademarks, patents, brand names, etc.

*5. Technical adjustments.* Technical adjustments are used to remove systematic over- or understatements of value. That is, when fair market valuations are consistently biased in one direction, adjustments to correct for those biases are necessary, which amount to market premiums or discounts being applied to fair market valuations.

*6. Objectives of buyer and seller.* Whenever there is a divergence of buyer and seller objectives, market premiums or discounts are used to compensate the party forgoing their objectives. This is an area where negotiation subteams invest time to understand the other side and create objectives opposite to the other party's so that moves toward the other side's objectives are compensated through premiums.

*7. Institutionalized practice.* Market premiums and discounts have a long history in acquisitions in the Western world. By virtue of the widely accepted view that price paid to close the transaction is invariably different than fair market valuation, negotiation parties routinely apply market premiums and discounts to fair market valuations.

*8. Severable intangible assets.* This type of premium is paid when one or more of the intangible assets can be separated from the selling entity and can be acquired along with the target company or a part thereof. Such assets are brand names, trademarks, patents, rights, and franchises.

*9. Customer, employment, and other contracts.* Premiums related to customer and employment contracts are applicable when long-term agreements are in place. The reason for this is that they add stability and predictability to the target company's cash flows. Agreements by the seller not to compete with the buyer in the target company's market also command sizable market premiums.

*10. Improving trends.* In industries characterized by increasing opportunities for growth and improving trends, one should ordinarily expect to pay a premium over fair market valuation. This, however, must be examined in the context of financial projections because improving trends are reflected in the market forecasts underlying the target's financial projections and in the fair market valuation.

*11. Tax considerations.* This premium is related to the approach used by the acquiring company in assigning values to different income items and depreciable assets. That is, a premium is paid when certain tax consequences result from the price allocation used. Premiums paid for tax considerations are directly related to the cost and benefits accruing to the seller and buyer of a company.

*12. Acquisition type.* Premiums are involved when the type of acquisition desired by the buyer is different than the offer of the seller. For an acquisition of assets to be effected, the fair market valuation may need to be enhanced to induce the seller to absorb the liabilities of the company being sold.

It is apparent that market premiums and discounts can be argued for and are always present in the determination of price to be paid. However, the magnitude and terms of payment for the premiums or the form in which discounts take place is subject to negotiations. Premium-related risks should be part of negotiations in order to reduce their magnitude by tying premiums to performance and expected outcomes as much as possible and continuously look for applicable discounts after understanding the benefits accruing to the other side.

### Valuation of Synergies

Our view is that synergies present in an acquisition rightfully belong to the acquiring company and the negotiations subteam should press this point. The seller will undoubtedly argue that it is the sale of the target that creates synergies and, therefore, the seller is entitled to share in them. The outcome is negotiated somewhere in the middle. For that reason, the implementation subteam must conduct a thorough investigation into the identification and quantification of expected synergies and the cost and likelihood of obtaining synergies to determine their value and how that value will be shared with the seller.

Cost savings in areas of R&D, product development, and operations and investment synergies are the first areas that need to be examined by the implementation subteam followed by revenue and other financial synergies. Synergies related to cost savings expectations must be verified against the business plan of the new entity, which includes additional expenses for implementation and expenses associated with consolidation of operations, such as severance pay and early retirement incentives.

Expected investment synergies are checked against capital requirements of the new entity's business plan and any financial synergies such as risk reduction and tax advantages should be thoroughly investigated and assessed in the due diligence. In the case of expected revenue synergies, the implementation subteam should demonstrate their existence and assess the benefit of realizing synergies. In all cases, however, the project team must ensure that synergy extraction and realization are not allowed to cannibalize the long-term viability of the acquired firm or the joint venture company.

### Acquisition Tax Impacts

The acquisition structure tax impacts play an important role in determining the price required to close the transaction. The gain or loss realized in a transaction has present tax consequences if certain IRS requirements are met to qualify an acquisition as a reorganization. Consequently, acquisition structures attempt to produce a new cost basis for the assets of the target company or to leave the tax basis of these assets unchanged. Asset acquisitions, stock acquisitions, and section 338 transactions are taxable acquisitions, whereas various types of reorganizations are non-taxable transactions because

---

*A 338 transaction is one where the acquiring company purchases within a year 80 percent of all shares and then elects to treat the transaction as if the target company's assets were sold to a new corporation at a price equal to the stock acquisition price.*

shareholders of the seller company are only changing the form of their investment or exchanging stock in one entity for stock in another.

In the case of an asset acquisition, the tax basis of the assets acquired, allocation of the purchase price to various assets, carry-over tax attributes, and investment tax credits determine how the buying company is treated and the impact on the target firm. To assess the tax consequences of a stock acquisition, the analysis needs to consider the purchase price, the recognition of gain or loss on the sale of assets, who pays the tax owed by the target, and the effect of liquidation of the target. As with other determinants of the acquisition price, the complexity of issues involved in determining tax consequences makes the help of legal tax experts and investment bankers necessary.

The discussion of tax impacts has thus far been limited to different acquisition types. However, there are tax consequences associated with different structures of joint venture companies as well. The tax status of joint venture companies varies significantly around the world and these differences produce widely different tax impacts. Here, the advice and guidance of legal tax experts is invaluable in structuring the most advantageous joint venture entity from a tax-impact perspective.

### Project Valuation Risks

Risks associated with project valuations have to do with the realization of expected conditions that led to premiums attached to the fair market valuation. These risks are real and are introduced by the negotiation subteam into the calculation of premiums. For example, even in the growing phase of an industry, expectations of continued growth need to be tampered by the risk that the maturing phase or decline may set in sometime after closing. Synergy premiums need to incorporate risks of expected synergies not being realized for a variety of reasons or realized with higher expenses, investment, and effort.

Project risks impact the stand-alone fair market value of a project through the acquired firm's business plan financials and need to be accounted for in that calculation. Usual approaches of including risk impacts in the project NPV are to raise the discount rate used in the financial analysis and valuation or follow a conservative approach in projecting financials and calculating residual value. They also include developing a project NPV weighted by probabilities of risk occurrence or incorporating the cost of developing and executing a risk management plan.

It is important that risk-related offsets are introduced in the negotiation process to negotiate a reduction in premiums, allocate risks to both parties in the project, and have the seller share the burden. Handling project valuation risks entails pursuing a prudent and multifaceted approach that produces conservative, but well-balanced financial projections and valuations that include all costs and benefits to the buyer and estimates benefits accruing to the seller due to the transaction. It may also entail allocating the new entity's business plan risks to both parties through the use of legal agreements, tying payment of synergy premiums to the value of synergies created, and earn-out formulas. However, it should provide incentives to induce the seller to share project risks.

## DETERMINING THE ACQUISITION PRICE

For an outsider to the acquisition processes and mechanics, determination of the acquisition price to close the transaction is an ad-hoc and confusing approach conducted under short time lines. Yet, as shown in Figure 15.1, there is order to the process and a sequence of steps involved to arrive at the acquisition price. The same approach is used in determining the value of a joint venture project and the price to be paid to acquire a partner's share in the joint venture.

**Figure 15.1**
**The Process of Determining the Acquisition Price**

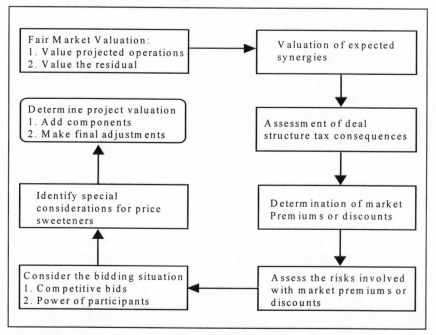

*1. Fair market valuation.* This step produces the starting range of value for the target on a stand-alone basis, which is the foundation upon which the negotiations subteam builds the price to be paid. For this step to be useful, the project team ensures that the stand-alone valuation range is defined by the least and most beneficial methods so that agreement can be reached somewhere in the identified range.

*2. Synergy quantification.* It is important to ensure that if synergies are included in the project valuation, they should be net synergies. That is, additional investments required and the cost of harnessing synergies need to be subtracted from expected benefits. Also, the project team needs to take a probabilistic view of being able to achieve expected net synergies, negotiate how they are to be shared between seller and buyer, and then add that synergy value to the fair market valuation range.

*3. Assessment of tax consequences.* The tax consequences of the acquisition deal structure are evaluated to determine how the parties benefit by a particular structure and how costs and benefits are shared. In this step, the value of tax savings determines the extent to which leverages are created for the buyer and seller and how large an addition or subtraction should be made from the value which includes the fair market value plus expected synergies.

*4. Market premiums and discounts.* At this stage, appropriate market premiums or discounts are determined and included in the value of step (3), which is the fair market value range adjusted by expected synergies and tax consequences. Attention is drawn not only to the company's operations within the industry, but also to comparable transactions and the industry of the target.

*5. Bidding situation.* The competitive nature of bidding for the target and the strategic importance of the acquisition are additional elements that enter the calculation of the valuation adjustment, which already includes market premiums or discounts. However, keep this adjustment to a minimum and do not pass much of the acquisition value to the seller simply because someone else may be willing to pay a higher price.

*6. Special considerations.* Unusual circumstances must be weighed carefully, but there are specific factors, which the buyer is willing to consider to enhance the bid price. For instance, in leveraged buyouts or foreign acquisitions for strategic purposes, the project team may view price sweeteners as a small cost to pay in order to achieve broader company objectives.

Once negotiation subteams have identified the components of the acquisition price, discussions center on how to close the valuations gap and determine the price to be paid to close the transaction. Often, if there are substantial differences in the valuations of the target, negotiations move from deadlocked positions through earn-out formulas whereby a certain price is agreed to under the condition that other terms are met. This, however, assumes that there is leftover value for the buyer to share with the seller.

## SUMMARY

The discussion of this chapter centers around project valuation because of its central role in opportunity assessment, quantification of synergies, preparation for negotiations, assessment of negotiated terms and conditions, and determination of the price required to close the transaction. The price paid to close the deal also determines project financeability, project economics, and shareholder value created. Hence, the central role of project valuation in corporate reviews and approvals.

The steps in the fair market valuation process are discussed to understand what is involved in coming up with a price range and the various valuation methods of a company's operations are reviewed. Here we note that each valuation method produces a different valuation, which is applicable under different circumstances. The valuation of a firm's productive capacity and operations beyond the forecast period are the subject of terminal value calculation discussion and extensive use of investment banker's expertise is recommended.

Market premiums are important in determining the price to close a transaction as are acquisition tax impacts and the benefits to buyer and seller. The issue of risks associated with valuations is introduced and we recommend bringing the risks into premium negotiations, which involve the seller in sharing those risks. The roles of project participants in the valuation process are discussed and we note that the price required to close the deal is subject to negotiation and is heavily influenced by how badly the parties want to complete the transaction.

# 16

---

# CHALLENGES OF
# INTERNATIONAL PROJECTS

## INTRODUCTION

International acquisitions and joint ventures, especially those in emerging countries, are undertaken with expectations of higher returns on investment for the higher risk involved and for participation in the local market growth. The basic principles of doing acquisitions and joint ventures apply equally well to international projects, but so far the discussion has centered around domestic projects where the rules of engagement are well established and known to participants. However, foreign projects present some peculiarities that project teams needs to understand. These special considerations motivate the discussion because they impact the project team's ability to execute projects successfully in emerging countries.

The execution of acquisition and joint venture projects in developing countries involves elements that are either new or different than domestic practices, and to be effective, the project team should familiarize itself with international project peculiarities. For instance, the project assessment, negotiation, and implementation processes are often not understood in developing countries where the main objective is to extract as much as possible out of the project immediately, with limited concern about the project's future. Also, financial and marketing concepts are not fully appreciated. Regardless of whether the process is understood, it is much longer and more complicated because decision making is a bureaucratic activity involving many organizations.

The significance of international project peculiarities is that they tend to distract and take the focus off issues that matter the most. Faced with many twists and turns in the process of doing a project, project teams not familiar with doing foreign projects are discouraged and pull out of projects prematurely. On the other hand, engaging in a project without understanding how things get done in developing countries results in the project team being engaged for a long time in marginal projects that do not have much upside potential for the company.

The discussion in this chapter centers around doing projects in developing countries because that is where the differences are most pronounced. We begin with a review of preparations necessary for foreign projects with emphasis on understanding the host country's legal and regulatory environment. Then, we discuss environmental analysis elements and their importance in determining whether to proceed with the project. Unique elements in project selection and due diligence in foreign projects are discussed with emphasis on strategic considerations and legal and regulatory issues, respectively.

Managing foreign cultures requires knowledge of the local character, the way of doing business in the host country, and ability to communicate with local project participants. Project negotiations in foreign acquisitions and joint ventures are far more interesting and complex because they involve many considerations not present in domestic projects. These topics are discussed along with participant contributions, expectations, and the need to manage both effectively.

The governance structure in foreign projects is crucial in project success and it is discussed before project risks, which in many cases come down to two considerations: ability to enforce legal agreements and ability to convert profits to hard currencies and profit repatriation. Foreign projects require using advisors and agents who are instrumental in getting projects done, but can create situations of conflict with U.S. laws. In concluding the chapter, we discuss this sensitive issue and offer recommendations.


## EMPHASIS ON EARLY ASSESSMENTS

### Preparation for Foreign Projects

Chapter 5 deals with issues around preparation for acquisition and joint venture projects, but does not discuss the special considerations associated with doing international projects, which the project team should understand to execute projects successfully. The first step to prepare for doing a project in a foreign country is to become acquainted with the basic elements of the foreign culture: that is, with that country's history, geography, dominant religions, natural resources and industry, educational standards, legal system, political system, government structure, and regulatory agencies. A good source of this type of information is the series of country profiles produced by the U.S. Department of State or the CIA country descriptions.

Once the project team is exposed to basic knowledge about the country, a two-to-three-day, high-quality cultural training program for the project team is advisable. The reason for this is to develop appreciation of cultural idiosyncrasies of the host country, understand what appearances mean, and the sensitivities and consider the key motives of the local party. While cultural training may not be that important for developed countries, it is essential in the case of emerging countries because in most instances, although those countries have little wealth, they have lots of national pride.

With basic country knowledge and cultural sensitivity training behind, the project team researches the host country business law, the rules and regulations applicable to the industry of interest, and various tax codes. The most reliable sources of information about these issues are the U.S. Department of State and the Commerce Department. Most of the time, doing foreign projects requires hiring local advisors and agents and the project team should obtain advice on hiring and using agents, consultants, and brokers from the U.S. Embassy in the host country. No project should be undertaken in developing countries before discussions and advice have been obtained from experienced advisors.

The reason input and advice obtained from experienced advisors is so important is to understand local business practices and potential conflicts with U.S. laws. In addition, the project team should use the host country's embassy information center in the U.S., research the foreign government makes available, and various investment promotion and incentive programs.

Preparation for international projects involves performing a thorough environmental due diligence before the project begins with focus on major issues that make a difference. In addition to using U.S. and host government resources to understand the operating environment and hiring local advisors and agents, it is a good idea for the project team to hire its own interpreter. This is necessary to understand what foreign participants are saying because a hired interpreter will also translate for the project team the entire meaning, not only the words spoken.

### Environmental Assessment

Environmental assessment for international acquisitions and joint ventures takes on a much greater significance in assessing the likelihood of successful operations. It is a kind of due diligence undertaken before the project begins to determine how risk factors related to the operating environment impact the project viability. The first factor to be investigated is the legal framework in the foreign country and the enforcement of legal agreements. The legal status of different types of companies and the pros and cons should be evaluated under the assumption of a long-term presence in the foreign country. The treatment of intellectual property is another consideration as is payment of royalties for licensed products or processes. These are particularly important in emerging countries where business law is still being developed, intellectual property rights and legal agreements are often violated, and contract enforceability is an issue.

If satisfied that the legal framework is adequate and contract enforceability does not present a problem, the project team looks at the business environment in that country to determine whether the way of doing business and common practices in that country are not going to create problems in terms of conflicts with U.S. laws and regulations; potential conflicts with local laws, rules, and regulations; violation of company codes of conduct; and compromising ethical standards of individual managers. After this test, living conditions in the foreign country are assessed to determine how difficult it will be to staff key positions with ex-patriate assignments.

Host country macro-economic conditions are examined by a professional to determine the impact of major macro-variables on the new-entity operations. Past and forecast growth of the economy and its sectors, price inflation and wage adjustments, import duties and other controls, and currency convertibility and foreign exchange rates are analyzed and potential risks and impacts on a project are evaluated. This also includes an assessment of tax laws, tax holidays, foreign investment incentives, and foreign exchange controls because of their impact on project economics and repatriation of profits.

The industry structure, competition, and the health of the industry under consideration in the foreign country are examined to understand the players and determine the source of competitive advantage of individual participants in that market. The demand for the product line envisioned and the market conditions are examined because it does not always follow that because products have done well in one country they will necessarily do well in another country. Also, the industry's regulatory agencies, rules and regulations, and their enforceability need to be understood to avoid unpleasant surprises in the future.

The most important element of environmental assessment is identification of the foreign government's objectives for the industry and its performance expectations of new entrants, especially foreign companies. These are crucial considerations in projects that involve either a joint venture with an agency of the foreign government or participation in the privatization of a government-owned company. In these cases, the views of the government on competition and the use of exclusivity are important in determining project success.

### Project Selection Considerations

In domestic acquisitions and joint ventures, a few selection criteria are applied consistently to projects, such as strategic fit, value created by the project, and ability to implement so as to harness expected synergies. International projects are undertaken with the expectation of higher returns on investment and participation in the local market growth, but emerging country projects entail additional considerations in the decision to undertake them. The first of these considerations is whether the project team can develop clarity of purpose and project objectives and maintain continuity of purpose in the midst of a changing foreign environment and rules.

Strategic and operational fit criteria are important in foreign projects, but the long-term, market share considerations and the likelihood of success need to be assessed in light of uncertainties in the operating environment. The stability of the foreign government and political support for the project need to be established at the start of the process. The reason for this is that in developing countries governments change frequently and unless there is broad political support for the project, the project is destined to fail because of roadblocks raised after the government that approved the project is not in power.

It is important that the foreign government agency reviewing the project be shown the benefits and that they be demonstrated to local project participants and the country. It is equally important to identify correctly the government's motives in the project and its expectations concerning hard-currency investment levels, technology transfer, local production and procurement, and performance obligations. All these considerations enter the decision criteria set because they impact project economics and the project team's ability to execute the project.

The ease of project implementation is a bigger issue in foreign projects in developing countries because of complicated host country government approval processes, difficulties in hiring qualified management talent and skilled labor, and high costs of ex-patriate assignments. The issue of ease of project implementation, especially related to living conditions in the host country and the cost of ex-patriate assignments, needs to be considered along with other criteria for project selection.

The concept of an exclusive operating license must be tested extensively to understand the definition of exclusivity by foreign participants. Exclusivity rights must be clarified and the length of the contractual agreements verified and tested repeatedly before assuming that they have the same meaning as in the U.S. or other developed countries. These definitions should be included in the decision criteria set, which needs to be viewed in its totality when selecting a project in a developing country. The project team also needs to understand the local project participants' views on the project and the value of the entity at the license or contractual arrangement expiration.

Owing to complexities in the decision-making process for foreign projects, it is recommended that the project team leader spend time with advisors in the host country. The reason for this meeting is to discuss the project with knowledgeable people who can be trusted, obtain input and feedback, ask for their perspective on issues surrounding the environment, and take their advice on the key factors that determine project success in the host country and their view of the project and likelihood of success. Also, advice should be solicited on the project and country risks over the project's expected life and the use of local agents and advisors.

A helpful approach in doing foreign projects is to take an evolutionary approach to the project, establish limited presence, and then leverage the established presence. Often, this approach produces good projects and minimizes project and country risk exposure. At the same time, it gives foreign project participants an opportunity to determine whether the project is indeed delivering the expected benefits. On the negative side, the foreign partner could base the decision to go with a different project simply because of a larger commitment by another party. We believe that most of the time this is a risk worth taking.

## IDIOSYNCRASIES OF INTERNATIONAL PROJECTS

### Due Diligence

The due diligence effort in a foreign country project starts earlier than in domestic projects. It actually begins before the project is fully developed and its scope defined by assessing the stability of the host country's national government. That is followed by verification of the functioning of the country's business laws and the local parties' ability to deliver on promised items. Special attention is given to the validation of project financials first because their definition may be different than in the U.S. or because true figures may be hidden or difficult to obtain. If financials are missing entirely, there should be no further discussion unless sufficient intelligence is generated through trusted local advisors to close data gaps.

The due diligence subteam for foreign projects includes the project team leader, a technical expert, the financial analyst, a seasoned lawyer, and foreign agent or advisor, and the interpreter hired by the project team. All areas traditionally covered in domestic due diligence need to be covered, but the scope of this effort is broader and requires specialized expertise. The enlarged due diligence effort includes determining the scope of the permits obtained, the rights and obligations of operating licenses, and the length and exclusivity of negotiated agreements. Second, it determines to what extent and at what costs compliance with labor law requirements and social fund contributions can be achieved and if various tax laws, tax holidays on foreign investments, and import restrictions and duties on capital goods apply.

The ability to convert local currency profits to hard currencies and repatriate profits generated in the host country —as opposed to reinvesting profits in the local entity— is investigated along with export requirements or restrictions on output produced, countertrade, and offset purchase requirements, technology transfer, local production, and purchase requirements. In addition, the foreign government social goals and objectives and performance requirements of the entity and the ability to enforce negotiated agreements and contracts when conditions change against the local parties are evaluated.

In addition to determining the project team's ability to obtain expected synergies and strategic returns on investment, the due diligence subteam must assess the reasonableness of the project, given the peculiarities of the foreign country's laws and expectations and requirements of the local parties. To arrive at that, the due diligence subteam identifies the project and country risks, examines those risks, and assesses the likelihood of occurrence.

### Managing Cultural Differences

In order to manage projects in different cultures, the project team needs to understand them and identify and deal with cultural barriers. In some cases, language is viewed as a barrier, but it is not really because most business is transacted in English and when it is not, the project team should use its own interpreter, and not allow discussions in the foreign language during business meetings. After hours, discussions in the foreign language could be helpful in developing personal relationships, but as a rule not while conducting a business meeting.

Differences in how other people view the role of businesses, social responsibilities of companies, and how others approach work and their work sensibilities often create communication barriers. However, once differences are understood and accepted for what they are, barriers come down. Here, a lot of emphasis is placed on personal relationships and connections with local project participants from high-level government officials to technical experts. Without personal relationships, executing a project becomes painfully difficult.

Technology and systems cannot be transplanted instantaneously to foreign countries. Hence, it is important to negotiate that technology needs will be transferred over time and systems adapted to local environments and requirements. The project team needs to be aware that there is resistance in developing countries to external influences and for that reason, transplanting company cultures and practices may not occur until local participants are convinced of their value. In some cultures, it takes longer to make decisions and this needs to be understood and accepted as a fact of life and part of the process.

The decision-making process takes on various forms in different cultures. In some countries, there is a well-defined approach in making decisions while in other cultures decision making is done at top levels. Regardless of how decisions are made in the foreign country, the project team must state the company's intent in clear and precise terms so that there is no uncertainty, and since some cultures have a low degree of tolerance for risk and ambiguity, clarity of signals is important.

In Western countries, there is a tendency for the initiating party to lead the discussions, which is carried over to discussions with foreign project participants. This ordinarily raises suspicion and is viewed as an attempt to obtain control even before projects are concluded. For that reason, the project team should move cautiously and let the local party lead the discussions while it is assessing what is being offered.

### Project Negotiations

Business dealings and negotiations in the U.S. are governed by complex laws, rules, and regulations and there is a tendency for project teams to use the same approach to acquisition and joint venture negotiations internationally. Presence of lawyers in the pre-agreement phases and a legalistic approach to doing projects creates suspicion and distrust and makes negotiations more difficult. Hence, the lawyer assigned to the project should operate behind the scenes in the early phases of the project.

As with other negotiations, foreign acquisition and joint venture project negotiations require that the project team knows what it wants to get out of the project, what it is willing to contribute, and what the local party needs to give in order to make the project a success. The difference with foreign project negotiations is that the project team should expect repeated setbacks and unusual developments and prepare for long, drawn-out negotiations. Also, negotiation approaches and styles may be different than in developed countries where information is standardized and the negotiation process follows unwritten, yet well-understood rules of conduct.

Negotiations in foreign projects take a long time to complete for a number of delay factors, such as the fact that the local project participants need time to understand what is being presented and the decision-making process takes longer than in the U.S. business world. Ordinarily, foreign government approvals are required prior to entering into negotiations and since the level of trust toward outsiders may be low, the foreign side may be moving cautiously through the process. Also, foreign participants' requirements are often outside the experience set of the negotiation subteam and working with interpreters more than doubles the time it would take. More importantly, long negotiations are to the foreign participants' advantage by wearing down the negotiations subteam, which wants to close negotiations as soon as possible and head home.

It is important to understand costs and benefits to the local side, even for less tangible things such as changing the name of a local company to a new name or offering technical advice to the local participants. The negotiation subteam needs to understand the value of national goals and aspirations, national security concerns, and political considerations. This is particularly important if the project involves a foreign government agency as a joint venture partner or the privatization of a company serving an important function, such as power generation or telecommunications.

The advice concerning foreign project negotiations is to expect and prepare for long negotiations, but show understanding and patience. Let the local party lead the discussions, but stay firm on developed positions and persevere. Respect the local culture, the approach and operating styles, and avoid confrontations. Treat people with respect, regardless of level or function and display trust so that relationships can develop through time spent after business hours. Instead of the negotiation subteam spending evenings by itself, share dinner and drinks with local participants at the conclusion of daily business. The more time and effort invested in personal relationships, the easier negotiations become and their conclusion far quicker.

All business is conducted in English with company-hired interpreters who understand Western business concepts. Besides bringing value to the table, the negotiation subteam needs to keep demonstrating benefits accruing to the other side by doing the proposed project under the offer at hand. It is important to remember that people are motivated by the same considerations, but needs may differ and it may be necessary to educate the other side. Insist on win-win arrangements, but be prepared to walk out when in doubt of the foreign participants' ability to deliver the agreed-upon terms.

A common practice in emerging countries is changing the composition of their negotiation subteam. Due to government changes, political agenda changes, changes in government agency responsibilities, legal structure evolution, or by design, new individuals are brought in the negotiations. This lengthens and complicates negotiations, additional time is required to bring new participants up to speed, new relationships must be created, and items negotiated with individuals no longer on the foreign team are not recognized. Therefore, the project team is advised to formalize understandings and agreements in written documents when certain milestones are achieved in the negotiations.

In acquisitions and joint ventures in emerging countries it is crucial that negotiated terms and conditions can be enforced and implemented. Terms of the contract and duration of the arrangement should be clarified and verified repeatedly to ensure no misunderstandings. Also, the negotiated agreement should include the method and process of project valuation at the end of the time horizon. In addition, it should contain termination and escape clauses to allow the company to exit the contract if expectations on either side are not met.

### Contributions and Expectations

Two important elements in foreign acquisitions and joint ventures that need to be clarified and verified are contributions of each participating entity and expectations of the other side. Failure to understand either one leads to conflicts, long delays, and eventual project failure. Therefore, it is a good idea to start a project by first having a clear understanding of what the company is willing to contribute and what it expects to get from the project. Then, communicate the company's views and obtain a similar understanding of the position of the foreign project participants.

The project team begins the evaluation of the foreign side's contributions in the personnel area. It examines the number and qualifications of individuals to be seconded to the entity being created. In the case of acquisitions, it needs to find out what the expectations are concerning retention of the target's management team and in the case of a joint venture, the number of individuals to be seconded to the new entity and their skills and qualifications. Expectations concerning present cash investments and in-kind contributions to be made by participants should be stated clearly and agreement obtained on the methodology to value in-kind contributions and patents, licenses and permits brought to the project. Furthermore, expectations concerning the local participant's ability to meet future capital calls need to be checked.

The earlier the expectations of foreign project participants are assessed concerning hard-currency investments, local content requirements, and technology transfers, the better. Issues such as export requirements of goods produced in the host country, countertrade expectations, and local purchases tied to the contract need to be identified and their impact on project financials assessed. When dealing with foreign government entities, it is essential to identify at the beginning government expectations related to performance levels and obligations of the new entity.

The project team's assumptions surrounding distribution of profits versus reinvestment in the entity must be verified along with currency convertibility, foreign exchange controls, and profit repatriation. In every project undertaken in developing countries, the project team should ensure that foreign project participant expectations are conditioned and managed appropriately through effective use of local agents and obtaining political support for the project. When the project team is unable to deliver the right messages to foreign project participants effectively, it is a good idea to use the bankers involved in the financing to deliver desired messages.

## INSTRUMENTS TO ENSURE PROJECT SUCCESS

### Organizational Structure Considerations

The governance structure of entities created by foreign projects is far more important than for domestic projects because in addition to setting strategic direction for the new entity operations, it plays an important role in the control issue, which is accentuated by distance. The composition of the new-entity board of directors is given special attention to ensure adequate representation regardless of share of ownership in it. Therefore, the steering committee is involved in the screening and selection of board of directors members even when the government of the foreign country is involved and nominates or appoints individuals.

The steering committee is involved in the creation of the new entity's organizational structure and staffing of key management positions as well. It is customary for the head of marketing, the chief financial officer (or treasurer), and the technical director to come from the company's management ranks and the other functional areas to be staffed by local personnel. Also, the steering committee monitors staffing of positions to preclude hiring of relatives and friends of the personnel director, ensure that qualified local talent is hired, and prevent abuses in hiring practices. In addition, it watches the wage and salary escalation in order to keep the new entity competitive not only within the host country, but in export markets as well.

The steering committee and the liaison subteam examine ex-patriate assignments versus local personnel deployment and balance project participant interests in light of the need to provide sufficient company representation throughout the new entity with highly qualified managers and the living conditions in the foreign country, especially living quarters and health care facilities. They consider incentives to be given to experienced managers to attract them to an assignment in an emerging country, the cost of the ex-patriate assignment given the significant wage and benefit difference with hiring local managers, and the need to satisfy local hiring requirements and give the new entity local character.

Next on the steering committee's responsibility set is the development of the new entity's strategy and outlining the operational setup and direction. The business definition of the new entity is created according to company project objectives and negotiated terms in legal agreements. The strategy of the new entity should be consistent with the company's strategy and created so that it promotes its interests, taking into account local interests and requirements. The scope and direction of operations is defined carefully in the negotiations and implemented accordingly.

Once legal agreements have been signed, project implementation begins and extensive involvement by the project team in foreign projects winds down mostly because of the foreign travel expenses. At that point, the company's liaison subteam represents the company and its major role is to ensure that project objectives are met and the company's interests protected. Because of reliance on the steering committee and the liaison subteam to ensure results, it is important to select seasoned managers for these positions who, as agents of change, also have the cultural sensitivity needed in foreign projects.

### Risks in Foreign Projects

Risks in acquisitions and joint ventures in emerging countries are a key screening criterion and determinant of value. Consequently, identification of project and country risks, likelihood of occurrence and quantification of impacts, and creation of risk management plans have a central role in the assessment of value created by a foreign project. In many instances, some identified risks do not lend themselves to quantification of impacts. For those cases, it is recommended that the risk be listed along with a potential impact statement in different areas such as, for example, ability to control the course of the new entity's strategy evolution, project implementation, and ability to harness expected synergies. This provides a basis for qualitative adjustments to project value.

Risks present in acquisitions and joint ventures in emerging countries, which consistently result in poor projects and require appropriate attention involve the following:

1. Absence of a governance structure that balances company interests with those of foreign project participants, which results in a strategy being tilted toward the objectives of foreign participants being realized.
2. Divergence of strategy, goals, and objectives of the new entity from those envisioned by the project team, which is reflected in the new-entity business plan. When this occurs, the negotiation subteam insists on safeguards around formulation and execution of new entity strategy consistent with company strategy and objectives.
3. Failure to manage the newly created entity to ensure targeted operational performance, quality control, and meeting the business plan objectives results in poor operational results and eventual sale to local participants.
4. The project team is unable to manage cultural differences sufficiently and conflicts may arise after signing of legal agreements, which make project implementation difficult, if not impossible.
5. Inability to enforce legal agreements. If this is determined early in the process, complete withdrawal from the project is recommended, but if the project team fails to determine this risk before implementation begins, it will cause the interests of the company to be compromised and the project value to decline.
6. Facing an inflexible regulatory environment that requires unreasonable performance criteria, prevents the new entity from pursuing planned activities, and sets prices and wages at uncompetitive levels.
7. Unreasonable foreign participant positions. This becomes a problem after project implementation and invariably results in value being shifted to local project participants. On some occasions, unreasonable positions are related to government requirements and can result in the project being terminated or interest in the new entity sold off.
8. Cancellation of operating licenses. While this is rare, it happens when stringent local government requirements are not met and results in termination of operations. Threat of cancellation of an operating license results in additional burdens being placed on the new entity, which decrease project value.
9. Reneging on exclusivity arrangements is not an unusual occurrence in projects in emerging countries and is usually related to false assumptions on exclusivity because of large investment requirements and little appreciation of foreign government objectives related to competition. Termination of exclusivity occurs when foreign project participants believe that excessive project value was given to the company, or when competitors are offering better terms and increased value to the local project participants.
10. Local competitors are given preferential treatment. When this happens, the new entity's management team needs to remedy the situation with whatever means are

required. If the new entity is meeting the terms of the agreements, but is systematically discriminated against, the steering committee may want to rethink the governance structure or even participation in the new entity.

11. Inability to import required technology. This does not happen frequently, but when it does, it results in paying exorbitant import duties, which impact project value. Inability to export high-tech equipment to hostile countries causes a change in the technology used or the project being terminated.

12. Technology transfer, local production to export, and local content requirements. These risks are real, but they are usually negotiated to acceptable levels. When technology transfer requirements are placed on proprietary processes and patents, the decision has to be made whether to terminate arrangements or obtain for offsetting compensation.

13. Misinterpretation or biased market research results. This occurs frequently, overstates project revenues significantly, and results in poor project performance.

14. Inability of qualified ex-patriates to get accustomed to local living conditions. Occurrence of this risk is frequent and it results in short assignments, frequent travel, and extended stays outside the host country. It also decreases the project value and causes difficulties in meeting operational performance targets.

From the discussion thus far, the need for risk management plans is apparent. To help the effectiveness of decision making, the project team uses sensitivity analysis and scenario assessment extensively to show the range of possible outcomes. In high-risk foreign projects, it is a good idea to develop a probabilistic NPV range for the project that takes into account the likelihood of risk occurrence and associated impacts. Because of their understanding of the local markets and various local players, obtaining input of experienced advisors in identifying risks, evaluating impacts, and developing risk management plans is essential.

### Financing International Projects

Financing of foreign acquisitions and joint ventures is more complex than domestic projects, especially for emerging country projects. This is because additional environmental factors are impacting the ability to execute the project successfully, there are increased project risks and uncertainty, the legal infrastructure may be partially developed, and contract enforceability may be an issue. In addition, impaired credit worthiness of foreign participants and inability to share project risks, or provide guarantees, necessitate involvement of third parties such as development banks. However, financial performance requirements may take second place to foreign government needs, political risks are high, and increased commercial risks continuously challenge the project team's ability to bring external financing to these projects.

The first step toward ensuring successful external financing for a foreign project is assessing the company's contributions and ability or willingness to provide guarantees in the project to cover the foreign project participants' share of risks. The next step is to engage a financing advisor, if the project involves third-party financing or off-balance-sheet financing. If the financing required is in excess of 100 to 150 million U.S. dollars, engagement of an independent project financing advisor to develop the financing strategy and execute the financing plan is recommended. Otherwise, investment bankers in the project can arrange the financing.

Engaging a seasoned project financing advisor with extensive experience in doing projects in emerging countries is essential; otherwise, the project is destined for long delays and possible failure. There are several reasons for engaging a seasoned financing advisor, the most important being:

1.  Understanding the needs of emerging countries, the process involved in bringing financing to credit-impaired countries, and what they can offer to get financing. Also, having ability to relate to foreign project participants in terms of project financing requirements they can appreciate.
2.  Contacts in regional development banks and funding institutions, export credit agencies, and unilateral and multilateral institutions and strong personal relationships in commercial banks, investment firms, insurance companies, and other financing institutions and individual investors.
3.  Guiding the project team through negotiations as they relate to risk sharing and financing agreements and countering the view in emerging countries that outside companies have the resources to help the local entity develop by providing financing support.
4.  Expertise in competitive sourcing, obtaining supplier financing, and shifting the burden to major suppliers in the project who may wish to establish local operations in the host country.
5.  Bringing independent assessment and the best financing approach under the constraint of balancing the interests of local participants while protecting company interests.

Key to successful foreign project financing are risk allocation and sharing, equity raising, and loan agreements for the project. The project team needs to be involved throughout the process, review financing plans with the financing advisor, and ensure no undue risk sharing is imposed and that the company interests are protected in every clause of the agreements. It is also a good idea to work with the financing advisor to develop a clear process for financing implementation and create systems to produce the required documentation to satisfy debt and equity contributors. Under no circumstances should the project team agree to take on local project participant risks in order to get the project done, unless there is offsetting compensation, project financials justify it, and there are overriding strategic considerations.

### Use of Local Agents and Advisors

Acquisition and joint venture projects in foreign countries require use of local agents and advisors in addition to investment bankers, due diligence experts, and external functional experts and consultants. The engagement of local agents and advisors is expensive even in emerging countries because without them, the chances of outside companies doing the project effectively on their own are nil. On the other hand, local agents and advisors perform some important functions, but the project team must direct their effort toward realizing the company's objectives.

The first function local agents and advisors perform is to guide the project team through the maze of foreign laws, rules and regulation, and business practices. Therefore, it is necessary that the project team work closely with local agents and advisors. The second major function performed is to communicate the objectives of the company and the project benefits to local participants in terms they can relate to, and the third one is to influence decision makers in the host country through their contacts and connections. Another valuable service agents and advisors provide is getting insights on what local participants value and helping the negotiation subteam obtain favorable terms and conditions.

The project team should look to local agents and advisors to help understand the sensitivities of the local project participants and, more importantly, to prevent the project from being undermined by competitors. However, for the project team to rely on local agents and advisors, they must be competent and trusted. For that reason, it is important to screen the credentials of local agents and advisors carefully, use only reputable agents with a good track record, and define their activities carefully. When possible, negotiate fees according to success in negotiating desired key terms and conditions, and monitor agent and advisor activities to ensure compliance with U.S. laws and company policies.

## SUMMARY

The execution of foreign acquisitions and joint ventures involves the processes in doing domestic projects plus some challenges that the project team needs to understand and prepare for prior to undertaking an international project. These challenges include ignorance of basic finance and market concepts on the part of foreign participants, longer time frames to do projects, need for careful assessment, different negotiation approaches, a distorted view of costs and benefits, and unenforceable legal agreements.

This chapter emphasizes project team preparation to do the project in an emerging country, starting with cultural training and exposure to different business practices. The elements of environmental assessments are discussed and attention is given to project screening and additional criteria involved in the selection process. In international projects, early due diligence is crucial to assess project feasibility and involves a lot of non-financial considerations, such as validating the scope of an operating license or required technology transfers.

Contributions and expectations of project participants are discussed because participants come to the project with unconfirmed assumptions of what they will do or not do. Then, we discuss the governance structure intended to protect the interests of the company and examine project and country risks involved in international projects. Projects in emerging countries are rarely completed without participation of local agents and advisors to facilitate the process and guide the project team through the intricacies of local processes and business practices. The project team leader should seek the advice of local agents and advisors on all aspects of a project, but especially on project risks and ways to mitigate them.

# PART IV

# THE MEANS AND TOOLS
# TO ENSURE SUCCESS

# 17

# RISK IDENTIFICATION, ASSESSMENT, AND MANAGEMENT

## INTRODUCTION

Risk is generally defined as the probability of occurrence of an event that impacts unfavorably the financial position of a company. When meaningful probabilities can be assigned to these events and impacts can be quantified, we call that a risk analysis. Risk in acquisitions and joint ventures includes project implementation risk, commercial or business risk, legal/regulatory risk, as well as country or political risk in the case of international projects. Risk management is the management of the project revenues, costs, assets, and liabilities so as to minimize adverse impacts on future cash flows when unfavorable outcomes materialize. Therefore, the purpose of risk management is to mitigate the impact of factors outside the project team's control and enhance the chances of a project being successful. Risk management is viewed as a form of insurance that brings some certainty to the project's financial performance.

While risk can be measured by the probability of a well-defined outcome, uncertainty describes a state of affairs where there is a likelihood of an ambiguous activity taking place or where the outcome is unknown. Consequently, while the impact of risks can be quantified, uncertainty simply cannot be measured. Usually, sensitivity analysis is performed when there is a high degree of uncertainty surrounding an event or activity. It is the recommended approach to assess how a key financial variable responds to uncertainty induced changes, changes in factors whose variation cannot be established, and changes in the assumed strength of relationships with those factors.

The discussion in this chapter begins with our approach to handling risks in acquisition and joint venture projects. We proceed to the identification of sources and causes of project risks and quantification of potential impacts. The discussion then moves on to the need for risk management, common practices in this area, and development of risk management plans. Because risk management plans involve substantial costs, the need for balancing costs and benefits in risk management plans is introduced.

Approaches, principles, and means of risk sharing, allocation, and mitigation are also discussed as well as the types of risks that cannot be managed. For instances where the impact of a risk is large, but the likelihood of occurrence small, the need for contingency plans arises, which is discussed along with a review of superior risk management plan characteristics.

## PROJECT RISK COMPONENTS

### Sources of Risk

The probability of successful acquisitions and joint ventures is small because one needs to structure a transaction appropriately to the satisfaction of both sides, at the right price, financed efficiently, implemented successfully, and operated according to business plan expectations. That is, there are many requirements to be met to have a successful project and, consequently, there are many areas where things can go wrong and cause a project not to meet expected performance or even fail entirely.

The main source of risk in acquisition and joint venture projects lies with the assumptions that describe the operating environment and relationships underlying financial projections, which, in turn, form the basis of project valuation and project implementation plans. Therefore, the project team needs to pay particular attention to assumptions behind key financial variables: revenues, expenses, cash flows, and fixed investment requirements. More specifically, assumptions must be compared with views of industry experts and modified appropriately to reflect a realistic state of affairs.

Another set of risks in acquisitions and joint ventures has to do with project financeability and the financing structure of a transaction. In the case of financing risk, the deal structures assumed may not be feasible due to a number of external factors. IRS disallowance of desired classifications of transactions, failure to reach expected agreement on the particulars of the deal structure, high costs of risk allocation, and unexpected credit enhancements and parental guarantee requirements could derail financing plans. When financing risks materialize, availability of financing comes under question and the range and efficiency of financing solutions decline drastically. In other words, the cost of financing the project becomes substantially higher, and for this reason, early assessment of project financeability followed by thorough review of the project financing plan is necessary.

Often, project implementation plans or target integration plans are incomplete or include implicit or unsubstantiated assumptions that contain several project risks. A major source of risks for acquisitions and joint ventures is ability to integrate a target or to implement a joint venture successfully. Our estimates place project implementation costs in the 7 to 12 percent range of project value, but rarely are such cost estimates included in business cases, except in world-class companies experienced in doing these projects.

Even when detailed implementation and business plans are developed, it is impossible to guarantee project success because a lot depends on management support, implementation team expertise, and chemistry created between the parties. In addition, ability to retain and attract new management talent, and strategy and scope of operations for the acquired company or the joint venture entity impact project success significantly. Also, it is difficult to guarantee success if it is taken for granted that there will be management support for the new entity, that there is expertise in the implementation subteam, and so on, whereas the opposite may be true.

Risks surrounding expected synergy realization create fears in every project team leader's mind because partial or no realization of expected synergies is viewed as directly responsible for failure of most projects. Sellers and their advisors study potential purchasers and have several synergy scenarios sketched out for each purchaser. These synergies usually contain claims of increased efficiency of operations, lower cost structure, higher market share, better product development, etc. Often, the underlying assumptions go unchallenged and the expenses and investments required to obtain synergies are left out. However, even though synergies belong to the buyer, in most projects they are used as instruments to increase the price to be paid to close the transaction.

Violation of formal understandings and legal agreements, revocation of permits or withdrawal of operating licenses, and governmental approvals are other major risks in acquisitions and joint ventures. These risks present a particularly acute problem in foreign joint ventures where the local partner happens to be a government entity of a developing country. It is a problem because few project participants understand the nature of risks and are able to convince others that basic assumptions concerning legal agreements must be challenged. Foreign joint venture companies have been declared unlawful because the person who signed the joint venture agreement was not the highest-level person authorized to sign or because governments changed and the new government refused to extend the former regime's approval to the project.

Operating business risks or business plan risks have to do with being able to deliver the operating and financial performance set out in the business plan of the new entity. To some extent, these risks are a residual of project implementation or related to assumptions not dealt with in the development of financial projections. Operating risks are considered part of any major scenario and what-if analyses because they originate in assumptions underlying relationships and associations postulated in the financial model.

### Risk Impacts

Project completion, implementation effectiveness, and speed of integration are areas in which the risk impacts are realized and reflected. Delays in project completion, joint venture implementation, and integration of the acquired company's operations are indications that some risks have materialized. The impacts of risks are captured in the difference between actual from expected project implementation and integration time lines and budgeted costs.

When risks begin to materialize in a project, there are immediate and direct effects on the project financials. Revenue and expenses are among the first financial variables to be impacted when risks materialize in the absence of risk management plans. Either the revenue or expense side can be impacted by specific risks, and one way to find out the extent to which a risk has materialized is to look at the deviation of revenues and expenses from predicted values. Market and industry changes are risks that often impact key elements of financial statements.

Increased capital requirements above and beyond the pro forma business plan projections are another avenue through which risk impacts make themselves known and affect forecasted cash flows. Projects experience additional fixed capital investment requirements when investments in new technology, equipment upgrades, and higher capacity requirements are necessitated by unanticipated market conditions and competition. In some instances, automatic capital calls kick off to offset the impact of risks on revenues and expenses, but instead, they produce compounding negative effects on the project cash flow.

In acquisitions and joint ventures, in addition to affecting financials, risks impact human resources and requirements in a number of other ways. For example, management that were induced to remain with the acquired company through earn-out arrangements observe their position deteriorate and begin to exit. Often, across-the-board adjustments in the new entity's labor force take place when its financial performance deteriorates and senior management compensation is impacted adversely. Also, inability to attract new management talent of the caliber required to operate the new entity successfully is another human resource risk.

Legal agreements and informal understandings are occasionally revised or even nullified when risks begin materializing. In other instances, parties to agreements and understandings look to exit from contractual obligations. When the risk impact is substantial, it is not unusual for legal agreements to fall apart because the affected party seeks relief under the agreement's exit clauses.

The combined effect of several risks being realized simultaneously impacts the ability of management to operate a newly acquired or a joint venture company. This outcome impacts the extent to which synergies are harnessed and the business plan is realized. When risks materialize, project valuation is impacted adversely. Hence, the need for risk management because of the relief it provides by mitigating or eliminating some risks and their impacts.

### Risk Identification

The perceived risk profile of an acquisition or joint venture project changes through the course of assessment and implementation because of increased understanding of project particulars, assumptions being used, and operating environment. Therefore, project risks are monitored continuously from project inception until successful implementation and integration are achieved. The major steps to identify project risks systematically are:

*1. Consistency of strategy and objectives.* The first area to look for risks is consistency of strategies and long-term objectives between target and acquiring companies and between joint venture partners. This investigation assesses if risks present in a project can cause it to fail because of conflicting strategic objectives among project participants. Also, it determines if and how potentially conflicting interests can be harmonized.

*2. Compatibility of cultures and expectations.* The assessment of how compatible are organizational structures, corporate cultures, and problem-solving approaches of the parties involved along with the chemistry present identifies potential risks that need to be flushed out. As importantly, assessment of expectation compatibility provides clear indications about risks in this area.

*3. Screening project participants.* When screening target or partner companies, the project team identifies risks concerning the state of the industry, their market position, and their future economic viability. Risks identified in this phase often translate into rejection of the proposed project or revised expectations about its economics and strategic value.

*4. Assumption set verification.* As the project financial analysis unfolds, the project team reviews and checks the reasonableness of assumptions behind key financial variables and relationships. This phase allows the project team to identify project risks and to quantify a range of impact through simulation of financial models using different assumptions.

*5. Stability of financials.* The stability of key financial drivers through time provides indications about risks involved in the operational phase of the project. Instability of financials is traced to two factors: misspecified relationships or missing influences on stated relationships. Often, this requires the project team to go back to identify the source of instability in the project financials and examine the nature of risks involved.

*6. Review of legal agreements.* The project team needs to ensure that agreements the parties have reached and legal documents drafted treat risks appropriately and do not create new risks or amplify the impact of existing risks, but instead they mitigate risks. Legal documents should specify unambiguously the risks involved and parties responsible for them. Since the project team is able to alter the risk profile of the project by changing the legal documents and agreements, it uses the negotiation process to accomplish that.

*7. External advisor input.* Evaluation of project risks by the independent assessment party and by outside advisors who are industry experts provides another perspective on the risk profile. That assessment could identify new risks, generate discussion, and result in more accurate quantification of risks.

*8. Due diligence findings.* In the due diligence phase, all information obtained and assumptions used are scrutinized and validated. In the process, inconsistencies and risks are identified, pointed out in the due diligence report, and recommendations are dealt with.

In identifying risks, the project team pays attention to emerging deviations of expectations from reality as the project unfolds. This means that it needs to develop the capability to monitor, communicate, and manage the project risks and the perception of senior management concerning project risks.

### Risk Quantification

Quantification of risk impacts is fairly straightforward if a risk is directly related to inputs used in a financial model. However, the project team needs to find ways to translate risk occurrence to something quantifiable and easily understood by project participants. In such instances, the starting point is to use the project NPV because of convenience. Occasionally, other measures are used such as market share of a target or dividend requirement for a joint venture company.

The basic methodology used in quantifying a risk, once it is established that the risk is connected to a financial model input variable or assumption, begins with the project base case using the consensus view on the most likely future state of affairs. Appropriate changes to the financial model inputs or assumptions are made to reflect risk realization in its entirety. Use a binary approach to risk realization (risk either happens or it does not), simulating the risk view to calculate the resulting NPV. The difference between the baseline view and the risk occurrence view NPVs is a quantification of risk, which occurs with 100 percent probability.

Since life is not that simple, the project team needs to come up with a probability of risks occurring and this necessitates revisiting changes in inputs and calculating an expected NPV related to a specific materialized risk. Comparison of the baseline with the probabilistic occurrence risk view yields a better assessment of the risk impact because it considers the likelihood of risk occurrence.

To quantify risks, the project team performs a series of sensitivity analyses by changing assumptions and variables impacted by risks one at a time and simulating the financial model to calculate resulting NPVs. These simulations quantify individual risk impacts one at a time. To get a comprehensive view of risk impacts, the project team generates what-if scenarios and looks at possible outcomes obtained by modifying a series of assumptions, model inputs, and probabilities to create a pessimistic scenario where several risks materialize simultaneously.

Project teams may not feel entirely comfortable with quantification of risk impacts and use external expert advice on the impact of various risks. In those cases, compare the risk impact views of external advisors with those of the project team to understand the causes of the differences and be selective in using risk impact views. Development of conservative risk scenarios is another way to show potential impacts on the project NPV. We advise against using overly conservative risk impact quantifications because they result in projects being rejected.

## ELEMENTS OF RISK MANAGEMENT

### Risk Management Approaches

The starting point in the risk management process is getting a good understanding of the company's strategy and its long-term objectives, the industry structure and trends, and the economic and operating environments. Another key element of successful risk management is understanding the marketplace, production processes, new technology and product evolution, and issues surrounding key financial drivers such as political considerations impacting the outcome of negotiations, regulatory rulings, issuance of operating licenses, or foreign government approvals. A good understanding of these elements collectively enables the project team to develop the company's position on how a risk should be handled.

A common way of mitigating acquisition or joint venture risks is for participants to share risks in some fashion acceptable to all. While this appears to be an equitable way of handling risks, who bears what share of the risk is a difficult question to answer and is settled through negotiations. Shifting project risks to other parties entirely is often a preferred approach to managing risk, but it is also done through the negotiation process and requires giving up something else in return. In some instances, the party best equipped to handle a risk assumes that risk, while in others the party benefiting the most absorbs the risk.

Yet another approach, if the participants in the transaction agree, is to shift risks to a third party, which is able and willing to bear risks. This approach involves close cooperation among project participants and some form of compensation to the third party for assuming the risk. Purchase of insurance to cover specific project risks shifts risks to a third party and is common in international transactions where political risk is best handled through insurance coverage. Legal agreements can also be used to shift risks to a third party through conditions that allow, for example, partners to exit a foreign joint venture if a license is not issued under expected conditions and to be reimbursed for their expenses.

Earn-out formulas are often used to manage risks in acquisition projects. This is a form of risk sharing where the seller benefits only when and to the extent the business plan projections of the new entity materialize. In those instances, the buyer compensates the seller for assuming this risk through higher price payments or some other form of enhanced remuneration. Earn-out formulas are also used to provide incentives for management teams staying with the acquired company or appointed to the management team of the joint venture.

Contingency plans should be developed to handle project uncertainties when the risks cannot be quantified or when risks begin to materialize and no other options are available to manage them. Contingency plans entail major changes in operational plans, they are used when there is substantial deviation from the course outlined in the business plan, and they involve large corrections. While effective if they are well thought out, once contingency plans are put into effect, they are difficult to reverse and they become a drag on the ability to manage project risks.

Some project teams approach risk management with the view that if they adopt rather conservative assumptions and financial views then risk is automatically mitigated or even eliminated completely. This is a view that is difficult to argue against except that it makes acquisition and joint venture negotiations difficult to conduct and often impossible to close. When such conservative views are adopted, the entire risk burden is borne by the other party without being compensated for sharing the risk. Under unusual market conditions or when a party has tremendous negotiation clout, this approach can be very effective, but under normal operating environments and conditions, it is ineffective.

Managing project risks through careful planning of assessment, negotiation, and implementation of a project along with creation of a sound business plan is the preferred approach to managing risks effectively. The reason that this method is effective is that risks are anticipated, impacts are included in financial and operational plans, and costs and benefits to the parties are balanced. When implementation plans include risk management, they become an effective approach to managing risks.

Another effective form of project risk management is through negotiations of balanced agreements whereby both sides share project risks. By recognizing identified project risks and incorporating them in the negotiations agenda, project participants internalize the need to handle project risks and find solutions acceptable to both sides. To the extent that acceptable solutions are negotiated and reflected in legal agreements, project risk allocation then becomes part of the project terms and conditions.

### Risk Management Plans

To most people, risk management in acquisitions and joint ventures means complete elimination of risk. In reality, risk management is the only systematic way to mitigate risks through planning and negotiations prior to occurrence. Risk management plans involve a series of after-negotiations steps that are part of project implementation. Consequently, the implementation subteam does most of the work because of their understanding of the project and what it takes to implement successfully. The following are the key elements that constitute the process of developing a risk management plan:

1. Create a risk management subteam made up of implementation and negotiation subteam members and assign risk management responsibility to this team.
2. Undertake thorough review of key assumptions used in developing project financials, legal documents, and agreements to identify risks.
3. Break down each risk in subcomponents and assign specific responsibilities to project implementation team members. Each subteam member responsible for a specific risk develops their own risk mitigation plan, but these plans are integrated at the project risk configuration level to ensure consistency of approaches.
4. Develop a good understanding of the project risk exposures and impacts. That is, understand the nature of major risks, what circumstances would trigger risks to occur, and the likelihood of that happening.
5. Analyze risks and quantify impacts on the measure of performance through financial

model simulations when possible or use expert advice and assessment.

6.  Establish the company risk management policy for the project. That is, develop the company position on risks to be assumed, risks to be shared, and risks to be shifted to third parties along with costs associated with each approach.

7.  Once the inventory of risk exposures is taken, define measures of project performance so that risk impacts are assessed using the same yardstick. The measure of performance used extensively is the project NPV.

8.  Create a mechanism to track the project's risk configuration. Basically, this entails assigning an experienced risk management subteam member to monitor risk exposure from project start though implementation and beyond.

9.  Outline alternatives to be pursued under different circumstances and communicate this information to the risk management subteam.

10. Coordinate with the negotiations subteam to help its members understand risks and potential impacts and engage appropriate parties in risk allocation negotiations.

11. Monitor the project risk management performance throughout its life cycle. Record risk occurrence events, corrective actions taken, and results that followed and update the risk profile of the project.

### Costs and Benefits of Risk Management

The nature of acquisitions and joint ventures is such that companies view these projects as a way to enhance their strategic and financial position, and because of that, they are willing to take risks. However, the project team should structure projects so that the company goes into them understanding the consequences and taking calculated risks. As with other business endeavors, risk management plans have costs and benefits associated with them and the key to successful risk management is achieving a balance between the two.

In addition to financial costs, the risk management subteam needs to develop an estimate of the strategic impact of risks that are part of the totality of project risk impacts. That is, it must answer the question of what major and strategic costs the company will suffer if various project risks occur. Note that strategic costs may be quantitative or qualitative assessments of consequences of risks materializing. Following that, the risk management subteam considers the likely financial impact of risks on cash flow uncertainty, which impacts the cost of financing and the project value.

The other element of the cost side is the expense involved in actual risk management, which should be weighed against the consequences of not managing project risks. Here, the project team includes the cost of resources dedicated to managing risk along with the cost of insurance against certain risks, cost of negotiating risk sharing, and cost of contingency planning.

Having looked at consequences of risks left unmanaged and the cost of managing project risks, the risk management subteam considers the benefits of expanding resources to manage project risks. To do that, the risk management subteam first looks at the strategic benefits of risk management. It determines in what major ways the company will benefit in the area of achieving its long-term strategy and objectives if the project is implemented successfully due to risk management efforts. Then, it assigns certain worth to preserving the project value through the risk management plan and compares that against the total cost of risk management.

The additional discipline that risk management brings to the area of project management should be counted as an important benefit because risk management considerations enable the project team to better structure acquisitions and joint ventures and increase the likelihood of project success. Further, improved financial performance, certainty of project cash flows, and more favorable financing terms need to be included in the benefits of risk management.

### Risk Sharing and Mitigation

There are no fixed rules about risk sharing and allocation, and how they are handled depends entirely on the nature of the risks involved in a given project. Often, negotiation subteams push for risk allocations based on the principles that risks are assumed by the party in the best position to manage or absorb risks or that risks are allocated to the party benefiting the most by the project. Since acceptable trade-offs to project participants can be developed in risk sharing and allocation, the negotiated agreement approach should be used as much as possible. However, there are other approaches to risk sharing and mitigation, the most common being:

*1. Legal agreements.* Risk may be shifted or allocated to various parties able and willing to assume the risk using legal documents and by fixing the financial model results to negotiated agreements. Risk sharing agreements and risk compensation agreements are other ways of using legal documents to manage risk and provide remuneration to the party assuming the risk.

*2. Earn-out formulas.* These are used extensively in acquisition agreements to shift a good part of financial risk from the buyer to the seller and also in management contracts in joint venture projects. The latter are a convenient risk mitigation mechanism and they usually work well in developed countries.

*3. Risk insurance.* In some instances, commercial insurance may be purchased to cover risks in various degrees. Insurance coverage tends to be expensive and its pricing varies with the likelihood of the risk occurrence and its potential impact. In the case of international projects, political insurance coverage is available from export credit agencies and investment insurance coverage by unilateral and multilateral institutions.

*4. Contingency plans.* These are plans dealing with the major risk issues and contain specific actions to be taken to alter the course of events or minimize the impact when a risk materializes. They contain the action, timing of the reaction to a risk beginning to materialize, and clear responsibility assignments for project participants.

*5. Adopting conservative views.* This approach may be appropriate in moderation or when negotiation conditions allow one party to impose conservative expectations and conservative financial assumptions on the other party. Use of this approach carried to extremes is discouraged, but using conservative views in planning activities and scenarios is recommended.

*6. Risk management through planning.* The importance and value added of a highly skilled implementation subteam has been long recognized. Sound implementation planning is the best way to ensure a successful project implementation and, consequently, the best way to manage risks. Also, a sound business plan anticipates operating risks and develops ways to deal with such eventualities. Finally, a good risk management plan brings plans together and mitigates project risks effectively.

## CONTINGENCY PLANNING

### Risks Not Easily Managed

Risk management enhances the chances of an acquisition or a joint venture being successful and should be undertaken in every project. However, there are instances in which risk management may not be feasible or in which risks cannot be managed but contingency planning helps. For example, when economic costs outweigh benefits of risk management or there are no strategic reasons, costly risk management does not make sense. Nor is it pursued for long-term foreign exchange risks where international cash flows beyond three to five years are involved and the cost of foreign exchange hedging or swaps becomes prohibitive. Other instances where risk management is not feasible are the following:

1. No markets exist for hedging or insuring risks. Operational risks are not insured in commercial insurance markets and there are no hedging instruments for emerging country currencies.
2. Foreign government interventions in future tax laws and performance requirements. These areas impact foreign joint ventures and are not included in political insurance coverage offered by unilateral or multilateral institutions.
3. New risks surface that were not anticipated in the business plan and risk management is not possible because of timing considerations.
4. Lack of partner cooperation in the presence of conflicting objectives. Being unable to get agreement, risks cannot be managed when there are conflicts of significant objectives and project participants cannot resolve them through negotiations.
5. The seller or the joint venture partner is unwilling to share risks. This risk is real and could surface in every project if negotiation teams have not prepared trade-offs or are inexperienced.
6. Legal, regulatory, and institutional constraints. Occasionally, regardless of efforts, risks cannot be managed because of unpredictable changes in rules and regulations or restrictions imposed on the new entity having to do with local practices.
7. Lack of risk management know-how. This surfaces often when project teams are inexperienced and advisors cannot provide direction and guidance.

### Contingency Plans

When the probability of risk occurrence is low and the impact of the risk is low, the preferred approach is to deal with the risk as it occurs. When the probability and impact of risk occurrence are high, risk management plans are appropriate to mitigate adverse financial impacts. However, when the probability of risk occurrence is low, but the financial impact is fairly large, contingency plans are necessary to deal with that risk if it occurs.

The development of contingency plans starts with identifying the set of events, situations, and activities that are high-impact, low-probability risks in the project and understanding what factors would cause them to occur. Identifying and defining trigger mechanisms for reaction follow. That is, specifying how project participants would recognize the risk occurrence, what signals the need for action, and when action should be initiated.

Contingency plans minimize damage to the project by eliminating uncertainty, confusion, indecisiveness, and delays in reacting to catastrophic events. Some additional steps in contingency planning are to:

1.  Define consequences to project financials or other objectives that requires assessment of project economics and key strategic and operational objectives.
2.  Define responses for alternative objectives and appropriate corrective actions. In this step, the reaction for each major objective being impacted is specified as well as what action should be taken to remedy the situation.
3.  Develop, test, and integrate individual contingency plans. For each major project objective being impacted, a contingency plan is created, validated for consistency, and integrated with other contingency plans into a cohesive overall plan.

## SUCCESSFUL RISK MANAGEMENT

### Characteristics of Superior Risk Management Plans

How risk configuration is laid out is the foundation of a risk management plan and determines to a large extent the risk mitigation possible. This requires the formation of a risk management subteam made up of implementation and negotiation subteam members assisted by functional experts. The first element of a sound risk management plan is the assignment of specific responsibilities to individuals accountable for managing specific risk elements.

Consistency of risk management across the project risk spectrum is another characteristic of superior risk management plans and requires an understanding of company policy to risk tolerance, consistency of guidelines, and consistency of risk management plans. An underlying element of risk management plan consistency in win-win arrangements is allocation or risk sharing acceptable to all parties involved. Acceptable risk sharing or allocation entails appropriate compensation for the parties that are assuming the risk in question.

Like other plans in acquisitions and joint ventures, a sound risk management plan has to have customer focus and orientation and be motivated by a desire to ensure uninterrupted customer satisfaction through the entire planning horizon. It must also protect the integrity of financial projections so as to result in a successful project and reflect a reasonable balance between costs and benefits of risk management over the planning horizon.

Stability and certainty of risk management plans is another important consideration. Presence of these characteristics in risk management plans requires balance of interest of the parties, legal agreements with reasonable escape clauses and that are sustainable under stressful events, and flexibility in enforcing agreements. Stability and certainty also require creating backup contingency plans in the event catastrophic events materialize.

Comprehensive treatment of project risks is another requirement for superior risk management planing. In addition, it should display high-level flexibility across all risk management components and subplans to be able to change positions as required by market conditions. Finally, a superior risk management plan must have wide acceptance by the project team, senior management, and external advisors.

## Recommended Project Risk Approach

Understanding and managing project risks are crucial in determining the likelihood of projects being successful in creating the shareholder value expected. Unless managed properly, risks materialize and result in poor project financial performance. However, in most acquisitions and joint ventures, project risks are not addressed until the financial analysis is performed. At that point, the range of valuation defined by a pessimistic and the baseline NPV scenario is where risks are treated, with the pessimistic scenario describing the state of all risks occurring simultaneously.

A better approach to handle project risks is one observed in world-class project teams, summarized in the following practices:

1. Begin identifying risks from the moment an opportunity is brought to the business development group.
2. Scrutinize the assumption set to determine the likelihood and magnitude of deviations from the assumed state.
3. Identify the project's key financial drivers and assess how they are linked to various risks.
4. Quantify potential impacts of major project risks identified for each key financial driver.
5. Perform extensive sensitivity and scenario analyses to understand the range of various impacts being realized.
6. Assess risks associated with achieving financial performance levels included in agreements and surrounding payment of premiums.
7. Prepare several trade-offs and help the negotiation subteam to handle risk allocation and sharing effectively.
8. Ensure balance of interests and incorporate elements of sound risk management in the project risk management plan.

Before negotiations begin, the project team should also identify uncertainties surrounding the project. Having done that, it uses the negotiation process to allocate risks to third parties or to share risks with the seller or the partner. Understandings reached concerning risks need to be reflected in legal agreements to eliminate some project risks. At that point, the project team can develop the kind of risk management and contingency plans outlined in this chapter.

## SUMMARY

It is true that risks left unmanaged always materialize. It is also true that project risks can be managed effectively so that the expected value created in a project materializes. We start this chapter with recommendations on how to approach risk in acquisitions and joint ventures, and emphasize the need for the project team to understand the sources and causes of risks and potential impacts on project value.

Risk management begins from the moment risks are identified, continues through the negotiations where risk allocation and sharing are determined, and ends with project closing and establishment of operations. A discussion on the elements of risk management follows the risk management section and we stress the need for balance between costs and benefits in risk management plans.

The common approaches and practices in risk sharing, allocation, and mitigation are discussed, but we recognize that there are certain risks that cannot be managed easily. In those cases, help from external experts is obtained so that solutions to risk allocation are found. Contingency plans are part of risk management plans and are also reviewed. If internal risk management experts are not available, engaging outside consultants to assist in this effort not at deal closing, but from the start of the project is strongly recommended. The chapter ends with the discussion of superior risk management plan characteristics.

# 18

# THE PROJECT DUE DILIGENCE PROCESS

## INTRODUCTION

Due diligence is the phase in acquisition or joint ventures that entails in-depth analysis of the target or partner company in order to generate sufficient and accurate information to support the decision to proceed with the project. This a required activity in every acquisition or joint venture because a company would risk financial losses by undertaking a project on inadequate or false information. When the due diligence stage is bypassed, acquiring companies invariably suffer negative consequences, but an effective due diligence verifies representations and determines whether a project is as good as it looks.

The scope of due diligence is to conduct a comprehensive investigation and audit of the target firm or the partner company. It is far more extensive in the case of acquisitions than in joint ventures for the simple reason that motivations and the assumption of liabilities are handled differently. If the target or partner is a privately owned entity, the due diligence is even more important and the higher the cost of a project, the closer the scrutiny of the information. The degree of information screening and verification also depends on other factors, such as the nature of the acquisition, time lines imposed, and availability of information.

The due diligence phase is crucial in creating a sound basis for the decision to proceed with a project and helps in ensuring project success. Experienced project teams begin the due diligence effort before full-blown project assessment begins and rely on external experts to complete it as negotiations are coming to an end. On the other hand, inexperienced project teams leave the due diligence effort until the negotiations stage. By that point, there is insufficient time to do a thorough investigation of the other side's representations and generate the information needed to make a sound decision.

The discussion in this chapter begins with the composition of the due diligence subteam and the process involved to produce the due diligence findings report. We take up in sequence several areas that the due diligence covers: corporate structure and legal issues; revenue, expense, profitability, and investment; human resources and organizational structure; product line, markets, and the competitive positioning; technical and product development; company culture, networks, and reporting systems; and customer and supplier relations.

In the sections that follow, we discuss each area and address key questions that need to be answered to ensure that adequate information is generated or verified. The due diligence report concludes the effort with an analysis of findings and recommendations of the due diligence subteam. This report and its significance are discussed and the chapter ends with a review of quality attributes that characterize effective due diligence efforts.

## DUE DILIGENCE SUBTEAM AND PROCESS

### The Due Diligence Subteam

Given that the due diligence effort covers a wide area of investigation, the knowledge and experience that reside in the due diligence subteam must span all aspects of doing business, and because this project phase is very important, it is headed by the project team leader. The other members of the subteam responsible for the due diligence effort are the financial analyst, functional and technical experts, external accountants and tax experts, and lawyers specializing in acquisitions and joint ventures.

Due diligence spans all areas of operations of the entity being investigated. Therefore, communications is a key element in successful investigations to obtain and disseminate information quickly and effectively to the project team. It also requires extensive teamwork and coordination. That is why the linkage with the core team is important and for that reason the project leader must possess strong interpersonal skills. The due diligence effort presents a good opportunity for the project team members to understand the business of the target or the partner company. It is also an opportunity to learn from external advisors how this function is performed and use the knowledge to become more effective in subsequent projects.

In addition to verifying information and representations made by the target or the partner company, the due diligence subteam produces a report of findings and develops a set of recommendations derived from those findings. This is really significant because it gives the green light to proceed with a project to the next phase. It is also important because it assures senior management and the project team that the basis of project evaluation is indeed sound. Otherwise, the due diligence subteam would recommend against going forward with the project.

## The Due Diligence Process

The due diligence process is unique for each acquisition and joint venture project in four dimensions: timing of the effort, focus, depth and breadth, and type of investigation required. In acquisitions, timing of the due diligence effort is negotiated with the seller and usually begins after evaluation of the project is completed and the decision to move forward has been made. In some cases, the seller may not allow inspection of its books until an acceptable bid has been submitted and accepted. On the other hand, the due diligence in joint venture projects starts earlier, and in most cases, by the time the decision to proceed with the joint venture formation is made, the due diligence effort is completed.

The due diligence involves a review of the target's accounting books, financial statements, legal papers, other company records, and face-to-face discussions with the target's representatives. The seller usually allows one to three days for inspection of the target's records and makes its finance and accounting team available to answer questions. The seller's representatives also take technical, operational, and marketing questions; if unable to answer them, they pass them on to appropriate managers who provide an official response.

**Figure 18.1**
**The Project Due Diligence Process**

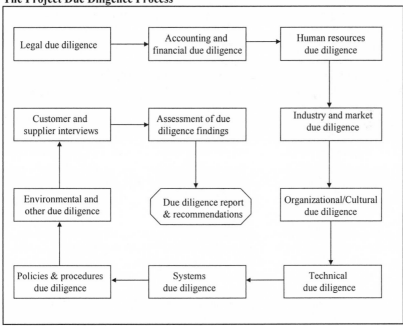

The focus of due diligence in acquisition projects is on uncovering hidden liabilities, verifying financial data, and obtaining market, technical, and operational information to support the decision-making process. In joint ventures, the focus is on organizational and cultural compatibility and on the ability of the partner to make required contributions now and in the future. In acquisitions, both depth and breadth of due diligence must be greater than in joint ventures in the financial area. Also, since the emphasis is on different issues, the due diligence is conducted differently: calculated and rapid in acquisitions versus cooperative and less structured in joint ventures.

## TYPES OF DUE DILIGENCE

### Legal Due Diligence

Due diligence involves several areas. Figure 18.1 outlines the process and shows the different types of due diligence required to arrive at the point where the due diligence subteam can deliver its findings and recommendations report.

The company background and history are the first elements in legal documents reviews. Here, the current company ownership structure, its asset holdings, and its evolution through time are examined along with senior management team contracts and external advisor engagements. Also, the development and performance of the company relative to government rules and regulations is evaluated to determine the degree of the target's reliance on government regulation to maintain its customer base and business.

Once management contracts are reviewed and costs of terminating or renewing them is understood, the due diligence proceeds to search for past and pending litigation against the company. Here, tax rulings and court judgments against the company are of significant interest. Then, customer and supplier contracts are reviewed to understand the terms and conditions governing these relationships, obligations of the firm, termination clauses, and costs of terminating or renewing contracts. Finally, an evaluation of present and future legislation and government rules and regulations is undertaken to establish the linkage between them and the firm's ability to function successfully.

The scope of legal due diligence is broad, and extends across a number of areas; because the scope of legal due diligence is so wide, experts in these areas are involved in verifying and assessing information. The most significant areas of legal due diligence are:

1. Corporate charter, ownership structure, past and current affiliations, subsidiary holdings, and claims on assets outside the target company.
2. Human resources legal issues, labor settlements, and union disputes and litigation.
3. Employment practices and policies and employment-related pending litigation.
4. Compliance with federal, state, and local rules and regulations.
5. Tax liabilities and provisions and past or pending litigation.
6. Target financial obligations, their terms, and seller obligations to be attributed to the target.
7. Product and service brands and licensing contracts and agreements.
8. Technology, patent, and intellectual property pending legal issues.
9. Market concentration considerations and competitive pricing and marketing issues.

The first question to be answered by legal due diligence is whether there is any litigation pending against the target or the partner company from either employee complaints, competitor lawsuits, or tax judgments. Whether legal representations to the firm's auditors are valid and whether the firm is compliant with various government agency regulations is the second question answered. The third is whether there are outstanding legal matters and the cost of remedying legal issues prior to deal closing. Another key question answered by legal due diligence is what legal problems might arise from the acquisition or the formation of a joint venture and how they impact project success.

### Financial Due Diligence

When business people think of due diligence, they think of financial due diligence of an acquisition because it is the most concentrated effort. Financial due diligence covers all aspects of revenues, expenses, and investments, along with a review and analysis of cash flows, profitability, dividend policy, tax status, and unit costs in order to assess or verify the financial health of the firm. Financial due diligence is linked closely with other due diligence efforts because all findings have financial impacts and ramifications that need to be included in the project financial analysis.

Verification of past financial statements is the starting point in financial due diligence, and then, financial projections are dissected to establish their validity. To do that, the assumption set underlying financial projections is scrutinized. The target company's tax status is verified as is payment of taxes due along with provisions for anticipated taxes. Items such as inventories, receivables, uncollectibles, financing policies, and depreciation practices are examined to establish compliance with accounting and sound business practices.

In addition to specific items being verified and facts established, financial due diligence evaluates the firm's financial practices and its financial management systems. This is important because it indicates how well the firm is operated and to what extent improvements are possible that translate to potential for value creation. Furthermore, the financial due diligence subteam must determine to what extent financial statements have been dressed up for the acquiring company's viewing.

The due diligence effort for international acquisition and joint venture projects is more complex because it involves review of foreign markets, business conditions, and practices. For international projects, the due diligence subteam needs to clarify a number of important issues, such as company registration requirements for the new entity, the foreign country's trade and investment requirements and restrictions, and tax treatment and holidays of different types of companies. In addition, it needs to understand the rules surrounding repatriation of dividends regulations, import duties on capital equipment brought into the country, foreign exchange controls and conversion costs, and financial reporting requirements of the host country's governing bodies.

To answer financial questions and establish the merits and foundations of project financials, the due diligence subteam has to answer the following key questions:

1.    How accurate and reliable is the financial information provided and how reasonable is the underlying assumption set? If information is inaccurate, what is the impact?
2.    What is the tax status of the company and are how tax liabilities being met?
3.    What has the balance sheet, income statement, and cash flow statement review revealed about the firm's operations? What is the financing and capital structure of the firm and its credit-worthiness?
4.    How are financial projections developed and to what extent are they reliable indicators of future financial performance? Are there risks facing the firm and what are its risk management plans and policies?
5.    How good is the financial planning, how sophisticated is the financial management of the firm, and what improvements can be made?

### Human Resources Due Diligence

Human resources due diligence is concerned with verifying information shared and answering questions concerning people and skills, wages and benefits, organizations and systems, and processes and networks. Human resources due diligence is conducted by personnel professionals with experience in acquisitions and joint ventures, the reason being that they can easily identify issues, assess the situation, and understand the kind of management talent needed and how to structure compensation packages.

Human resources due diligence begins with an organizational structure review to understand the target or partner company's management and reporting structure, determine compatibility of organizational structures, and establish what changes are needed to effect compatibility. Then comes the phase of verifying representations made concerning management and labor force skills and a review of the firm's labor relations history. This is especially important in cases where the labor force of the target is unionized.

Employment and compensation contracts of senior managers are reviewed along with their backgrounds and incentive plans to determine if and what changes may be required in the new entity's senior management team packages. Following that, the rest of the management team is reviewed in terms of training, skills and experiences, and compensation and incentive plans. Reviews take place with three things in mind: Is the right management team in place to run the new entity's operations successfully? Are there fair and adequate incentives to produce desired behaviors and if not, what is required to do that? And how compatible is the target or partner management team with the company's?

A company-wide human resources review and skills inventory then takes place where company statistics are reviewed and verified, such as number of employees by sex and age, educational backgrounds and training, wage and salary classification, and so on. The purpose of the skills inventory is to determine how compatible is the compensation of the firm with industry averages and whether discrepancies in this area translate to labor force dissatisfaction. In the review process, it can be established whether the firm's human resources can be a source of competitive advantage and how it might be changed to produce that advantage.

The human resources policies and procedures of the firm are reviewed concerning hiring, employment on a part-time and temporary basis, promotions, and dismissals as well as compensation, benefits, and incentives for the labor force of the firm. Review of policies and procedures of the target is undertaken to determine whether they are compatible with those of the acquiring company and adjustments needed to achieve compatibility. It can also predict the likelihood of implementation success and the challenges that must be overcome.

Another important element of the human resources due diligence is to evaluate how sound is the decision-making and goal-setting process, what may need to be changed, and how these changes would impact the new entity. This evaluation is important because the project team faces one set of challenges in project implementation if all decisions are made by one individual, but a different set of challenges if decisions are made by consensus. Likewise, if goals are dictated from above, it represents one approach to managing strategic and operational issues versus the approach of developing goals and objectives based on input from operational experts.

There can be no closure to the human resources due diligence before compliance with all federal, state, and local government rules and regulations is established and violations and outstanding litigation noted. In the case of foreign projects, the human resources due diligence must also understand the country's employment laws and practices and assess financial impacts of commencing operations in that country, ongoing costs, and costs associated with terminating employment contracts in the event exiting from the project is necessary.

Finally, a review of systems, networks, and processes of the target or the partner company takes place to assess effectiveness and determine compatibility with corresponding systems, networks, and processes in the company. Systems and networks include computer, accounting, and information reporting systems. This review is important because it reveals the changes and adjustments needed to make them compatible with those of the company and the impacts of changes on costs and people.

## Technical Due Diligence

Technical due diligence examines the R&D and technical capabilities of the firm in question to determine its ability to develop products and services on an ongoing basis. R&D, technology application, and product development capabilities are a source of competitive advantage. Hence, the due diligence in this area determines the source and degree of advantage, to what extent the advantage can be sustained over a number of years, and what it would take to ensure sustainability of that advantage over the long run.

The R&D activities of the firm are a good place to begin technical due diligence. Here, technical experts review the nature of R&D activities, backgrounds of professionals involved, and purpose and direction of their activities. A number of considerations are important in this review beginning with determining to what degree the R&D team has produced technical innovations in the past and whether it can continue to do it in the future. Understanding its linkages to the marketing and finance organizations to assess efficiency of commercializing products is important as is assessment of leadership, teamwork, and orientation of the R&D team and incentive plans.

R&D due diligence also entails a review of patents, licenses, and rights to technologies that have been commercialized. Assessment of the firm's technical platforms and capabilities is another area of technical due diligence to determine compatibility of systems and direction of R&D efforts in this area. It also involves an assessment of the firm's technology evolution and obsolescence and how new technology improves the quality of products and services developed.

Technical due diligence involves an in-depth evaluation of product development and commercialization cycle policies and practices of the firm. Care and skill are needed in this area to determine:

1. The time span from the conception of ideas to product development cycle and the management of that cycle.
2. How technological evolution and innovation impact industry changes and competition.
3. New-product commercialization processes and incentive schemes to ensure that it is in line with world-class competitors
4. Expected impacts of technological innovation and change on future capital requirements, product pricing and marketing, and competitive product and market positioning.

Technical due diligence is a pre-requisite to performing an industry and market due diligence because it determines how technological change and innovation affect the industry structure. In most instances, technological changes define the rules of competition in a given industry, depreciation policies, and unit cost structures. Hence, it is suggested that the industry and market due diligence take place after the technology due diligence effort is completed.

### Industry and Market Due Diligence

The scope of industry and market due diligence extends from the point where technology ends to where finance begins. It encompasses review and assessment of the firm's industry; evolution, changes, and trends; the firm's competitive environment and new entrants; product line and customers, marketing, pricing, promotion, and distribution channels; and the firm's ways of dealing with competitive pressures. It is an essential element of due diligence and it is important because it has a direct bearing on the assessment of financial projections.

A good approach to initialize the industry and market due diligence is to develop an understanding of the firm's customer preferences, followed by a product line and product life cycle review to determine how customer needs are being met and what product changes or introductions are needed to better serve customer needs. Product life cycle review is also useful in determining the position of products in their life cycles and future demand patterns. In addition, the firm's distribution channels are evaluated for adequacy, proximity to customers, and quality of service.

Market due diligence involves in-depth assessment of several factors and variables starting with industry structure and the degree and nature of competition. The firm's total market size and growth patterns over the past three to five years and projected growth rates are reviewed along with the firm's past and projected market position and share of total market to establish sustainabilty of the firm's market position and market share. The key drivers of customer demand for its products, the respective elasticities of demand, and how they are evolving through time are examined in light of pricing and promotion policies, discounting practices, and the demand response to changes in these variables. Finally, the financial, technical, and marketing capabilities of existing competitors and new entrants are evaluated.

Industry and market due diligence focuses attention on understanding forces of change in the firm's competitive position. Hence, it looks at industry changes and underlying factors as well as at the firm's response to those changes to assess how they impact its profitability. Here, it is essential to evaluate the evolution of competition and the role of technology in order to determine how technology defines industry changes. The assessment of evolution of competition, however, requires a close examination of barriers to entry and the power of market participants.

The importance of industry and market due diligence lies primarily with enabling the project team to determine to what extent the firm's position will change over time and how those changes will impact its profitability. Industry and market due diligence is important because it helps the implementation subteam to develop a business plan that is reflective of market conditions, helps in harnessing of synergies, and provides intelligence to determine and quantify the financial impacts of industry and market changes on the firm.

### Cultural Due Diligence

Cultural due diligence is part of the human resources due diligence, but because of its importance, it is treated separately and the significance of different factors in contributing to project success is emphasized. The scope of cultural due diligence is broad and seeks to determine the state of chemistry in the firm and in external relations. Starting with the target's organizational structure and setup, the due diligence subteam assesses the compatibility with the company's management team; consistency of missions; strategies, goals, and objectives; and the philosophy permeating senior management thinking.

The chemistry among senior managers is observed closely as are relationships among middle-level managers. The decision-making process, the escalation approach in decision making and conflict resolution, and the policies of the company concerning personnel and operational management are evaluated. Then comes evaluation of the development of management objectives process, linkages between accomplishment of objectives and compensation, productivity growth and incentive plans, and internal management control systems. Finally, operational processes and procedures, views and policies toward competition, and relationships in the industry are evaluated.

The organizational structure and the temperament of the management team of the target or partner firm are assessed for compatibility with the company's organizational setup and management temperament because without it, implementation is difficult and synergies not likely to materialize. The management philosophy and operating approach of senior executives, the chemistry among senior managers, as well as relationships among middle-level managers are important to understand to assess which senior managers should be retained beyond implementation. Another reason is to determine to what extent personalities involved are susceptible to changing their views so as to fit those of the company management team's views. The third reason is to assess what changes may be needed to eliminate inheriting undesirable middle-level-management conflicts.

Determining consistency of missions, strategies, goals, and objectives is important in order to assess the new entity's degree of autonomy, if autonomy is desirable. If autonomy is not viewed in a positive light, the due diligence subteam assesses the likelihood that harmonious relationships can exist when each company pursues its own strategy, goals, and objectives. In the absence of such consistency, project motives should be revisited to determine whether it makes sense to proceed or terminate the project at this point.

The decision-making and escalation process needs to be evaluated by the due diligence subteam to understand how decisions are made, i.e., fact-based versus senior management's determinations, autocratic versus consensus, systematic process based versus ad-hoc. How decisions are made helps the subteam determine how well a firm is run, how consistent the decision-making processes are with the company's processes, and how crucial some managers may be to the success of the new entity.

The development of objectives process, linkages of objectives to compensation, and productivity growth and remuneration are key areas of evaluation because they determine how well the firm is managed internally and the extent to which financial incentives are in place to motivate desired behavior. It also facilitates evaluation of existing plans to increase the productivity of the firm's human and capital assets on a continuous basis, and the possibility of developing a competitive advantage after the deal closes by making appropriate changes in these areas.

Internal management control systems and operational processes and procedures are evaluated to determine how well the firm is operated and whether synergies can be created in this area. The views of the firm toward competition and its industry relationships are examined to understand how changes in the ownership and management structure could impact the success of the entity under a new structure. Because cultural due diligence is broad in scope and requires a long time to complete, it should start as soon as contact is established with the target or the partner company.

### Other Due Diligence

In projects involving manufacturing, there are other areas of due diligence to be covered, such as environmental due diligence, evaluation of the condition of plant and equipment, and inspection of physical inventories and their valuation. Items such as unfunded pension and benefit contributions, hidden product, and other liabilities must be uncovered in the due diligence phase. Also, product and service reputation, internal performance monitoring and control systems, and external interfaces are assessed. Finally, relationships with government agencies, community involvement, and interactions with regulatory bodies are reviewed to uncover potential problem areas.

As every industry is characterized by rather specific operational and financial attributes, each project has areas of due diligence that are unique to it. Also, to the extent that a project is motivated by specific goals and objectives, areas impacting those goals and objectives should become the focus of in-depth due diligence. Foreign projects involve due diligence of country risks, operating business environment and practices, business laws and regulations, transfer pricing issues, and foreign tax liabilities. Therefore, the due diligence subteam should understand the areas that are the subject of due diligence for a specific project and pursue each area.

### Customer and Supplier Interviews

A key area of due diligence is the set of customer and supplier interviews because they yield unedited input and answers to fundamental questions. On the customer side, one determines how satisfied the customers are with the functionality of the firm's products, product quality, and customer service. It is an opportunity to understand what customers want changed in the product line and functionality to better meet their needs and how they feel about the price-to-value relationship. Through this effort, the due diligence subteam determines the relationship customers have with the target and how likely they are to remain customers after the change in the ownership.

On the supplier side, the due diligence subteam verifies supplier arrangements and assesses the terms and nature of the relationship with the target. The interview with suppliers is important because it enables the due diligence subteam to establish the target's payment practices and find out what suppliers project the demand of the target for their products is likely to be. This is significant because the demand for inputs is highly correlated to the target's estimates of its output or revenue in the future. The terms of supplier agreement are reviewed to verify that the target is getting the best possible deal.

The target's relationship with its supplier is important to understand because it is indicative of its payment policies and practices. However, a key element that comes out of supplier interviews is their unique assessment of the target and how it compares with its competitors in terms of past and future growth, its ability to meet financial obligations on time, and the future of the industry. This is probably an unbiased assessment of the target's ability to grow in the future.

Because the purpose of the customer and supplier interviews is wide, but important in developing a good assessment of the target's current position and future potential, it is recommended that these interviews be conducted by experts. The reason for this is that such interviews entail sensitive information that needs to be obtained in the spirit of helping the target firm set itself on a sound growth path. Hence, the findings of these interviews contribute a lot to improving customer and supplier relations.

## DUE DILIGENCE ASSESSMENT AND QUALITY CHARACTERISTICS

### Assessment of Findings and Report

The information-gathering and verifying aspect of due diligence is half of the work needed in order to benefit by it. The other half is evaluating the findings and developing recommendations on whether to proceed with the project and what changes may be required to make the target a better-run operation. The latter is a unique contribution of the due diligence effort and the more that is invested in the due diligence phase, the greater the ability to implement the project successfully and harness expected synergies.

To be effective, the information and findings of the due diligence subteam have to be organized by due diligence category. A highly effective approach is the due diligence report and assessment matrix of Table 18.1. The various items listed are new data and information obtained; items verified and referenced; unusual transactions, accounting practices, and methods of recording; irregularities in transactions or reporting; and positive and negative findings.

**Table 18.1**
**Due Diligence Report and Assessment Matrix**

| Area of due diligence | New data and inform- ation. | Items verified and referen- ced | Unusual practices and trans- actions | Reporting irregular- ities | Positive findings | Negative findings |
|---|---|---|---|---|---|---|
| Legal | | | | | | |
| Financial | | | | | | |
| Technical | | | | | | |
| Human resources | | | | | | |
| Industry and market | | | | | | |
| Cultural | | | | | | |
| Policies, procedures | | | | | | |
| Environm. and other | | | | | | |
| Customer interviews | | | | | | |
| Supplier interviews | | | | | | |
| — | | | | | | |

Analysis of information, materials, and input obtained takes place to evaluate the target in its entirety. Once the analysis is completed, the evaluation of impacts is summarized in the due diligence report. The due diligence report brings together findings, analysis, and implications of findings and outlines a set of recommendations.

The due diligence report must be concise and show the assessment of findings and their impact on the new entity and the acquiring or partner company. Recommendations of the due diligence report should be specific and clearly articulated to the project team. Once the project team has digested the report and its recommendations, a briefing of the sponsor takes pace. At that point, the project team makes its own recommendation whether to proceed with the project based on its assessment of due diligence findings. Since the due diligence recommendations have significant impacts on the target or partner firm as well as on the parent company, the subteam evaluates the impact of its recommendations prior to sharing them with senior management.

### Due Diligence Quality Characteristics

The due diligence effort must be broad enough to cover all areas that need to be investigated. At the same time, it is an in-depth investigation and the earlier it is performed, the better. The purpose of due diligence is to provide assurances that the information on which the decision to undertake a project is based is sound and reliable. Therefore, when reviewing information and examining evidence, the due diligence subteam challenges major assumptions and looks for evidence to support or modify those assumptions.

Objectivity in analysis and interpretation of findings is another key quality characteristic of an effective due diligence, which requires experience and industry knowledge to assess issues properly. In acquisition projects, an effective due diligence must also be speedy and bring issues to conclusion rapidly. Also, the due diligence report should include recommendations concerning ability to obtain expected synergies and how to harness new ones.

The last two elements of quality are completeness of due diligence and effective communications during and after the effort. The due diligence recommendations must be supported by facts and communicated in such terms that the meaning is conveyed clearly, but the language does not create overly negative impressions. That is, the basis of recommendations is included in a minimum impact phrasing developed for external purposes. Finally, the communication of recommendations internally and externally is handled by appropriate team members and external advisors.

## SUMMARY

This chapter discusses the areas of due diligence and the significance of its recommendations in decision making and in synergy realization. The due diligence effort is an essential part of the joint venture process, but it is far more significant in the case of acquisition projects. However, this does not mean that joint venture projects do not require thorough analysis of the potential partner to determine whether a partnership is viable. In both types of projects, the key areas of the due diligence effort are legal, financial, human resources, technical, industry and market, and cultural due diligence, and customer and supplier interviews. Projects may also require special attention such as, for example, environmental due diligence, evaluation of plant and equipment, or valuation of physical inventories.

In addition to the usual scope of due diligence, systems, processes and procedures, and policies and practices are reviewed to develop a complete and accurate picture of the firm in question. This is done to ensure that the assessment of the project is based on a solid foundation. Because the due diligence effort involves working under extreme pressure and with sensitive information and situations, external advisors should be engaged to lead this effort and present the subteam recommendations.

The due diligence report recommendations strengthen the decision-making foundation to proceed with a project, define under what conditions, and suggest what actions are required in the future to enhance the new entity's operations. Also, the due diligence findings form the basis of legal agreements. Thus, its recommendations contribute a great deal to project success through the synergy realization and creation effort.

# 19

---

# ACQUISITION AND JOINT
# VENTURE AGREEMENTS

## INTRODUCTION

Success of acquisitions or joint ventures depends in part on the legal agreements negotiated. The purpose of legal agreements is to formalize understandings reached by project participants, memorialize negotiated terms and conditions of a transaction, and assign benefits or liabilities to appropriate parties. Another key function of legal agreements is to create appropriate exit clauses in the event certain conditions are not met or a party wishes to adjust its ownership or leave entirely. Legal documents and agreements also form the basis for developing financing for a project, especially when the project financing approach is pursued.

Because it is difficult to understand what various legal terms mean, legal agreements are often left entirely up to lawyers to draft and negotiate. World-class project teams, however, take a more active role because drafting and negotiating legal agreements is not entirely the legal staff's responsibility and because a more appropriate sharing of responsibility is required to create superior agreements. The reason for this is that the project team has a better understanding of strategic, business, and operational issues involved, while the legal team has a better appreciation of legal consequences of terms and conditions being negotiated and knows how to structure agreements best. Therefore, it is only when project teams work closely with lawyers assigned to projects and invest time in negotiations that sound agreements are created.

There is a process involved in drafting and evaluating legal agreements that dictates the timing of creating legal documents and what they contain. While standard legal documents exist for acquisition and joint venture projects and are modified to cover particulars of a project, the most effective agreements come from clearly defined objectives and close cooperation between the legal staff and the project team to capture accurately what has been agreed. Such legal documents are formed with input from project subteams and by exchange of information with project lawyers. That input and interaction is reflected in Figure 19.1, which shows inputs to the legal document creation process.

The discussion begins with the legal document creation process and is followed by the types of agreements involved in acquisitions and joint ventures. Confidentiality agreements, which are among the first legal documents produced, cover information exchanged between the parties involved and are reviewed here. Then, the memorandum of understanding (MOU) and the letter of intent are reviewed.

The key points included in competition agreements are treated before the discussion turns to joint venture and acquisition agreements. Owning to the importance of the implementation phase and new-entity ongoing operations, retained or seconded management contracts are discussed. Other types of contractual and agreements present in these projects are discussed and the characteristics of good agreements are examined. The role of the project team in the creation of legal documents is reviewed and the discussion proceeds to conditional agreements and the need for simple language in agreements.

## THE LEGAL DOCUMENT CREATION PROCESS

The legal document creation process starts with a briefing of the project team lawyer on the nature of the project and a clear articulation of project objectives. Once the lawyer becomes part of the core team, he/she participates in identification of business needs to be addressed and covered through legal documents. Then, the company positions on key issues are discussed with the lawyer and recorded for use in the various legal documents. Briefings on the project status, risks and issues, and discussions follow to ensure effective transition of responsibility for drafting legal documents takes place and continuity of purpose is preserved. Figure 19.1 depicts how better documents are created when a lawyer is part of the core team, rather than called upon at the end.

Figure 19.1 shows the extensive input, feedback, and interaction between various project subteams and the lawyer to create legal documents required to close a transaction. Notice that senior management is part of the process by reviewing a summary of the legal documents produced and helping in the resolution of difficult issues.

The legal document creation process for acquisitions and joint ventures starts with input from subteams on key business issues, the creation of the first draft, and a core team review and comment. Legal documents produced are presented to the other side's legal team, which comments on and revises the draft documents. Negotiations on the revisions to legal documents follow and a new draft is presented to the project team. The process repeats itself and a second project team review and changes to the new draft take place. This is followed by a review of revised legal documents by the other side, and so on, until convergence is reached and the final legal documents are produced that are satisfactory to the parties.

**Figure 19.1**
**The Legal Document Creation Process**

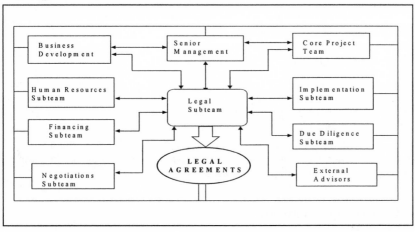

## THE MANY KINDS OF LEGAL AGREEMENTS

Many times in the early stages of acquisitions or joint ventures, agreements among senior managers are verbal and not recorded in any documents. However, as the project unfolds, verbal agreements are formalized and constitute a foundation to build on and a starting point blessed by senior management. While written documents provide assurance to project participants, this does not necessarily make them legally binding agreements unless they are drawn up specifically for that purpose.

The several agreements concluded to support closing of acquisition and joint venture projects are intended to balance and protect the interests of the project participants. The most important agreements in executing and implementing projects are the following legal documents:

1. Non-disclosure or confidentiality agreements where parties agree not to disclose shared information outside their organizations.
2. Memoranda of understanding that formalize commonality of purpose in early discussions.
3. Letters of intent, which are stronger than MOUs because they state intentions of the parties to proceed to outlined steps.
4. Non-competition agreements to limit the parties' ability to compete in certain markets for a specific time frame.
5. Exclusivity agreements, which refer to exclusivity in acquisition discussions and in doing business with a certain party.
6. Joint venture legal agreements, which are binding agreements between the partners in a project.
7. Acquisition purchase agreements formalizing the acquisition terms and conditions and bringing the project to closure.
8. Risk-sharing agreements, which are a means of risk allocation and assignment of responsibilities to project participants through legal documents.
9. Loan agreements, which are agreements between a banking institution and a

company assuming debt to fund the project.
10.  Management contracts, which are employment agreements for retained managers or seconded managers to an entity.
11.  Supply contracts or agreements outlining terms and conditions of transactions between the entity and its suppliers.
12.  Sales contracts or off-take contracts, which show the agreed-to terms and conditions between the entity and buyers of its output.

There are different types of acquisitions and joint ventures, and legal agreements are tailored to the needs of each arrangement. However, because the negotiating style is more open and cooperative in joint ventures, the agreements tend to be flexible. On the other hand, the competitive and closed nature of acquisition negotiations usually produces rather rigid and precise legal documents. Generally, some form of these legal documents is created to support closing of acquisitions and joint ventures.

### Confidentiality Agreements

The confidentiality of information shared and exchanged is often addressed in MOUs or letters of intent. When the nature of the information is sensitive or the technologies and the assets shared can lead to competitive advantage, stand-alone confidentiality agreements are executed to protect the proprietary nature of information shared. This is particularly true when a small firm is dealing with a much larger company.

Confidentiality agreements are recommended for all projects, regardless of level of trust involved, to prevent misunderstandings among future project participants. These agreements are essential for projects involving proprietary technologies and sensitive information, but they are a must in the case of projects in developing countries where notions of copyrights, royalties, intellectual property, and related concepts have different meanings than in industrialized countries.

The commonality of elements covered in confidentiality agreements begins with a description of items covered by the agreement and what information is considered confidential to make agreements enforceable. Provisions to handle the transfer of intellectual property and by-products are included so in the event the transaction is never completed, these provisions help avoid litigation. Other common clauses are control of confidential information and permissions to release information to parties outside the project participants, the time span covering agreements, and conditions describing their termination, including return or destruction of shared documents. Also, understandings of relief, the conditions for injunctions, and damages for breach are sometimes incorporated.

### MOUs and Letters of Intent

MOUs and letters of intent are discussed under legal agreements even though it is generally the case that participants want to burden themselves with few legal obligations. Hence, the prime legal objective is to ensure no unintended binding obligations. MOUs are the first substantive documents created in early acquisition or joint venture discussions. They are typically not construed as legally binding documents, but are extensively used in foreign joint venture projects and it is best practice is to state explicitly that MOUs do not create legally binding obligations. MOUs are intended to articulate goals of pursuing a common undertaking further, define some project scope, outline steps to advance to the next phase, and communicate the nature of understandings to participating companies' senior managers.

MOUs are often prepared by working level and signed by high-level managers with the idea in mind that they will serve as a foundation for project teams to build upon and, if warranted, to move projects through appropriate assessment, structuring, and implementation processes. The project lawyer should at least do a cursory review of the MOU prior to signature, and on large projects, they should do the drafting. MOUs often define the nature of participant contributions and outline their responsibilities and as such are useful tools to communicate obligations of parties to project teams and senior management. However, they should not be viewed as anything more than rough road maps to move projects forward.

Letters of intent are a step beyond MOUs and are used to formalize preliminary verbal agreements and move negotiations forward. Letters of intent can be used in lieu of MOUs and like them, they are frequently signed without legal review though a cursory review is recommended. Letters of intent are also sometimes referred to as term sheets and set forth the proposed structure of the transaction, define a price or a price range, and how it would be paid. They also consider special accounting or project tax considerations, specify conditions to conclude the transaction, and outline regulatory requirements and internal approvals. Letters of intent also condition the transaction on due diligence results and make a mutually satisfactory agreement a condition of consummating the transaction.

Letters of intent for joint ventures outline the reasons for joint venture formations and the purpose of agreements. As such, they define the joint venture company's scope in terms of geography and activities, outline objectives in the arrangement, and define responsibilities for partners. Joint venture letters of intent address commitments of financial and human resources at approximate levels and define deal structures for joint venture companies. They also specify in generic terms the governance structure of the joint venture, rights and exclusivity, and confidentiality and non-competition issues.

Letters of intent create a sense of moral commitment to a project although they should routinely state that they are not binding legal documents for most aspects of a transaction except for provisions of confidentiality, sharing of expenses, and refraining from negotiating with other parties. They are signed so that parties have a good sense of terms involved before they engage in due diligence or enter into lengthy negotiations that use a lot of valuable resources.

## Non-Competition and Exclusivity Agreements

The first exclusivity agreements in acquisitions and joint ventures are exclusive negotiation commitments in which the parties agree to limit discussions to the party signing the agreement. Another type of exclusivity agreements are those intended to prevent a party from engaging in business with an entity other than the one that signed the agreement.

Non-competition arrangements among project participants may occasionally be desirable to ensure project financial viability. However, in order for such agreements to be enforceable, they must not limit industry competition or impact consumer interests adversely. Typical key points in non-competition agreements include the following:

1. Coverage of specific items, such as non-competition in a certain geographic area, a certain technology, or a certain market.
2. The time span for which non-competition arrangements are in effect and conditions under which they terminate.
3. No raiding of personnel of parties involved for a specific and reasonable time in order to maintain confidentiality of information and protect proprietary technology.

Exclusivity agreements are a form of non-competing and cooperating arrangements, which grant one party alone the benefits of conducting business with the other party. The essence of these agreements is to limit the impact of one party's ability to transact business with others and bestow advantage to another party through the exclusive arrangement. As in the case of non-competition, exclusivity agreements cover the scope of arrangement, geographic area or market, time span of the agreement, and conditions for termination.

### Acquisition Agreements

Because acquisitions are risky business, acquisition agreements are essential to protect the interests of the parties, but especially the interests of the buyer. Hence, acquisition agreements are structured to be legally binding. Drafting and negotiation of these agreement is motivated by a preference to shift risks to other parties or be compensated for assuming risks others do not wish to accept. To ensure balance for both parties, acquisition agreements define the legal and tax structure and the terms and conditions of the transaction, represent fairly important financial and legal aspects about the target, and capture relevant information about the seller and buyer. They also determine how issues related to insufficient disclosure get resolved in the post-closing period and bind the two sides to complete the transaction, but also allow for exiting if representations and warranties of the seller are not factual.

Two major issues in completing the negotiations of an acquisition project are what conditions relieve a party from the obligation to close and what events after closing can cause refunding part of the purchase price. However, interests of seller and buyer are different, and to address concerns of both sides, acquisition agreements cover the legal and tax structure, the price, and the process of ownership transfer, representations and warranties of seller and buyer, and covenants before they are obligated to close the transaction. Additionally, they include the conditions to be satisfied before closing can take place, indemnification or establishment of liability for problems surfacing after closing, and other legal clauses peculiar to a specific acquisition.

Unlike joint venture agreements, acquisition agreements are very complex legal documents to draft and negotiate. Therefore, it is important that the project team and the lawyer assigned to the project work closely to hammer out a solid acquisition agreement.

### Joint Venture Agreements

In the process of evaluating and forming a joint venture, the parties get agreements solidified without realizing this is taking place. The reason for this is that to assess a joint venture, one needs to define the scope of that entity, a governance structure, contributions and obligations of the parties, and several operational responsibilities. Hence, by the time legal documents are drafted to formalize understanding and arrangements, agreements have more or less been shaped to the liking of the partners' project teams.

Joint ventures are successful when the right chemistry is present and clearly defined goals and objectives are shared by the partners. Therefore, joint venture agreements are of limited value because if partners need to use legal agreements to resolve issues and conflicts as they arise, then the joint venture is not likely to survive the test of time. Joint venture agreements tend to be relatively straightforward and the basic elements included are the legal structure of the joint venture and the objectives, scope and geographic coverage, markets, and technologies.

Other elements of joint venture agreements include financial, in-kind, human resource contributions, patents, licenses, and permits partners bring to the joint venture. They also contain assignment of major partner responsibilities and contractual obligations, non-competition and exclusivity clauses, and limitation of liabilities for obligations of the partners. The governance structure of the joint venture entity, minority partner preemptive rights to preserve their equity share interests, and definition of termination clauses, triggers, exit rights, and force majeure are also key elements.

### Management Contracts

Success of acquisitions and joint ventures depends on ability of the acquiring or the joint venture company to keep or attract key management talent to implement the project and operate the new entity. Hence, the need to develop management contracts in acquisition and joint venture projects for key senior managers. These contracts can be viewed as achieving a form of non-competition or exclusivity agreements with managers even though that was not the intended reason for them.

Management contracts cover engagements for specific functions and responsibilities to ensure stability over the transition period and take advantage of the expertise of talented managers. Thus, the terms of engagement specify functions to be performed in the transition or operation periods, length of engagement, and compensation schemes. For managers on secondments to joint venture companies, buyback contracts are drafted to ensure that managers are able to return to the parent companies once assignments in the joint venture expire. Although buy-backs are criticized as compromising the manager's dedication to the joint venture, they are essential to accomplish secondments in the first place.

Compensation of individuals under management contracts is based on some earn-out formula. That is, it is directly tied to performance of the new entity managers help implement and operate. The more successful the new entity, the higher the compensation. However, earn-out formulas have termination clauses attached to them and compensation of managers under contracts at that point becomes comparable to other managers in the new entity. Finally, management contracts themselves have renewal options attached and expiration and exit clauses to give parties the opportunity to continue cooperation or part ways.

### Other Agreements and Contracts

In some acquisitions and joint ventures other agreements and legal documents are needed before closing and financing of the project can take place. They include risk-sharing agreements, loan agreements, supply contracts, and sales contracts or off-take contracts. Risk-sharing agreements are intended to mitigate risk exposure of participants by having the party best equipped to handle project risks assume those risks. Risk-sharing agreements, therefore, deal with how project participants assume project risks and how they are compensated for potential liabilities. Loan agreements are among lenders and the borrowing party to pay for the acquisition or the formation of the joint venture. These are lengthy legal documents with terms and conditions that determine when, how, and under what conditions funds can be drawn down, how debt is repaid, and what happens in case of default.

Supply contracts, sales contracts, and off-take contracts are intended to ensure the new entity is supplied essential inputs to its production process under favorable terms and that its output is purchased by a party that has the ability to pay. Sales contracts usually refer to selling part of the goods or services produced and off-take contracts refer to purchase of the entire output, usually of a large plant. Often, such contracts are essential to secure financing of the new entity, and when backed by appropriate guarantees, they become bankable contracts.

### Conditional Agreements

Completeness of acquisition and joint venture agreements and legal documents is a requirement. However, because changes in operating environments and business conditions occur all the time and one cannot anticipate all eventualities, agreements depend on certain conditions being satisfied. For instance, the price to be paid for a target is a function of future operational performance or some financial indicator. In the case of management contracts, earn-out formulas condition management compensation on operational performance.

Conditional agreements are also used to motivate cooperative behavior on the part of foreign government entities that are partners in foreign joint ventures.

While conditional agreements may be prudent, care is exercised to ensure that terms are adequately defined, that adequate escape clauses are included, and that treatment of interests and issues is symmetrical. This is a requirement of good agreements that makes them implementable and enforceable.

## IMPORTANT FACTORS IN DEVELOPING AGREEMENTS

### Characteristics of Good Agreements

Acquisition and joint venture legal documents are easier to monitor and manage when their essence is developed by the project team and drafted by legal staff experienced in negotiating such agreements. The first requirement of good agreements and legal documents is clarity of purpose and addressing issues directly in a brief and concise manner.

Completeness of coverage of important issues and precise definitions and descriptions of representations and warranties, rights, responsibilities, and obligations of the parties along with clear assignment of benefits is another important consideration in good legal documents. However, superior legal agreements are permeated with balance of objectives and interests and symmetrical treatment of issues, rights, and responsibilities. Because of their nature, such legal documents incorporate elements of flexibility and are easier to negotiate, monitor, and manage.

In addition to flexibility, sound legal agreements have adequate escape clauses and well-defined termination or exit conditions to allow parties freedom in choosing ways to meet obligations and ensure interests of all parties are protected. Finally, clear language is a requirement for good legal documents for the implementation subteam to monitor and manage or execute terms and conditions of legal documents. That is, good legal documents contain understandable language and minimal amounts of legalese.

### The Role of the Project Team

In world-class companies, project teams play an important role in shaping and drafting the agreements to make them easier to negotiate, manage, and monitor throughout their lives. The reason for active involvement is that because legal agreements are used to manage formal relationships and transactions, project teams are in the best position to understand business issues and identify concerns to be addressed and provide appropriate input to lawyers.

The project team must ensure consistency of agreements with intended business purpose for the project to achieve its objectives. Therefore, the project team, and especially the implementation subteam, should participate in drafting and review of agreements, their negotiation, and revisions subsequent to negotiations. The project team should examine agreements with a critical eye to identify potential problems and negotiate appropriate solutions with help from the legal staff and project advisors.

Internal corporate approval processes routinely require management approval of acquisition and joint venture agreements and other legal documents.

Hence, management reviews negotiated agreements and legal documents to support the internal project approval process. Management approvals of acquisition and joint venture agreements are a prerequisite for the preparation of an offer memorandum, if it is required to attract equity participants in the project and in getting financing. Consequently, the project team stays involved in the process to ensure sound agreements are developed for management to authorize closing the transaction.

Once legal documents have been approved and signed, the implementation subteam is charged with turning paper documents into real entities and operations. Also, a good part of the responsibility to monitor agreements, raise and resolve issues, and manage contracts remains with the implementation subteam. The implementation subteam and legal staff assess how well agreements and contracts are functioning and make revisions to agreements and documents to reflect the reality of the situation. Additionally, the implementation subteam is involved in terminating agreements and exiting from contracts and other legal obligations.

### Language of Agreements

Acquisition and joint venture legal documents tend to be verbose and use complex sentence structures even when dealing with simple issues. In world-class project teams, legal documents are drafted in shorter sentences, which are easier to understand and monitor. Therefore, the project team should ensure that legal documents contain clear language because if the project team does not understand the language of the agreement, chances are the implementation subteam cannot manage that agreement.

Unlike joint venture agreements that formalize a series of understandings up to a point, acquisition agreements are usually negotiated and drafted during a confined time period. Therefore, there is heavy involvement by legal staff and investment bankers supporting the negotiation manager. However, if discussions take place in legalese and documents are written in legalese, then the negotiation manager takes second place and the legal staff manage project negotiations. There may be exceptions to this, for example, in the tax or intellectual property licensing areas, but these should be kept to a minimum. Negotiation subteams are, therefore, advised to simplify the language of legal documents to the maximum extent to make them understood by the project team.

### SUMMARY

Legal documents and agreements in acquisitions and joint ventures are intended to capture all understandings and formalize them in legal documents. They reflect negotiated terms and conditions in formal agreements, eliminate uncertainty concerning intents on both sides, allocate risks, capture risk-sharing agreements in legal documents, and protect the interests of participants.

In this chapter, we discuss the types of legal agreements needed in acquisitions and joint ventures and look at the role of MOUs and letters of intent. A brief discussion follows on confidentiality agreements and the legal document creation process is reviewed. After non-competition agreements, we focus on joint venture and acquisition agreements where balance of costs and benefits to parties involved and stability of arrangements is emphasized and contracts for retained or seconded management are discussed.

Characteristics of good agreements are reviewed and a discussion of the project team roles ensues. Since not all terms and conditions of agreements materialize by the time legal documents are prepared, conditional agreements are created to cover these situations. Since the majority of legal documents produced are rarely understood by project participants, it is recommended that the language of the agreements be simple, direct, and succinct. Emphasis should also be placed on extensive input and interaction of the project team with lawyers, clarity of objectives and continuity of purpose to ensure the positions on business issues are reflected in legal documents, and complete coverage of issues impacting project value.

# 20

# FINANCING ACQUISITION AND JOINT VENTURE PROJECTS

## INTRODUCTION

In most acquisitions, the acquiring company purchases the stock or assets of the target for cash, stock, securities, and other financial instruments or considerations. The tax implications of the transaction need to be understood first and then the deal structure decided. After that, the project team along with the investment bankers and external advisors look seriously at the financing issue. Financing acquisitions and joint ventures comes after definitive agreements are signed, but if funding does not materialize, projects never get implemented.

Acquisition targets are easier to finance than joint venture companies because target companies have been in operation and have track records indicative of their value. Also, the security offered by access to the target's assets that produce the cash flow allows development of several options to finance the acquisition. Financing a joint venture involves the same steps as an acquisition, the difference being how comfortable lenders are with the joint venture's financial projections. Regardless of the strength of the project, foreign acquisitions and joint ventures are more complicated and take longer to complete the financing.

Financing acquisition and joint ventures is an important consideration because it impacts the degree of project success. It determines whether projects are funded or not, the type of funding raised, and the cost of funds. Since financing costs and fees are a significant part of total project costs, the type of financing obtained affects project success. That is, financing impacts the cost of capital, the discount rate used in financial analysis, and the project valuation. It impacts project success because financing enhancements required place limitations and restrictions on the company's ability to raise additional capital and increases its cost. Also, financing is impacted by how project risks are allocated among project participants.

The emphasis in this chapter is on the financing process because of the complexity and multitude of steps involved in developing and implementing financing. The discussion begins with an exposition of elements determining whether a project is financeable and types of financing possible. The steps in the actual process of developing financing are reviewed next and the types of financing generally available in funding acquisitions and joint ventures discussed. The various financial instruments are considered along with sources of financing.

As not all projects are financeable without some kind of credit enhancements, financing enhancements normally required are discussed. The specific factors that determine what kind of financing can be obtained are examined after that. Financing based on project cash flows, or project financing, is discussed next. The roles and responsibilities of participants in financing are reviewed, and the chapter closes with the assessment of financing plans.


## BASIC CONCEPTS OF FINANCING

### Financeable Projects

Financing acquisitions and joint ventures are well-publicized events and one often gets the impression that whether projects get financed, or how they get financed, depends on the financing advisor engaged. The competence of the financing advisor is one element determining how effectively a project gets financed. However, there are additional elements the project team pays attention to in order to make a project financeable, such as:

*1. Reasonableness of assumptions and financial projections.* Equity holders are willing to take risks, but debt holders need to have assurance about repayment of interest and principal. Consequently, they scrutinize the assumption set and review financial projections and project economics closely.

*2. Strong project economics and cash flows.* In the absence of a strong business case, financing is problematic even if some forms of security are in place. Strong cash flows are expected in terms of magnitude and also certainty or variance of cash flows.

*3. Sound implementation plan.* This is a requirement because it shows potential funding sources that questions have been answered about how the project will be executed, how synergies will be harnessed, and how the new entity will be integrated with the buying company or the partners' operations.

*4. Reasonable business plan.* A good business plan with reasonable assumptions shows how the new entity will be operated in the post-closing period and how it will accomplish the financial and strategic goals set out in the business case.

*5. Acceptable risk allocation.* Potential funding sources assess project risks and look at how various risks are dealt with. Their interest in how risks are allocated among project participants is motivated by the need to have a stable and sustainable risk allocation scheme over the planning horizon.

*6. Solid and enforceable agreements and contracts.* Acquisition and joint venture agreements formalize understandings and negotiated terms and conditions in projects. Therefore, sound agreements and enforceable contracts with reasonable escape clauses are needed to deal with contractual obligations and risk elements managed through legal agreements.

*7. Sufficient securities.* While equity participants will ordinarily require higher returns on their investment, debt holders require adequate securities and guarantees to ensure principal and interest repayment. Parental guarantees are particularly important in cases of weak project economics.

*8. Balance of project participant interests.* The reason that reasonable and acceptable sharing of costs, risks, and benefits among project participants is a requirement to make a project financeable is that it ensures sustainability of arrangements and agreements. Other than the strength of project cash flows, balance of project participant interests does more to produce a financeable transaction than anything else in the project.

When these considerations are addressed adequately, possibilities and financing options for a project expand substantially. Therefore, it is recommended that the project team develop a sound business case and negotiate appropriate risk sharing and deal with these issues when developing financing strategy and plans.

### The Financing Process

The financing process for acquisitions and joint ventures entails a wide spectrum of activities to prepare the information required to convince potential debt holders and equity participants of the project value. Following is the series of steps that the project team goes through to develop financing for a project.

*1. Selecting a financing advisor:* This is probably the most important element in obtaining appropriate financing for the project. In searching for a financing advisor, the project team leader is looking for a seasoned individual in financing these types of projects and someone who is independent and not tied to certain financing solutions. However, in most projects investment bankers engaged to provide deal structure advice and independent assessment end up being the financing advisor. In such cases, the project team should monitor closely the financing solutions proposed.

*2. Deal structure review.* A review of project legal documents, legal and tax structure implications, and negotiated terms and conditions is undertaken once the financing advisor is engaged. Understanding the deal structure, the terms and conditions of the acquisition or the joint venture, and operational objectives enables the financing advisor to create a balance between financing requirements and objectives.

*3. Debt-to-equity requirements.* The debt-to-equity ratios of the buying or the partner company are reviewed to determine what adjustments may be made to achieve the objectives of project participants. The stand-alone and the combined debt-to-equity ratios are assessed to understand the possibilities for enhancing financing for the project.

*4. Pledges, collateral, and mortgages.* With the help of the financing advisor the project team determines what pledges and collateral will be required to secure debt financing. Also, the implications of mortgaging various assets of the company need to be evaluated in light of strategic and operational objectives.

*5. Review of agreements.* A thorough review of agreements takes place to determine the level of assurance potential debt holders and equity participants can have in the project. The contractual obligations of the parties involved are examined, as well as exposure to risks and how exposure is covered through agreements. Frequently, the financing advisor provides input and advice on how to restructure agreements to enhance financing.

*6. Evaluation of costs and benefits.* At this juncture, preliminary costs of various financing alternatives and possible benefits associated with these alternatives are evaluated. The project team is interested in total costs involved and not only expected return on each type of financing for the project.

*7. Risk allocation.* Once agreements are firmed up, ways in which various project risks are shared or managed are examined to determine whether investors can be assured of expected returns and repayment of principal. In this phase, the financing advisor provides input on how risks need to be allocated to achieve desired objectives.

*8. Business case.* The financing advisor is familiar with the project feasibility and assists the project team in the business case development. The advisor's objective here is to create credibility with external project participants by providing a complete and objective analysis that addresses all sources and uses of funds and risks involved.

*9. Options and strategy.* Having completed the business case, the financing advisor and the project team are now in a position to develop reasonable financing objectives, some financing options, and a strategy to implement these options. One option is selected that meets financing objectives in the most effective manner. The selected option must reflect the reality of the situation and the strategy steps should be documented, understood, and agreed upon by the project team.

*10. Guarantees and insurance.* Having completed a sound business case enables the financing advisor to look for various security, guarantee, and insurance schemes to provide adequate coverage for the risks the company is not in a position to assume. Once appropriate credit enhancement is identified, costs are estimated and included in the business case.

*11. Expected tenors.* The strength of the project cash flows, the availability of credit enhancements, and the cost of different loans determine the loan tenors appropriate for the financing of debt. Tenors vary inversely with risks, but traditional financing loan tenors tend to be shorter than limited-recourse financing loan tenors.

*12. Project rating.* When it is determined that project cash flows are exceptionally good or that there is no way to get around it, the project is rated by a rating agency, such as Standard and Poors. Investment-grade and above ratings make debt placements easier and less expensive because of objectivity associated with a rating agency project assessment.

*13. Costs of financing.* At this point, the focus is on calculations of total costs associated with different approaches and types of financing. Comparisons of all financing cost elements are made against a benchmark, which is usually the opportunity cost of financing through internal funds. While the emphasis is on numbers, ease of implementation and other considerations come into the picture as well.

*14. Information memorandum.* This is equivalent to a prospectus, or an external business case, intended to show potential investors or lenders what the project is all about and convince them of the project value. This is an area where expertise of the financing advisor comes into play to put things in an objective, but positive light and in terms that potential participants are able to grasp immediately.

*15. Raising equity.* After the company's or the partners' equity contributions, equity elements are commonly raised based on requirements of the financing option selected and the project's tax implications. The reason for this is that lenders like to see substantial equity participation by the acquiring company or the joint venture partners because it is viewed as strong commitment to the project. Other things being equal, the higher the equity portion of financing, the higher the comfort level of debt holders.

*16. Raising debt.* Debt placement and underwriting follows the underwriting of equity and takes on the form of loans, public debt, and private debt placement. Again, as in equity financing, the terms and conditions, pledges, restrictions, and security implications need to be well understood for negotiations with the financing institutions to be effective.

*17. Negotiation of terms and conditions.* With different types of debt come different restrictions that lenders attach to loans for acquisition and joint venture projects. Loan agreements contain clauses to protect the interests of lenders against default. Here, the expertise of the financing advisor and the lawyer on the project team is invaluable, but the need to understand loan agreement terms and conditions cannot be overemphasized. The goal in these negotiations is to preclude loan agreement restrictions from impacting the long-term growth of the entity being funded.

*18. Legal review.* A number of agreements are required in financing of acquisition or joint venture projects. While legal documents are drafted by lawyers of the funding institutions, they are reviewed and modified by lawyers of the acquiring or the partner companies. Reviews of legal documents related to financing must also be conducted by the project team and advisors to ensure that company interests are protected in every eventuality.

*19. Internal approvals.* Approvals of the financing package from the acquiring and the target company treasury organizations is required because of the need to coordinate activities leading to closing and financing implementation. Likewise, in the financing of a joint venture, the financing package should be reviewed by the partner companies so that obligations of each party are understood and activities coordinated to ensure smooth financing implementation.

*20. Financing implementation.* This refers to closing on financing and getting access to actual equity and debt funds. Financing implementation takes place when the financing package is approved by the affected stakeholders, agreements related to financing are signed, and conditions preceding the availability of a facility have been met. In the case of foreign projects, approvals by foreign government authorities may be required to ensure, among other things, availability of foreign exchange for debt repayment and dividend repatriation.

### Roles of Project Participants

In financing acquisitions and joint ventures, the buyer and seller and the joint venture partners are the major parties in the financing and they are responsible for negotiating the deal structure resulting in definitive agreements. The project team develops the feasibility study and the business case analysis to create the information memorandum in cooperation with the financing advisor. It also works with the financing advisor and internal organizations, such as corporate treasury and tax groups, to develop financing options and obtain internal approvals.

Lawyers draft documents and with the project team review legal documents related to financing a project. Lawyers are also involved in negotiations with financing institutions and are supported by the project team. The financing advisor and legal experts specializing in financing act as internal consultants and guide the project team in negotiating financing terms and conditions. Lawyers also support the financing advisor and are involved in risk-sharing negotiations, creation of loan agreements, and closing on the financing.

The financing advisor and the project team leader are responsible for bringing together the elements involved in financing and play a key role in determining the legal and funding structure for the project. The financing advisor is responsible for developing and assessing financing alternatives, creation of the financing strategy, and developing the information memorandum. Ordinarily, the financing advisor is responsible for initiating discussions on risk sharing and negotiating risk allocation. The financing advisor also negotiates with debt and equity sources and acts as a consultant when dealing with unilateral and multilateral institutions and insurance underwriters.

Independent technical experts and consultants play a key role in financing because they provide unbiased opinions and guidance to the financing advisor or the financing institutions. Independent technical experts and consultants are seasoned industry experts who provide objective assessments, whose judgments are trusted by the parties involved, and who serve as advisors to lawyers working with the project and the project team. Investment bankers are usually retained to provide independent financial assessments of projects and from time to time, they serve as financing advisors on the project.

Commercial banks and debt and equity underwriters play key roles in financing projects and set basic requirements and terms and conditions for the financing they provide. These parties interface with the project lawyers and the financing advisor and work with each other to create the loan agreements. These institutions conduct their own project due diligence and arrange or coordinate risk-sharing arrangements among themselves. Finally, commercial banks and debt and equity underwriters work closely with the financing advisor and project lawyers to finalize financing agreements.

Unilateral and multilateral institutions are major players in the financing process and provide the guarantees, insurance, and other programs needed to implement financing for projects in foreign countries. Without support from unilateral and multilateral institutions it may not be possible to provide coverage and finance some projects without major impacts on the project financials. The financing advisor works closely with unilateral and multilateral institutions to develop financing options and with the lawyers to ensure that appropriate counter-indemnities are in place to protect the parties against default.

## FINANCING ACQUISITIONS AND JOINT VENTURES

### Generic Types of Financing

Acquiring companies and joint venture partners usually have the option to finance all or part of a project through internally generated funds or through external sources of funds. In joint ventures (and some acquisitions) once the decision to go with external funding has been made, the project team needs to determine whether financing should be on an off-balance-sheet basis after the costs and benefits of each approach have been considered. That is, limited-recourse versus full-recourse financing is evaluated to determine the most effective approach.

Seller financing may be an option available in the case of an acquisition if the parent company is willing to hold securities issued by the buying company, such as bonds, promissory notes, and mortgages. In the case of joint venture projects involving exports of goods and services, Export Credit Agency (ECA) support in enhancing credit and financing is another viable option. Also, investment insurance is available for foreign projects to enhance financeability.

In joint venture financing, to what extent the joint venture partners contribute equity to the new entity is considered versus bringing in additional partners or strategic investors to enhance financing effectiveness. Supplier financing is another type of financing available in some cases where either equipment purchases are a condition or an ongoing provision of inputs and supply of goods and services is secured through contractual arrangements with suppliers. In the case of joint ventures with foreign government partners, the Build- Own-Transfer (BOT) type of project financing or any of its variants may be appropriate.

Regardless of financing pursued, the question of debt versus debt-equity financing combinations and resulting costs and benefits need to be addressed. Once the debt-to-equity ratio is determined, the particular form of debt and equity issue is decided subject to negotiations with other project participants. The project risks are assessed and allocated as effectively as possible to guide the creation of various financing alternatives.

> *BOT financing is a type of project financing tailored for companies that design, engineer, and develop projects mostly in developing countries in partnership with a foreign government entity, although they are also used to construct large infrastructure projects in industrialized countries. As the name suggests, companies invest in the project, build the plant, install the equipment needed, operate the new entity for a negotiated period long enough to recover their investment, and then transfer ownership in the project to a another entity.*

### Sources of Financing

On the equity side of financing, the acquiring company's or joint venture partner's equity is a major source of funding projects. However, strategic partner equity is often obtained to lessen the burden of financing on project participants and on some occasions it is supplemented with equity contributions by customers or suppliers. Equity contributions by customers and suppliers are used to strengthen the relationships with the company being financed.

Initial public offerings (IPOs) are commonly used to fund start-up and joint venture companies, especially if they involve a respected foreign local partner. While expensive, IPOs are a good way to receive publicity and advertising for new companies and their operations. Venture capital is expensive (35 to 50 percent expected return) and is not used to fund ordinary acquisitions and joint ventures. However, if such projects are highly speculative, venture capital may be a good approach to finance the project. Private or closed investment funds may also be used in funding projects, but only a fraction of financing comes from such investment funds. Insurance companies and pension funds are another source of equity capital when they have already loaned funds to a project on a fixed-rate basis because they can protect their positions against unanticipated inflation through equity participation.

Insurance companies and pension funds are increasingly involved in equity positions in acquisitions and joint venture projects, but they prefer equity instruments like convertible preferred stock and warrants. In some cases, seller equity investment in the buying company's stock is a source of funding the acquisition. For joint venture projects, direct partner equity investments are essential, form the foundation, and determine the type of financing to be developed. That is, the higher the partner equity contribution, the more financing options become available because potential participants in the financing derive additional assurance from large equity contributions by the partners.

The largest source of secured and unsecured debt financing for acquisitions and joint ventures are large international commercial banks. For foreign projects, local commercial bank loans are a good way to finance a project and establish local banking relationships. Commercial bank financing ranges from short-term credit to 30-year mortgages and interest rates vary according to the security involved. Insurance company loans of 7 to 15 years are available and their cost is fairly competitive —usually, treasury plus a default risk premium. Insurance companies like to lend to projects with high future potential on a subordinated debt basis with common stock conversion privileges to maximize their return.

Pension funds now participate in subordinated or even equity financing and are looking for the same kind of returns and terms as insurance companies. An advantage that pension fund debt has over commercial bank debt is that it does not have financing fees attached to it. Venture capital firms occasionally lend to acquisition and joint venture projects on a subordinated debt basis with conversion to common stock privileges. In addition, leveraged buyout (LBO) funds are another source of financing because of their ability to fund the equity portion of a much larger-value company. However, LBO financing is expensive because of the increased risks assumed.

The seller of the target company is a good source of debt financing, which, when available, gives the buyer additional assurance about the profitability of the acquired company. Often, earn-out arrangements are present when seller debt financing is involved because the seller enhances returns by helping the acquiring company be successful. Finally and more importantly, placement of public debt and increasingly private debt (144A placements) are premier sources of funding acquisition and joint venture projects because of the efficiency of this market.

In financing foreign acquisitions or joint ventures, in addition to traditional financial instruments, the project team and the financing advisor should be prepared to consider a number of non-traditional means of financing the project. Because foreign local capital markets may not be well developed, in-kind contributions, countertrade, offsets, and forfeiting may be appropriate although they are expensive and inefficient means of financing projects.

### Financing Enhancements

Acquisition and joint venture projects are risky and financing them requires providing assurance to potential investors and lenders. This takes the form of financing enhancements, which refer to support provided to enhance the credit worthiness of the borrower and make financing possible. It also refers to incentives given to lenders to make financing a project more attractive. The most important enhancements available are in the area of debt financing and take on the form of collateral, guarantees, and insurance against debt repayment default. Collateralized debt, parental and joint venture partner company guarantees, and insurance to cover project risks make financing quicker to obtain and lower its costs.

In international acquisitions and joint ventures, financing becomes possible through various credit enhancements provided by various unilateral agencies of governments, such as Export Credit Agencies (ECAs), or through multilateral institutions, such as regional development banks and the World Bank. Foreign investment insurance is available through unilateral agencies, such as the Overseas Private Investment Corporation (OPIC), or through multilateral agencies, such as regional development banks. Many guarantee and insurance programs are available to cover a wide variety of risks and projects around the world.

ECA support in financing comes into play when there are exports of goods and services from the country of the particular ECA. Multiple ECA coverage is possible and can often result in financing of 100 percent of the value of exports involved in a project even with ECA country content requirements. ECA guarantees and insurance programs cover lenders against political and commercial risk and ordinarily require foreign government counter-indemnities. While very attractive, ECA guarantee and insurance programs take longer to implement than other credit enhancement options or financing and tend to be cumbersome.

Investment insurance form OPIC or the World Bank covers a large majority of foreign acquisition and joint venture projects. OPIC covers investments of U.S. companies abroad and this coverage indirectly translates into protection of equity participants in the project against expropriation and other political risks. Most World Bank programs insure participants in projects with governments of developing countries, but other World Bank insurance programs are available for projects with private companies in these countries.

Regional and Islamic development banks offer guarantees and insurance programs that make the difference between a project being financeable or not. As in the case of World Bank involvement, a number of country development and technology transfer requirements apply when regional development banks or Islamic development institutions are involved. Furthermore, compliance with these requirements and negotiations with various financing participants take a long time to complete.

Co-financing and complementary financing may also be possible for certain types of joint venture projects in developing countries that qualify for World Bank or regional development bank loans. Under this scheme, the multilateral agency provides seed money for the project to be used in conjunction with loans from commercial banks so that default on commercial bank loans constitutes default on multilateral agency loans. Co-financing arrangements have low default rates because a default on a private loan is also viewed as default on a loan from a multilateral agency, which is rare.

### Factors Determining Financing

Many considerations determine the kind and form of financing brought to an acquisition or joint venture project. The following are key determinants of financing:

1. *Legal and tax considerations.* Numerous considerations go into the decision to pursue an acquisition under a certain legal and tax structure, but the resulting structure impacts how financing is done. For example, if it is determined that the best structure for an acquisition to take place is through a merger of equals, then the exchange of stocks at the appropriate ratio of values is all that needs to be done.

2. *Credit worthiness of the entity.* The types of financing possible in a given transaction are determined by the credit worthiness of the parties involved and the new entity. Other things being equal, a small company acquiring another company is facing an altogether different set of financing options than two large companies forming a joint venture.

3. *Ability to use the balance sheet.* On-balance-sheet financing is an option often used in financing acquisition and joint venture projects. It is indicative of the company's financial strength and ability to borrow. The reason that it is used frequently is that the financing costs under this approach are lower than if a company's balance sheet is not used in the financing.

4. *Adequacy of cash flows.* The business plan of the acquired or the joint venture entity is a key determinant of financing. Of particular significance is the magnitude and timing of cash flows because they determine the ability to repay debt and pay dividends according to expectations.

5. *Cost of financing.* The cost of financing alternatives plays an important role in what type of financing is selected once that cost and availability of desired facilities are balanced against other considerations, such as certainty and ease of financing. Cost of financing includes not only interest, but also various types of fees, commissions, expenses, and other charges to be paid.

6. *Expected financing coverage.* Availability of expected coverage and certainty of that coverage are important considerations especially when quick closing needs to take place. Usually, certainty of coverage at expected levels is arranged before a transaction closes, but certainty carries higher commitment and arrangement fees.

7. *Third-party guarantees.* The availability and quality of third-party guarantees make the difference as to how expensive debt financing is. The more protection offered to lenders and equity holders, the less the cost of financing and the quicker the closing.

*8. Nature and project size.* Certain acquisitions and joint ventures lend themselves to certain types of financing and the size of projects dictates certain options. For example, an acquisition of a small, but highly profitable target by a AAA-rated company can be funded entirely through senior debt. On the other hand, a joint venture formed to produce electricity in a developing country will require some form of limited recourse financing with a mix of debt and equity instruments to satisfy requirements of various participants.

*9. Risk allocation.* How risks are shared among project participants is a significant consideration because it determines the sustainability of arrangements and the ability of the parties assuming the risks to deliver on their obligations. Also, when risks are allocated appropriately, potential debt and equity participants derive assurance and are induced to part with their money.

*10. Unilateral and multilateral support.* In the case of international projects, investment insurance programs, various types of guarantees, and credit enhancement programs of different agencies are used to make financing possible or improve the terms of financing.

*11. Nature of agreements.* In large projects where limited-recourse financing is used to fund the project, various supplier and customer contracts, labor agreements, agreements with government entities, loan agreements, and other types of agreements are examined closely. The reason for such close review is that if agreements are knit together properly, they can give potential equity and debt holders a good idea as to how successful the entity being funded is likely to be.

*12. Credit enhancements and insurance.* Private and government insurance programs are intended to make financing possible and improve the terms of financing. A competent financing advisor searches for different insurance programs and credit enhancements to get better financing by involving the appropriate parties. When different forms of insurance are in effect or when credit enhancements are brought into a project, a lot of doors previously closed are now open.

*13. Constraints of financing.* Loan tenors, loan covenants, conditions precedent, requirements of project participants, and other constraints often preclude certain financing solutions from coming into effect and limit the set of financing options.

*14. Market conditions.* Market conditions when financing is needed influence the types of financing available and the cost of financing. Competent financing advisors monitor acquisition and joint venture projects closely and pay attention to the timing of the transaction closing and the financing available at closing.

*15. Risk appetite.* The extent to which the parties involved in the project are interested in assuming elements of risk for appropriate remuneration also affects what options are possible in financing of acquisitions or joint ventures.

### Limited-Recourse Financing

Project financing or limited-recourse financing is an off-balance-sheet financing approach used primarily in funding new, large infrastructure projects around the world, but it can also be used to finance acquisition and joint venture projects. Project financing refers to financing that is dependent on neither the credit support of the acquiring company or the joint venture partners nor on the value of the assets of the target or the joint venture companies. In project financing there is limited or, in a few cases, no recourse to the borrowing entities, but with it come risk-sharing negotiations, lengthy and complex agreements, and higher interest costs and fees because of higher lender exposure.

There are several advantages in pursuing limited or non-recourse project financing, the most important being that obligations of the borrowing entity to support the project do not appear on its balance sheet with the exception of financial guarantees, which appear on the balance sheet footnotes. Also, under this type of financing, lenders assume part of the risk that the borrower would assume. In the case of foreign joint venture companies, the treatment of capital investment, tax allowances, and tax holidays may be additional benefits from the creation of a project company to borrow under a project finance structure. Finally, project financing allows a company that is restricted from borrowing on a secured or mortgage basis to engage in non-recourse financing.

Under a project financing approach, the lenders do not require loans to be secured by assets, but they do require substantial equity investment to reduce the debt burden obligation of the project. Project financing is more expensive than on-balance-sheet financing because of the time involved in evaluating a project, negotiating agreements, developing documentation, and the costs of obtaining guarantees or insurance coverage. In addition, costs associated with monitoring the project and loans during their life and higher returns required to induce lenders to assume higher risks make limited-recourse financing more expensive.

The two fundamental project financing structures are a limited or non-recourse debt that is secured and paid back by the cash flow stream or debt backed by the purchase of the new entity's output. These two basic project finance structures can accommodate various financing techniques, such as export credit financing, lease financing, and issue of securities backed by guarantees. Variants of the build, operate, and transfer (BOT) project financing approach are often used in joint venture projects with foreign governments to enable a foreign government that does not have the financial resources to undertake the project, to attract foreign investment and affect some technology transfer.

Project financing was previously used almost exclusively to fund the development and construction of large infrastructure projects such as power plants, roads, and telecommunications networks around the world. Now, project financing is used to fund all types of projects that involve a directly attributable and adequate cash flow with some reasonable risk characteristics. Project financing for acquisitions and joint ventures is used extensively by companies building infrastructure projects in developing countries for reasons such as inability to use the acquiring or joint venture partner companies' balance sheet or their unwillingness to assume risks associated with funding under a full-recourse scheme. Also, limited availability of internal funds because other projects are undertaken simultaneously and shifting project risks to other entities are issues the project team needs to consider.

Project financing is based on a series of agreements among project participants where risks are allocated, shared, shifted, and mitigated according to ability to handle the risks and negotiating position of the parties. In such a scheme, various forms of insurance, securities, and guarantees play a crucial role in making the parties willing to accept different risks. Because of the risk assumption element by third parties and the negotiation of several agreements, project financing uses a lot of highly skilled human resources, it takes a long time to complete, and it is more expensive than traditional financing approaches.

The key requirement for a project to qualify for project financing is adequate strength and predictability of cash flows. Project cash flows must also be characterized by some stability, certainty, sufficient magnitude to cover debt repayment, and certain dividend distribution over the planning horizon. Because of consultant, legal, and advisor fees involved in the due diligence, negotiations, and drafting of legal documents efforts, project financing is only contemplated for projects over $100 to $150 million. A third requirement of project financing is conditioning management expectations to a long time span between project assessment and financing implementation. It is not uncommon for project financing in emerging markets to take as long as five or seven years to bring to completion.

### Assessing Financing Plans

The key to successful financing of acquisition and joint venture projects is a sound financing plan, which, in turn, is characterized by sound financing strategy given the goals and objectives of project participants. Therefore, whether the project financing requirements are assessed accurately and the needs of project participants seeking financing are correctly identified and appropriately met determines to a large extent the success of financing.

Simple, but timely and efficient, financing is another dimension of a good financing plan. The simpler the financing structure, the better it is understood by the project team, and the easier to implement. However, the project team must not sacrifice financing efficiency to obtain simplicity. Efficiency of financing refers to the totality of cost to carry out the financing strategy and the financing plan. It includes issuing debt and equity costs; all types of banking, underwriting, and broker fees; costs of guarantees and insurance; out-of-pocket expenses for legal, advisor, and consultant fees; and the opportunity cost of internal staff engaged in the financing activity for the project.

Unconditional availability or certainty of debt facilities, equity underwriting capacity, and clearly articulated and well-understood conditions are desirable attributes of financing. This is so because parties seeking financing in acquisition and joint venture projects are counting on the certainty of the agreed-to financing amounts, types, and conditions thereof. That is, no one likes to encounter surprises or hidden costs and fees, but certainty of financing comes at a premium.

Successful financing for an acquisition or joint venture project also entails solid agreements, stability of arrangement, and appropriate risk sharing among project participants. Balance of costs and benefits among parties, sharing risks is essential for stability of the financing arrangement; without it, financing implementation becomes difficult. The impact of financing costs on the entity obtaining financing should not be disruptive, but should have a low impact on the company's cash flows and its financial position. Finally, successful financing requires superb orchestration and execution of functions to be performed and adherence to pre-established processes. External financing introduces additional discipline in the decision-making process through stringent tests that the project must pass to qualify for financing.

## SUMMARY

Because of the complexity and the multitude of steps involved in financing acquisitions and joint ventures, the emphasis in this chapter is on process. To understand what makes a project financeable, we examine the elements that determine financeability and review steps involved from selecting a financing advisor to the implementation of financing. The sources of financing available to a company are discussed along with financing instruments commonly used.

External sources of financing are reviewed to determine which are appropriate for funding, given the project economics, goals, and objectives. Often, credit enhancements such as parental guarantees or purchase of project insurance are required to provide assurance to creditors and investors, and these are discussed as well. The determinants of financing are reviewed to provide insights to the elements that are important to financing institutions. Because of its prominent position in financing especially for infrastructure projects in developing countries, we discuss limited-recourse financing.

The role of participants in project financing and the importance of assessing financing plans are discussed as the chapter comes to an end. Successful financing of acquisition and joint venture projects requires superb orchestration and execution of various functions performed and adherence to pre-established processes and plans. External financing brings additional discipline in the decision-making process through tests that the project must pass to qualify for financing. That is, the rigor of financial analysis by funding institutions requires thorough review of project assumptions, financials, and risks involved.

# 21

# ACQUISITION AND JOINT VENTURE PROJECT IMPLEMENTATION

## INTRODUCTION

The price paid for an acquisition or the cost of forming a joint venture is an important consideration, but in most cases success of a project is judged by several factors beyond financial considerations. These factors are close strategic fit, strengthening of the core business, and creation of competitive advantage. Other factors with significant impact on project success are a smooth and efficient project implementation, ability to extract expected synergies, and profitable ongoing operations. While strategic fit, strengthening of the core business, and creation of competitive advantage can be shaped to some extent in the early phases of a project, smooth and effective project execution, ability to harness synergies, and the basis for efficient ongoing operations are shaped in the project implementation phase.

The implementation of a project follows the implementation plan, while the operations of the new entity are guided by the business plan. One of the most important elements in acquisitions or joint ventures is a competent implementation subteam and not a bargain acquisition price, a low-cost joint venture company, or even potential synergies to be harnessed. The reason for this is that unless a target company is effectively integrated into the buying company's operations or a joint venture established and set on a proper course, low transaction cost and potential of future synergies are not sufficient to produce success.

In executing project implementations successfully, the emphasis is on continuity of purpose and effective transition of responsibilities, reliance on findings of the due diligence subteam and its recommendations, and validation of synergies and quantification of costs and benefits. Reasonable legal agreements that balance costs and benefits of project participants help in implementing projects as do a sound implementation plan and reasonable business plan. Experienced implementation, liaison, and new management teams are essential along with strong parent company support, appropriate incentives, and remuneration for the implementation subteam and the new entity's management team.

The focus of the discussion in this chapter begins with elements of implementation planning. Following that, the composition and responsibilities of the implementation subteam are discussed along with the human resource requirements for project implementation. The role of the steering committee and the liaison subteam and their contributions are reviewed because of the major role they play. The different phases of implementation are introduced in a sequential fashion, followed by a discussion of the preparation of the new-entity business plan. The creation and characteristics of sound business plans are discussed followed by what is involved in operationalizing the business plan. Then, implementation costs are reviewed and the chapter closes with keys to successful project implementation.

## CONSIDERATIONS IN PROJECT IMPLEMENTATION

### Implementation Planning

Implementation planning is required because there several functions that need to be performed and coordinated in the midst of organizational change, unclear direction, and potential conflicts of interest. Also, because the parent company and the new entity bring different strengths and weaknesses, potential, and limitations, the implementation subteam needs to understand them. Hence, planning is undertaken to maximize the strengths and potential brought to the new entity and minimize the weaknesses and limitations while, at the same time, dealing with organizational change and emotions associated with change.

The objectives of implementation planning are first to achieve the goals and objectives of the acquiring company or the joint venture partners and balance them against the interests of the target or joint venture company, respectively. A second objective is to create the most effective organizational structure from the mix of elements the project participants bring with a minimum amount of disruption. Implementation planning also sets the foundation for the operational plan to obtain expected synergies, minimize conflict of strategies and interests, and ensure the new entity is set on a course to successful ongoing operations. Also, it ensures adequate financial and human resources support from the acquiring and the joint venture partner companies to make the transition effective.

The scope of implementation planning covers all aspects of executing the agreements and transforming plans into organizations, systems, and functions. Senior management expectations are that it all be done with a minimum amount of disruption and within established time frames. The tools used to do this are the implementation workplan and the business plan for the new entity. The workplan lays out the activities that need to take place in specific time frames to get the new entity started while the business plan is the blueprint for its operations.

It is essential that the implementation subteam of the acquiring or the partner company be matched with the tasks of making the acquired or the joint venture company operational in order to properly identify and understand the nature of key management tasks involved. Skill matching involves evaluating the needs of the new entity against the management team of the target company or the management team proposed by a partner company. It determines which target company managers are retained under what conditions and what additional resources and talent needs to be brought in. Additionally, it requires determining the appropriate organizational structure and motivating the newly established management team.

## Implementation Subteam Composition and Responsibilities

The implementation subteam consists of managers from the project team who are functional experts responsible for managing the change from paper agreements to a new entity. The job of the implementation subteam is to manage and facilitate the process of implementing an acquisition or the formation of a joint venture company. The implementation subteam managers need to have thorough knowledge of the company's or the joint venture partners' strategy, their strengths and weaknesses, and understand their objectives, technical competence, market position, cost structure, and financial position.

The focus of the implementation subteam is to transform paper agreements into functioning organizations. Therefore, strong competence of subteam members in respective functional areas is required to deal with issues at hand. Additionally, because many of the implementation subteam responsibilities deal with organizational issues and necessitate extensive cooperation, the makeup of implementation subteam members must be such that they can deal effectively with the human element of change. This is where the contribution of the implementation subteam lies.

The specific responsibilities of the implementation subteam begin with planning the transition to create organizational structures, effect change, and decide whether to integrate the acquisition target or let it operate autonomously. A second set of responsibilities includes managing transition conflict, dealing with politics of change, creating the joint venture entity and staffing it appropriately, and establishing an interface with the new entity and ensuring support from the acquiring or the partner companies. This subteam also creates the business plan for the new entity and helps turn that business plan into reality. It establishes operational objectives and targets to monitor performance, and develops feedback systems and management control mechanisms for the new entity. In most cases, the implementation subteam is involved in all activities that have to do with getting from closing to the new entity being operational according to the business plan.

### Human Resource Requirements

The project team is responsible for determining the number of experienced managers to implement the project, and other human resources needed. The human resource needs assessment examines the functions required to achieve success in the project, reviews personnel records of effective managers to determine whether they possess appropriate skills, and identifies needs gaps and ways in which they could be filled. The main reason for the needs assessment is to identify the appropriate organizational structure to handle the challenges of the transition and the ongoing operation of the new entity. Once the right organization is developed, the skill set requirements to staff the organizational structure are identified.

If it is determined that key managers from the target should stay in the post-acquisition period, the implementation subteam and the lawyers develop terms and conditions for contracts and secondment agreements with buyback provisions from the originating organization. A lot of effort goes into developing compensation packages for retained and seconded managers to ensure adequate incentives are included to motivate desired behavior.

In addition to staffing and the creation and management of compensation plans, the implementation subteam is responsible for new entity's training and development programs in this phase. Another important issue at this point is development of migration plans from management contracts to the new-entity-wide compensation plan. Also, movement to and from the new entity is planned by the implementation team to ensure that enough management talent is available to bring to the new entity specialized expertise and knowledge.

Human resource processes and procedures are transplanted into the new entity's operations and interfaces are established to maintain ongoing support of the acquiring or parent company for the new entity. Here, the implementation subteam ensures that appropriate management is installed and controls are in place to monitor the operational performance of the new entity. Also, the experience gained from the implementation of a project is institutionalized and the knowledge and lessons learned from doing the project are incorporated in the project process.

## KEY FACTORS IN PROJECT IMPLEMENTATION

### Implementation Phases

The project implementation process is best described in terms of the sequence of steps shown in Figure 21.1. The first phase in implementing a project is to understand the objectives and what needs to be done to transform agreements into an operating entity. After understanding the operating environment, opportunities, and challenges it presents for the new entity, the implementation subteam lays the foundations for project implementation. At this point, the implementation workplan is created with specific responsibilities assigned to subteam members and other stakeholders. At the same time, a command and control structure is created to oversee the project implementation. This structure includes a manager from the new entity, a senior manager from the buying or the parent companies, the implementation team leader, and the steering committee leader.

**Figure 21.1**
**The Project Implementation Process**

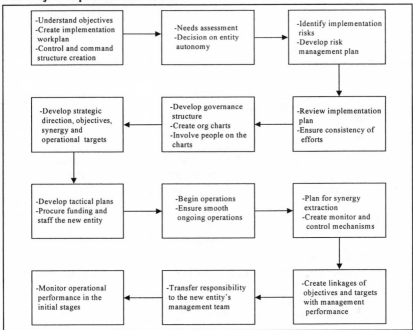

After an implementation command and control structure has been created, strengths and weaknesses are verified and ways to minimize weaknesses and capitalize on strengths are addressed. Here, the decision of whether to fully integrate the target company or to give it autonomy of operations is made and communicated. After the needs assessment, the identification of risks and issues related to project implementation is performed and ways to deal with these risks and issues are devised. Also, sanity checks are performed along with a review of the implementation workplan.

Next in this phase is development of the new entity's governance structure and organizational charts with names of management team individuals now filling the boxes. As boxes in organizational charts are filled, managers become involved in the process and assume responsibilities assigned to their posts. At that stage, the steering committee begins developing the new-entity strategy, while the implementation subteam creates objectives and synergy and operational targets and sets expectations of the new entity's management team.

Strategies for specific areas of operations are created and checked for internal consistency and compatibility with each other. That is, human resources, production and operations, R&D, marketing, and financial strategies are developed not in isolation, but as part of the new entity's strategy. This sets the stage for creating the business plan and setting up the target company as an autonomous entity or forming the joint venture company. However, at this juncture adequate funding and staffing for the new entity is required to make it operational. With adequate funding and staffing, the new entity begins operations and the first item is to ensure that operations proceed according to plan with minimal disruptions. Once smooth operations are established, the focus of the implementation subteam shifts to addressing synergies.

Once the challenge of synergies is addressed and progress begins to take place, the implementation subteam creates monitoring, feedback, and control mechanisms for the new entity. This involves setting up organizational, operational, and financial reporting structures to the acquiring or parent companies and tracking systems. The recommendation is to track operational and financial performance and how much progress is made toward accomplishing strategic returns on investment established at the start of the project. Monitoring the following areas is recommended:

1.  How market strength of the acquiring or parent company is impacted by the new entity's operations.
2.  How organizational capabilities are augmented and operational efficiency improved in terms of profitability and cost reductions.
3.  Whether better processes are implemented, know-how increased, and progress made in operating efficiencies.
4.  How the competitive advantage position of the acquiring or parent companies has been altered by the new entity's operations.

The last step in the implementation process is to create linkages from objectives and targets to operational performance, that is, to develop management objectives driven by targets set against which management performance is measured. This ensures attention to the short-run issues, while measuring performance against strategic return on investment considerations directs attention to the long-term viability of the new entity. The consistency of the new entity's strategy and long-term objectives are checked repeatedly against those of the acquiring or the joint venture parent companies.

### Implementation Costs

Our estimate of average project implementation costs derived over several acquisition and joint venture projects is in the 5 to 10 percent range of project value. While this is a high cost component to include in project financials, the project team should also consider the impact of not planning versus including implementation costs. Including implementation costs in the final business case is necessary as is allocating those costs among various project participants according to agreements.

The most significant elements to be included in the project implementation costs include the following:

*1. Financial and human resource costs.* These costs include capital expenditures and expenses incurred in the course of planning and executing project implementation. They also include the cost of management contracts to be retained and the cost of human resources dedicated to implementation.

*2. Integration costs.* These are costs incurred in the process of actually combining the organization of the target with that of the acquiring company. They may include incentive packages, cost of closing plans and facilities, cost of exiting from various contractual agreements, and so forth.

*3. Costs of setting up the new entity.* This cost component includes items such as legal fees, costs of designing and setting up an organization, administrative costs, and expenses incurred in securing space and starting operations. It also includes the cost of the steering committee and the liaison subteam, if these costs are not included in the project team costs.

*4. Costs of reporting, monitoring, and control systems.* These are costs incurred by both sides to set up and manage monitoring processes and reporting systems as well as administering control mechanisms to ensure adherence to the business plan. Ordinarily, they also include replacement costs of existing systems that are not compatible with those of the acquiring company.

*5. External consultant and advisor fees.* This category includes fees paid to investment bankers, external due diligence experts, financing advisors, and consultants helping the implementation.

*6. Cost of management talent drain.* Calculation of this cost is difficult because it involves estimating the impact of management talent moving from the acquiring or the parent company to an autonomous acquired company or a joint venture entity. Secondment costs are also included here.

Beyond the estimation of the implementation costs above, the implementation subteam assesses the cost of the leakage of technology and trade secrets to an autonomously operating acquired entity or a joint venture company. Quantification of such cost is difficult, but a qualitative treatment gives a better picture of total implementation costs and makes it more realistic.

### The Business Plan

A business plan is a document that is used to guide the new entity created by an acquisition or joint venture project. Here, the project team realizes that a business plan is nothing more than a planning tool that summarizes decisions made for the new entity to operate successfully. Therefore, the business plan lays down the important actions to be taken in a prescribed manner in order to meet the challenges and opportunities in accordance with expectations set out by the implementation subteam.

Business plans vary by project and are shaped by many considerations, but the basis of business plans is the development of the mission, goals, and objectives of the new entity consistent with the strategy, goals, and objectives of the acquiring or the parent company. Understanding the new entity's operating environment through industry analysis updates and environmental scans and updating or performing a gap analysis to understand its strengths and weaknesses is the second layer. Then, articulation of organizational and management, R&D, production and distribution, market, and financial strategies follow.

Creating a production and operational plan to guide the new entity through its initial stages and lay the groundwork for successful ongoing operations is another building block. Also, a marketing, sales, and distribution plan is developed in sufficient detail so that it becomes a tactical weapon in implementing the strategy of the new entity. The human resources plan identifies key areas and functional skills to be strengthened along with training and development, compensation packages, and other incentive plans.

The business plan includes a fairly detailed financial plan describing the timing and quantities of key financial variables with respect to revenues, expenses, capital outlays, and cash flows. However, providing performance targets and monitoring operational performance, linking management objectives and performance with operational performance, and describing a feedback and control mechanism to assess the new entity performance versus expectations and targets are value-added characteristics.

The business plan is an important communication tool for delivering a consistent message concerning acquiring or parent firm expectations, goals and objectives, priorities, and operational targets of the new entity. Another useful function the business plan performs is to lay out requirements and issues that need to be addressed, coordinated, or resolved. Finally, as the environment and operating conditions change, the business plan provides the structure to evaluate the impact of changes on strengths and weaknesses of the new entity.

### Characteristics of Sound Business Plans

Basically, what makes a business plan good is the thought that has gone into the decision process for the purpose of creating a successful new entity. The first indication of a sound business plan is a clear strategy for the new entity, a concise business definition, and focus on supporting the core business. This is followed by realistic and clearly articulated goals and objectives. In addition, it is essential that the business definition, strategy, and goals and objectives of the new entity are consistent with those of the buying or the parent companies.

A good business plan includes a reasonable environmental assessment to understand challenges and opportunities, an objective new-entity analysis of the strengths and weaknesses, and a good outline of what is needed to be successful. This, in turn, requires reasonable production, operation, marketing, human resources, and financial strategies. A sound business plan also provides adequate incentives to motivate desired behavior to reach desired targets, but its projections and expectations should be realistic and have wide stakeholder support.

Another important element in a sound business plan is brevity coupled with enough direction for line managers to understand what needs to be done, but not overly detailed to stifle initiative and creativity. Just as importantly, it needs to make provision for sufficient working capital funding and quality of human resources dedicated to the new entity. It should be implementable with effort, but not impossible to achieve; otherwise, it will de-motivate the new entity's work force.

A good business plan addresses and anticipates a lot of issues likely to come up and plans for them. That is, it has a thorough risk assessment performed, including risk management and contingency plans. Since a business plan must always look backward and forward, it must have performance targets, management objectives tied to performance, and linkages to performance tracking. Also, because a business plan is a key internal communication tool, it is a living document and should be flexible and adaptable to environment changes. Finally, a sound business plan is brief, concise, and uses simple language to communicate the significance of teamwork and communication needed to ensure success.

### Keys to Successful Implementation

The most important element to successful implementation is excellence of the implementation subteam. Excellence refers to breadth and depth of skills, experience, and understanding how to implement acquisitions and joint ventures with emphasis given to ability to deal with organizational issues and managing relationships. Even though implementation particulars are different in each project, following established processes and world-class practices helps ensure successful implementation.

Understanding of acquiring or parent company strategy, a sound needs assessment, and a gap analysis help in identifying correctly the opportunities and challenges facing the new entity. Creating a clear strategy and business definition is a key requirement, but setting realistic goals and objectives and reasonable targets is a must. This leads to development of a solid business plan that is used as a blueprint in the project implementation. Often, implementation subteams are pushed to implement projects as soon as possible, but without a reasonable workplan and time lines, successful implementation cannot happen.

Continuity of purpose and effective transition reinforce discipline and are crucial in implementing successfully. Starting with clearly articulated goals and objectives communicated at each transition point, continuity of purpose involves clearly defined roles and responsibilities, accountability to well-defined reporting channels, review of project status, and stated expectations on deliverables. Managing expectations of internal and external project participants, controlling information outflow, and managing relationships and chemistry are other key requirements to successful implementation. All this requires continuous and unimpeded horizontal and vertical communications.

Focus on the strategic return on investment approach to synergy realization and comprehensive monitoring, reporting, and control mechanisms are crucial to successful implementation. Additionally, in order for any project to be implemented successfully, it must enjoy strong management support of the new entity's management team and its business plan. This involves embracing the new entity's management team, providing direction and guidance, and allocating human resources and financial support to execute the business plan. Well-thought-out and adequate incentive plans and compensation must be offered to serve as catalysts.

## THE ESSENCE OF PROJECT IMPLEMENTATION

### Creating Linkages to the New Entity

The linkages between the parent company and the new entity are the liaison subteam and the steering committee. These two subteams are a group of talented, highly thought of, and influential managers from the parent companies who are charged with the interface and liaison responsibility to the new entity and to each partner company. Steering committee managers come from business development groups and liaison managers from personnel organizations, but both are experienced in transitioning, project implementation, and issues facing new entities. The responsibilities of the steering committee are governance and strategy related, while those of the liaison subteam are mostly operational.

Steering committees are mostly created to handle implementation and interface issues, monitor, and support an acquired or newly formed target company to develop strategy and business definition consistent with those of the parent company. On the other hand, the liaison subteam is valuable because in the early phases of implementation, there is an intense need to address new-entity governance issues, but after that it handles conflict resolution and ensures adequate support from the parent companies. The skill requirements of the liaison subteam and the steering committee are different; the former requires heavy communication skills, and the latter experience in governance issues, overseeing establishment of new organizations, and creating strategy.

While the new joint venture company is formed by the implementation subteam, the steering committee stays involved, monitors progress closely, and serves as a deal maker and catalyst to see the process to successful completion. The steering committee fine-tunes the governance structure of the joint venture, but because of its experience and interaction with the parent and partner management teams, it serves in an advisory capacity to the new entity's board of directors.

The steering committee and the liaison subteam work closely with the implementation subteam during the new entity's formation. However, as the implementation subteam gradually phases out, the steering committee takes a more active role to ensure success of managing the joint venture and continuity of operations. The role of the steering committee also changes with time. As the joint venture company is established and operations are working smoothly, the steering committee's involvement lessens and eventually is phased out.

The liaison subteam's key contribution is ability to resolve conflict among partners and between partners and the joint venture company, and deal with operational partnership issues. Another important function is to represent the joint venture in parent company meetings and to support joint venture requests to the parents once it is fully operational. The third area of value added by the liaison subteam is to monitor new-entity performance against the business plan and parent expectations and explain variances from targets. A fourth area of liaison subteam contributions is reviewing management compensation versus operational performance and recommending adjustments.

### Operationalizing the Business Plan

The implementation subteam works with the steering committee and the liaison subteam to make the business plan a reality. To do that, it executes the decisions made by the project team and follows a step-by-step approach using the implementation workplan as a blueprint to operationalize the business plan. To ensure success in this endeavor, the implementation subteam involves impacted project stakeholders in its development to obtain buy-in. Also, it needs to obtain management commitment and support to execute the business plan and that support comes in three forms: embracing the new entity's management team, adequate funding to be able to implement the project, and dedicating appropriate human resources.

Reviewing or updating the gap analysis determines the needs to be filled for the new entity to be successful. However, it is in the process of operationalizing the business plan that decisions are made concerning structuring the organization, hiring or replacing management talent, setting operational targets, and executing the financial plan. In acquisitions, operationalizing the business plan often involves consolidation of facilities and closing down operations. This is difficult because it impacts human beings; for that reason, the implementation subteam must be able to deal with issues surrounding change. In addition, it shares the business plan targets and translates them to expectations of individuals while motivating the management team to meet the new entity's objectives and targets.

Throughout the effort of operationalizing the business plan, the emphasis is on creating a sound organization to capture expected synergies and set the new entity on its long-term course with minimal disruption. This requires raising the consciousness about expected performance, attention to be paid to financials, and tracking how close actual performance comes to targets each month. It also requires continuous and unimpeded horizontal and vertical communications and motivation to make appropriate adjustments to the business plan to meet operational targets and accomplish long-term objectives.

## SUMMARY

Effective project implementation is a key element in creating a successful project and realizing the expected shareholder value. The main themes of this chapter are continuity of purpose and effective transitioning, experienced implementation and liaison subteams and steering committee, and strong support from the parent company's senior management team. Successful implementation requires flawless orchestration and execution of various activities and functions, adherence to process, and ability to extract expected project synergies and create new ones, but above all is ability to manage change and communicate effectively.

The discussion of how to get from legal agreements to actual operations begins with implementation planning, the composition of the implementation subteam, and its roles and responsibilities. The human resource requirements for project implementation, linkages to the new entity, and liaison subteam and the steering committee contributions are discussed.

The elements of the business plan and their importance are reviewed as are the characteristics of successful business plans and how a business plan is operationalized. Implementation costs are a substantial part of total project costs and we discuss the need to evaluate those costs early in the process to determine whether sufficient value is created by the project. Finally, we examine the keys to successful implementation and stress the need for strong support from the parent company's senior management team.

# 22

# HARNESSING PROJECT SYNERGIES

## INTRODUCTION

In acquisitions and joint ventures, synergy is the notion of the parent company and the new entity working together such that the combined results of their actions are greater than the sum of the two acting separately. Hence, the expression $1 + 1 = 3$. In reverse acquisitions or divestitures, the synergy math is expressed as $5 - 1 = 7$. Another, more concrete definition of synergy is the incremental increases in free cash flow that come about because of the combination or the joint venture creation. The definitions of synergy express the idea that when two parties work together and cooperate, their combined efforts produce results that neither could obtain on their own.

It is recognized that one of the main reasons for acquisition and joint venture failure is inability to harness expected synergies that made the project attractive at the start. A typical acquisition project that resulted in bankrupting the combined company is described in a *Business Week* article dated March 17, 1997 where the acquiring was unable to integrate the target company quickly and effectively. The problem of being unable to realize synergies for which premiums were paid is so widespread and costly that it is often the focus of senior management.

Harnessing synergies is important in order to generate cash flows to pay for the premiums and make the parent company more competitive and profitable. Hence, obtaining expected synergies is essential to ensure project success. Many factors contribute to synergies not being realized and root causes of project failures were discussed earlier. It is important to note that in most projects, after the deal closes, the seller is paid, and investment bankers and advisors collect their fees, the acquiring company is left to harness synergies on its own. The project team needs to ensure that the acquiring company contributes something significant to help the target realize synergies and make the seller part of the synergy problem solution: that is, getting the seller to commit to active participation in synergy extraction, and if a premium is to be paid, ensuring that payment of the premium is tied to the degree to which synergies are realized.

In this chapter we discuss various types of synergies that are possible, major reasons for the inability to harness synergies, impediments to the effort, and ways to identify synergies in different project stages. The question of whether the acquiring company should pay a premium and how payment should be made is brought up again. The theme is that for the project team to be successful in harnessing synergies, the seller has to be part of the solution, and effective transitioning and continuity of purpose are key. Another theme is that if after deal closing no synergies are apparent or are minor, the project team must find sufficient new synergies to improve the company's competitive position. Finally, we discuss the responsibilities of obtaining synergies and the need to balance costs and benefits.

## KEY CONSIDERATIONS IN HARNESSING SYNERGIES

### Types of Synergies

A good approach to obtain synergies is to look at the type of acquisition or joint venture first to determine possible synergies in horizontal, vertical, or concentric expansion projects. For example, if a project involves a new entity that can be vertically integrated into the company's production process, then synergies are generally possible in improving the cost structure, better pricing, and increased competitiveness. When a project involves an expansion horizontally, synergies become possible through economies of scale, by sharing overhead costs, in finance and taxes, and in distribution channel efficiencies. Possible synergies in concentric projects are more difficult to identify because the new entity and the parent company are in unrelated businesses. In this case, synergies may be found in increased purchasing power, finance, and sharing certain overhead costs.

In each acquisition and joint venture, several synergies are possible, the first and possibly most important being strategic synergy. This kind of synergy refers to results of a close strategic fit that creates the right conditions for the company to extract additional value through appropriate implementation and management of the new entity. That is possible because companies complement each other's strengths and gaps are filled by the other firm. When such synergies are present, the strategy of one firm reinforces the strategy and market positioning of the other company and the end result is creation of sustainable competitive advantage.

Operational synergies refer to synergies brought about by the integration of operations of two entities. In most cases, operational synergies are created by combining R&D facilities and production processes, product line rationalization, eliminating redundant functions, consolidating operations, downsizing organizations, and increasing the scope of distribution channels. The main fruits of operational synergies are cost reductions and efficiency of operations.

However, the nature of operational synergies is short-lived, must be extracted soon after project closing, and leveraged into some other advantage for the company.

Technical and R&D, product development, and marketing and distribution synergies are quite common and sellers are eager to point them out to prospective buyers. These synergies are similar to operational synergies and are harnessed extensively, but the project team must be mindful of the costs and the long-term impacts of changes needed to create these synergies. As with other aspects of acquisitions and joint ventures, long-term success is based on balance of costs and benefits, and harnessing synergies is no exception.

Economies of scale in operations, procurement, and product branding are synergies that are fairly easily obtained. The first two have to do with achieving a lower cost structure through expanded output and declining marginal costs. The third refers to the enhanced image of the company's products through association with the new entity. To obtain the first two, the operations of the two entities must be integrated. To obtain the third, the image of the two firms' products must be similar. Financial and tax synergies are possible when a project is well structured and executed properly. Financial synergies include lower cost of capital, increased leverage of the combined entities, tax savings on interest payments, and debt and equity flotation and transaction costs. However, pursuing a project for financial synergies is not recommended.

### The Synergy-Harnessing Process

The synergy-harnessing process starts with the business development group, which defines the project, develops preliminary project goals and objectives, and outlines synergy areas to be explored as the project goes through evaluation, negotiation, and implementation. The work of the business development group is transitioned to the project team for its identification and quantification of synergies, which passes it to the due diligence subteam and external advisors for their verification, evaluation, and assessment. Figure 22.1 shows key areas of responsibility for each project subteam and the process flow of synergy harnessing.

Once external advisors pass judgment on the rationale for synergies and the validity of magnitudes involved, responsibility is transitioned to the due diligence subteam and the core project team. The due diligence subteam gathers information, verifies data, and validates or modifies the expectations concerning synergies. The due diligence subteam recommendations concerning areas of operational improvements, financial synergies, technical and R&D efficiencies, and other synergies are related to the core team and the implementation subteam.

The core project team works with the negotiation subteam to identify buyer or joint venture partner costs and risks in extracting synergies, assess seller views, and generate acceptable trade-offs of synergies. The negotiation subteam determines whether there are reasons to pay for synergies and negotiates the level of synergies, costs involved, and risks the seller needs to share in. It also negotiates the approach in which the seller will share in synergy extraction,

**Figure 22.1**
**The Synergy-Harnessing Process**

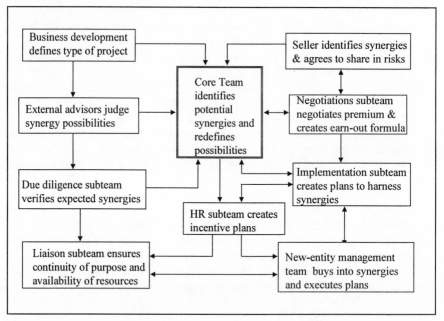

earn-out formulas that tie magnitude of payment to the level of synergies obtained, and seller commitment to help the acquiring company obtain synergies above premiums paid.

The negotiated issues surrounding synergies are transitioned from the negotiations subteam to the core team and the implementation subteam. By this point, synergy expectations are based on the business case analysis and are firmed up and plans to harness synergies are developed by the core team and the implementation subteam. Resource requirements are identified, organizational designs take form, and experienced managers are approached to harness synergies.

The human resources subteam works closely with the core team and the implementation subteam to finalize the new-entity organizational structure and interfaces with the parent company. It also identifies talent needed from both the target and the parent company, and negotiates retained management contracts and secondments to the new entity. This linkage is significant in creating and realizing synergies because the synergy-harnessing responsibility is assigned to individuals qualified for the challenge. Additionally, incentive plans are developed in this phase, to reward managers according to progress in accomplishing synergy goals and objectives.

The human resources subteam transitions responsibilities to the liaison subteam and the management of the new entity and due diligence subteam recommendations are conveyed to the liaison subteam, which ensures availability of resources to implement the synergy-harnessing plans. The liaison subteam contribution is significant because it shares in the responsibility of extracting expected synergies with the new entity's management team and relates progress to the core team and senior management.

The management team of the new entity obtains implementation and synergy-harnessing plans and works with the implementation and liaison subteams to harness synergies. Through these two subteams, the management of the new entity has access to the entire project team and can secure support needed to obtain expected or create new synergies. Since objectives and performance of the new entity's management are tied to success in operating the new entity and obtaining expected synergies, compensation and incentive plans should reflect the extent of synergy accomplishment.

The seller of the target identifies synergies for the buying company in order to make the case for getting a premium for the target and the project team must do the same for the seller. That is, it must identify benefits and synergies to be obtained by the selling company and engage in the development of $5 - 1 = 7$ math in order to counter the seller's claims. To obtain the synergy premium the seller is looking for, the seller needs to share the costs and risks involved in obtaining the synergies it outlined. Otherwise, value is transferred to the seller that rightfully belongs to the acquiring company.

### Cost of Harnessing Synergies

In acquisitions and joint ventures, attention is given to benefits of synergies, but costs and investment requirements are rarely talked about. Yet, these costs and investment requirements have equal weight in determining whether synergies are worth pursuing. However, synergy costs and benefits are a second-order question; the first-order question is whether the parent company is likely to extract expected synergies. It can be answered by looking at the availability of management talent and skills required to harness synergies.

The cost of human resources that need to be expanded to obtain synergies should be examined in two ways: the actual cost in engaging in synergy-related activities and the opportunity cost, i.e., the value of what such highly skilled and talented managers could be doing instead. In addition to human resources required to harness operational synergies, costs and benefits of integration need to be evaluated versus those of autonomy.

The investment and operating cost requirements of new systems, system enhancements, or changes to make systems workable are included. Systems include computer, payroll, financial reporting, and personnel systems. Other system costs include market information and promotion tracking, distribution, technical and operational performance reporting, monitoring and control, and customer satisfaction monitoring systems. The costs of instituting or changing processes and procedures to obtain synergies are more difficult to estimate, but need to be included as well.

Additionally, the impacts on production and distribution processes need to be evaluated before decisions are made to pursue a certain synergy area. The impact on people and morale due to consolidation of operations, organizational changes, relocation, and force reductions need to be figured into the cost of obtaining synergies. Through balance of costs and benefits of harnessing synergies the project team can ensure that synergies obtained are worth the effort and expense.

### Impediments to Harnessing Synergies

Frequently, project teams are unable to extract expected synergies because of the presence of impediments. In some projects, lack of effective communications results in confusion about how to realize synergies and what groups have which responsibilities. Projects in which high-synergy premiums are paid, but few synergies are realized, are projects in which inexperienced project teams are involved. Lack of experience in identifying, quantifying, validating, negotiating, planning for, implementing, and extracting synergies is the major cause of failure to realize synergies.

Inadequate project assessments and partial and incomplete due diligence result in overstatement of potential synergies causing too much value attributed to synergy benefits without appropriate consideration for costs and investments involved. Incomplete due diligence results in unvalidated synergies and operational improvements not being identified.

Often, senior management expectations are set so high —by external parties or the seller— that it is impossible to capture the expected synergies to the degree expected. For that reason, the project team should engage early on in active management of synergy expectations. Also, inadequate or passive business unit involvement and support are responsible for inability to harness expected synergies, which may be due to internal politics or the project's failure to meet the particular business unit's needs. Such causes need to be identified early and eliminated immediately.

Slow project implementation and integration of the new entity's operations are a major impediment to extracting synergies in a project, and ineffective transitioning and lack of continuity of purpose cause slow integration. Where there is unclear purpose, confusion and inability to extract synergies result and conflict due to slow integration causes delays in executing synergy plans. This problem is further aggravated by lack of cooperation from the new entity's management team if it feels cut off from the parent company's operations.

If there are conflicting strategies, goals, and objectives between the parent and the new entity, synergy extraction becomes extremely difficult. When the project team fails to detect strategic fit conflicts, it is impossible to be successful in synergy extraction. When goals and objectives of parent and new entity differ considerably, the implementation team is almost certain to fail in its efforts to plan and extract many synergies. Conflicts in strategy, goals, and objectives coupled with an inexperienced liaison subteam and lack of parent company support result in synergies not being obtained and project failure.

Finally, project teams fail to extract synergies when the parent company ignores the new entity after deal closing, and one wonders why the parent company invested resources in the project only to end up abandoning the new entity to struggle on its own. The explanation usually given is that so much energy has been expended in doing the project that none is left for the post-deal-closing requirements, but we disagree with this conclusion. Lack of senior management involvement and strong direction are rooted in other problems. Namely, acquired firms and joint ventures are ignored primarily because of inexperience with this type of project, ignorance of process, ineffective transitioning of responsibilities, and lack of continuity of purpose.

### Paying Synergy Premiums

Establishing the presence of synergies and paying for them are emotional issues, which impact project participants and the project itself. Ordinarily, the idea in synergy discussions is to raise possibilities offered by the acquisition of a target firm or the creation of a joint venture company. Once the synergy possibilities are raised, the issue becomes one of how they impact the value of the target or the joint venture. The impact of synergy possibilities on the project value becomes a requirement in synergy premium estimation. The synergy premium then becomes the subject of negotiations and is settled according to which party needs the transaction most.

Sellers extract synergy premiums when the project team is inexperienced in this area. To deal effectively with the synergy issue, the project team should consider the following viewpoints in negotiating and deciding to pay a premium and how much that premium should be:

1. For some acquisition and joint venture experts and impartial observers, synergies are not real, but a device to extract a higher price.
2. Reality is that synergies in most projects amount to insignificant contributions because they are small or because of high costs to extract or inability to harness synergies.
3. Synergies occur in the future and the target's future is with the buyer not the seller. Therefore, synergies rightfully belong to the buyer despite arguments that synergies are part of valuation today.
4. If the seller is convinced of the synergies and there are no risks involved in getting them, the seller should gladly share in the synergy extraction risk.
5. The seller obtains benefits other than the price paid for the target such as more efficient operations, better financial performance, and higher stock price because of the sale of a division. If the seller requires premiums for value created through the sale, the buyer should also require premiums for synergies accruing to the seller.
6. Substantial costs are involved in harnessing synergies in terms of human resources, expenses, and capital investments to realize them. These requirements are not apparent until the opportunity to validate synergy possibilities is raised and costs are assessed.
7. The acquisition process is highly pressurized and time lines imposed from the outside do not allow sufficient time to assess the synergy issue and claims. Therefore, the project team must be prepared to deal with the synergy issue effectively.
8. A process should be established to identify, assess, quantify, and validate synergies expeditiously. That is, the team leader should steer the team through this issue quickly and carefully.
9. Often, synergies are used to fill the gap in project valuation and show a positive NPV. If the value of synergies is substantially less than what the team believes possible, the project team should consider exiting negotiations if the seller insists on premiums reflecting higher synergy levels.

There is a long-standing debate as to whether synergies are for real, what the rationale is for paying premiums, how much the premiums should be, and under what conditions the buyer should not pay synergy premiums. The reality of the situation is that some kind of synergy premium is involved in closing a project. That being the case, the negotiation subteam should be well prepared. If the buyer must pay a synergy premium to close a project and the project has strategic and financial value for the company, then the project team should insist on agreements that contain earn-out and risk-sharing formulas. In calculating synergy premium payments, these formulas should include the cost of obtaining synergies and the value of synergies accruing to the seller deducted in the case of reverse mergers.

The discussion here centers around acquisition projects and synergy premiums required by the seller of the target, but the same principles apply in joint ventures. A joint venture partner may require a premium disguised in many different forms —usually high valuations for in-kind contributions to the joint venture— to participate in the joint venture. More importantly, since joint ventures are short-lived, one of the partners may wish to sell its interest in the joint venture. That being the case, synergy issues comes up again and they impact project value the same way acquisition premiums do.

## HOW TO ENSURE THAT SYNERGIES MATERIALIZE

### Identifying and Quantifying Synergies

Identifying project synergies is not something that starts after deal closing and ends when new-entity operations begin. Instead, it is an activity which, like continuity of purpose in the project, relationship development, and communication, starts with project inception and has no end. In the screening and selection phase, the business development group outlines some of the apparent project synergies, which, in the subsequent project evaluation stage, the project team defines in more detail and identifies other possibilities for synergy creation. During due diligence, identified synergies are validated and new areas of operational improvements are identified. Also, during independent project assessment, identified synergies are examined closely.

Every time there is a review of project rationale, goals, and objectives, identified synergies need to be scrutinized and new ideas sought about synergy creation. Also, in the review of strategic fit, synergies are revisited and new ones identified. The reason for bringing up synergies issues in these reviews is to understand the possibilities offered by the new entity and assess the likelihood of obtaining identified synergies.

Effective project execution requires that throughout acquisition and joint venture transitioning, the project team maintain continuity of purpose. In each phase, it seeks to understand strengths and weaknesses of the parties involved, identify new synergies, and validate the ones expected. While identification of synergies is usually easy, validation is far more complex because it requires quantifying synergy benefits, human resource requirements, and financial costs and investments.

Quantification of synergy costs and benefits is done in the business case phase, but is refined by the due diligence subteam. Using the due diligence subteam's findings, soliciting input from business unit heads, and obtaining unbiased input from external sources are essential in doing a thorough job in synergy identification and validation. Also, obtaining input from functional experts at fairly high management levels is recommended as are customer and supplier input and suggestions.

Arguments can be build that synergies due to an acquisition are in the future and belong to the acquiring firm. Therefore, once the seller requires a synergy premium, synergies become a symmetrically treated issue in that the seller should also pay a premium for synergies obtained by the sale of the target. Since synergies are subject to negotiations, the project team leader should promote understanding on both sides concerning key synergy and growth drivers.

Most of the work in verifying the value of expected synergies and planning for synergy harnessing takes place during the implementation phase. The implementation and business plans serve as blueprints of how expected synergies are to be obtained and measure costs and benefits of harnessing synergies. The implementation subteam benefits by comparing the planned new entity with operational characteristics and attributes of competitors in the industry to judge what synergies should be obtained to make the new entity more competitive. The final link in identifying and validating synergies is transitioning to the new-entity management team. In the review of goals and objectives and status of various issues, expected synergies are discussed and views of the new entity's management team are obtained. The new entity's management team should be in a position to validate the expected and identify additional synergies.

### Transitioning and Continuity of Purpose

Earlier we discussed the importance of appropriate transitioning of responsibilities and continuity of purpose throughout the project process. Effective transitioning and continuity of purpose are key elements to success in obtaining synergies; another is having the right individuals in the implementation and liaison subteams, and appropriate incentives. In synergy extraction, effective transitioning and continuity of purpose means the project team reviews the project goals and objectives and communicates the status of various issues. It also means it goes over the identification and quantification of expected synergies and outlines the responsibilities of harnessing synergies to the project subteams.

The importance of effective transitioning and continuity of purpose in the synergy area and how much they contribute to project success is demonstrated by observing what happens if transitioning of responsibilities is done improperly and there is no continuity of purpose. In those cases, a number of confusing situations and unpleasant results are observed, such as:

1. The project team goals and objectives are vaguely understood by project participants; that is, team members do not know what they should be looking for.
2. Responsibility for harnessing synergies rests with the entire extended project team;

that is, nobody specifically.
3. Synergy expectation possibilities are not spelled out clearly; that is there no specific and quantified targets.
4. There are no plans and directions on how to harness synergies; that is, not everyone is pulling in the same direction and often in opposite directions.
5. The liaison subteam is told to make synergies happen; that is, react to the need to create synergies without having participated in the assessment or planning for synergy realization.
6. The new entity's management team is expected to deliver expected synergies without appropriate preparation; that is, not having been part of the project, they operate in the dark.

The conditions described are characteristic of ineffective transitioning, and possible synergies in acquisitions and joint ventures are lost. If no premiums were paid, the severity of value loss would be less than when synergy premiums were paid and the expected synergies are not realized. For that reason, the project team leader needs to ensure effective transitioning and continuity of purpose and senior management needs to remain engaged in the project until synergies are indeed realized to expected levels.

### Responsibility for Harnessing Synergies

The first group that is involved with identifying and quantifying project synergies is the business development group. When a business unit brings in a project, synergies are identified early to strengthen the project rationale and make the project financials more robust. When opportunities are brought from external sources, synergies have already been identified and packaged to enhance the attractiveness of the target.

After identification comes synergy quantification whereby the project team looks into how synergies are obtained and the costs and benefits involved are developed. This is the responsibility of the financial analyst assisted by the rest of the project team. Here, assumptions are examined, synergy financials are built, and premium scenarios quantified. The project team spends a fair amount of time on the verification of assumptions to build a reasonable case for project synergies. Based on those assumptions, financial projections are made that measure the level of expected synergy benefits.

The core project team is responsible for assessing the likelihood of synergies being realized by the company. That is, it evaluates risks associated with extracting synergies in addition to human resource requirements and financial costs and investments to determine whether there is a reasonable chance the expected synergies will materialize. Another responsibility of the core project team is to coordinate the synergy identification, validation, planning, and extraction efforts and ensure effective transitioning and continuity of purpose. However, the core team's most important responsibilities are communications about the synergy effort and management of expectations.

The negotiations subteam's primary responsibilities are to negotiate terms and conditions related to synergies, arrive at a synergy premium solution acceptable to both parties, and negotiate synergy risk-sharing and earn-out formulas. The negotiation subteam works with the core team to obtain support related to the synergy financials and the likelihood of being able to extract synergies. It also argues synergies accruing to the seller because of the project and negotiates an agreement on sharing costs and benefits of synergy extraction.

The due diligence subteam is responsible for verifying information and data shared, uncovering hidden information, and assessing the reasonableness of financial projections. In the process of doing so, the due diligence subteam identifies synergies and areas to improve operational performance. The due diligence subteam, therefore, assists the core team in the assessment of assumptions and quantification of synergies since it has experts to validate the likelihood of synergies materializing.

The implementation subteam is responsible for several areas starting with verifying potential for synergy realization and identifying costs and investment requirements. It plans for harnessing expected synergies through the implementation plan and the new-entity business plan and is a key player in transitioning synergy responsibilities to the new entity's management team. Synergy realization depends to a large degree on the human resources subteam for design of organizational structures and incentives and compensation plans that make expected synergies a reality. The human resources subteam is also responsible for identifying required talent to extract synergies and staff key positions in the new entity and the liaison subteam.

The liaison subteam is responsible for ensuring satisfactory issue resolution between the new entity and the parent company and that resources are available to obtain expected synergies. This subteam works closely with the human resources group to initiate secondments to the new entity and obtain required management skills from the parent company. It also coordinates efforts with the steering committee, which is responsible for guiding the new-entity management team and ensures diligent pursuit of extracting expected synergies in the early phases of the new entity.

Paradoxically, the party ordinarily left out of synergy extraction is the seller of the target. The recommendation is to make the seller an important party in realizing project synergies through the following means:

1. Identifying synergies accruing to the seller due to the project and scenarios of operational improvements after the sale and negotiating a reverse premium or discount.
2. Bringing up the issue that if the seller is convinced of synergy potential then the seller should be willing to share in the risk of obtaining the synergies.
3. Identifying costs and investments required in extracting synergies and subtracting them from expected benefits.
4. Making synergy premiums conditional on realization of synergies, that is, if claimed synergies are realized, then synergy premiums are paid accordingly. Otherwise, no such payment is made or the payment is graduated.
5. Requiring ongoing involvement by the seller to obtain synergies for which a premium is paid, but creating incentives for the seller to help in harnessing of synergies by negotiating earn-out formulas.

Once transitioning from the implementation subteam has taken place, the new entity's management team is responsible for executing the synergy plans working with the implementation, human resources, and liaison subteams. The new-entity management team faces challenges in accomplishing synergy objectives and the continued engagement of the parent company's senior management team after deal closing is important. It is important to embrace the new-entity management team, recognize its efforts and contributions in harnessing synergies, and provide direction and guidance when needed. This is crucial to ensure project success.

### How to Extract Synergies

In acquisition and joint venture projects, extracting synergies is as important as negotiating a reasonable price for the new entity. However, unlike price being determined mostly by market conditions, synergy extraction is determined by established processes and plans and ability to follow and execute them. One way to ensure being on the right path to harnessing synergies is to understand and follow the due diligence subteam' s recommendations, because this subteam has examined expected synergies and financial impacts closely. The project team leader then ensures that the due diligence recommendations are reflected in the implementation plan and the new entity's business plan for synergy extraction to proceed efficiently.

After deal closing, it is important to implement the project and integrate quickly and effectively to eliminate uncertainty and resistance being build up from the new entity's management team. Effective transitioning and continuity of purpose contribute a great deal to extracting expected synergies whether the new entity is integrated or remains autonomous. In the case of autonomy, synergy extraction becomes more difficult to accomplish, and for that reason, most experts recommend immediate and complete integration of operations.

Regardless of integration or autonomy of operations, it is crucial to move quickly through the implementation phase to eliminate uncertainties and embrace the new entity's management team into the parent company family. When we talk about implementation and integration we talk about integrating organizations made of people, systems, policies, procedures, and of plants, facilities, and other components. However, to implement and integrate effectively, the implementation team, functional experts, and the new entity's management team need to examine productivity drivers carefully. This allows them to determine which have the most impact and focus on those few drivers.

Another way to extract synergies is to assess and implement suggestions by customers and suppliers. Customers and suppliers that have a long record of doing business with the new entity know what needs to be done to enhance its operational efficiency, improve customer and supplier relations, increase customer satisfaction, and enhance its competitiveness. Customer suggestions are particularly significant in the area of product functionality, delivery, customer service, and product quality.

Using earn-out formulas in agreements with the seller and even with the joint venture partner to provide incentives to support the synergy-harnessing effort is an effective way to get help from the other side. That, however, is not sufficient unless the effort starts with a good implementation plan, and a sound business plan is created. Sanity checks of synergy extraction plans need to be developed and plan requirements reviewed and validated.

Initiating secondments to the new entity and encouraging learning and mobility of people and other resources contribute to extracting synergies by bringing in the right individuals to work the issues. Aggressive pursuit of expected synergies will backfire unless it is based on a balance of cost and benefits of obtaining synergies. Hence, the project team should ensure that benefits outweigh the costs and investment requirements of obtaining synergies before pushing aggressively for synergy extraction.

If synergies are an important element to make the project succeed, then assigning seasoned and experienced managers to the liaison subteam and the steering committee is essential. To extract synergies, teamwork and communications are promoted, management objectives with operational performance linkages are established, and incentives linking compensation with performance are developed. Only seasoned managers should be assigned to those positions because these activities take place in the midst of organizational changes and conflicting interests and objectives. Finally, seasoned liaison managers are required to re-examine the organizational structure and end-to-end operations and assess the need for changes to make the new-entity operations more efficient.

The last linkage in extracting synergies in a project is the new entity's management team. For this team to be able to extract expected synergies, it needs to be embraced, accepted, supported, and given direction by the parent company's senior management team. It also needs teamwork and support by the liaison and human resources subteams and the entire project team and external advisors if needed. Finally, the project team needs to guide the new entity's management team through the implementation and business plans and compensate it for performance.

### If Synergies Don't Exist, Create Them

Occasionally, there are no synergies to be obtained or the cost of expected synergies may be too high to pursue them. After agreements are signed and no synergies are apparent or are too costly to obtain, world-class project teams create synergies to offset the premiums paid. This is not impossible, but it is difficult and requires skill in developing synergies. The business development group reminds everyone that there is always room for improvement because there is no such thing as flawless operations.

The project team may start a joint venture project with one purpose in mind, but if the performance of the joint venture entity is below expectations, the steering committee should direct the entity's focus on different areas where it is able to create substantial synergies. While changing the focus of the new entity routinely is not recommended, the project team, the liaison subteam, and the management team of the new entity need to be flexible to take advantage of opportunities previously not considered. This applies to those instances where focus on the original goals and objectives is not yielding the synergy results and returns expected. In these situations, the liaison subteam should review the systems, policies, and procedures in place to determine whether new synergies can be created.

The next step in creating synergies that were not identified in the project evaluation process is to use due diligence findings related to operational performance and improvements. In addition, the core project team should conduct a thorough business process analysis with assistance from external advisors to determine what consolidations are feasible and what process improvements may result in significant synergies. If customer and supplier recommendations were not implemented, it is a good idea to assess them and implement whatever changes seem appropriate. Seeking input and feedback of new-entity employees helps create operational synergies, and understanding and leveraging assets and relationships of the new entity creates synergies not previously entertained.

The business development group monitors the synergy effort and should be involved in the event there no apparent synergies or they are too expensive to extract. Then, it looks for new strategic, operational, and financial synergies through scenario analysis. The various scenarios re-define the scope of the project and look at all horizontal, vertical, and concentric possibilities and create new opportunities. Then, possible synergies are identified and quantified. After that, they are validated by subteams involved, and if necessary, the focus is re-directed to change the business definition of the company and/or the new entity.


## SUMMARY

In this chapter, we discuss the importance of synergies and their contribution to project success. The synergy possibilities associated with vertical, horizontal, and concentric acquisition and joint venture projects and the types of synergies ranging from strategic to operational, to technical and R&D, to consolidation of operations, to economies of scale, to financial and tax synergies are examined. We begin with identification of synergies early in the project process, move to the quantification stage, then on to validation by the core team, external advisors, and the due diligence and implementation subteams.

We discuss the role of each subteam and synergy planning involved in the work of the implementation subteam. The elements we introduce in synergy negotiations include the seller in the sharing of synergy risks and the synergy premium being offset by gains accruing to the seller from doing the deal. We also describe how to identify synergies and emphasize the importance of due diligence findings and recommendations in identifying, quantifying, and validating expected synergies. Furthermore, we stress identification of costs and investment associated with extracting synergies to determine the net present value of synergies and decide whether they are worth pursuing. We end the synergy discussion with impediments to the process and what needs to be done to eliminate them in order to extract expected synergies.

# 23

# MONITORING PERFORMANCE AND PROJECT SUCCESS

## INTRODUCTION

Monitoring performance of a newly acquired entity or a joint venture is undertaken to ensure effective management of the new organization, realization of company or partner objectives in the project, and recognition for accomplishments by management teams involved. The traditional approach of monitoring performance is confined to tracking and reporting financial variables and measurements with heavy emphasis on comparison of actual versus budgetary figures and a tremendous amount of effort going into explaining variances. However, the traditional tracking approach is of limited use because it has no linkages to strategic returns on investment objectives, other than profit.

For world-class business development groups, monitoring performance and judging success of an acquisition or a joint venture project is more comprehensive than reporting financials and explaining variances between budget and actual measurements. To begin with, it entails setting strategic return on investment targets and monitoring performance against those targets. Then, it requires developing a system that links operations, measurements, and objectives along with a feedback and control mechanism to initiate corrective action. Under this approach, a system to recognize accomplishments of objectives and meeting of strategic and performance targets is also established.

The reasons for and importance of monitoring performance are the starting point of this chapter and the discussion proceeds to setting new-entity objectives. We show the need to develop entity objectives to encourage appropriate behavior and reach pre-determined levels of performance, but setting performance criteria is not sufficient to ensure success and these criteria must be linked to project and management objectives.

> *Reminder:* *Strategic return on investment targets includes an entity's financial performance, its market position, technological leadership, customer satisfaction, and progress toward development of competitive advantage.*

Creating operational targets is primarily done by the implementation subteam and requires a thorough understanding of the company's operations and needs, industry averages, and the strengths and weaknesses of the new entity. This issue and the variables to be tracked are discussed and the need to track strategic returns on investment to determine project success is emphasized. That is, in addition to project profitability, the liaison subteam must track market positioning, technological leadership, customer satisfaction, and other project attributes that can create a competitive advantage. A brief discussion on tracking systems and systems integration follows along with ideas behind feedback and control mechanisms used. Also, characteristics of sound performance monitoring and how project success is judged are discussed.

## MONITORING RATIONALE AND PRINCIPLES

### Why Monitor Performance?

The first reason for monitoring performance is to determine the extent of project success, but the ultimate motive for monitoring new-entity operational and financial performance is to ensure effective management of that entity. This, in turn, requires consistency of strategies, goals and objectives; adherence to business plans; and compliance with pre-established rules, policies, and practices. Another reason for monitoring new-entity performance is to provide the right incentives for the management team to deliver expected operating performance on an ongoing basis.

By monitoring the new-entity operational performance, the implementation subteam can assess how well the project implementation has been and measure the extent of the realization of company objectives in the project. Also, through monitoring of performance the project team can measure how the project supports the company's strategies and goals. Alternatively, through performance monitoring one determines the level of project success, and for this to be effective, it necessitates a broad approach that goes beyond monthly financial reporting.

Monitoring of performance means having targets to work toward, establishing reporting systems, developing feedback mechanisms, and controlling various processes that generate the resulting performance. That is, monitoring allows the project team to determine how closely targets have been met and how corrective action may be instituted to bring performance to expected levels. In addition, monitoring is done to recognize accomplishments of project participants and the management team of the new entity.

Another important reason for monitoring new-entity operational performance is to satisfy the requirements of legal agreements related to earn-out formulas and financing of the project. Financing agreements require tracking and reporting progress in a number of areas, the most important being project implementation; construction of facilities, plant, and equipment; acceptance of newly constructed facilities; commercial operations; and financial performance. In addition, financing agreements require reporting on the extent of expected project synergies being extracted and on operational performance relative to business plan expectations.

### Properties of Sound Performance Monitoring

A good tracking system is a performance-monitoring system that links entity objectives and targets to performance because in well-managed and successful entities, performance determines management compensation. An effective monitoring system captures the new entity's objectives, operational targets, and strategic return on investment objectives in a clear and concise manner. It also identifies potential performance and compares that with targeted and with actual performance. In addition, it is a holistic and comprehensive monitoring system that encompasses traditional financial measurement variables, strategic return on investment concepts, and broad new-entity productivity measures.

A sound monitoring system links expectations of the owners to management objectives and the new entity's performance and focuses on key variables that are reliable measurements and reports on a regular and consistent basis. It defines what constitute acceptable ranges of deviations from targets, performs variance analysis, and contains adequate explanations and is a tool to communicate results and a feedback and control mechanism. It also possesses flexibility to reflect changes in organizational structures, the operating environment, and reporting requirements and reflects responsiveness to acquiring or parent company reporting, analysis, feedback, and control needs. Finally, it is used in conjunction with other management tools to encourage desired management behavior and contribute to the project's success.

## MONITORING PERFORMANCE AND PROJECT SUCCESS

### Setting Entity Objectives

Regardless of the reason for the acquisition or the joint venture, to ensure long-term success, the new entity must develop operational objectives. In the approach we recommend, performance objectives are created to assist the new entity's management team do a better job in creating and maintaining a common vision among project stakeholders and effect shareholder value creation on a continuous basis going forward. Performance objectives enable project participants to capture and maximize project expected synergies, measure the health of the new entity in a holistic approach, and assess customer satisfaction levels and the entity's market leadership position. Additionally, they help determine to what extent the project has been financially attractive, understanding how to strengthen the entity core business, and how to create a competitive advantage.

The starting point for developing new-entity objectives is creation of a reasonable mission statement. The mission statement is a brief and concise statement regarding what the new entity stands for and what it aspires to become over the long run. It is important that the mission statement aims high enough to focus the new entity's management team to develop challenging objectives in moving the new entity from the implementation to the operational phase. After the new-entity mission is articulated, the long-term goals and objectives become apparent as does the strategy required to achieve those objectives.

The strategy of the new entity must be consistent in its key aspects with the acquiring or parent company's long-term objectives regardless of the degree of autonomy granted to it and, like the mission statement, it should provide reasonable challenges to the management team. The new-entity strategy must be clearly articulated and communicated continuously throughout the organization so that it provides the focus needed. In addition, it must be easy to operationalize; that is, to create the tactics to apply in meeting the entity's objectives.

The new entity's management objectives are developed to enable the entity to accomplish its business objectives. This is a fairly straightforward, though not easy, process, because it starts with strategic return on investment objectives. Namely, it begins by creating objectives for the financial performance of the new entity; its market position and strength; its state of innovation, its technological know-how, and product introduction ability; organizational capabilities to be developed; and the approach to creating a competitive advantage. Once strategic return on investment objectives are set, appropriate management teams are assigned responsibilities for meeting specific objectives not only individually, but also collectively.

On a few occasions, the main reason for undertaking acquisitions and joint ventures is to create some form of competitive advantage for the company. Therefore, setting objectives for the new entity must be done after assessment of the new-entity strengths and weaknesses. In the early stages of the new entity's operation, the liaison subteam needs to identify the entity's weaknesses and make their elimination part of its management team's objectives on an ongoing basis.

### Linking Performance to Objectives

Comparing results to targets is required to assess operational performance, but we recommend that monitoring performance go a step further and link operational performance to management objectives. To ensure that there is agreement on both sides and ensure consistency of objectives, linkage of performance to management objectives should be undertaken in both the entity and the acquiring or parent company. The schematic in Figure 23.1 shows how this linkage works in the case of a joint venture.

**Figure 23.1**
**Linking Operational Performance to Management Objectives**

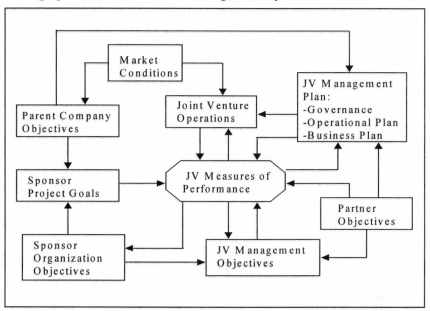

The same linkages hold true for linking performance of acquired companies. The reasons for the linkage of performance to objectives are to assign responsibility and create accountability at all levels, encourage appropriate behavior to nurture and grow the new entity, and achieve the project objectives by realizing business plan expectations. Also, it helps to obtain expected synergies and create new ones, direct and focus management effort in the right areas, and remunerate managers according to how well objectives are met.

### Creating Operational Targets

Operational targets are specific levels of performance in organizations or functional areas serving as goals to meet or exceed expected outputs and motivate group behavior toward accomplishing those objectives. Before creating operational targets, the first step is to establish the important business plan elements to monitor and decide which variables to track. Also, a review of industry benchmarks, metrics, and measures of performance is conducted and entity potential levels of performance in line with world-class companies are developed.

The reason for establishing potential performance targets is to ensure they are set at levels comparable to world-class companies and objectives. Also, operational targets are developed to make progress toward meeting potential performance targets, and direct behavior toward creating a competitive advantage for the new entity. Creating a competitive advantage ensures survival and is pursued in all functional areas. In the operational phase, new entity performance targets are set by its management team with the business plan as a guide and input from the liaison subteam and line managers. Performance targets should be easy to understand and set at challenging levels, but with incentives attached to them. That is, management and labor compensation plans should reward exceptional performance relative to business plan expectations.

Operational targets also need to be linked to strategic return on investment targets; that is, the entity's detailed financial performance, its market position, technological leadership, customer satisfaction, and progress toward development of competitive advantage. The reason for this is so that everyone understands how each organization impacts the new entity's overall performance and determines where the new entity is headed based on recent performance. While the new entity should have its own objectives, the common financial targets are revenue and expenses per employee, unit costs for each product or service offered, and entity contributions to the acquiring or parent company's net income.

Market position targets ordinarily include market share, market share gains or losses, and market growth. Technological leadership targets include number of new products and innovations introduced, time of product development and introduction to market, quality and reliability of products, and cost savings by technology introductions. Customer satisfaction targets include customer reaction to product quality and reliability, perceived value for the price paid, and customer care services. Competitive advantage targets include unit costs compared to those of top competitors, development of unique capabilities, processes enhancements and new technologies, and ability to differentiate the entity's products or services. They also include measures of efficient entity management such as timely approval of the entity's annual business plan, positive and improving customer survey responses, and plans to resolve operational conflicts.

### Variables to Track

In order to understand where the new entity is headed, project participants need to monitor both operational and strategic return on investment variables. The reason for this is that unless one knows the linkage between operational variables and strategic return on investment, one cannot judge how well the project serves the interests of the company or the future course of the new entity. The most important operational variable to track is customer satisfaction because it tells how effectively the new entity's resources are organized around producing a good product and serving the customer well. The next most important variable to be tracked is economic value added created by the project. Economic value added is defined as the value created above the cost of capital invested in the project.

In addition to economic value added, it is a good idea to monitor improvements in total project NPV as a result of implementing a particular business plan. Also, the NPV of synergies included in the business case should be monitored to ensure that value is created according to expectations. These are high-level measures of financial performance and one should examine lower-level variables to get an understanding of the entity's financial picture. That is, one needs to look at the key financial statement variables and identify trends on a monthly basis. Revenue, cost, and capital invested per employee along with the standard financial ratios should be monitored and trends identified to provide warning signals. Unit costs and the difference between best in class and own costs deserve special attention because they are indicative of the entity's ability to operate efficiently and create and sustain a competitive advantage. Also, some measure of productivity should be defined and tracked on a monthly basis.

Market position variables ordinarily are monitored on a monthly basis and include market share, market share gains or losses, and market growth. Technological leadership variables to monitor include the number of significant new products and innovations introduced, the time of product development and introduction to market, the quality and reliability of products, and cost savings of technology introductions. Customer satisfaction variables include customer reaction to the quality and reliability of products, perceived value for the price paid, and rating of customer care services.

Competitive advantage variables include, in addition to unit costs versus those of top competitors, development of unique capabilities, processes, or technologies, and ability to differentiate the entity's products or services. Furthermore, measures of efficient entity management, such as timely approval of its annual business plan, positive survey responses, and plans to resolve operational conflicts, should be included in a sound monitoring system of new-entity performance.

### Tracking Systems

Effective monitoring of performance requires development of a tracking system whose objectives are to capture operational performance targets, monitor performance of important metrics or variables, and report performance measurements versus the identified targets and objectives. Tracking systems are management tools and part of the entity's operating systems to report performance on a regular basis, usually every month, unless there is a need to look at a variable more often to respond to market changes.

While a tracking system is usually an extension of a financial reporting system and has the ability to produce reports on as-needed basis, it is important that tracking systems of a new entity have a strategic return on investment monitoring capability. They should also have the capability to perform a potential versus target versus actual comparisons. A good tracking system is not only a computer system reporting numbers, but a broader system that allows for intelligent comparisons, feedback, and qualitative assessment.

Because of its value in judging project success and the many requirements it should meet, tracking systems should be developed with input from the implementation subteam. The reason for this is that tracking systems are management tools and not simply a financial reporting system that does budget versus actual comparisons. Also, the implementation subteam has a full appreciation of what makes the new entity successful; that is, it knows what should be monitored and how it should be reported.

### Feedback and Control

A good monitoring system should be used not only as a performance or a financial reporting system, but as a communication tool as well. When monthly operational and financial data come in, it is important to conduct an operational review along with an examination as to how well the new entity is performing with respect to the strategic return on investment targets. As reviews of operational data show areas that need attention, so do assessments of strategic return on investment data point to potential deviations from long-term goals and objectives.

Communication of monthly results and the entity's management interpretation of their implication are important in beginning discussions, obtaining input from the stakeholders involved, and initiating the feedback process from the parent to the new entity. While the implementation subteam plays a key role in defining entity targets, the liaison subteam and the steering committee evaluate the operational and strategic return on investment performance. The liaison subteam leads the assessment of entity performance, conducts the review and communication sessions with the parent company, and is responsible for reporting the performance of the entity's management team.

Because the liaison subteam is charged with managing the relationship between the owners and the new entity, it is also the body responsible for providing the parent company's feedback to the entity and mediating when required. This does not mean that there is intervention on a monthly basis. It does mean, however, that when major deviations occur from the expectations set out in the business plan, there should be a joint review of results with the entity's management. Also, when major changes occur either in the entity's organization or in the operating environment, the liaison subteam works with all stakeholders and the entity's management to reset expectations and define appropriate intervention.

Part of the liaison subteam's charter is to provide input to the new entity and the parent company on how to translate the feedback obtained into actionable items and to devise ways to control entity performance. Changes of objectives and operational targets are also communicated to the new entity by the liaison subteam as well as initiatives to motivate behavior changes so as to obtain desired results.

### Judging Project Success

The presence of a sound monitoring system is crucial in order to judge the overall degree of success of acquisitions or joint ventures. Project success encompasses different elements and must be measured on many dimensions in a holistic approach. Although project NPV and economic value added are essential in judging project success, there are a number of other dimensions the project team must pay attention to in order to determine whether the project has indeed met the expectations of the acquiring or the parent companies.

Again, strategic return on investment measures are included in the set of criteria for judging project success because focus on current financial measurements does not tell senior management how well the company is positioned to compete in the future. However, there must be a balance between short- and long-term, operational and strategic, financial and market, and technology and competitive advantage criteria to determine project success. Hence, in addition to strategic return on investment measures, the recommendation is to include other measures in the criteria used to judge project success. These criteria are weighted according to importance to the entity's owners:

1. Effective management of new entity from the board of directors down to line managers and extent of realization of management objectives and linkage to actual performance.
2. Degree to which the new entity is able to harness synergies expected in the business plan and develops additional synergies.
3. Sustainability of management agreements, customer contracts, supplier arrangements, and marketing programs
4. Incentive programs and the parent company's commitment and financial backing to ensure viability of the new entity.

## SUMMARY

The discussion of this chapter centers around monitoring project performance to track financial success, overall project success, and determine creation and likelihood of maintaining competitive advantage. The emphasis is on linking operational performance with management objectives, on integrating tracking systems, and on extending the continuity of purpose in the monitoring and control areas.

The need to monitor new entity performance stems from the need to satisfy project financing requirements, track financial performance, and determine how successful the project is in producing strategic returns on investment expended. Setting entity objectives consistent with the project objectives prior to developing operational performance targets is stressed as is the need for a process to link operational performance with management objectives. Effective tracking system requirements and integration of systems are discussed as is the need for feedback and control mechanisms. Characteristics of sound performance monitoring and ways of judging project success are also outlined.

# PART V

## MANAGING APPROVALS AND LEARNING

# 24

# IMPEDIMENTS TO PROJECT APPROVALS AND IMPLEMENTATION

## INTRODUCTION

In the second chapter, we demonstrated that the probability of creating a successful project is very small because there are many elements in the process whose individual likelihood of successful execution determines the overall chances of projects being successful. We have stated repeatedly that acquisition and joint venture projects are difficult and expensive propositions because the sequence of challenges in these projects is long and the challenges so many that few experienced project teams are able to meet them successfully.

Aside from challenges inherent in doing acquisitions and joint ventures, several internal barriers and difficulties arise in moving projects effectively to the approval stage. These difficulties have their roots in poor communications, ignorance or inexperience, and fear of potential changes by some project stakeholders. These difficulties become obstacles and require additional energy and effort to overcome and advance the project. However, the project team leader with support from the entire team must deal with these obstacles and remove them to avoid contamination and damage to the project team's morale and project success.

A main objective of the project team is to deliver a project that proceeds to the approval stage quickly and effectively. Hence, we begin the discussion with project approvals and the process to obtain approvals, and their importance is underscored by the follow-up discussion of characteristics of a sound approval process. Then, we examine the causes of internal impediments to getting to corporate project approvals efficiently. Quite often, presence of internal politics creates impediments to the approval process; hence, the need for impediment management. These two topics are discussed and the chapter ends with ways to deal with impediments.

The emphasis is on factors that create an efficient project approval process, namely, assessing alternatives presented completely and objectively through agreed-upon criteria; obtaining input, buy-in, and consensus from the individual business unit heads right from the start, and involving key internal stakeholders in major decisions. We also stress the requirement to communicate company needs and project benefits effectively, ensuring continuity of purpose and effective transitioning, and relying on facts, evidence, and due diligence subteam recommendations for effective corporate approvals.

## AFTER NEGOTIATIONS COME APPROVALS

### Project Approvals

Different companies, or even different business units within a company, have different project approval requirements, processes, and criteria for what exactly needs to be approved to authorize investment in a project. There are different authorizations, concurrence, or approvals commonly required to get a project from the idea stage to its implementation depending on investment thresholds, purpose of the project, and risks involved. The most common types of corporate approvals involved in the project process are:

1.  Authorization or approval to sign a non-disclosure agreement, an MOU, or a letter of intent to begin involvement and assessment of a proposed acquisition or a joint venture project.
2.  Authorization of the business development group to form a project team, engage in evaluating an opportunity, and obtain appropriate funding for this effort.
3.  Review and approval of the feasibility study, which allows the project to move to the business case development stage and appropriates additional funds for that engagement.
4.  Approval of the interim project business case, which contains the analysis needed to make the decision to proceed to project execution. This authorization enables the company to make an offer to the seller or to commit to forming a joint venture company subject to certain due diligence conditions being satisfied.
5.  Review and approval of the acquisition or joint venture agreements, which create further commitment to the project, allow implementation planning to begin, and financing to be pursued.
6.  Corporate approval of the final business case, which authorizes investment in a project and funds to cover project implementation expenses.

To move an acquisition or joint venture project from one stage to the next, approvals are required and the project team should have good tools to communicate the nature of the project and progress made. Such tools include the MOU or a letter of intent, the project feasibility study, the interim and final business cases, the independent assessment and the fairness opinion letter, and the definitive project agreements.

The corporate approval process varies from company to company, but in every case approval processes define clearly who reviews, concurs, and approves what documents and decisions at which point in the project process. The process to be followed and the sequence of events and conditions to be met to move the project through the approval channels are specified along with the expense, investment, and risk thresholds for authorizations and approvals. The set of criteria, the evaluation that a project must pass, and the wording of the recommendation needed for approvals are spelled out. Instructions are given concerning the documentation package required, such as a business case, an independent assessment report, a due diligence report, a fairness opinion, and certain external approvals along with the format and the way the business case must be presented. The roles and responsibilities of the project team, the project sponsor, senior management, and the board of directors in the approval process are outlined in conjunction with the role of external advisors and investment bankers. Any conditions attached to approvals must have follow-up and subsequent completion, and how the project will be monitored and success measured against expectations is delineated.

## Characteristics of Efficient Approval Processes

Some projects fail to get through the approval process not because of poor economics, but rather due to external as well as internal politics. While there may be valid reasons for internal participants not to support a project, if the approval process is contaminated with internal politics, the process becomes ineffective and projects are not completed. Therefore, the first requirement and characteristic of a sound approval process is absence of territorial struggles, turf battles, and internal political posturing. For this not to happen, a wide buy-in of the project's value by internal stakeholders is necessary.

Another important characteristic of an effective approval process is a consistent corporate policy specifically addressing acquisition and joint venture projects, that is, a schedule of authorizations that is clear about the threshold levels of expense, investment, and project risk approvals and that requires consistent application of policy. The schedule of authorizations should also be clear about the process, timing, and required senior managers' concurrence, authorizations, and approval signatures for different types and size of projects.

A sound approval process should be characterized by constant, open, and unimpeded horizontal and vertical communications among all project participants and stakeholders. At the same time, it should assign specific roles and responsibilities in the approval process to specific project participants with experience in respective functions. It should also be characterized by flexibility in terms of process and timing requirements to facilitate busy schedules of senior managers.

Another characteristic of a sound approval process is that it has several milestones and contains sanity checks at lower approval levels. Part of this requirement is that the approval process ensures adequate review of key aspects of a project and provides a thorough and unbiased independent assessment. This enables senior executives to delegate interim approvals to lower management levels, to minimize business case and legal document reviews, and to keep the number of senior management signatures to a minimum.

## MANAGING THROUGH PROJECT IMPEDIMENTS

### Impediments and Their Causes

It is important for the project team leader to recognize early in the process the presence of impediments to the approval process and take steps to eliminate them immediately. Regardless of origin, impediments to the approval process are likely to persist into the implementation phase of the project and make that process difficult to complete successfully. For that reason, it is recommended that the project team leader deal with impediments as soon as they are identified and remove them from the project along with individuals creating impediments.

There many reasons that impediments to acquisition and joint venture project approvals and successful implementation arise almost on a regular basis. Besides large project stakeholder egos, the main causes and manifestations of impediments are the following:

*1. Lack of strategic motive and objectives.* Lack of corporate strategy and/or understanding of the company objectives in the project is responsible for confusion and delays because there is no benchmark and things are never clear.

*2. Limited appreciation of strategic fit.* Insufficient understanding of the new entity's position in the company's long-term strategy and how it can support the acquiring or parent company's business leaves business unit heads and managers wondering how the project will impact their organizations and creates anxiety, which is then manifested in resistance to the project and barriers being raised.

*3. Ignorance of process.* Because some managers do not seek help to understand the project process, ignorance or, rather, not admitting ignorance of the acquisition and joint venture formation process causes frustration and delays to project approvals and in subsequent implementation.

*4. Turf battles and politics.* Internal and external project politics are usually responsible for most projects being derailed, rejected, or executed improperly. Fear of losing control, turf battles, and power struggles cause uncooperative and aggressive behavior in project stakeholders. When turf politics is combined with other impediments, the project is headed for failure and the project sponsor is advised to step in.

*5. Lack of training and experience.* Acquisitions and joint ventures are expensive, difficult, and risky business and require skilled managers to evaluate and implement them. Inexperienced project teams cause delays in the approval process and lack of management talent is responsible for unsuccessful project implementation. The absence of experienced talent results in projects drifting without focus and development of impediments.

*6. Poor communications.* Ineffective or limited communications always lead to misunderstandings and make the approval process difficult and lengthy. This is especially true for ineffective vertical communications, which leave project participants without direction and focus.

*7. Unreasonable time lines.* Artificial time lines and restrictions on the project are usually externally imposed and are motivated by selfish reasons and for the benefit of certain project participants. Unreasonably tight project time lines cause shortcuts to be taken instead of following pre-established processes and this results in poor quality of deliverables, delays, and self-promoting behavior.

*8. Limited management involvement and support.* Weak sponsor and/or lack of management interest and project support allow divisive behavior among competing business unit interests to surface because in the absence of focus, some project participants tend to pursue their own interests more than those of the project. Lack of management interest and support for a project also translates into limited funding for effective project assessment and successful implementation.

*9. External conflicts.* Conflicting buyer-seller and joint venture partner objectives are another cause of impediments that tend to disappear when appropriate resolution of issues takes place. For this reason, it is imperative that the goals and objectives of buyer, seller, or joint venture partners are identified at the beginning of the project and handled in the negotiations. If not fully resolved, they cause impediments to develop at any point in the evaluation and implementation phases.

*10. Poor documentation and legal agreements.* Unbalanced legal agreements or inadequate documentation of negotiated terms and conditions causes confusion and delays in the negotiation phase, in the financing effort, in the approval processes, and in the implementation of the project. The reasons for such legal documents may vary, but are usually traced to inexperienced project teams.

### Project Politics and Origins

World-class business development groups value innovation and emphasize quality project assessments and discipline in decision making. In these organizations, politics has no place in the processes and principles of quality decisions are applied consistently. On the other hand, some experts maintain that project politics is good because it generates discussion and re-thinking of a project's goals and objectives. Regardless of whether project politics is good or not, it is an impediment in every acquisition and joint venture project because, unlike other causes of impediments, once it is allowed to develop it is difficult to contain.

In most companies, individual business units usually look for insiders to the organization to handle acquisition and joint venture projects. World-class companies, however, have independent business development groups with strong linkages to the business units that operate with organizational politics kept at minimum levels. The reason for this is that the emphasis is on teamwork and sharing common project responsibility in order to ensure success. When politics dominates a project, teamwork suffers and responsibility for managing the project to completion is not shared among project stakeholders. Consequently, internal project politics causes the quality and effectiveness of project evaluation to suffer, approvals take longer than necessary, and project implementation becomes difficult and expensive.

Some motives underlying impediments to approvals and successful implementation are difficult to deal with because they are outside the project team leader's circle of influence and require help from the project sponsor and senior management. The three major motives in this category are personal objectives not being consistent with project objectives, turf protection and power struggles between heads of different organizations, and positioning of various managers to benefit by the project execution. Sometimes, internal project politics have their origin in a number of issues that could be handled or avoided with appropriate training, experience, communications, and project process. One such issue is failure to invest time up front to communicate the long-term growth needs of the company to business unit heads, explain how the proposed project meets the strategic and operational needs, and obtain consensus on the proposed project.

Another source of impediments is the appointed project sponsor not having a positive reputation, not commanding much respect company-wide, not enjoying strong senior management support, and not being well acquainted with the power structure within the company. Failure to include key stakeholders in the strategic and operational gap analysis, the screening and selection process, and several decisions made in the project evaluation and negotiations phases causes friction. Also, if the alternatives to the proposed project were not evaluated according to clearly defined and communicated criteria or the proposed project was selected without considering existing internal or external initiatives the project will face opposition.

Inexperienced project teams usually fail to communicate effectively progress on the evaluation and negotiations phases to internal stakeholders and demonstrate how the project and the negotiated terms and conditions meet every stakeholders needs. Also, ignorance of the acquisition and joint venture formation process causes delays and frustration when it is coupled by a project team that does not have time to explain the process and its requirements to everybody. Additionally, complex matrix management reporting structures often create confusion because inconsistent directions are given and are expected to be followed by inexperienced project team members.

Some of the common manifestations of project politics are uncooperative behavior, mistrust and conflict, and limited sharing of information or even wrong information being released. Other indications of project politics are restricted vertical and horizontal communications, limited interaction and relationship building, and extensive management interference with project details that ordinarily are left to the discretion of project team members. Outer signs include conflicting signals concerning management support or support being conditioned on terms inconsistent with project goals. They also include long delays in the feasibility study review process and the interim business case beyond what is considered reasonable, senior management indecision, and inability to take a definite position and provide direction and guidance.

Project politics are not limited to internal politics; external politics is also present, but its cause is different and its impact on the project is usually much less significant. Quite frequently, project politics is rooted either in personal objectives being inconsistent with project objectives or in power plays and turf battles. While ignorance of process and communication problems may allow politics to develop, the project team can take steps to eliminate that problem. However, other underlying problems, such as inconsistency of personal with project objectives and a rigid matrix management structure imposed on the team, are outside its ability to resolve and result in politics disabling the project team.

### Impediment Management

Dealing with project approvals and implementation impediments requires experience and project stakeholder management. The starting point for dealing with impediments is providing awareness about the project and how it meets the strategic and operational needs of the company. Inclusion of key stakeholders in the screening process, using agreed selection criteria, and obtaining agreement on company strategy and project objectives also help. The second step involves ensuring consistency and harmonization of strategies and objectives among business units impacted by the project, which is helped by continuity of purpose and effective transitioning of responsibilities. Step three entails nominating a strong project sponsor who enjoys strong senior management support, with authority and responsibility to proceed without having to go back to various committees for approval on smaller issues, and with experience in doing acquisitions and joint ventures.

Once the project team is formed and project stakeholders are identified, roles and responsibilities of subteams are defined and education of project participants concerning all aspects of the project process begins. When project participants are well informed, building relationships and trust becomes possible. By addressing participants' concerns through open and uninhibited communications and enlisting their support, consensus building emerges. However, the project sponsor must take a leading role in handling project politics with help from the project team and senior management.

To neutralize the impact of politics, the project team must ask for considerable project sponsor and senior management involvement in the project. For that involvement to be effective, the project team needs to ensure balance of costs and benefits and presence of win-win arrangements to satisfy the needs of project participants. No one's interests, positions, or fears should be discounted;

they need to be addressed to disarm the potential for politics to fester. In addition, to neutralize politics, the project team needs to operate under the "demonstrate, communicate, escalate" principle at all times. That is, to take a project through the approval process and implementation effectively, there must be continuous feedback and communication. When all else fails, the project team should demonstrate damage being inflicted on the project and have the impediments removed.

### The Role of Project Participants

Acquisitions and joint ventures impact most business units or groups within a company and in some cases, the objectives of stakeholders may be in conflict with those of the project. The project team leader is responsible for identifying the potential for conflict and initiates actions to manage the impact of impediments developing down the road. Areas of potential conflict should be brought to the project sponsor's attention before project assessment begins so that appropriate positioning of the project takes place to ensure buy-in from all stakeholders.

Appropriate positioning of a project with stakeholders begins with a clear articulation of objectives and an outline of how each organization is impacted by the project. When negative impacts are identified, compensatory schemes are developed to leave impacted stakeholders as well off as prior to the project being undertaken. To ensure that this happens, the project team leader needs to monitor progress on the project and steer changes in the right direction. The project team leader has to observe project team performance and behavior of other participants and stakeholders so that he or she can intervene immediately and influence project dynamics before conflicts develop; however, intervention should be infrequent and measured in nature. If the situation is not controlled immediately, the intervention will be greater and likely to cause additional erosion of support for the project.

Once project goals and objectives are understood and agreed upon by all stakeholders, the project workplan with specific responsibilities assigned to each participant along with expected results serves as a control mechanism. This helps the project sponsor and the team leader to take control of the process, intervene when appropriate, and re-assign responsibilities to eliminate impediments and move the project forward. It is important that the project sponsor communicates progress to senior management and outside stakeholders and maintains the support of business unit heads with a common focus. The project sponsor secures senior management support for the project and communicates deviations from initial objectives, project value, and negotiations on a regular basis. The project team communicates progress on the project, internally on a continuous basis through the project team leader and externally on as-needed basis through the project sponsor. When project evaluation, negotiation, and implementation are completed, the project team leader needs to take the pulse of stakeholder organizations to sense how they feel about the project in each phase.

Corporate project approvals usually involve concurrence by business unit heads and finance officers and the project sponsor's influence goes a long way toward obtaining those approvals. Since approvals are required, the project sponsor ensures that assessment is done before approvals are required so that there will be no last-minute surprises and appropriate "selling" of the project takes place. However, in some instances the influence of the project sponsor may not be sufficient to resolve conflicts due to adverse project impacts on some organizations. In those cases, the project sponsor may escalate to ensure that all stakeholders are pulling in the same direction.

While there are no clear prescriptions on how to eliminate project impediments, the business development group can help manage impediments through the following practices, which produce positive results:

1.  Select seasoned, respected, and well-connected project sponsors and engage the heads of organizations impacted by the project from the start.
2.  Use experienced project team leaders and core team members who can recognize impediments and can deal with issues appropriately. Also, obtain agreement on screening criteria and involve stakeholders in the selection process using those criteria to screen alternatives.
3.  Invest ample time in communicating project goals and objectives and benefits to all stakeholders and in building trust and relationships through win-win arrangements.
4.  Demonstrate the impacts of project impediments and cause ineffective reporting structures to be torn down and inappropriate behavior eliminated. When all else fails, escalate the problem to ensure removal of impediments.

## SUMMARY

This chapter deals with the mundane issue of obtaining project approvals and impediments present in acquisition and joint venture projects. The causes of impediments are many and varied, but their impacts are always long delays and, in some cases, project elimination. We review the steps to obtain corporate project approvals and discuss the characteristics of sound approval processes, the key being absence of internal politics and resulting conflicts. Because of damage that project impediments can cause, we discuss the causes of impediments in general and the project politics and its origins. Management of project impediments is discussed and some ideas are offered to help in handling this issue, while roles of project participants are also reviewed.

There are no clear prescriptions on how the project team can eliminate all project impediments, but world-class practices produce positive results. Hence, we recommend selecting seasoned, respected, and well-connected project sponsors; engaging heads of organizations impacted by the project from the start; and using experienced project team leaders and core team members who can recognize impediments and can deal with issues appropriately. We also recommend obtaining agreement on screening criteria and involving stakeholders in the selection process, communicating the project goals, objectives, and benefits to stakeholders, and trust and relationship building through win-win arrangements. All impediments must be removed and inappropriate behavior eliminated.

# 25

# PROJECT POSTMORTEM AND FEEDBACK

## INTRODUCTION

The last, and often omitted, step in acquisitions and joint ventures is the project postmortem analysis, which is a thorough review of the entire process of a recently completed project by experienced business development professionals. It examines every step of the project process to identify what was done or not done according to pre-established process, understand the reasons behind major actions, and report significant findings. It is a process that examines events and facts from initial contact to establishment of new-entity operations.

The project postmortem analysis is left out of the acquisition and joint venture process for two reasons: (1) it is work after the fact; that is, additional work after a project has been completed, which is not appreciated by most stakeholders because it involves further expenditure of resources, and (2) when projects are not done according to process and negative findings surface, individuals do not appreciate having their involvement associated with negative findings. However, world-class business development groups consider postmortem analysis an integral part of doing a project because of dividends it yields. They invest in professionally performed postmortem analyses and reports and include the report recommendations in the business development process to improve future performance.

The overarching goal of postmortem analyses is to help identify areas of improvement in the evaluation, negotiation, and implementation of acquisitions and joint ventures. However, there are other reasons for it, which open the discussion of this chapter. Then, discussion focuses on the scope of the postmortem analysis, which includes assignment of responsibilities among subteams and individual members, verification of appropriate transitioning and continuity of purpose, and identification of impediments to various project functions. Other elements included in the postmortem are a review of project team successes and failures in performing assigned tasks, investigation of root causes of failures, and judging discipline and speed of the decision-making process.

The importance of screening input and feedback in fact finding in order to balance views and ensure fair assessment is considered next. Distilling lessons learned is a key element of the postmortem function and the need to incorporate them in the report's recommendations is discussed here. Also, the means of transferring knowledge and use of knowledge derived from the postmortem analysis is discussed and attention is given to postmortem costs and benefits considerations.

In characterizing successful postmortem analyses, we emphasize adherence to pre-established processes, continuity of purpose and effective transition of responsibilities, and discipline in the decision-making process. Also, senior management support and direction for the new entity's management team, the performance of subteams and individuals, and inclusion of lessons learned in the process to be used in future projects are stressed repeatedly.

## KEY CONSIDERATIONS IN POSTMORTEM ANALYSIS

### Purpose of Postmortem Analysis

The main reason for a postmortem analysis is to review the project execution from start to finish through the pre-established process so that learning takes place from project experiences. Postmortem analysis is ordinarily performed by the corporate business development group because it has the most experience in doing projects correctly, it can abstract from business unit interests and politics, and it is a centralized organization that provides continuity of learning and experience to the company.

The first area of postmortem analysis is to identify the positive aspects and approaches used in the project process and what was done right at each step. The second area of the analysis is to identify problem areas, what went wrong, and why. Then, the team assigned the postmortem responsibility distills lessons learned from doing the project. After fact finding and analysis are done, the team's purpose becomes to report the results of the analysis, communicate to management the lessons learned, and integrate them in future projects.

The lessons learned are examined in the context of assessing project success, which extends beyond project execution. That is, while the postmortem analysis concentrates on project execution, it is not complete unless it continues beyond project implementation into the operational phase. The idea in postmortem analysis is to learn from past mistakes, prevent their recurrence in future projects, and transfer newly acquired knowledge. All this is done to institutionalize knowledge and improve the effectiveness of the acquisition and joint venture process.

## Scope of Postmortems

The corporate business development group is usually charged with the responsibility of conducting the postmortem analysis. To undertake a project postmortem analysis, the business development team given this task examines the assignment of individuals and respective roles and responsibilities of both internal and external project participants. Then, it assesses the performance of various subteams based on pre-established criteria. In addition, it looks behind events and actions of project participants that resulted in major failures to identify the reasons for them and apparent motives. That is, the subteam conducting the postmortem needs a plan for approaching the analysis, which outlines steps involved and creates criteria of judging performance.

The scope of postmortem analysis is fairly broad. The team performing it reviews what took place from the moment contact with a target company or a joint venture partner was initiated, who was involved, what were the key issues, how things were handled, and what the outcome was. Concurrently, it looks at the pre-established process to determine to what extent process was followed, and whether appropriate individuals were involved, and assesses the outcome in each step of the process.

In postmortem analysis, the key elements of the acquisition and joint venture project process and related activities are reviewed and evaluated. The elements given attention in this review are the following:

1. The level of preparation before undertaking the project, both in terms of the project team knowledge of process and in terms of internal analysis capabilities.
2. The actual process used to evaluate, negotiate, and implement the project and associated workplans.
3. Development of project objectives based on strategic and operational gap analyses and evaluation of alternatives and screening based on agreed-upon criteria to select among competing projects.
4. The distribution of responsibilities between various subteams and articulation of expectations on deliverables.
5. Assessment of how close pre-established process was followed and how the project team performed.
6. The findings and recommendations of the due diligence subteam, especially those related to expected synergies and new areas of improvement.
7. The performance of individual team members, outside consultants, and investment bankers as well as that of the project team, the business development group, the steering committee, and the senior management team.
8. Continuity of purpose throughout the process and how the transition of responsibilities was effected at each junction.
9. The quality of the business case analysis including strategic fit, project valuation, risk allocation and management, implementation planning, the new-entity business plan, and the assessment of overall project success.
10. The assessment of causes of process, subteam, and individual successes and failures and the identification, management, and elimination of project impediments.

Although not exhaustive, this list is a fair representation of the postmortem analysis scope. For large projects or for projects where several things went wrong, we recommend engaging outside experts to assist the business development group perform an objective postmortem analysis and develop specific and implementable recommendations. Also, because external experts are considered impartial, they should be used to communicate postmortem findings and recommendations. However, the business development group is responsible for incorporating the postmortem recommendations in the updated acquisition and joint venture process.

### Postmortem Costs and Benefits

Conducting a sound postmortem analysis requires investment of additional resources in a project that has already closed, regardless of whether it went through the entire process or was eliminated in the evaluation stage. An experienced business development group strives to balance the costs involved in performing a postmortem with expected benefits from that analysis. The guiding principle here is to develop implementable recommendations so that future projects can benefit from the postmortem analysis and the recommendations.

Postmortems involve both financial and human resource costs. The most significant cost elements considered in the decision of how detailed the postmortem analysis should be are the following:

1.  Financial costs and the human resource commitments involved in interviews, feedback, and communication of the postmortem report recommendations.
2.  Exposure of poor subteam and individual project participant performance may cause political casualties and fallout. These costs need to be considered carefully.
3.  The need for action to remedy the process, remove impediments in the process, and introduce changes may require drastic measures, additional financial costs, and create unpleasant situations.
4.  The financial cost of benchmarking best processes and practices can be substantial and in some cases, the experience gained may not be easily transferable.
5.  The cost of maintaining a central depository of knowledge gained and updating it as new lessons are learned and experience is gained.
6.  The costs of implementing the postmortem analysis recommendations involve not only financial costs, but costs of restructuring organizations and processes.
7.  The cost to the company of either not doing a postmortem analysis for a project or doing a poor assessment of what happened in the last project.

Postmortem analysis recommendations result in positive changes in the project process and yield several benefits to the company. To begin with, there is an increased awareness and accountability that the project participants' roles and responsibilities will be reviewed and their performance evaluated relative to assigned objectives. Knowing that the postmortem analysis will identify sources of excellence, shortcomings in the process, and subteam and individual performance, the participants tend to follow process and perform well.

The postmortem analysis determines the extent of discipline in the decision-making process and how quickly decisions are made. When this comparison with world-class practices is well documented, it leads to improvements in the way projects are executed. Incorporating new learning in the acquisition and joint venture processes produces more successful projects and over the long run, it creates a competitive advantage. Postmortems also identify exceptional individual performance, encourage duplication of such behavior in following projects, and reward world-class practices. Finally, postmortems result in enhanced communication among subteam members and between subteams and ensure continuity of purpose, effective transitioning, and accountability in future projects.

### Successful Postmortem Characteristics

Project postmortem analyses are great learning and communications tools when done appropriately and characterized by world-class practices. The assessment of discipline in decision making, the speed of project execution, and adherence to pre-established process versus the project being driven by external and artificial time lines are the primary focus of postmortem analysis. However, for the assessment to be effective, extensive feedback from participants concerning continuity of purpose and appropriate transitioning of responsibilities is required. Thorough and objective review and analysis of events, expectations, and behavior of project participants add tremendous value to the postmortem analysis, which also ensures direct input and feedback from all project participants on the key steps of the acquisition or joint venture formation process.

A good postmortem identifies the positive elements and behaviors in the project, recognizes contributions and praises them, and lists events and functions that went wrong in the evaluation, negotiation, and implementation phases of the project. It also investigates the root causes of problem areas and shortfalls without attempting to assign blame. The postmortem also examines the roles and responsibilities of various subteams and subteam members and how transitioning of responsibilities was effected to determine whether continuity of purpose was maintained. In the process, it assesses individual participant performance relative to workplan expectations, given the roles and responsibilities assigned to individuals.

The postmortem report summarizes the internal findings of the analysis. However, a good report also includes an evaluation of external stakeholder involvement, contributions, and performance assessment of consultants and functional experts. The recommendations of the postmortem analysis report should be drafted expertly to enhance discipline in the decision-making process. However, the report should be based on a sound basis in that it has looked at root causes of problems, reasons for failures, and remedies to repair the process elements that caused failures. The postmortem report also distills the lessons learned in clearly articulated and concise recommendations to be incorporated in the acquisition and joint venture process. The report is widely distributed and lessons learned are effectively communicated through meetings with project participants.

For the postmortem to be effective, senior management should review the report and understand the findings and the recommendations. Hence, the postmortem report should contain clear, specific, and implementable recommendations that can be integrated into the project process. Institutionalized learning is a quality characteristic and is effected by the postmortem analysis and incorporation of lessons learned in the project processes. Benchmarking practices of world-class companies and comparison of the project team's performance relative to world-class benchmarks are used to identify areas of improvements through training and experience.

Identification of superior performance by any subteam and its members, what is responsible for that performance, and how it can be duplicated by other subteams are elements present in sound postmortems. In addition, evaluation of current reward systems that provide incentives for cooperation, teamwork, and other appropriate behaviors is undertaken. Finally, an effective postmortem report shows cost-benefit considerations of postmortem analysis as part of the process.

## VALUABLE LEARNING AND KNOWLEDGE INTEGRATION

### Project Feedback and Screening

The project team leader monitors progress on the project continuously by obtaining input from internal and external sources involved in the project. At each step of the process, the project team leader obtains feedback as part of communicating progress ensuring that pre-established process is followed. The feedback screening done by the project leader is a continuous process from the start of the project, but at the postmortem stage, it is concerned with evaluating the totality of inputs on events and actions taken.

In the postmortem phase, the project team leader obtains feedback from the core project team, the negotiation and implementation subteams, external advisors engaged, senior management, the project sponsor, and business unit heads. It also solicits input from employees retained by the new entity, joint venture partners, the liaison subteam and the steering committee, participating financing institutions, and independent project assessors. In addition, feedback is obtained from the acquired company's or the joint venture's management team and through established performance-tracking mechanisms.

To ensure consistency and reconcile conflicting views of events from different participants, the team leader engages in active screening of the input provided. This screening involves examining independent or external assessments to determine retrospectively how diligent they were and how closely the project team followed their recommendations. Some helpful considerations in obtaining feedback and input and screening are the following:

1.   Abstract from personalities and emotional attachments to the project, internal politics, and ulterior motives.

2.    Identify repeated input and comments, common themes raised, and repeated patterns in the feedback obtained and note consistent patterns.

3.    Seek and examine as much as possible objective evidence and facts in addition to verbal input. Ask for supporting documentation and evidence to establish credibility.

4.    Screen all input and feedback obtained on subteam and individual performance to eliminate politically motivated feedback.

5.    Get behind the common or recurring themes in project team and other stakeholders' behavior, but do not dwell on isolated instances and events.

6.    Summarize feedback obtained by area of concern and present findings in a clear and concise manner.

After input and feedback has been obtained, it is summarized and related back to the individuals who provided it and ask for validation of the input. This step helps eliminate misconceptions in the input and feedback phase.

### Distilling Lessons Learned

Distilling lessons learned from a completed project and using them to update the acquisition or joint venture process is the most important contribution of the postmortem analysis. The distilled lessons learned ordinarily relate to the following considerations:

1.    What function or activity was done well, how it was done, and how it impacted project team performance and the success of the project.

2.    What function, activity, or step in the process was not done in a manner it should have been done, the reasons for this, and how it impacted the project.

3.    What function or activity was performed poorly, the reasons for the poor performance, and how it impacted the project.

Lessons learned also include understanding how good the pre-established process was for the project, how closely it was followed, and the rationale for deviations from it and to what extent continuity of purpose and effective transitioning of responsibilities took place throughout the process. In addition, they include the performance assessment of external participants, reasons for good or bad performance, and how it impacted project success.

The practices that yield results in distilling lessons learned start with focus on identifying and shaping lessons learned and not on identifying scapegoats and assigning blame for failures. Then a benchmarking study of best practices in the postmortem area is conducted to obtain input from business development groups in world-class companies. This is required to establish a reference point to judge project participants performance. When comparing subteam and individual performance against best practices performance, gaps are identified that need to be addressed. Instead of a multitude of items, four or five big impact items are presented as lessons learned from doing the project, expressed in clear and specific terms.

Lessons learned become tools of change when the project team leader briefs senior management on the findings of the postmortem analysis and recommendations for changes needed to improve the process for future projects. This requires the project team leader to demonstrate how such changes would benefit the company, communicate the new learning extensively with internal project participants, and share the recommended changes in the processes to be used on a going-forward basis.

### Transfer and Use of Knowledge

Performing the analysis and distilling lessons learned from doing the project is the first step in the postmortem process. This is followed by transfer of knowledge and institutionalizing learning so that it can be used successfully in future projects. How the knowledge transfer takes place and how it is used in future projects depend on the structure of the business development group. The means commonly used by business development groups to transfer the knowledge and experience gained vary, but it is effected through written reports containing lessons learned, which are distributed internally, and through external participant reports or assessments of consultants engaged to assist in the postmortem analysis.

Internal meetings on knowledge transfer are the main venue using various communication tools, including presentations to different project participant groups and sharing the postmortem report analysis and recommendations with internal stakeholders. The business development group institutionalizes knowledge via incorporating lessons learned and updating the business development process, and they do it by building a library of reports containing experiences gained in every project. The main issues include problems that arose, unique situations, how they were resolved, and lessons learned.

How the knowledge and experience gained from doing a project is used in future projects varies according to the experience of the business development group and individuals in the core project teams. Following are some of the ways the knowledge included in the postmortem report can be used to create a competitive advantage for the company:

1.  Increase the business development group's knowledge base and incorporate it in the thinking of likely key project participants in future projects. Incorporate lessons learned and recommended changes in existing processes to make them more effective. If required, create new subprocesses to handle unique issues and problems.
2.  Share the postmortem study and results of benchmarking studies related to the project process. Also, make reference to success stories of other business development groups and positive experiences that can be duplicated by project teams in future projects.
3.  Share postmortem analysis reports, lessons learned, experiences gained, and approaches to close knowledge gaps in future projects with individual participants before projects start to enhance effectiveness.
4.  Introduce additional discipline and rigor in the decision-making process through benchmarked best processes and practices and reduce the probability and number of

future failures, errors of judgment, inappropriate handling of issues, and conflicts in future projects through institutionalized learning.

5. Increase senior management awareness of the evaluation, negotiation, and implementation process requirements, what can go wrong, and why assessments and executions can be faulty. Also, enhance management's ability to make informed decisions by sharing the body of knowledge accumulated through postmortem analyses of projects to date.

## SUMMARY

Because it is the last step in the acquisition and joint venture process, postmortem analysis is often omitted entirely or executed poorly. The recommendation is to invest in postmortem analysis to understand the strengths and weaknesses of a process and the project team so that strengths can be leveraged and weaknesses eliminated. This leads to a competitive advantage when world-class practices are duplicated and experience is accumulated through execution of a number of projects.

The purpose and reasons for the postmortem analysis starts the discussion in this chapter. A discussion of the breadth and scope of postmortem analysis follows and we discuss how feedback is obtained and screened by the project team leader conducting the effort. On distilling lessons learned, we emphasize the need to focus on a few key lessons and the importance of establishing world-class practices benchmarks to identify gaps in the process and individual and subteam performance.

Transferring the lessons learned and insitutionalizing knowledge obtained from doing the project are discussed and the importance of disseminating new learning throughout the business development organization and the project team participants is stressed. Like a secret formula or process that produces a new product, lessons learned need to be documented and transferred to appropriate organizations in the company. Experience gained by doing acquisitions and joint ventures benefits individual participants, but knowledge gained is institutionalized to benefit the company because it was paid for and it is company intellectual property.

Conducting postmortem analyses is costly, but they are undertaken with the expectation of producing large benefits for the company. The costs and expected benefits need to be balanced in determining the detail of analysis to perform. The discussion on this important step of the acquisition and joint venture process closes with what characterizes successful postmortem analyses and stresses the need for specific recommendations to be incorporated in the future project process.

# 26

---

# SUMMARY AND CONCLUSIONS

## INTRODUCTION

By now, it is apparent that acquisitions and joint ventures are complex transactions and a large number of these projects fail with amazing regularity. However, the success rate of acquisition and joint venture projects is increased significantly when pre-established practices are followed, corporate strategy drives project objectives, and the project subteams have sufficient training and experience in doing acquisition and joint venture projects.

Successful project teams are characterized by extensive cooperation and teamwork, world-class professionalism, and uninhibited 360-degree communications. Project participants understand what is involved in doing acquisition and joint venture projects, know their roles and responsibilities, and what is expected of them and other team members. Continuity of purpose and effective transitioning of responsibilities are essential in maintaining focus on the goals and objectives and executing the implementation flawlessly. In addition, to ensure project success, the project team leader and project sponsor must focus on key areas and provide strong leadership and support.

In the closing chapter, we summarize important areas that participants need to focus on to ensure project success. First, we review the main determinants of value creation in acquisitions and joint ventures. Then, the discussion evolves around clarity of purpose and objectives in the project and the need for continuity of purpose throughout the project evaluation, negotiation, and implementation phases. After clarity of purpose and objectives comes the emphasis on preparation and following pre-established processes designed to help in professional executions.

Because discipline in decision making is a major requirement to create value for a project, we summarize the key considerations and emphasize the need for decisions to be based on facts and evidence. Characteristics of excellent project teams are discussed, and the need for quality in project assessments is raised again. Elements of effective negotiations are distilled; as we concluded earlier, win-win arrangements are the model to strive for. The financial assessment of a project is a complex undertaking involving many steps and considerations, which we summarize here.

The factors of effective implementation are reviewed briefly and the need for parent company senior management support for the new entity is brought up because it is crucial in ensuring effective transitioning and project success. Without teamwork and effective communications, acquisitions and joint ventures are likely to fail and for that reason, we review key considerations in teamwork and communications. Finally, we discuss the need to benchmark and adopt best practices in doing acquisitions and joint ventures, copy the behavior of world-class project teams, and end the chapter with a brief conclusion.

## CONDITIONS FOR CORPORATE VALUE CREATION

Corporate shareholder value is created by strategic business development projects if, and only if, these projects are strategy-driven and successfully executed. Success, in turn, is determined by several conditions that must be satisfied, the most important being:

*1. Picking the right target or joint venture partner.* To pick the right target or joint venture partner requires a good understanding of corporate strategy, a knowledgeable business development team, and a sound, pre-established screening and selection process.

*2. Strengthening and enlarging the core business.* The strategic and financial strength of acquisitions and joint ventures must be guided by the principle of strengthening or expanding the core business or areas in which the company has a comparative advantage.

*3. Obtaining adequate strategic returns on investment.* Strategic and financial strength of acquisition and joint venture projects must be accompanied by enhanced market and technological positioning and enhanced competitiveness of the parent or the new firm.

*4. Successful implementation.* Turning paper agreements into successful entities is crucial in integrating a target or setting up joint venture operations because in addition to understanding operational issues, it requires ability to manage change and conflict.

*5. Harnessing synergies.* Because acquisitions involve premiums above the market value of an acquisition target and because joint ventures involve costs usually unaccounted for, harnessing expected synergies or creating new ones is key to ensure strategic and financial success of the new entity.

*6. Creating a competitive advantage.* Unless an acquisition or joint venture can confer some form of competitive advantage through increased skills, more effective processes, or some other form of enhancement, the new entity is not likely to be viable.

## RECURRING THEMES IN SUCCESSFUL PROJECTS

### Clarity of Purpose and Objectives

In addition to the requirements stated above, the creation of corporate value begins with clarity of purpose and objectives and continuity of purpose throughout the project process. A number of fundamental principles, which are central for clarity of purpose and project objectives, are summarized below. However, even if these principles are satisfied, success is not ensured unless there is continuity of purpose throughout the project and effective transitioning of responsibilities.

*1. Understanding strategy and objectives.* This includes the strategy and objectives of the acquiring or the parent company, gaps in their strategy, the strategy of the new entity, and project-specific goals. Often, this principle is violated for the sake of expediency with the result always being project failure.

*2. Consistency of strategy and objectives.* This principle is so important that if the strategy, objectives, or project goals of the parent and the new entity are in conflict, the project team must harmonize them or consider abandoning the project.

*3. Knowing what you want to get out of the project.* If the project team does not have clear project goals and objectives, there is no way of knowing how successful the project is or whether good terms and conditions have been negotiated.

*4. Stakeholder buy-in of mission and objectives.* This involves clear articulation and extensive and uninhibited communication among participants in order for the project mission and objectives to be understood, clarified, and accepted as the guiding force in the project.

*5. Close strategic fit.* The new entity created by the project should strengthen the company's core business, satisfy customer needs that are currently not being met, have common or consistent strategic objectives, and produce strategic returns on investment.

### Emphasis on Pre-established Process

Acquisition and joint venture projects are executed under short time lines and extreme pressure to complete the transactions. Because of this, it is crucial that project teams know and put emphasis on the process to be followed. More specifically, project teams must adopt the following approach:

*1. Apply past experiences.* Use past experience and lessons learned to do the project in a manner best suited to the company's culture and operating environment. There may be some room for experimenting, but the project team should rely on tried and tested approaches to execute the project.

*2. Create a sound workplan.* Develop an agreed-upon workplan with clearly articulated roles and responsibilities for project participants. The workplan should state expected deliverables by participant, quality expectations, time lines involved, and how output from one individual relates to the rest of the process.

*3. Adhere to pre-established process.* This is key to doing acquisitions and joint ventures properly. Consequently, timelines should not determine how things get done, but serve as one input to the workplan agreed to by all participants.

*4. Channel external pressures.* Re-directing external pressures is necessary to get things done right. That is, resist pressures to meet artificial deadlines and focus people's creativity and influence on doing things right to ensure project success.

*5. Provide a common base.* This requires commonality of definitions and is done through a pre-established process where each project participant knows where he stands in the process, who delivers what, to whom, when, and how.

*6. Ensure smooth transition.* Continuity of purpose in the project and effective transfer of responsibilities at each step of the process is the glue that holds the process together.

While reliance and adherence to process help in executing acquisitions and joint ventures, it takes extensive preparation to meet the challenges presented by these projects. Preparation involves investment of time to communicate the need for and the benefits of the proposed project to obtain internal support. Team building and training on the process and best practices and developing an understanding of strengths and weaknesses of the parent company are required to create an effective team. Creating channels of effective communication, defining the project scope, assessing resource requirements for its execution, and creating and conditioning appropriate management expectations are additional areas to address before project execution.

### Discipline in Decision Making

Successful projects do not happen by chance; they are done under a decision-making process where information, evidence, and analysis underlie all decisions. This is what we call disciplined decision making, which entails the following key considerations:

*1. Get agreement on definitions.* Developing a common knowledge and definitions among project participants right at the project start eliminates confusion later on and makes the process more efficient.

*2. Test the assumptions.* Understanding assumptions underlying the development of market and financial data and projections is essential. Understanding of assumptions often involves testing the assumptions or comparing them with industry-wide averages or obtaining input from external advisors and consultants.

*3. Understand risks.* Assessing the environment in which the project is executed is important to assess market stability and to what extent assumed conditions are likely to persist in the planning horizon. Environmental and risk analysis involves assessment of major factors outside the new entity's control that can influence and shape its future performance.

*4. Manage expectations.* This includes managing participant expectations concerning new entity performance, responsibilities of the parent and the new entity, quality of outputs and deliverables, time lines associated with key activities, and terms and conditions to be negotiated. Expectations must be conditioned at the start of the project to avoid lengthy discussions as the process unfolds and participants develop firm views.

*5. Rely on facts and evidence.* Base decisions on factual information and evidence, but do not discount qualitative information. This is an essential element to ensure project success and it is always a good idea to obtain input from several sources to ensure that personal biases are minimized.

*6. Quantify synergies and strategic returns on investment.* Time and effort required to perform this task pay back handsome returns because they force discipline on the evaluation process. The view is that if you can't quantify it, you don't really understand it, and if you don't understand it, you can't manage it, and if you can't manage it, your project will not be successful.

## Excellence of Project Teams

Project teams in world-class companies are put together by the business development group and consist of experts in functional areas. These project teams share several common characteristics that result in flawless executions and successful projects:

*1. Functional expertise.* Expertise, training in functional areas, and ability to relate functional knowledge to specific projects are expected in every project. However, a clear definition of roles and responsibilities of participants is essential so that contributions of individual members are maximized.

*2. Team above personal interests.* This refers to ability to work in teams where common interests supersede individual self-interest. This requires selecting the right team members and ability to communicate effectively with all levels of management.

*3. Experience in business development projects.* This requirement is rarely fulfilled, but having team members go through training and study of several acquisitions and joint ventures helps in shortening the learning curve, understanding the issues, and handling the project challenges.

*4. Knowledge of project process.* Knowing the sequence of events, who should be involved in what, and focusing on important elements of the project is important. When there are deviations from pre-established process, the team can assess the impact of deviations and whether a course correction is needed.

*5. The right implementation team.* Project team members are equal contributors to project success. However, a lot of emphasis must be placed on the selection of project team members who are responsible for turning definitive agreements into real operations because of the skills required to manage organizational change.

*6. Successful negotiation subteam.* Negotiation subteams succeed only if they have exceptional support from the rest of the project team and prepare extensively. Senior managers should not participate in negotiations, especially without extensive coaching, input, and guidance from the project team.

*7. Seasoned steering committee and liaison subteam.* These subteams represent the company in the transition phase, but are established to ensure balance of interests and provide interfaces between the parent and the new entity.

## Quality Assessments

Quality project evaluations are a component of disciplined decision making where thoroughness and objectivity are essential. Quality assessments contribute to successful acquisitions and joint ventures and require adherence to process, which involves a number of steps, the most important being:

*1. Quantification of information.* Environmental assessment, qualitative information, and expectations require quantification. This is followed by thorough strategic fit assessment, which has more credibility when based on a sound assessment and quantitative data.

*2. Checking the basis of the assumptions.* This refers to thorough and complete review to establish that the financial analysis is based on an unbiased and reasonable assumption set. This enables the project team to determine potential for value creation, course of negotiations, and how to influence the closing price range.

*3. Process sanity checks.* These checks are essential in the development and evaluation of market and financial projections; without them, even expert project teams are led astray. Sanity checks are performed at each point of responsibility transfer to another subteam.

*4. Independent assessment and fairness opinion.* These evaluations performed by competent internal or external advisors and consultants are needed to ensure that no significant elements have been overlooked, the analysis performed by the project team is objective, and corporate project approvals have been obtained.

*5. Adequate due diligence.* Validation of seller or target claims and verification of financial information are important in assessing future performance. Adequate due diligence is a requirement for joint ventures as well as inclusion of costs associated with new-entity formation and ongoing support.

*6. Sensitivity and scenario analysis.* It is a good idea to incorporate this analysis in the assumption set assessment and to determine the impacts of risks. That is, perform sensitivity and scenario analysis to assess the financial impacts of events outside the assumption set that could occur and impact the project adversely.

### Win-Win Negotiations

The basic purpose of negotiations is to find solutions to different issues that are acceptable to all stakeholders so that closing occurs and transfer of ownership takes place. While the style of acquisition negotiations is more aggressive and pressurized, joint venture negotiations take place throughout the project and are more personable. However, successful negotiations have several common elements, the most important being:

*1. Know exactly what you want to get in the negotiations.* At the same time, the project team must also know what can be given up in exchange in order to get what is really significant. This is important to create acceptable solutions and to determine to what extent negotiations are successful.

*2. Create the right chemistry.* The right chemistry between negotiation subteams involved is almost as important in acquisitions as it is in joint venture projects. Good relationships and the right chemistry must be established from the start of the project among functional experts on both sides.

*3. Understand the other side.* Spending time with the other side is probably one of the best investments because it enables the negotiation subteam to find out what is really important to the other side and evaluate what trade-offs they would accept.

*4. Search for win-win arrangements.* They are key to successful negotiations and pay back large dividends in the negotiation and the implementation phase of the project. Strive for win-win arrangements and avoid exploiting seeming weaknesses. At the end of the day, if the other side realizes that negotiations were not conducted in good faith, further negotiation and implementation are far more difficult.

*5. Facilitate closing.* The ultimate goal of negotiations is to arrive at a closing under fair terms and conditions; hence, the negotiation subteam needs to develop acceptable ranges of solutions on the key issues for both sides.

*6. Identify and quantify trade-offs.* Not only does the negotiation subteam need to know the company's position on various issues, but it also needs to identify trade-offs that would be of interest to the other side and have their value quantified.

*7. Share and balance costs and benefits.* Regardless of the project, successful negotiations involve sharing project benefits and costs in different degrees. The negotiation subteam should embrace this idea on all issues including future synergies: It may share with the seller some synergy benefits, if the seller commits today to share the costs and risks of extracting synergies.

*8. Draft comprehensive and balanced legal agreements.* The project team knows the company positions, the negotiated terms and conditions, and works with lawyers to draft legal documents. Insist on comprehensive legal documents and do not accept one-sided agreements because they are unstable solutions.

*9. Use external consultants as advisors only.* Do not let external consultants conduct face-to-face negotiations on your behalf but, if necessary, use them sparingly in that capacity. Also, have the negotiation subteam monitor discussions and accept only those terms and conditions that are reasonable for you, not what the market will bear.

*10. Obtain input and advice from the project team.* The negotiation subteam should practice politics of inclusion and use the expertise residing in the project team to brief and prepare its members. In addition, it should use the project team as a sounding board to check the course of negotiations.

### Sound Financial Evaluation

Ordinarily, the foundation of the fair market valuation of an acquisition or joint venture is the future economic capability of the new entity as indicated by the NPV of its cash flows. To arrive at the negotiated price to close a project, market, synergy, and tax savings premiums are added. The project team is involved in activities related to financial assessment of the new entity and determination of premiums involved in the project. A sound project financial assessment involves the following elements:

*1. Develop reasonable and objective assumptions.* This is essential in developing a reasonable set of pro forma financial statements for the target or the joint venture. Assumptions should be scrutinized and when possible tested against past experience, industry averages, and market intelligence.

*2. Create demand and price components.* Creating sound revenue components entails market assessment, industry analysis, and development of most likely demand and price forecasts given the product life cycles and expected technological changes.

*3. Include relevant cost information.* To ensure this, the financial analyst must take a broad view of the project in order to determine what present and future operating costs and capital investments should be included in the project business case.

*4. Quantify the value of trade-offs.* This requires modeling trade-offs, but armed with them, the negotiation subteam becomes effective in negotiating desired terms and conditions.

*5. Ensure assessment and allocation of risks.* Identification and quantification of project risks is absolutely crucial in determining likelihood of project success. How risks are shared determines the degree of project success, which is reflected in the project financials.

*6. Evaluate expected synergies.* This is an important component in determining the project value and negotiating sharing the value of synergies. However, ensure that the costs and investments required to extract the expected synergies are included.

*7. Perform sensitivity and scenario analysis.* This is an effective approach to test key assumptions and quantify the impact of project risks and the allocation of risks among different participants if appropriate scenarios are created.

*8. Prepare the new entity's business plan.* The business plan of the new entity is developed with pro forma financial statements and extensive analysis of the entity's projected operational performance. Check for growth enablers and constraints.

*9. Perform fair market valuations.* Based on the new-entity financial projections and the risk allocation negotiated, a fair market valuation is developed. A range of fair market valuation should be created using different valuation methods.

*10. Use industry averages and comparable transactions.* To determine the basis and the amount of premiums likely to be involved in a project, comparable industry transactions need to be monitored and understood.

*11. Obtain advice and independent assessment.* The best sources are investment bankers and external advisors. This step is important to ensure that information obtained is accurate and complete and that there are no errors and omissions in methodologies used and resulting calculations.

*12. Determine the final project valuation.* Once the earlier steps have been completed, the project team is in a position to recommend ranges of premiums and price to be paid to close the transaction.

### Effective Implementation

One of the greatest challenges in acquisitions and joint ventures is project implementation. The reason for this challenge is the organizational changes involved and departure from past practices that complicate turning legal agreements into operations. However, there are a number of things that help make project implementations effective, such as:

*1. Good implementation plan.* Such a plan is created by balancing project objectives with new-entity interests. A good implementation plan is executed quickly and effectively before confusion and conflicts arise within the ranks of the new entity's management team.

*2. Reasonable business plan.* A reasonable business plan for the new entity is the blueprint for its operations. In addition to clear mission and strategy, it includes operational targets and parent company support.

*3. Effective implementation subteam.* The implementation subteam must be composed of seasoned managers of change who have done this type of work before and are able to deal with conflict and organizational issues.

*4. Clear implementation strategy and objectives.* To develop these, the implementation subteam needs to determine early on the extent of the new entity's autonomy in terms of business definition, strategy, operations, and development of future objectives.

*5. Development of relationships.* Relationships at all functional levels and creation of the right chemistry and communications between project and management teams are essential to implement a project successfully. This includes embracing the new entity's management team and providing support and guidance.

*6. Retaining key managers.* Retaining top-notch managers from the acquired company and attracting talent from the parent companies to the new entity are required for effective implementation and involve negotiating contracts with appropriate incentives.

*7. Sound new-entity governance.* The steering committee creates an effective governance and sound organizational structure for the new entity and ensures ongoing support. Effective governance structures include adequate representation and balance of interests of the parties involved.

*8. Synergy extraction.* Ability to harness expected synergies and create new ones under the constraint of balancing costs and benefits requires an experienced implementation subteam, effective liaison subteam, and appropriate incentives for the new entity's management team.

*9. Management objectives.* Development of management objectives and creation of appropriate operational performance targets for the new entity are the first step in ensuring sound management of operations, the other step being linking compensation to operational target realization.

*10. Incentive systems.* Adequate rewards and incentives for the implementation subteam and the new entity's management team are necessary to motivate appropriate behavior. Rewards should be tied to operational targets and financial performance.

*11. Continuity of purpose and objectives.* Continuity of purpose and project objectives as well as effective transitioning of responsibilities in every step of the process are required to ensure that the project meets the initial objectives.

*12. Parent company management support.* Without strong support, direction, and guidance from the parent company's senior management team, effective implementation cannot take place because the new entity's management team feels left out of the mainstream decision-making process.

### Senior Management Support

As is the case with project participants, the roles and responsibilities of senior management must be clearly defined at the start of the project in order for the acquisition or joint venture process to work smoothly and effectively. In this area, the following principles are helpful in facilitating effective project execution:

*1. Management team education.* The project team leader should help management understand the steps of the process, approaches to be used, and different requirements to make the project successful. Also, management should understand the allocation of responsibilities among subteams and the roles of external participants.

*2. Project sponsor support.* The role of the project sponsor is to communicate to senior management the status of the project, obtain approvals to proceed to the next step, and ensure that adequate financial and human resources are allocated to the project. The project sponsor is not involved in day-to-day project management; instead, his or her role is to oversee and monitor progress and intervene when requested by the project team.

*3. Senior management briefings.* The project team leader should deliver regular project updates and communicate progress to the project sponsor. The project sponsor, in turn, communicates to senior management the project status on a regular basis and obtains feedback.

*4. Senior management support.* Senior management needs to understand that their support for the project on an ongoing basis is required for the project to succeed. This is key to ensure that sufficient financial and human resources are dedicated to the project. Without such senior management support, projects die.

*5. Removal of project impediments.* One of the project sponsor functions is to ensure that project impediments are removed as soon as they are identified. Impediments refer to lack of interest and cooperation, project politics, artificially tight time lines, lack of sufficient external support, and lack of dedicated resources.

*6. Measured management involvement.* There should be limited senior management involvement in the day-to-day management of negotiations or other project phases. This rule holds true for all cases except when senior management assistance is requested in stalemate situations.

*7. Corporate project approvals.* Corporate approvals are usually required for acquisitions and joint ventures and senior management support in the approval process is crucial. This is especially important when there are competing alternatives in the background being pushed by aggressive business unit heads.

### Teamwork and Communications

Acquisition and joint venture projects are complex and challenging assignments and to be successful, they require an inordinate amount of teamwork, cooperation, and communication. The key considerations in this area are:

*1. Spirit of project teamwork.* Teamwork, communication, and cooperation among and between project team members, business unit heads, the project sponsor, senior management, internal functional experts, external advisors, and consultants are essential ingredients for success.

*2. Absence of politics.* Internal politics and related impediments must be removed as soon as they are identified. Nothing hurts the effective project evaluation and implementation more than project politics, but this is routinely ignored.

*3. Unimpeded communications.* 360 degree communications are essential to ensure that participants understand the strategy, goals and objectives, roles and responsibilities, deliverables, and time lines. The flow of information among project participants must not be interfered with or interrupted in any way, but rather encouraged and facilitated.

*4. Briefings and progress reports.* Regular project team briefings and internal meetings and gatherings to share information and project progress are important communication tools and should be encouraged. External briefings and communications should be controlled by the communications subteam and intended to deliver specific and consistent messages.

5. *Chemistry within and between teams.* Creation of the right chemistry among project participants is important not only in joint venture projects, but in acquisition projects as well. The right chemistry facilitates effective project team functioning, the project team leader is responsible for it, and the project sponsor provides support.

6. *Relationships between counterparts.* Relationships between functional experts and counterparts on both sides is the most effective way to create the right chemistry and should be encouraged because they pay handsome dividends.

7. *Right interfaces and tracking systems.* In addition to the creation of appropriate governance and sound interface and support structures, the right tracking and control mechanisms are needed to ensure teamwork. Of the three, interface and support structure between the new entity and the parent company and between joint venture partners is probably the most important. However, the appropriate management structure and monitoring and control mechanisms are just as important in creating successful projects.

8. *Stepwise approvals to the final project approval.* This approach allows for sanity checks to be introduced between steps with minor disruptions should it be decided to terminate the project. Its advantage lies with the implicit commitment of resources conditioned on the outcome of the phase being executed.

### Adopting Best Practices

The business development group does benchmarking of world-class practices on a regular basis and project team performance is compared with best practices in the postmortem analysis. Results of the postmortem analysis are shared with project participants to understand what was done well and how, what went wrong and why, the impact of things being done the wrong way, and key lessons learned. Once this takes place, the business development group incorporates lessons learned in the project process used in subsequent projects. This is an effective way to benefit by lessons learned.

In addition to benchmarking and putting lessons learned from previous projects to work, adopting best practices involves several key elements:

1. *Encourage specialization.* Concentrate strategic business development in the corporate business development group and limit frequent entry and exit of managers from that organization. Encourage specialization in business development and creation of expertise in all aspects of executing acquisition and joint venture projects.

2. *Contact with the best in the business.* The business development group should maintain contact with world-class business development teams to exchange experiences and learning. Perform benchmarking studies to find out

what processes world-class companies use, how they approach issues, and implement best practices that fit the company's particular needs.

*3. Develop a learning organization.* Hire the best professionals, train them extensively, and ensure that lessons learned from past projects are incorporated in the process for future projects. Finally, reward the project team for world-class performance.

The expectation is that if not present, a strong corporate business development group should be created to handle acquisition and joint venture projects on behalf of all business units. A strong business development group has the ability to assemble a good project team and functional experts from inside and outside the company. A knowledgeable project team, if it is appropriately trained and follows pre-established processes, is likely to deliver successful projects on a consistent basis.

## CONCLUSION

Since acquisition and joint venture projects are risky and their probability of success is small, once the decision to proceed with a project is made, the project team must ensure that every item impacting project success is executed flawlessly. Such execution requires a wide range of expertise and experience to be brought together in the project team under a strong project sponsor and a competent project team leader. Clear project objectives and continuity of purpose must be present throughout the process and effective communications and transition are essential to ensure success.

All acquisition and joint venture projects must be strategy driven and undertaken for the right reasons. Experienced managers should participate in project teams and those without prior practical experience should be trained. Only trusted and seasoned experts should be assigned to the liaison subteam and the steering committee. Preparation and adherence to process are important and project participants should know exactly what should be done and how to do it at any point in order to be effective. Otherwise, it pays to include in the project team an external consultant who specializes in acquisition and joint venture project selection and execution to facilitate the process and ensure success.

# BIBLIOGRAPHY

Abell, D. F., *Defining the Business: The Starting Point of Strategic Planning*, Prentice-Hall, Inc., Englewood Cliffs, N.J, 1980.

Advanced Issues Conference, "All-Purpose Alliances: Joint Ventures to Cut Risks or Penetrate Tough Markets," *Mergers and Acquisitions*, November/ December 1988, p. 73.

Advanced Issues Conference, "The Disclosure Dilemma: Guidelines on Deciding Whether to Announce Merger Talks," *Mergers and Acquisitions*, November/December 1988, p. 66.

Advanced Issues Conference, "Europe's Merger March: The Urge of Foreign Firms to Acquire at Home and Abroad," *Mergers and Acquisitions*, November/December 1988, p. 68.

Advanced Issues Conference, "The Focus on Cash Flow: How Asset-Based Lenders Are Shifting Their Approaches," *Mergers and Acquisitions*, November/December 1988, p. 71.

Advanced Issues Conference, "Friendly Bidding Wars: Paying What it Takes to Buy a Target in Demand," *Mergers and Acquisitions*, November/December 1988, pp. 64–65.

Advanced Issues Conference, "The Leading Edge in Mergers and Acquisitions," *Mergers and Acquisitions*, November/December 1988, p. 63.

Advanced Issues Conference, "One Eye on Competition: Going Beyond Conventional Values in Pricing Acquisitions," *Mergers and Acquisitions*, November/December 1988, p. 69.

Advanced Issues Conference, "The Ratners Acquisition of Sterling Inc.: How an LBO Turned a Small Jeweler into a Coveted Target," *Mergers and Acquisitions*, November/ December 1988, pp. 74–75.

Advanced Issues Conference, "In Search of Protection: Fraudulent Conveyance Pressures and Solvency Letters," *Mergers and Acquisitions*, November/ December 1988, p. 72.

Alpert, G., "Is Market Structure Proof of Market Power?" *Mergers and Acquisitions*, Summer 1984, pp. 47–51.

Altman, E.I., and Nammacher, S.A., *Investing in Junk Bonds: Inside the High Yield Debt Market*, John Wiley and Sons, New York, 1986.

Andersen Consulting, "Communications Executives Predict New Partnerships for Interactive Services But Are Wary of Them," *Business Wire*, June 27, 1995.

Anderson, E., "Two Firms, One Frontier: On Assessing Joint Venture Performance," *Sloan Management Review*, Winter 1990, pp. 19–30.

Anslinger, P.L., and Copeland, T.E., "Growth Through Acquisitions: A Fresh Look," *Harvard Business Review*, January-February 1996, pp. 126–35.

Baker, D.I., and Blumenthal W., "Demystifying the Herfidahl-Hirsschman Index," *Mergers and Acquisitions*, Summer 1984, pp. 42–46.

Bartek, D., "Shift in Focus for Strategic Alliances," *Electronic Business*, March 19, 1990, pp. 58–60.

Baum, L. and Byrne, J.A., "The Job Nobody Wants: Outside Directors Find That the Risks and Hassles Aren't Worth It," *Business Week*, September 8, 1986, pp. 56–61.

Bleeke, J., and Ernst, D., "Is Your Strategic Alliance Really a Sale?" *Harvard Business Review*, January-February 1995, pp. 97–105.

Bleeke, J., and Ernst, D., Eds., *Collaborating to Compete: Using Strategic Alliances and Acquisitions in the Global Marketplace*, John Wiley and Sons, New York, 1993.

Boisi, G.T., Good, D.J., Higgins, J.F., Kay, D.G., Wagner, W.J., and Waters, S.M., "Roundtable: New Techniques in Deal Structuring and Pricing," *Mergers and Acquisitions*, March/April 1986, pp. 26–36.

Brennan, W.F., "Mergers: Follow Prescription for Successful Merger," *Law Practice Management*, Vol. 18, No. 6, pp. 50–52.

Brooks, J., *The Takeover Game*, Truman Talley Books: E.P. Dutton, New York, 1987.

*Business Acquisitions and Leveraged Buyouts*, Coopers and Lybrand, New York, 1989.

Byrne, J.A., "The Best and Worst Boards," *Business Week*, November 25, 1996, pp. 82–98.

Campbell, D., Ed., *Commercial Alliances in the Information Age*, John Wiley and Sons, New York, 1996.

Carrington, N., and De Araujo, P., Eds., *Acquiring Companies and Businesses in Europe*, John Wiley and Sons, New York, 1994.

Carter, J.D., Cushman, R.F., and Hartz, C.S., Eds., *The Handbook of Joint Venturing*, Dow Jones–Irwin, Homewood, IL, 1988.

Carver, J., *Boards That Make a Difference*, Jossey-Bass Publishers, San Francisco, CA, 1990.

Chance, Clifford, *Project Finance*, IFR Publishing, London, 1994.

Chatterjee, S., "Types of Synergy and Economic Value: The Impact of Acquisitions on Merging Rival Firms," *Strategic Management Journal*, Vol. 7, 1986, pp. 119–39.

Coale, K., "Planning Is Key to Successful Mergers," *Infoworld*, February 24, 1992, p. 51.

Coley, S., Reinton, S., and Welch, J., "The High Mortality Rate in Playing Unfamiliar Turf," *Mergers and Acquisitions*, July/August 1987, pp. 56–59.

Contractor, F.J., *International Technology Licensing*, Lexington Books, Lexington, MA, 1981.

Copeland, T., Koller, T., and Murrin, J., *Valuation: Measuring and Managing the Value of Companies*, John Wiley and Sons, New York, 1990.

Corley, L.M., Halpern, M., Ferenbach, C., Rice, J.L., III, and Shaykin, L.P., "Roundtable: The Leveraged Buyout Market," *Mergers and Acquisitions*, Summer 1984, pp. 26–40.

Cozzolino, J.M., "Joint Venture Risk: How to Determine Your Share," *Mergers and Acquisitions*, Fall 1981, pp. 35–39.

DeYoung, H.G., "Piecing Together Successful World-Class Partnerships," *Electronic Business*, May 28, 1990, pp. 32–40.

Doler, K., "Cisco's Secrets to Successful Acquisitions," *Investors Business Daily*, November 1995, p. A8.

Ebin, R., and Rosenbloom, A., "Countdown to Acquiring in the U.S.," *Acquisitions Monthly*, October 1989, pp. 44–47.

Economist Group, "Foreign Investment Differences in Ex-USSR," *Business Eastern Europe*, July 6, 1992, pp. 321–22.

Economist Group, "Strategic Alliances in L.A: New Opportunities for Profit," *Business Latin America*, April 29, 1991, pp. 137–43.

Economist Group, "Western Firms Organizing Business with Ex-USSR," *Business Eastern Europe*, June 22, 1992, pp. 297–99.

Economist Intelligence Unit, "Global Company: EIU Report on Keys to Acquisition Success," *EIU, Electronic Publishing*, January 30, 1996.

Ehr, A., "Have Takeovers Gone Too Far?" *Fortune*, May 27, 1985, pp. 20–24.

Eley, P., and Barlett, T., "Act of Desperation, or Smart Move in a Competitive Environment?" *Acquisitions Monthly*, October 1989, pp. 30–31.

Ernst and Young, *Mergers and Acquisitions,* 2d Ed., John Wiley and Sons, New York, 1994.

Fast, N.D., "Pitfalls of Corporate Venturing," *Research Management*, March 1981, pp. 21–24.

Fogg, J.G., III, "Takeovers: Last Chance for Self-Restraint," *Harvard Business Review*, November-December 1985, pp. 3–8.

Franco, L.G., *Joint Venture Survival in Multinational Corporations*, Praeger Publishers, New York, 1971.

Gaddis, P., "Taken Over, Turned Out," *Harvard Business Review*, July-August 1987, pp. 8–18.

Garner, D.R, Owen, R.R., and Conway, R.P., *The Ernst and Young Guide to Financing for Growth*, John Wiley and Sons, New York, 1994.

Gaughan, P.A., *Mergers, Acquisitions, and Corporate Restructurings*, John Wiley and Sons, New York, 1996.

Gilbert, E., "Analyzing Corporate Culture Key to Successful Mergers," *National Underwriter*, March 13, 1995, p. 13.

Goldberg, S., *Hands across the Ocean: Managing Joint Ventures with a Spotlight on China and Japan*, Harvard Business School Press, Boston, MA, 1988.

Gullander, S., "Joint Ventures and Corporate Strategy," *Columbia Journal of World Business*, Summer 1976, pp. 104–14.

Hamilton, G., "Managing by Acquisition," *Management Today*, May 1985, pp. 45–48.

Hamilton, G., "Start Your Acquisition Program Ten Minutes from Now," *Business Horizons*, September/October 1985, pp. 12–16.

Harrigan, K.R., *Managing for Joint Venture Success*, Lexington Books, Lexington, MA, 1986.

Haspeslagh, P.C., and Jemison, D.B., *Managing Acquisitions: Creating Value through Corporate Renewal*, Free Press, New York, 1991.

Hazell, P., "Strategic Alliances: An Alternative to Outright Ownership," *Acquisitions Monthly*, February 1990, pp. 48–49.

Hill Samuel Bank Limited, *Mergers, Acquisitions and Alternative Corporate Strategies*, W.H. Allen and Company, London, 1989.

Hooke, J.C., *A Practical Guide to Doing the Deal*, John Wiley and Sons, New York, 1996.

Houlder, V., "Neglect of the New Addition: Most Acquired Businesses Are Ignored by Their New Parents," *Financial Times*, February 5, 1997, p. 11.

Howard, M., "British Merger Policy: Tilt toward the Free Market," *International Mergers and Acquisitions*, March/April 1986, pp. 74–78.

Ivancevich, J.M, Schweiger, D.M., and Power, F.R., "Strategies for Managing Human Resources during Mergers and Acquisitions," *Human Resource Planning*, Vol. 10, No. 1, pp. 19–35.

Jarell, G.A., and Easterbrook, F.H., "Do Targets Gain from Defeating Tender Offers?" *New York University Law Review*, Vol. 59, May 1984, pp. 277–96.

Jemison, D.B., and Sitkin, S.B., "Acquisitions: The Process Can Be a Problem," *Harvard Business Review*, March/April 1986, pp. 107–16.

Jemison, D.B., and Sitkin, S.B., "Corporate Acquisitions: A Process Perspective," *Academy of Management Review*, Vol. 11, No. 1, 1986, pp. 145–63.

Jensen, M.C., "Takeovers: Folklore and Science," *Harvard Business Review*, November/December 1984, pp. 109–21.

Johns, B., "Executives Cite Trust as Linchpin for Successful Joint Ventures Abroad," *Journal of Commerce*, September 27, 1993, p. 4A.

Just, A.A., Kata, E.J., Long, J., and Olenzak, A.T., "Roundtable: Corporate Techniques in Acquisitions and Divestitures," *Mergers and Acquisitions*, Spring 1985, pp. 24–36.

Kayaloff, I.J., *Export and Project Finance*, Euromoney Publications Plc, London, 1988.

Killing, P.J., "How to Make a Global Joint Venture Work," *Harvard Business Review*, May-June 1982, pp. 120–27.

Kintner, E.W., *Primer on the Law of Mergers*, Macmillan, New York, 1973.

Kirkland, R.I., Jr., "When Paying Off a Raider Benefits the Shareholders," *Fortune*, April 30, 1984, pp. 152–55.

Kitching, J., "Why Do Mergers Miscarry?" *Harvard Business Review*, November/December 1967, pp. 84–101.

Klueger, R.F., *Mergers and Acquisitions: A Practical Guide to Taxation, Corporation, and Securities Law*, John Wiley and Sons, New York, 1989.

Kogut, B., and Singh, H., "Entering the U.S. by Acquisition or Joint Venture: Country Patterns and Cultural Characteristics," paper presented at the Orsa/Tims meetings, Boston, 1985.

Lee, C., and Beamish, P.W., "The Characteristics and Performance of Korean Joint Ventures in LDCS," *Journal of International Business Studies*, Third Quarter 1995, pp. 637–54.

Lehn, K., "Public Policy towards Corporate Restructuring," *Business Economics*, April 1990, pp. 26–31.

Leighton, C.M., and Tod, R.R., "After the Acquisition: Continuing Challenge," *Harvard Business Review*, March/April 1969, pp. 90–102.

Lucas, A., "I Want a Divorce: Failed Corporate Mergers and Acquisitions," *Sales and Marketing Management*, Vol. 148, No. 11, November, 1996, p. 17.

Lynch, R.P., "Building Alliances to Penetrate European Markets," *Journal of Business Strategy*, March/April 1990, pp. 4–8.

Lynch, R.P., *Business Alliances Guide: The Hidden Competitive Weapon*, John Wiley and Sons, New York, 1993.

Lynch, R.P., *The Practical Guide to Joint Ventures and Corporate Alliances*, John Wiley and Sons, New York, 1990.

Main, J., "Making Global Alliances Work," *Fortune*, December 17, 1990, pp. 121–26.

Marren, J.H., *Mergers and Acquisition: Will You Overpay?*, Dow Jones–Irwin, Homewood, IL, 1985.

Marsden, P., and Heibron, J., "Case Study: Eyes Down for a Full House," *Acquisitions Monthly*, October 1989, pp. 32–33.

May, C.R., "How to Determine True Value of Acquisitions," *Pension World*, February 1989, pp. 20–22.

Maynard, R., "The Makings of a Successful Alliance," *U.S. Chamber of Commerce, Nation's Business*, May 1996, p. 26.

McDouglas, G.E., and Malek, V.F., "Master Plan for Merger Negotiations," *Harvard Business Review*, pp. 71–82.

McIntyre, D.A., "Mergers and Acquisitions," *Financial World*, November 15, 1988, p. 88.

McLean, R.J., "How to Make Acquisitions Work," *McKinsey Quarterly*, Autumn 1985, pp. 65–75.

Mennil, T., "Acquisitions Risk Management Demands Due Diligence: Planning a Successful Acquisition," *Canadian Chemical News*, Vol. 48, No. 8, September 1996, p. 23.

Metzger, R.O., and Ginsberg, A., "Lessons from Japanese Global Acquisitions," *Journal of Business Strategy*, May/June 1989, pp. 32–36.

Morris, J., Ed., *Mergers and Acquisitions: Business Strategies for Accountants*, John Wiley and Sons, New York, 1995.

Morrison, I., "People, Not Price, Key to Successful Merger," *The Herald* (Glasgow), February 1, 1996, p. 22.

Muradian, V., "First 100 Days Critical to Merger Success, Firm Says," *Defense Daily*, Vol. 191, May 30, 1996.

Nathans, L.J., "The Merger Wars Are Turning Downright Friendly," *Business Week*, October 1989, pp. 116–17.

Neumann, E., "Whirlpool and Philips: Successful Joint Venture, Successful Financing," *EUI Business International Money Report*, March 18, 1991.

Nevitt, P.K., *Project Financing*, 5th Ed., Euromoney Publications Plc., London, 1989.

Nigh, D., Walters, P., and Kuhlman, J.A., "US-USSR Joint Ventures: An Examination of the Early Entrants," *Columbia Journal of World Business*, Winter 1990, pp. 20–27.

Nisse, J., "Auctions and Sealed Bids: An Increasingly Popular Method for Handling Corporate Disposals," *Acquisitions Monthly*, October 1989, pp. 25–28.

Nussbaum, B., and Dobrzynski, J.H., "The Battle For Corporate Control," *Business Week*, May 18, 1987, pp. 102–9.

O'Reilly, A.J.F., "Establishing Successful Joint Ventures in Developing Nations: A CEO's Perspective," *Columbia Journal of World Business*, Spring 1988, pp. 65–71.

Orsino, P.S., *Successful Business Expansion: Practical Strategies for Planning Profitable Growth*, John Wiley and Sons, New York, 1994.

Pettibone, P.J., "Negotiating a Joint Venture in the Soviet Union: How to Protect Your Interests," *Journal of European Business*, November/December 1990, pp. 5–12.

Petty, J.R., "Shell Oil's Carroll Gives Recipe for Successful Strategic Alliances," *Houston Post*, March 29, 1995, p. C3.

Petzinger, T., Jr., *Oil and Honor: The Texaco-Penzoil Wars*, Berkley Books, New York, 1988.

Piper, T.R., and Fruhan, W.E., Jr., "Is Your Stock Worth Its Market Price?" *Harvard Business Review*, May/June 1981, pp. 124–32.

Porter, M.E., *Competitive Strategy: Techniques for Analyzing Industries and Competitors*, Free Press, New York, 1980.

Porter, M.S., "Most Acquisitions Fail, CandL Study Says," *Mergers and Acquisitions Report*, November 18, 1996, p. 2.

Porter, M.S., "Post-Merger Savvy Needed for Success," *Mergers and Acquisitions Report*, November 4, 1996, p. 3.

Rajan, M.N., and Graham, J.L., "Nobody's Grandfather Was a Merchant: Understanding the Soviet Commercial Negotiation Process and Style," *California Management Review*, Spring 1991, pp. 40–57.

Rappaport, A., "Strategic Analysis for More Profitable Acquisitions," in D.B. Crane, Ed., *Financial Management*, John Wiley and Sons, New York, 1983, pp. 345–65.

Rappaport, A., *Creating Shareholder Value*, Free Press, New York, 1986.

Reed, S.F., and Lane and Edson, P.C., *The Art of M&A: A Merger Acquisition Buyout Guide*, Dow Jones–Irwin, Homewood, IL, 1989.

Reingold, J., "Anatomy of a Bankruptcy: Why Were Warning Signs at MobileMedia Overlooked?" *Business Week*, March 17, 1997, pp. 77, 80.

Rock, M.L., Ed., *The Mergers and Acquisitions Handbook*, McGraw-Hill, New York, 1987.

Rock, M.L., Rock, R.H., and Sikora, M., *The Mergers and Acquisitions Handbook*, 2d Ed., McGraw-Hill, New York, 1993.

Rosenbloom A., and Ebin, R., "Countdown to Acquiring in the U.S.," *Acquisitions Monthly*, October 1989, pp. 44–47.

Salter, M.S., and Weinhold, W.A., "Choosing Compatible Acquisitions," in D.B. Crane, Ed., *Financial Management*, John Wiley and Sons, New York, 1983, pp. 366–81.

Salter, M.S., and Weinhold, W.A., "Diversification Via Acquisition: Creating Value," in D.B. Crane, Ed., *Financial Management*, John Wiley, N.Y, 1983, pp. 327–43.

Sankar, C., Boulton, W.R., Davidson, N.W., Charles, A., and Ussery, R.W., "Building a World-Class Alliance: The Universal Card–TSYS Case," *Academy of Management Executives*, Vol. 9, No. 2, May 1995, pp. 20–29.

Saul, R.S., "Hostile Takeovers: What Should be Done?" *Harvard Business Review*, September-October 1985, pp. 4–8.

Sexton, O.G., "Measuring the Value Gap: A Survival Exercise for Management," *M&A Europe*, September/October 1989, pp. 33–37.

Shrallow, D.A., "Managing the Integration of Acquired Operations," *Journal of Business Strategy*, Vol. 6, Summer 1985, pp. 30–36.

Sletten, E., *How to Succeed in Exporting and Doing Business Internationally*, John Wiley and Sons, New York, 1994.

Slowinski, G., "The Human Touch in Successful Strategic Alliances," *Mergers and Acquisitions*, July/August 1992, pp. 44–48.

Smith, A., "The Effects of Leveraged Buyouts," *Business Economics*, April 1990, pp. 19–25.

Smith, G.V., and Parr, R.L., *Intellectual Property: Licensing and Joint Venture Profit Strategies*, John Wiley and Sons, New York, 1993.

Smith, J., Allen, J., and Durham, M., "A Structured Market-Entry Analysis for the Former Soviet Union," *Journal of European Business*, May/June 1992, pp. 13–18.

Sunoo, B.P., "Wedding HR to Strategic Alliances," *Personnel Journal*, Vol. 74, No. 5, May 1995, pp. 28–35.

Telesio, P., *Technology Licensing and Multinational Enterprises*, Praeger Publishers, New York, 1979.

Triantis, J.E., "Forecasting for Acquisition and Joint Venture Projects," *Journal of Business Forecasting*, Fall 1996, pp. 3–6.

Tuller, L.W., *The McGraw-Hill Handbook of Global Trade and Investment Financing*, McGraw-Hill, New York, 1996.

U.S. Department of Commerce, *Introductory Guide to Joint Ventures in the Soviet Union*, Washington, DC, 1990.

U.S. Department of Justice, *Merger Guidelines*, Bureau of National Affairs, Inc., Washington, DC, 1984.

Vogt, S., and Weidenbaum, M., "Takeovers and Stockholders: Winners and Losers," *California Management Review*, Vol. 29, No. 4, Summer 1987, pp. 157–67.

Walter, J.E., *Financial Strategies for Managers: Techniques for Success*, John Wiley and Sons, New York, 1990.

Ware, J.P., "Bargaining Strategies: Collaborative versus Competitive Approaches," *Harvard Business School Case Services*, 1980.

Wassner, N.A., "Non-Taxable Methods" in S.J. Lee and R.D. Colman, Eds., *Handbook of Mergers, Acquisitions, and Buyouts*, Prentice-Hall, Englewood Cliffs, NJ, 1987, pp. 191–203.

Weston, F.J., and Chung, K.S., "Takeovers and Corporate Restructuring: An Overview," *Business Economics*, April 1990, pp. 6–18.

"Why Too Many Mergers Miss the Mark," *Economist*, January 4, 1977, pp. 57–58.

Willens, R., "Benefits of Cash Option Mergers Include Favorable Dividend Taxation," *Journal of Taxation*, May 1989, pp. 272–74.

Williamson, J.P., Ed., *The Investment Banking Handbook*, John Wiley and Sons, New York, 1988.

Zweig, P.L., Perlman Kline, J., Anderson, F., and Gudridge, K., "The Case against Mergers," *Business Week*, October 30, 1995, pp. 122–30.

# INDEX

**About the Author**

JOHN E. TRIANTIS is Managing Director of Forerunner Consultants Inc., Morristown, N.J. Dr. Triantis is also Associate Director, Association of Business Forecasting, and an editorial board member of *Review of Business*.